Scribal Publication in Seventeenth-century England

Scribal Publication in Seventeenth-Century England

HAROLD LOVE

CLARENDON PRESS · OXFORD

Oxford University Press, Great Clarendon Street, Oxford OX2 6DP
Oxford New York
Athens Auckland Bangkok Bogota Bombay Buenos Aires
Calcutta Cape Town Dar es Salaam Delhi Florence Hong Kong
Istanbul Karachi Kuala Lumpur Madras Madrid Melbourne
Mexico City Nairobi Paris Singapore Taipei Tokyo Toronto Warsaw
and associated companies in
Berlin Ibadan

Oxford is a trade mark of Oxford University Press

Published in the United States
by Oxford University Press Inc., New York

First published 1993

British Library Cataloguing in Publication Data
Data available

Library of Congress Cataloging in Publication Data
Love, Harold, 1937–
Scribal publication in seventeenth-century England/Harold Love.
Includes bibliographical references and index.
1. English literature—Early modern. 1500–1700—Criticism. Textual.
2. Literature publishing—England—History—17th century.
3. Authors and readers—England—History—17th century.
4. Music—Publishing—England—History—17th century.
5. Manuscripts. English—History—17th century.
6. Scriptoria—England—History—17th century.
7. Manuscripts, English—Editing. 8. Transmission of texts.
9. Scribes—England. I. Title.
PR438.T42L68 1993 820.9'004—dc20 92–43510
ISBN 0–19–811219–X

3 5 7 9 10 8 6 4 2

Printed in Great Britain by
Antony Rowe Ltd, Chippenham, Wiltshire

PREFACE

THE realization that this book needed to be written emerged from an interest in the editorial problems posed by the writings of Rochester and other Restoration authors of libertine and state verse. The period since 1960 has seen a remarkable growth in our understanding of the importance of manuscript copies to the circulation of these writings, and the first serious attempts by editors to reconstruct lost authorial texts from the highly variant copies. However, most of these attempts limited their concern to the individual poems, excluding any but the most perfunctory investigations of the larger manuscript anthologies in which most of them were to be found. This was understandable in that traditional approaches to recensional editing offer no satisfactory methodology for determining the relationships of such complex and heterogeneous wholes; but it also meant that the editorial enterprise was considering only one part of the available evidence.

It seemed obvious that if answers to this problem were to be found it could not be through any narrow technical analysis of variant readings, but had to embrace an understanding of the culture of transmission within which the proliferation of copies took place. It was equally clear that this culture was a very sophisticated one with links back to the period before the invention of printing when all texts were circulated in handwritten copies. From this realization that a wider context had to be found for a textual problem came the awareness that the context was a topic of even greater interest than the problem.

This account of the origins of my interest in the subject will explain the way in which it has been approached. Where the book draws on my own research into manuscripts and their transmission, this is mostly from the field just indicated; otherwise, in considering the periods and areas of the vast, multiform enterprise that I call by the name of scribal publication, my contribution has largely been one of collecting and interpreting the work of other scholars. The appreciation that such a book was necessary might just as easily have come to a worker in a very different speciality—say parliamentary compilations, cathedral music or scribally transmitted prophecies—and the resultant perception of the nature of scribal publication would necessarily have been a different one, not simply because of differences in the expert knowledge brought to bear, but because the very subject has no objective status independent of the point of view from which it is constructed. What is presented is to be seen as a model to aid in seeking solutions for practical problems but one that will itself continually require modification in the light of the solutions arrived at.

The decision to restrict this study to seventeenth-century examples followed from my initial concern with the generation of Rochester: to look any further into the past would make it difficult to assume continuity of practices. Obviously, much of what is said would also hold true of the generation of Sidney and Spenser, and examples have occasionally been borrowed from the 1590s. Yet it will be evident from what follows that the accession of James I precipitated a situation in which, for a variety of reasons, texts of great political and intellectual importance were deliberately reserved for the scribal medium. At the other end of our time scale, the accession of Anne provided a natural terminus, not because texts ceased to be circulated in manuscript, but because such texts (with the possible exception of John Dyer's newsletters) had lost the centrality to ideological debate which can still be claimed for them in the 1690s.

The chance to lay a foundation of research for this book was offered under ideal circumstances by the Cambridge University Library through the award of the Munby Fellowship in Bibliography for 1986–7. Among the many individuals who contributed guidance and suggestions during that year I owe a particular debt to David McKitterick, who encouraged the publication of an early summary of my findings in the *Transactions of the Cambridge Bibliographical Society*, and Sheila Lambert, who guided my first attempts to acquire an understanding of the scribal publication of parliamentary documents, as well as passing on invaluable references to her own and others' writings. Beyond that, Anne Barton, Howard Erskine-Hill, Paul Hartle, Mary

Hobbs, Robert D. Hume, Ian Jack, Peter Jones, Elizabeth Leedham-Green, Richard Luckett, Jeremy Maule, Don McKenzie and Arthur Sherbo all contributed helpful advice or useful leads for which I am grateful. At a later stage, following a break to complete a book on a nineteenth-century topic, I was able to draw on the vast expertise of Peter Beal and Hilton Kelliher. But my greatest debt is undoubtedly to Keith Walker, who heroically read the entire typescript, besides being a continual source of wit, wisdom, hospitality and obscure journal articles which would otherwise have escaped my notice.

It was my great fortune during the period of writing to have the services of two enthusiastic and highly skilled research assistants, Meredith Sherlock and Dianne Heriot. Their contribution both to this book and to the edition of Rochester in which I hope to apply its discoveries has been very considerable. I am also much in debt to my colleagues in the Monash University English Department, Philip Ayres, Geoff Hiller, Clive Probyn and Chris Worth, all of whom made valuable comments on draft chapters, and Denise Cuthbert and Mark Allinson for many useful leads regarding Marvell and Donne respectively. Wallace Kirsop and Brian McMullin of the Monash Centre for Bibliographical and Textual Studies and Richard Overell, Monash's Rare Books Librarian were generous, as always, in answering bibliographical and booktrade enquiries.

This book draws widely on my 'Scribal publication in seventeenth-century England', *Transactions of the Cambridge Bibliographical Society* 9 (1987), 130–54. An early version of Chapter 7 appeared as 'The editing of Restoration scriptorial satire' in *Editing in Australia*, ed. Paul Eggert, Canberra, 1990, pp. 65-84, while the opening section of Chapter 4 draws on my 'Manuscript versus print in the transmission of English literature, 1600–1700', *Bibliographical Society of Australia and New Zealand Bulletin* 9 (1985), 95–107.

References cited at any stage by short-title are included in the bibliography; others should be sought through the index.

Clayton, Victoria H.L.

CONTENTS

ILLUSTRATIONS

ABBREVIATIONS

BIHR	*Bulletin of the Institute of Historical Research*
BL	British Library
BNYPL	*Bulletin of the New York Public Library*
BSANZ Bulletin	*Bulletin of the Bibliographical Society of Australia and New Zealand*
CSP(Dom)	*Calendars of state papers: domestic series*
CTB	*Calendars of treasury books*
ELN	*English language notes*
EMS	*English manuscript studies*
HMC	*Historical Manuscripts Commission*
IELM	Beal, Peter, comp. *Index of English literary manuscripts. Volume 1 1450–1625* and *Volume 2 1625–1700* (London, 1980–92)
M&L	*Music and letters*
MLR	*Modern languages review*
N&Q	*Notes and queries*
PBA	*Proceedings of the British Academy*
POAS (Yale)	*Poems on affairs of state. Augustan satirical verse, 1660–1714*, gen. ed. George deF. Lord 7 vols. New Haven, 1963–75.
P&P	*Past and present*
PRO	Public Record Office
RES	*Review of English studies*
SB	*Studies in bibliography*
SEL	*Studies in English literature*
SP	*Studies in philology*
STC	*A short-title catalogue of books printed in England, Scotland and Ireland and of English books printed abroad 1475-1640*, first comp. by A. W. Pollard and G. R. Redgrave; 2nd edn, rev. and enlarged by W. A Jackson, F. S. Ferguson and Katharine F. Pantzer (London, 1976–86)

PART I

SCRIBAL PUBLICATION

I

THE PHENOMENON

In publishing this Essay of my Poeme, there is this great disadvantage against me; that it commeth out at this time, when Verses are wholly deduc't to Chambers, and nothing esteem'd in this lunatique Age, but what is kept in Cabinets, and must only passe by Transcription . . .

Michael Drayton (1612)[1]

I might have had one Word here by Way of Reflection upon the happy Times we are just now coming to; Times I remember very well to have seen before, when Printing being not in use, I mean as to News-Papers, State-Tracts, Politicks, &c., Written Scandal shall revive, and the Nation shall swarm with Lampoon, Pasquinade, written Reflections, Characters, Satyrs, and an inconceivable Flood of written News-Letters.

Daniel Defoe (1712)[2]

THAT many of the texts known to an educated English reader of the seventeenth century would have been encountered in manuscript rather than in print is hardly news: the collections of major British and United States libraries contain many thousands of testimonies to this fact. That some of this material was the creation of professional scribes, whose work was distributed through organized markets, while less widely known, is also a matter of record—the advent of the press did not extinguish older

[1] 'To the generall reader', *Poly-olbion*, in *The works of Michael Drayton*, ed. J. William Hebel (Oxford, 1961), iv, p. v. The idea is repeated in his 'To . . . Henery Reynolds Esquire', ll. 187–95 (ibid., iii. 231).

[2] *A review of the state of the British nation*, viii. 708 (facsim. ed. A. W. Secord (New York, 1938), book 21).

methods of publication through manuscript. That certain seventeenth-century poets, among them Donne, Corbett, Strode, King, Carew, Pestell, Marvell, Cotton, Katherine Philips, Traherne, Rochester and Dorset, wrote primarily for scribal transmission is amply acknowledged by their editors and confirmed by the formidable list of sources for the best-known of these given in Peter Beal's volumes of the *Index of English literary manuscripts.*[3] What is lacking to date has been an awareness that each of these things is a part of a larger phenomenon—scribal publication—which had a role in the culture and commerce of texts just as assured as that of print publication. The aim of this book is to explore the nature of this phenomenon and to propose terms for its further investigation.[4]

In doing so it will be necessary to draw connections between fields of enquiry which, for reasons that invite consideration, have not been seen as related. Between 1952 and 1978 the Clarendon Press published the distinguished Gardner and Milgate editions of Donne's poetry.[5] The main textual sources for these were manuscript collections circulated during Donne's lifetime, others written after his death, and a first printed collection which was itself reliant on scribally published exemplars.[6] Over much the same period David M. Vieth was working on his path-breaking study of the scribal transmission of Rochester's verse, *Attribution in Restoration poetry*, and the edition which drew on its findings.[7] The earlier volumes of the Donne edition were available to Vieth, and

[3] Peter Beal, *Index of English literary manuscripts. Volume 1 1450–1625. Volume 2 1625–1700* (London, 1980–).

[4] These matters were originally raised in my 'Scribal publication in seventeenth-century England', *Transactions of the Cambridge Bibliographical Society* 9, no. 2 (1987), 130–54. There is a also a lucid statement of the issues in Hilton Kelliher's review of Beal, *IELM*, i/1 and 2 in *Library*, 6:4 (1982), 435–40.

[5] John Donne, *The divine poems*, ed. Helen Gardner (1952), *The elegies and the songs and sonnets*, ed. Helen Gardner (1965), *The satires, epigrams and verse letters*, ed. Wesley Milgate (1967) and *The epithalamions, anniversaries and epicedes*, ed. Wesley Milgate (1978). The poems are currently being re-edited for the Variorum Donne to be published by the University of Missouri Press.

[6] Discussed in Alan MacColl, 'The circulation of Donne's poems in manuscript' in A. J. Smith, ed., *John Donne: essays in celebration* (London, 1972), pp. 28–46; *The first and second Dalhousie manuscripts: poems and prose by John Donne and others, a facsimile edition*, ed. Ernest W. Sullivan II (Columbia, Mo., 1988), pp. 201–8 and Beal, *IELM*, i/1, 243–568.

[7] David M. Vieth, *Attribution in Restoration poetry: a study of Rochester's 'Poems' of 1680* (New Haven, Conn., 1963); *The complete poems of John Wilmot, Earl of Rochester*, ed. David M. Vieth (New Haven, Conn., 1968).

his own work to the Donne editors for all but their first volume. The two projects were concerned with very similar traditions of copying and distribution and faced identical problems in endeavouring to construct texts from a multiplicity of witnesses. Yet neither cites the findings or textual arguments of the other or shows any sign of having drawn on them. The example is far from unique: editors of seventeenth-century poetry have generally shown a quite staggering lack of interest in authorial traditions other than the one in which they were directly engaged.

This is hard to understand when, as is so often the case, the most characteristic mode through which verse was circulated to its readers was the miscellany containing work by a number of writers, rather than the manuscript devoted to the work of a single poet. Miscellanies have usually been treated simply as quarries for texts of individual writers and as providers of dating evidence. Rare is the editor who, like Vieth in his study of the major Rochester source Yale MS Osborn b 105, pauses to consider how the larger context provided by the miscellanies may have influenced the writing or reading of the individual poem.[8] From the earlier Stuart period, only Mary Hobbs's study of miscellanies circulated by Henry King and Arthur F. Marotti's of the social context of Donne's poetry can be said seriously—and successfully—to have confronted such questions.[9] To Hobbs the miscellany is a communal as well as an individual construct, to be read for what it shows us about the communities in which it was created and revised. The interest of the case is heightened by the fact that King was himself a scribal publisher of miscellanies, presenting his own poems intermixed with those of friends. Marotti emphasizes that miscellanies (whether manuscript or printed) 'often give the impression that they retain a sense of the social environment of the verse they collect' in presenting 'courtly or satellite-courtly poems written on particular (if conventionalized) social occasions'. Removed from this setting the poems

[8] See Vieth, *Attribution*, pp. 56–100 and *passim*.

[9] Mary Hobbs, 'An edition of the Stoughton manuscript (an early seventeenth-century poetry collection in private hands, connected with Henry King and Oxford) seen in relation to other contemporary poetry and song collections', London University Ph.D. thesis, 1973 and 'Early seventeenth-century verse miscellanies and their value for textual editors', *English manuscript studies 1100–1700* 1 (1989), 182–210; Arthur F. Marotti, *John Donne, coterie poet* (Madison, Wis., 1986), pp. 5–13.

suffer a decontextualization which it is one of the tasks of the historicist critic to reverse.[10] The possibilities of interpretation open to an early reader would always have been governed by the wider context provided by the miscellanies, and the fact that particular poems would tend to cluster with others from the same circles. Any attempt to enter that first reading experience must always take account of the company poems were accustomed to keep.

It must also be stressed—genealogical analysis of variants hardly being an exact science—that the transmissional history of the poem can often be understood only through that of the miscellanies in which it is encountered. It is certainly the case that the ability to derive a whole family of miscellanies from a particular scriptorial archive vastly simplifies the task of creating stemmas for their individual items. For the Restoration period, Vieth's pioneering work on the scribal publication of verse in the 1670s and 1680s is valuably supplemented by W. J. Cameron's detailed analysis of the surviving output of a scriptorium of the 1690s specializing in verse miscellanies.[11] If Cameron's findings are correct, which I believe to be the case, the texts of Restoration state and libertine verse contained in a substantial body of manuscripts can be assumed, in the absence of countervailing evidence in the variants themselves, to derive from single archetypes. Unfortunately, scholarly information about these matters is not abundant, and when it does exist is too often ignored. Cameron's hypothesis has drawn no follow-up work prior to the present study. Even Hobbs's important findings languished for many years in an unpublished Ph.D. thesis. The problem is not simply one of editors and critics being too absorbed in particular authors, works or manuscripts to reach out to the wider culture of transmission, but of a blindness to the nature and persistence of this culture.

This observation is not intended to denigrate editors. Editing is hard enough work as it is without adding new methodological requirements. There are also many practical difficulties affecting research. The manuscript heritage is now widely dispersed over

[10] Marotti, pp. 12, 11.

[11] W. J. Cameron, 'A late seventeenth-century scriptorium', *Renaissance and modern studies* 7 (1963), 25–52 and 'Transmission of the texts' in *Poems on affairs of state. Augustan satirical verse, 1660–1714*, gen. ed. George deF. Lord (New Haven, Conn., 1963–75), v. 528–38. Collations by the present author of texts from the manuscripts concerned have always supported Cameron's results.

Britain, North America, Europe and even Japan. Microfilms (necessarily regarded by many libraries as a means of fund-raising) and travel are both expensive. While most libraries with large manuscript collections give strong support to the work of scholars, others, through tradition or penury, insist on restrictive rules for the use of their materials. Frequently funds for an expensive acquisition may only be available if first publication is reserved for the purchasing institution, which will not necessarily possess the scholar best fitted for the job. Above all, awareness of the existence of problems is something which is itself dependent on the progress of scholarship. It was not until such editions as the Oxford Donne and Suckling, Vieth's and Keith Walker's editions of Rochester, the monumental Yale *Poems on affairs of state* series and Ernest W. Sullivan's edition of the Dalhousie miscellanies were in existence that the transmissional challenges posed by scribal publication fully revealed themselves to literary scholars.[12] As late as 1955 it was still possible for an Oxford edition to dismiss the manuscript tradition of a scribally published poet with the remark: 'most of the manuscripts containing poems written by or attributed to Corbett are commonplace books of little authority, and sometimes compiled, in part at least, from printed sources', and to refer the reader to 'the printed catalogues of the great libraries' for further information.[13] Finally, it should be remembered that literary editors normally work to provide the kinds of texts required by critics. An author-centred critical ideology will assign less importance to the wider structures that connect sources than one which is concerned with the intertextual workings of language, or which, in foregrounding the role of the reader, requires that more information be given about the historical circumstances of reading.[14]

It will also be evident that the making of historical connections is

[12] *The works of Sir John Suckling*, ed. Thomas Clayton and L. A. Beaurline (Oxford, 1971); *POAS (Yale)*; Vieth, *Complete poems*; *The poems of John Wilmot, Earl of Rochester*, ed. Keith Walker (Oxford, 1984); Sullivan, *Dalhousie manuscripts*. For the other editions mentioned see nn. 5 and 6 above.

[13] *The poems of Richard Corbett*, ed. J. A. W. Bennett and H. R. Trevor-Roper (Oxford, 1955), p. lvii. For a refutation of these assumptions, see Hobbs, 'Early seventeenth-century verse miscellanies', pp. 183–4.

[14] These relationships are further explored in D. C. Greetham, 'Textual and literary theory: redrawing the matrix', *SB* 42 (1989), 1–24 and '[Textual] criticism and deconstruction', *SB* 44 (1991), 1–30.

hindered by the existence of scholarly lines of demarcation, of which the most glaring is the year 1660. Vieth, as well as neglecting the example of Donne, makes no reference to Carew, who performed a literary role in the court of Charles I which was a direct model for that which Rochester was to adopt at the court of Charles II, and whose work was distributed through similar modes of scribal publication.[15] The reason for this is not hard to seek. Literary scholars working on the earlier Stuart period define themselves as Renaissance specialists, inhabiting a different conceptual as well as historical world from those working on the later Stuart period who define themselves as Augustan specialists. Those Renaissance specialists who concern themselves with Caroline authors further define themselves as studying the end of a process of development which reached its highest point with Shakespeare, while Restoration scholars see themselves as occupied with the beginning of a process which is to reach fruition in Pope and the eighteenth-century novelists. Despite the existence of the *Oxford book of seventeenth-century verse* there is no such subject as seventeenth-century literature in our academies. Historians acknowledge the same divide. W. K. Jordan, writing in 1960, could think 'of no scholar who has done really significant work on both sides of the watershed, who has moved easily and freely in both historical environments'.[16] It is not hard today to think of exceptions to this generalization, especially in the fields of economic, ecclesiastical and legal history, but it still has force. Differences in interest and professional approach become hypostatized into a belief that there was a sharp and decisive break in the development of English culture in 1660—a year which, in actuality, saw a massive attempt to obliterate all political change that had taken place since 1641. But, if chronological and ideological divisions within one discipline are enough to blind literary scholars and some historians to continuities in scribal practice, how much more serious are those that separate them from scholars in other disciplines—from musicologists, historical socio-

[15] The similarity extends to the first printed edition of each writer's verse having been an unauthorized collection of mixed authorship hastily set from a scribally published miscellany immediately following his death.

[16] *The restoration of the Stuarts, blessing or disaster? A report of a Folger Library conference held on March 12 and 13, 1960* (Washington, DC, 1960), pp. 47–8.

logists, historians of science and medicine, legal scholars and codicologists, and these from each other? For the scribal transmission of verse is something that can be treated only when we have a sense of the very much wider enterprise of which it was only one part. The same agencies, both private and professional, which created the verse miscellanies were employed in a large variety of other fields, all of which throw light on each other, but few of which have been studied comparatively.

Scribal publication, then, is a perfect example of what Don R. Swanson has called 'undiscovered public knowledge'. By this he means knowledge that exists 'like scattered pieces of a puzzle' in scholarly books and articles, but remains unknown because its 'logically related parts . . . have never all become known to any one person'.[17] In the remainder of this chapter, I will demonstrate this principle, and the method to be followed in the rest of the book, by bringing together scattered pieces of work on two fields which to date have only been studied as isolated phenomena—the scribal publication of parliamentary proceedings and the provision of manuscript copies of viol consort music—and then by pointing to some ways in which these illuminate both each other and the larger phenomenon. This will also be an opportunity to consider what use is to be made of such knowledge once assembled.

NEWSLETTERS, SEPARATES AND PARLIAMENTARY COMPILATIONS

Political documents—state papers, short polemical tracts, and reports of parliamentary proceedings—were copied in larger quantities than any other kind of scribally published text and, for that reason, reveal more about the production of copies in general. But before we consider the case of the proceedings, it will be necessary to review the history of two contributory sub-types of the scribally published text, the manuscript newsletter and the 'separate'.

At the beginning of the seventeenth century the practice was

[17] Don R. Swanson, 'Undiscovered public knowledge', *Library quarterly* 56 (1986), 116. See also Roy Davies's review of this and other papers by Swanson in 'The creation of new knowledge by information retrieval and classification', *Journal of documentation* 45 (1989), 273–301.

already established of country gentlemen receiving news and political information on a regular basis from a town informant. Lawrence Stone notes that 'by the 1590s Peter Proby was writing regularly to the Earls of Shrewsbury, Derby, Pembroke, and Hertford, and many others of the nobility during their absences from Court'.[18] The extensive correspondence between John Chamberlain and a circle of friends headed by Dudley Carleton, Ralph Winwood and Lancelot Andrewes represents a stage before this custom had become professionalized. Chamberlain, an enquiring Londoner, traded information largely acquired in Paul's Walk for friendship, influence and more information, and not for money; yet he was operating in a mode which was already being pursued as a means of livelihood.[19] The advent and growing influence later in the century of the printed coranto and newspaper did not initially affect the newsletter trade, as much more could always be said in a letter than could be uttered in print. The very secretiveness of the operation cast a gloss over what might otherwise have been regarded as rather ordinary news. A 'Factor of newes for all the Shieres of *England*' in Jonson's *Newes from the new world discover'd in the moone* (1620) acknowledges this when he complains: 'I would have no newes printed; for when they are printed they leave to bee newes; while they are written, though they be false, they remaine newes still.'[20] A well-organized newsletter writer, with good sources of information, would soon build up a network of customers, who would pay a subscription to receive the letters. John Pory received a remarkable £20 a year from Lord Scudamore for his weekly letters in 1631–2, and Edward Rossingham was rumoured in 1640 to be charging 'not under' the same sum.[21] (Another source estimated Rossingham's income at £500 a year, suggesting a clientele of about the maximum size that could be written to on a weekly basis by a

[18] *The crisis of the aristocracy 1558–1641* (Oxford, 1965), p. 388.

[19] For Chamberlain, see *The letters of John Chamberlain*, ed. N. E. McClure, 2 vols (Philadelphia, 1939) and Wallace Notestein, *Four worthies* (New Haven, Conn., 1957), pp. 29–119. His 'knot of friends', a small 'scribal community' of the kind that will be discussed in Ch. 6, is treated in Notestein, pp. 37–8.

[20] *Ben Jonson*, ed. C. H. Herford and Percy and Evelyn Simpson (Oxford, 1925–52), vii. 514–15. The idea is repeated in *The staple of newes*, I. v. 46–50 (ibid., vi. 295).

[21] William S. Powell, *John Pory 1572–1636. The life and letters of a man of many parts* (Chapel Hill, NC, 1977), p. 55; *Proceedings of the short parliament of 1640*, ed. Esther S. Cope in collaboration with Willson H. Coates, Camden Society, 4:19 (London, 1977), p. 35.

single writer who also had to devote time to information gathering.[22]) After the Restoration Henry Muddiman charged £5 a year for a weekly letter, Giles Hancock between £4 and £6, and Will Urwin a reputed £10, while the average price for written news in 1709 was '£3 or £4 *per annum*'.[23] If demand for services should outstrip the power of the writer's own pen, clerks would be employed to duplicate a standardized form of the letter. However, the fiction was usually maintained that the letter was a personal communication between gentlemen, and in two surviving files of Rossingham's letters duplicated passages are supplemented by other material apparently unique to the recipient.[24] When in 1696 Ichabod Dawks's newsletter reached a circulation that made the transition to print unavoidable, he tried to retain something of the old exclusiveness by having a special script typeface cast.[25]

Despite this air of confidentiality, the circulations of some newsletters may have risen to several hundred copies. Jonson's fictional factor writes his 'thousand Letters a weeke ordinary, sometim⟨e⟩ twelve hundred', supplying his customers, to order, with Puritan, Protestant or 'Pontificiall' [i.e. Catholic] news.[26] This is no more to be taken literally than the outrageous claims of the other news-gatherers in this and *The staple of newes*; but the real-life model for the satirical portrait was genuine enough: a body of scribal journalists engaged in a profitable trade, some of whom will have specialized in personalized service to a small group of clients (and charged accordingly) and others in the distribution of a cheaper, standardized product to as many as practicable. In 1688 Sir Roger L'Estrange noted on an inflamma-

[22] Stone, p. 389. The claim was made by William Cavendish, Duke of Newcastle, in a memorandum to Charles II written shortly before the Restoration.

[23] Peter Fraser, *The intelligence of the secretaries of state and their monopoly of licensed news 1660–1688* (Cambridge, 1956), pp. 40, 128; HMC, 11th rep., app., vii. 20; Henry L. Snyder, 'Newsletters in England, 1689–1715, with special reference to John Dyer—a byway in the history of England' in Donovan H. Bond and W. Reynolds McLeod, eds, *Newsletters and newspapers: eighteenth-century journalism* (Morgantown, 1977), p. 8.

[24] Cope, p. 36. Of course, it is possible that what appears to be unique in the files, those to Lords Scudamore and Conway, was differentially recycled in other letters of the same week.

[25] Described in Stanley Morison, *Ichabod Dawks and his 'News-Letter'; with an account of the Dawks family of booksellers and scriveners, 1635–1731* (Cambridge, 1931), pp. 18–32.

[26] *Ben Jonson*, vii. 514. Cf. *The staple of newes*, I. v. 13–17 (ibid., vi. 294). The rivalry between newsletter and newspaper suppliers may be overstated. John Pory, a leading newsletter writer, maintained a close relationship with Nathaniel Butter, the pioneer coranto publisher.

tory newsletter: 'The Paper Enclosed is an Original of One Dyer, a Coffee-man in White-Fryers. There cannot upon a Fair Computation be so Few as Five Hundred Copies of it Spread over ye Kingdom.'[27] In this case what we have is not satirical exaggeration, but an educated guess by a well-informed official. In the case of the official newsletters issued during the reign of Charles II as a domestic counterpart to the printed *London gazette*, circulations of well over a hundred are recorded. During the late 1660s, Joseph Williamson, under-secretary to secretary-of-state Arlington, sent letters to 122 correspondents within Britain and fifty-four overseas (though not to all of these simultaneously).[28] A staff of five clerks was required to maintain this output. Henry Muddiman's letter had a circulation of around 140 at the close of 1665 when it was still issued from Arlington's office, but undoubtedly increased this after February 1666 when it came under the patronage of the other Secretary.[29] Giles Hancock, the leading Whig newsletter writer of the 1680s, often brought 'above thirty letters to the post', a figure which to Fraser suggests a total of 'well over a hundred correspondents'—there being by this time three posts a week out of London as well as an efficient daily delivery system within the metropolis and surrounding boroughs.[30] From the 1650s there was a brisk demand from coffee houses, which were in effect also reading rooms. In 1683 Nathaniel Thompson recorded that the (mostly Whig) newsletter writers had 'foisted their Shams . . . at the constant Pension of 4, or 5*s*. a week from each Coffee-house'.[31]

The newsletter, then, was a stable and successful genre of scribal publication and one that maintained a function for some decades after the advent of the printed newspaper. However, it was not the

[27] BL MS Add. 41805, f. 93. This appears to be the earliest reference to Dyer's famous letter. For its later history, see Snyder, 'Newsletters'.

[28] For their names and addresses, see Fraser, pp. 140–4, 153–5.

[29] J. G. Muddiman, *The king's journalist 1659–1689: studies in the reign of Charles II* (London, 1923), pp. 258–64. Muddiman had originally produced his letter for Williamson, but changed masters after a dispute over the mixed public and entrepreneurial nature of his operation (Fraser, pp. 30, 34, 49). Williamson's ideal was one of a confidential exchange of information with the recipients of his letters.

[30] Fraser, p. 128, citing William Cotton's memorandum, *CSP (Dom.) 1683–4*, pp. 53–4.

[31] *Loyal Protestant and true domestic intelligence*, no. 239, 1 March 1682/3, p. 2. See also Fraser, pp. 114–21 and Muddiman, p. 219. Fearing competition from Thompson's printed newspaper, the newsletter writers arranged for a 'scandalous Villain' to harrass his hawkers and customers.

only scribal source of information on current happenings. Individuals who subscribed to newsletters were also likely to have large collections of the documents that historians call 'separates' and that were sometimes referred to in their own time as 'pocket manuscripts'.[32] Bibliographically the separate is an individually circulated short manuscript which was written as a unit, and not assembled from elements copied at varying times and places (which would be an 'aggregation'[33]). In the usage of historians it refers exclusively to texts of a political or ideological nature, but there is no reason why it should be restricted to this sense and it is convenient to be able to speak of poetical or theological separates. The most common format was the same as that favoured for the newsletter—a whole or half-sheet bifolium with the first three pages written on and the last left blank for addressing—but texts written over two or three sheets and quired or stab-sewn may also be so described. (Anything beyond this would comprise a manuscript book.) A separate usually contains a single text such as a speech or short treatise, but will sometimes present a 'linked group' of closely related items—for example epigrams on the same subject. Any more heterogeneous assemblage of texts becomes a 'compilation'.[34] In practice any text initially published as a separate, and that had a reasonably wide circulation, is likely to be known today both from true separates, as just defined, and from later copyings into compilations, commonplace books or volumes of 'collections'.

That political separates were produced in enormous numbers is made clear by the quantity that survive today: some can still be found in fifty or more contemporary copies. (Several tracts by a single author, Sir Robert Cotton, survive in such numbers.) While we can only speculate about the number that were once in circulation, the evidence of newsletters, whose surviving copies can be measured against an estimate of total circulation, would suggest that the loss rate has been considerable. Conservatively assuming a circulation of 200 a week for Dyer's letter, the 300 copies located by Snyder (pp. 8–9) for 1709–10 would represent

[32] e. g. on the title-page of Burleigh's *Certain precepts* (London, 1617).

[33] For this term, see Cameron, 'Scriptorium', p. 27.

[34] A compilation, as a single manuscript with heterogeneous contents, is distinct from an aggregation, which is joined together from a variety of pre-existing manuscripts.

only 1.5 per cent of those produced. For earlier separates the additional hazards of the Civil War and the great fire would have to be allowed for, as well as the fact that 'loose papers' were in constant demand for a variety of domestic uses. (An important Mary, Countess of Pembroke autograph was acquired 'among other broken books to putt up Coffee pouder'.[35]) These copies circulated by a variety of means. Chain copying by private individuals was probably the most important, but there is also evidence for commercial production by law scriveners and by booksellers, particularly those in the vicinity of the Inns of Court who dealt in legal manuscripts as well as printed books. The separate might also circulate as an adjunct to the newsletter, as is noted by Powell in his study of John Pory:

> In addition to payment for his regular newsletters, Pory also sold his patrons copies of 'excellent discourses' which he copied from various sources available to him in London. The speech of Sir Benjamin Rudyerd, 28 April 1628, may have been such an item. On 22 September 1631, in a postscript to a regular letter to Sir Thomas Puckering (which was also shared with Sir Thomas Lucy), he offered for ten shillings each an assortment of 'discourses' by Mons. de Rohan, a 'character' of Cardinal Richelieu, an 'apology' of the cardinal, and 'a pathetical Remonstrance' of the princes assembled before the Holy Roman Emperor in Leipzig. Lucy agreed to share the cost of these with Puckering. Several pieces which must have been prepared in this category are included among Pory's letters: the Rudyerd speech of 28 April 1628; Dr Mainwaring's submission, 21 June 1628; the king's speech to both houses, 26 June 1628; 'Certain speeches whereof one Mr Melvin a Scottishman is accused', 26 June 1628; and 'A true recital of what hath passed', 30 October 1630.[36]

The pieces named include four parliamentary reports of a kind which received very wide circulation in manuscript and which survives today both as actual separates and as transcripts entered from separates into albums and compilations.[37]

[35] Samuel Woodford's note, cited in *The triumph of death and other unpublished and uncollected poems by Mary Sidney, Countess of Pembroke (1561–1621)*, ed. G. F. Waller (Salzburg, 1977), p. 24. Jayne Ringrose records how Richard Rawlinson rescued several important collections of papers which had been sold to be used as waste. (' "I collect and I preserve": Richard Rawlinson 1690–1755 and eighteenth-century book collecting', *Book collector* 39 (1990), 36.)

[36] Powell, *John Pory*, p. 56.

[37] See, for example, the list of manuscript sources for speeches given in *Proceedings of the short parliament*, pp. 292–318.

The most extensive study to date of the political separate and newsletter in their relationship to larger unities was published in 1921 by Wallace Notestein and Frances Relf in the introduction to their edition of the commons debates of the 1629 parliament.[38] Once again, their discussion concentrates on one particular mode and occasion of scribal publication, only intermittently raising its gaze to the wider picture, but the material is of such richness that a great deal is suggested about that picture. More importantly, the hypotheses advanced by Notestein and Relf and the discussions of their findings by other historians permit us to consider how far practices observed in a particular field of scribal publication can be assumed to apply in other fields where evidence for them may not be so strong. The question is a vital one in that it is only if a positive answer is given, and the conditions defined under which such an answer would be valid, that we can hope to use a generalized model of the procedures of scribal publication in the search for historical explanations.

Prior to 1921 the proceedings of the parliament had been known from the scribally published *A true relation of every day's proceedings in parliament since the beginning thereof being the 20th of January 1628* [i.e. 1628/9]. This is available in print in editions of 1641, 1654 and 1707 and the 1751 *Parliamentary history*, as well as having been reproduced in part by Rushworth in the second volume of the *Collections*.[39] But the texts of the three editions differ from each other in a great many details, and also from the text in the *Parliamentary history* which appears to have been conflated from 1707 and two manuscript sources. The editors discovered that none of the printed editions possessed authority, but that they were simply taken from whatever manuscript happened to be available to the printer. Their own edition drew on forty-eight contemporary manuscripts of the *True relation*, the survivors of what must have been a much larger body once in circulation. A new census would undoubtedly uncover additional sources.[40]

Circulation on this scale of a scribally published text is not in

[38] *Commons debates for 1629* (Minneapolis, 1921), pp. xi–lxv.

[39] *CD 1629*, p. xv.

[40] One such, purchased from a law bookseller in the year of the parliament, is described in Edward Hughes, 'A Durham manuscript of the *Commons debates* of 1629', *English historical review* 74 (1959), 672–9.

itself unusual, but the nature of its contents makes the *True relation* a valuable witness to the processes of its creation, production and distribution. For a start it should be noted that it is neither a newsletter nor a separate but a compilation formed out of independently circulating separates of parliamentary speeches, messages and declarations, together with linking passages of a diary-like nature.[41] The 1921 edition lists fifty-eight copies then known of seventeen elements found in the compilation, which survive independently of it as separates or miscellany transcripts *from* separates. While a few may have been copied from the *True relation* itself, there can be no doubt that most of this transmission was distinct from and, in its origins, prior to that of the compiled text. Notestein and Relf differed from most editors of historical documents in possessing practical skills in the genealogical analysis of textual variation. This allowed them to dispose very quickly of an earlier hypothesis that the manuscripts were descended from a single archetype which could be reconstructed by applying the method of Lachmann. Instead they diagnosed a situation similar to that to which some contemporary Chaucer scholars attribute variations in the order of the *Canterbury tales*: namely that several compilers created differing versions of the larger text (four in the case of the *True relation*) by making their own selection and ordering of the currently available materials.[42] According to this view, the differences arose from variations between the summaries (of which for one period two were available) and differences in the choice and placing of separates.

As regards the general availability by 1629 of separates of parliamentary speeches and declarations, there was no shortage of evidence. Despite regularly renewed attempts to enforce the ancient principle of secrecy, such materials had been freely circulating since the time of Elizabeth. For the reigns of James I and Charles I they survive in 'untold numbers'.[43] Moreover, these are generally of quite a different cast from the brief versions of the same materials found in the 'newsletter' sections of the *True relation*

[41] *CD 1629*, pp. 271–2.

[42] For the possible Chaucerian parallel, see Ralph Hanna III, 'The Hengwrt manuscript and the canon of *The Canterbury tales*', *English manuscript studies 1100–1700* 1 (1989), 64–84.

[43] *CD 1629*, p. xxii.

or the hurriedly scribbled accounts sometimes found in members' personal diaries. Notestein and Relf observe:

The separates are obviously the product of leisure. They have, most of them, full, rounded sentences, they are not at all conversational in style, but rather oratorical and flowing. They are full of delightful allusions to scripture and to the classic writers. They reveal in every way the fact that they have been 'written up'. They give the names of the speakers in full and present the speeches in a formal, full-dress pattern. They are finished productions intended for a wide circulation.[44]

Among a wealth of attendant evidence gathered from the period 1610–42 were cases where members circulated their speeches in a different form from that in which they had been delivered, or even speeches which had never been delivered at all. At other times, speeches were deliberately misattributed under illustrious names or compiled on the basis of second-hand reports.[45] It is clear that there were many active note-takers in parliament who could probably have passed on a fair report of a speech; but it is equally clear that the circulation of speeches by the author was an important form of political activism. The editors cite comments by Simonds D'Ewes, Peter Heylyn, Bulstrode Whitelock and John Nalson relating to this practice, as well as the following from the preface to Thomas Fuller's *Ephemeris parliamentaria*:

Some *Gentlemen, Speakers* in this *Parliament*, imparted their *Speeches* to their *intimate Friends*; the transcripts whereof were multiplied amongst others (the penne being very procreative of issue in this nature:) and since it hath happened that the *Gentlemens Originalls* have in these *troublesome* times miscarried, yet so that the *fountain* (as I may say) being dried up, hath fetch't this water from the *channell*, & they have again supplied their losses from those to whom they civilly communicated a *copy* of their paines.[46]

Some parliamentary documents, including legal arguments, were available to members from the Clerk's book and could be copied at their request in the Clerk's scriptorium. This material was of

[44] *CD 1629*, pp. xx–xxi.

[45] *CD 1629*, pp. xxii–xli.

[46] Thomas Fuller, *Ephemeris parliamentaria* (London, 1654), ¶¶1^{v}; cited *CD 1629*, pp. xxviii–xxix. Lord Digby's speech on Strafford's attainder was given by him 'to John Moore a com[m]on writer to write 20 copies' (ibid., p. xl; BL MS Harl. 163, f. 396^{v}).

particular interest to the legal profession, and there is every reason to suppose that copies were sought by legal stationers for further duplication. Separates of actual speeches would appeal to a much wider public, embracing leading county families (many separates show marks of mailing), foreign diplomats, politically involved clergymen, and members of both houses, some of whom possessed large collections of separates.[47]

Some separates of speeches show signs of being compiled by outsiders with an imperfect grasp of parliamentary procedure. This, together with the very wide circulation achieved by the standard separates and the apparent rapidity with which they became available, led Notestein and Relf to hypothesize that professional 'venters of manuscripts' played a significant role in their multiplication.[48] This was certainly so by the early 1640s when Samuel Pecke, a scrivener, actually had a stall in Westminster Hall for the sale of parliamentary speeches and proceedings, though one would be surprised if this was a location of long standing.[49] Stationers or newsletter writers might acquire a copy directly from the author (in which case, as with Sir John Eliot's speeches, the resulting text would be a good one), might draw on notes taken from a member, or might cobble up a version of their own from verbal reports. A Commons resolution of 25 January 1641 drew a lively picture of 'loose beggerly schollers who did in Alehowses invent speeches of and make speeches of members in the Howse' which were then sold to stationers.[50] None the less, the *CD 1629* editors' claim that separates were 'parliamentary speeches, etc., gathered by ignorant, careless and often unscrupulous scriveners in roundabout ways and hastily put together for immediate circulation' (p. xli) probably underestimates the amount of what will subsequently be called 'author' and 'user' publication involved. More caution should also have been extended with regard to the time range of the evidence cited (much of which is from the early 1640s) and of the manuscripts

[47] *CD 1629*, pp. xxxi–xxxiv.

[48] p. xxxiv. Evidence is presented from the D'Ewes diaries and the Borlase 'newsletters' suggesting that separates were normally received 'about a week after the delivery of the speech' (p. xxxiii).

[49] Muddiman, p. 10.

[50] BL MS Harl. 162, f. 351^{v}; *CD 1629*, p. xxxv.

themselves—bearing in mind that material relating to the parliaments of Charles I continued to be copied for several decades.[51] As regards the dating of sources, it makes sense to assume that a separate that survives as a separate is probably fairly close to the event: the average life expectancy of unbound separates before and during the Civil War years is unlikely to have been high.[52] It was separates aggregated into bound volumes or texts recopied into compilations or personal miscellanies which were more likely to be preserved to the present day. The 1629 *True relation* is itself one of these larger compilations and in some sources has become incorporated into others of still wider scope. However, the dates of surviving sources are of little significance when a later copy simply replaced an earlier one. The real problem to be resolved is whether the overall population of copies shrank from a large base, grew from a small one, or maintained a roughly stable profile over the crucial decades. At present there is no way of choosing between the three models. Genealogical analysis can demonstrate the existence of lost intermediaries but has no method for estimating the number of texts intervening between a surviving document and the nearest common ancestor. In the end we must rely on a broader assessment of the vitality of the trade in separates and compilations at the time of the parliament, a matter in which evidence from fields of scribal publication other than the political has to be considered.

As well as investigating the circulation of separates, Notestein and Relf also had to explain the diary-like accounts of proceedings in which the separates are embedded, and for which they use the term 'newsletters'. This reflects their belief that these were compiled outside the House by newsgathering professionals drawing on information from members. There are examples of parliamentary newsletters in an account by Pory of a day in the

[51] However, the copy cited in Hughes, 'A Durham manuscript' was certainly written in the year of the parliament, being inscribed 'August the 10th, 1629, John Heath empt Londino a W. Walbanck'. The parties to this transaction seem to have been John Heath of Durham who entered Gray's Inn on 8 August 1620 and Matthew Walbanck, bookseller at Gray's Inn Gate, or a member of his family.

[52] Some reasons for this have already been suggested. More generally P. J. Croft observes that '"Loose papers"—i.e. manuscripts written on unbound sheets—are the most intrinsically vulnerable of all types of record, and survive only when they become incorporated with other papers at an early date' (*Autograph poetry in the English language* (London, 1973), i, p. xv). Parliamentary separates would have suffered further as documents which some would regard as risky to keep.

1610 parliament (of which he was himself a member) and material forwarded in 1640 by Rossingham.[53] Newsletter-like accounts also survive for the 1628 parliament (BL MS Stowe 366, 367) and for the Short and Long Parliaments, but none external to the *True relation* for 1629.[54] This is not an overwhelming objection to the newsletter hypothesis, since such material would be expected to have a low survival rate, especially once it was also available in larger retrospective compilations. Moreover, it is possible that newsletter accounts (which were technically in contempt of parliament) would have been burnt after reading—a practice enjoined on his customers by Pory.[55] On the other hand, a circulation on the scale envisaged by Notestein and Relf would surely have left some trace of itself in the form of a particular letter or two bearing an address. In the absence of this, the strongest evidence for the newsletter hypothesis remains the one that first suggested it—namely the presence of the diary-like material in each of the four recensions of the *True relation*, with the implication that four separate compilers (whether stationers, newsletter writers or private individuals) were independently in possession of copies. However, Notestein and Relf fail to consider, and by this failure do not exclude, the possibility that the summary of proceedings may only have become available after the end of the session. Neither do they consider whether the four recensions may have arisen within a single scriptorium.

Validation (though not proof) for the last possibility is provided by an account of two scriptoria of the 1670s run by the Whig booksellers Thomas Collins and John Starkey which specialized in the provision of exactly this kind of material:

> There are two booksellers shops (viz. John Sterkey's and Thomas Collen's, living neer Temple Bar) that poyson both City and country with false newes.
>
> To these shops are sent every afternoon
>
> I. All novells and accurents so penned as to make for the disadvantage of the King and his affairs.

[53] Powell, pp. 65–9; Cope, pp. 36–7.

[54] *CD 1629*, pp. xlii–xlv. For the Stowe MSS, see *Commons debates 1628*, ed. Robert C. Johnson, Mary Frear Keeler, Maija Jansson Cole and William B. Bidwell (New Haven, Conn., 1977–8), i. 20–3 and below.

[55] Powell, p. 54.

II. All resolutions of Parliament that are either voted or a preparing for vote in either House, perfect true, or artificially corrupted, or penned by halves on purpose as may make most for the Faction.

III. All speeches of the most eminent members of each House that way affected, upon every business, are also sent them.

IV. Addresses also intended and at any time preparing by either House are here to be had in copies.

All these are thus disposed as followeth.

To these shops, for those things, every afternoon do repair severall sorts of people.

1. Young lawyers of both the Temples and the other Inns of Court, who here generally receive their tincture and corruption.

2. Ill-affected citizens of all sorts.

3. Ill-affected gentry.

4. The emissaries and agents of the severall parties and factions about town.

Against the time of their coming the Masters of those Shops have a grand book or books, wherein are registred ready for them, all or most of the forenamed particulars; which they dayly produce to those sorts of people to be read, and then, if they please, they either carry away copies, or bespeak them against another day.

These take care to communicate them by Letter all over the kingdome, and by conversation throughout the City and suburbs.

The like industry is used by the masters of those shops, who together with their servants are every afternoon and night busied in transcribing copies, with which they drive a trade all over the kingdome.

You may at present there have a copy of the intended address to his Majesty which the Houses have not yet agreed to.[56]

What is described here is exactly the kind of organization which

[56] BL MS Egerton 3329, fol. 57; Andrew Browning, *Thomas Osborne, Earl of Danby and Duke of Leeds 1632–1712* (Glasgow, 1944–51), iii. 2–3. A file of Collins's newsletters for 1688 is preserved in BL Add. MS 34487. For the scribal publication of parliamentary votes and proceedings after 1660 see Fraser, pp. 124–6. The 'Preface to the reader' of *A coppy of the journal-book of the House of Commons for the sessions of parliament begun at Westminster the 21. day of October, 1678. and continued until the 30. day of December next following* (London, 1680) justifies the printing of proceedings from the currency of inaccurate manuscript copies: '*Besides which there are many other most remarkable passages worthy our curiosity and knowledge, and very instructive both as to what has past, and towards what is to come; none of which should have been thus exposed (though this juncture of time gives so great a liberty to the Press) had not this very thing been handed about in Manuscripts to the great charge, as well as the great abuse of inquisitive Gentlemen, by imperfect Coppies; for what that Honorable House thinks fit to be lock'd up in their* Archives, *ought not to be exposed without their leave; but when any such secrets; are stolen abroad, it can be thought no ways unbecoming to make them speak the truth, and correct the mistakes that are incident to a hasty pen; so that here you shall find onely such Lapses as are inseperable to the Press*'

might have given rise to all stages of the creation of the *True relation* and perhaps even its division into four separate recensions. This division could have happened as the result of copying by several scribes simultaneously from an exemplum in the form of loose sheets, or from copying over a longer time span from an exemplum whose constituent elements were not stable (what will later be described as a 'rolling' as opposed to a 'static' archetype), or, designedly, as the result of preparing recensions to suit the knowledge and interests of particular customers.[57] It is true that the date of the document is 1675 not 1629 but the claim is not made here that the existence of the Starkey and Collins operations at a later period implies that of a predecessor using the same techniques—simply that, now the new model is admitted, the existing textual evidence requires to be reassessed and new evidence sought that would permit us to test the possibility. This cannot be performed from the *CD 1629* record of variations which, as a matter of policy, omits all readings 'whose only service would be to show the worth of particular manuscripts' (p. 3). Moreover, not all sources were collated in their entirety (p. 276). None the less, it remains possible that the advanced techniques of genealogical analysis which are described in Chapter 8, if applied to a fresh collation, could permit a preference to be established for one model over the other.

To say this is to assert that the *True relation* still remains a document in need of explanation, and that this explanation can only be provided when we possess a much fuller understanding not only of its own textual history but of the regularities (such as they may have been) of scribal publication over a much broader prospect.

(*A*2^{r}–2^{v}). A Commons debate of 29 October 1678, cited by Fraser (p. 124), mentions a Mr Cole (perhaps Elisha Cole the author and writing master) as a supplier of parliamentary separates and that they were available 'sometimes for 6*d*. sometimes for 12*d* according as they were considerable'. The theme is renewed in the preface to *A true copy of the journal-book of the last parliament* (London, 1680), A3^{r}: '*The purchace of so many written Coppies as have been dispers'd at so great rates (notwithstanding the many imperfections they are fraught withal) demonstrates sufficiently, the vallue curious people sets upon them; how much more acceptable therefore must they needs be when purged from their Errors, and brought down to such a reasonable price, as to afford Gentlemen the benefit of them in their Libraries, without any great Tax upon their Purses*'.

[57] Cope, pp. 35–7, regards this last possibility as the most likely cause of the variations among texts of the diurnal of the 1640 parliament.

THE SCRIBAL PUBLICATION OF CONSORT MUSIC FOR VIOLS

My other example of a specialized study of scribal publication is the admirable *Thematic index of music for viols* published by the Viola da gamba Society of Great Britain.[58] Although the index includes printed as well as manuscript sources, its interest for us lies in its being an exhaustive inventory of surviving examples of a particular class of seventeenth-century, scribally circulated text. Within this class, our concern will be with the sources of consort music written for three to six viols.

The consort of viols was introduced into England by Italian court musicians during the reign of Henry VIII. During the later years of Elizabeth it became a favourite with amateurs, with the result that the reigns of James I and Charles I saw an outpouring of fantasias for the combination by Alfonso Ferrabosco II, Orlando Gibbons, John Coprario, John Ward, Richard Deering, William Lawes, John Jenkins and a number of lesser lights. The viol fantasia with its 'perpetuall grave course of fugue' maintained its popularity through the Commonwealth, when, as Roger North put it, 'many chose rather to fidle at home, than to goe out, and be knockt on the head abroad'.[59] However, after the Restoration, a shift of taste towards a lighter, more homophonic idiom based first on French and later on Italian models led to the neglect both of the instrument (in favour of the violin family) and the fantasia style. Purcell's fantasias, written in the early 1680s, are the last significant contribution to viol consort literature.

Consort music was and remains primarily players' music, giving each performer both an individually rewarding voice in the ensemble and a unique spatial perception of the interrelationship of the musical lines. It is most satisfactorily performed with the players in a ring facing inwards towards each other, the role of the listener, if any, being that of an eavesdropper. Roger North found an ideological value in this '*respublica* among the consortiers', contrasting it with the 'unsociable and malcreate behaviour' of 'some violin spark, that thinks himself above all the rest, and above

[58] Comp. Gordon Dodd, first instalment (London, 1980), with further instalments 1982, 1984 and 1987.

[59] *Roger North on music*, ed. John Wilson (London, 1959), pp. 25, 294.

the musick itself also, if it be not screwed up to the top of his capability'.[60] Such music encoded an idealized image of the gentry as a community of equals while, at the same time, providing release from the tensions of hierarchy in the state and in the family. In refusing a dominant role to any single part it was also asserting—even when played by musicians who were political royalists—a consensual conception of the ideal state.[61] The culturally and ideologically competing ideal of a dominant, ornate melody line supported by a subservient chordal continuo was frowned on by admirers of the viol, though most of their favourite composers eventually adjusted to it.[62] It also altered the social relationships of playing, making the accompanists subordinate to the soloist and the soloist in turn subordinate to the listener.

The kind of circle in which the consort style was cultivated is indicated by the learned nature of its counterpoint and the fondness of composers from Lawes onward for striking dissonances and bold modulations. It is not surprising to find either that Oxford maintained a strong tradition of consort playing or that several composers for the medium held appointments in the private music of James I and Charles I.[63] This was music for educated, often intellectual, music lovers who would themselves in most cases have been players. Seeing that to play the five and six part fantasias, which were the crown of the repertoire, required the continued presence of a group of competent performers in one place, there was a strong tendency for consort music to be associated with music-loving gentry families such as the L'Estranges, Norths,

[60] North, *Roger North*, p. 222. His words acquire interesting resonances from Patrick Collinson's use of the term 'republic' in *De republica Anglorum, or history with the politics put back* (Cambridge, 1990), pp. 18–35.

[61] This was not lost on left-wing musicologists of the 1930s and 1940s. See in particular Ernst Meyer's pioneering studies of the consort repertoire, *Die mehrstimmige Spielmusik des 17. Jahrhunderts in Nord- und Mitteleuropa* (Kassel, 1934) and *English chamber music* (London, 1946; rev. edn as *Early English chamber music* (London, 1982)), and John Manifold, *The amorous flute* (London, 1948), p. 14.

[62] For opinions to this effect see North, *Roger North*, p. 222 and Thomas Mace, *Musick's monument* (London, 1676), pp. 233–4.

[63] For music at Oxford, see Bruce Bellingham, 'The musical circle of Anthony Wood in Oxford during the Commonwealth and Restoration', *Journal of the Viola da gamba Society of America* 19 (1982), 6–70. Court appointments of the principal viol composers are detailed in *Records of English court music*, ed. Andrew Ashbee (Snodland, 1986–), greatly extending the work of H. C. de Lafontaine, *The king's musick* (London, 1909). The 'private music' was the inner circle of court musicians who played in the sovereign's own apartments.

Brownes, Packers, Bolles's, Cliffords, Hattons, Fanshawes, Hamonds, Maules and Pastons.[64] Children would be instructed and consorts directed (from the organ) by visiting music masters who in many cases were also composers for the medium.

The Viola da gamba Society's index demonstrates how profoundly reliant the players of viol consort music were on manuscript transmission. Of hundreds of surviving fantasias for the instruments written between 1600 and 1680, only a few in three parts by Gibbons, Lupo, Coprario, Young and Locke and some lightweight four and five part pieces by Michael East ever appeared in print.[65] The rest were published scribally by their

[64] The L'Estranges are discussed in Pamela Willetts, 'Sir Nicholas Le Strange and John Jenkins', *Music and letters* 42 (1961), 30–43 and 'Sir Nicholas Le Strange's collection of masque music', *British Museum quarterly*, 29 (1965), 79–81, and Andrew Ashbee, 'A further look at some of the Le Strange manuscripts', *Chelys* 5 (1973–4), 24–41; the Norths in North, *Roger North*, Pamela J. Willetts, 'John Lilly, musician and music copyist', *Bodleian Library record* 7 (1962–7), 307–11 and Margaret Crum, 'The consort music from Kirtling, bought for the Oxford Music School from Anthony Wood, 1667', *Chelys* 4 (1972), 3–10; the Brownes and Packers in Andrew Ashbee, 'Instrumental music from the library of John Browne (1608–1691), clerk of the Parliaments', *Music and letters* 58 (1977) 43–59, Nigel Fortune (with Iain Fenlon), 'Music manuscripts of John Browne (1608–91) and from Stanford Hall, Leicestershire' in *Source materials and the interpretation of music: a memorial volume to Thurston Dart*, ed. Ian Bent (London, 1981), pp. 155–68, and David Pinto, 'William Lawes' music for viol consort', *Early music* 6 (1978), 12–24. Information on other families will be found in Margaret Urquhart, 'Sir Robert Bolles Bt. of Scampton', *Chelys* 16 (1987), 16–29 and *Sir John St Barbe Bt. of Broadlands* (Southampton, 1983); Lynn Hulse, 'John Hingeston', *Chelys* 12 (1983), 23–42 (the Cliffords of Skipton Castle); David Pinto, 'The music of the Hattons', *RMA Research chronicle* 23 (1990), 79–108 (the Hattons and Fanshawes); Margaret Crum, 'A seventeenth-century collection of music belonging to Thomas Hamond, a Suffolk landowner', *Bodleian Library record* 6 (1957–61), 373–86; Calum McCart, 'The Panmure manuscripts: a new look at an old source of Christopher Simpson's consort music', *Chelys* 18 (1989), 18–29 (the Maules); Pamela Willetts, 'Musical connections of Thomas Myriell', *Music and letters* 49 (1968), 36–42 and 'The identity of Thomas Myriell', *Music and letters* 53 (1972), 431–3; Philip Brett, 'Edward Paston (1550–1630): a Norfolk gentleman and his musical collection', *Transactions of the Cambridge Bibliographical Society* 4 (1964), 51–69; and Andrew Ashbee, 'A not unapt scholar: Bulstrode Whitelocke (1605–1675)', *Chelys* 11 (1982), 24–31. John Harper, 'The distribution of the consort music of Orlando Gibbons in seventeenth-century sources', *Chelys* 12 (1983), 3–18 discusses the collections of Thomas Myriell, John Merro, John Browne and Narcissus Marsh (with bibliography). Craig Monson's valuable *Voices and viols in England, 1600–1650: the sources and the music* (Ann Arbor, Mich., 1982) discusses a wide range of surviving sets of manuscripts including those of Myriell, Hamond and Merro. Sets of unknown provenance are closely analysed for clues as to their geographical and institutional origins.

[65] Collections of dances, masque tunes and pieces arranged for broken consort did appear in print and may have been used by viol ensembles (as were madrigals) but were not primarily meant for them. The small corpus of printed ensemble music for lyra viol represents a separate tradition of the instrument.

composers for direct sale to players (some of whom will have been their pupils) or as part of their work for their patrons. Collections of fantasias consolidated into part books were also available, with some pieces evidently composed as sets for this purpose.[66] Once available in this form, new compositions moved quickly through the network of music-loving families, either by private copying or by purchase.

An insight into the quantity of material in circulation may be gained from the most popular of the composers, John Jenkins, whose entries in the *Thematic index* occupy seventy-six pages. The manner in which Jenkins operated as a publisher of his own music is illustrated by Roger North (born in 1651) who as a young man was closely associated with the by then elderly composer. North's account is of special interest because Jenkins's methods of reaching his public need not have been very different from those of a poet, a scholar or a writer of political tracts. By this stage of his life, Jenkins had long been a pensionary of a succession of music-loving, royalist households who welcomed his visits and would often have a room permanently reserved for his use. During his stays Jenkins would instruct the children of the house, supervise consort playing, copy and compose. North speaks of 'horsloads' of his works being 'dispersed about' and states that 'the private musick in England was in great measure supplyed by him'.[67] North himself occasionally acted as Jenkins's distributor by delivering copies of new compositions to the viol virtuoso, Dietrich Steffkins.[68] Transmission was not restricted to England. On one occasion

> A Spanish Don sent over to the late Sr P. Lely, the leaves of one part of a 3 part consort of his, with a desire to procure the rest, *costa che costa*; for his musick had got abroad and was more esteemed there than at home. I shewed him the papers, but he could tell nothing of them, when or where they were made, or might be found, onely he knew they were his owne.[69]

[66] Examples are the sets of six six-part fantasias by Orlando Gibbons and William White. The production and sale of partbooks of vocal music by a well-organized scriptorium of the late sixteenth century is discussed in Philip Brett, 'Edward Paston'; however, that all the manuscripts discussed were written for Paston is to be doubted. As with the verse and political miscellanies, there was considerable overlap between the different collections offered for sale, forcing assiduous collectors of new material into purchasing items they already had.

[67] North, *Roger North*, p. 345.

[68] Ibid. 21, 298, 347.

[69] Ibid. 296.

The channel of communication in this case is likely to have been Henry Butler, an English viol player at the Spanish court whose pupils included Philip IV and his son Don Juan.[70] Apart from some pieces said to have been contributed to Christopher Simpson's *The division viol* in 1659, there is no evidence that Jenkins sought print publication for any significant body of his music.[71] He was content with scribal publication and lived in comfort on the proceeds from it. It was Nicola Matteis, according to North, who made the discovery that higher returns could be made from printing music than from selling it in manuscript.[72]

What the case of Jenkins demonstrates is exactly what we would expect from the rich scribal heritage revealed by the *Thematic index*. Viol consort music, along with the related lyra-viol repertoire and fantasia suites and airs for violin, bass viol and organ, circulated through an extensive and well-organized network of copyists to a scattered but enthusiastic amateur clientele to whom it offered both an aesthetic and, as suggested earlier, an ideological satisfaction. But this circulation represented only one aspect of a much wider participation by the families concerned in the culture of scribal publication. That this was the case is evident at every turn; but for the moment a few instances must suffice. The first of these is the career of Roger North as writer for the scribal medium. North, besides his activity as a player and copyist of music, was a voluminous author of tracts, treatises and essays most of which remained unprinted during his lifetime. As a lawyer he belonged to a profession still predominantly dependent on the handwritten word; but in the long years of his retirement his conception of himself was clearly as an essayist, philosopher and family historian. He was also an inveterate reviser and reworker of material, deriving later treatises out of the materials of earlier ones.[73] Franciscus Korsten advances the opinion that North was his own

[70] Ian Woodfield, 'The first Earl of Sandwich, a performance of William Lawes in Spain and the origins of the pardessus de viole', *Chelys* 14 (1985), 40–2; Elizabeth V. Phillips, 'Henry Butler and the early viol sonata', *Journal of the Viola da gamba Society of America* 21 (1984), 45–52. Butler was active at the Spanish court between 1623 and 1652. Charles I of England was also a competent viol player.

[71] North, *Roger North*, p. 347.

[72] Ibid. 356. See also pp. 64–5 below.

[73] See Wilson on this point in *Roger North*, p. vii, and Mary Chan, 'Roger North's *Life* of Francis North', *RES* NS 42 (1991), 191–211.

sole intended reader; but this seems to be contradicted both by the public nature of the forms he chose for his writing and their frequently pedagogical tone.[74] While it is possible that he wrote with the expectation of posthumous print publication, it is more natural to see him as an heir to the tradition, which will be discussed in subsequent chapters, of the scribally published treatise, bearing in mind that such texts were frequently restricted by design to a single copy.[75] If Korsten is right, it may only be because North was a scribal author who had outlived his natural readership. For his deep identification with the culture of the inscribed word, the fifty-six volumes of his manuscripts in the British Library are sufficient evidence.[76]

A wider involvement in scribal publication was also displayed by another of Jenkins's patrons, Sir Henry North, baronet of Laxfield, Suffolk.[77] The evidence for this lies in the personal miscellany of John Watson, a fellow of Queens' College, Cambridge who in 1661 became vicar of Mildenhall in the same county.[78] Watson's manuscript, which will be discussed in more detail later, is of special value because it records the donors of separates that were copied into it, together with the date of copying. Among the contributors of texts was Jenkins himself, bringing poems by Sir Henry and his chaplain Clement Paman, as well as two poems of his own, one being an elegy on Lord Digby North.[79] However, Sir Henry and his wife Sara are also present in the volume as writers or transmitters of poems and inscriptions. Among these is 'Tush, look for no ease from Hippocrates', marked 'A Song in Sr H. North's Eroclea. transcribd

[74] F. J. M. Korsten, *Roger North (1651–1734): virtuoso and essayist* (Amsterdam, 1981), p. 23.

[75] See below, pp. 70–2.

[76] BL Add. MSS 32,500–32,551. For descriptions of these, see Mary Chan and Jamie C. Kassler, *Roger North. Materials for a chronology of his writings. Checklist no. 1* (Kensington, NSW, 1989), pp. 65–91. The whereabouts of other Roger North manuscripts are given in ibid. 50 and P. T. Millard, 'The chronology of Roger North's main works', *RES* NS 24 (1973), 283–94. North's (anonymous) print publications are described in Korsten, pp. 24–5.

[77] The Norths of Laxfield and Mildenhall were descended from Henry, second son of Roger, second Baron North (1531–1600). The Norths of Kirtling (Roger's branch) derive from John, the eldest son. There is an account of the family in Dale B. J. Randall, *Gentle flame: the life and verse of Dudley, fourth Lord North (1602–1677)* (Durham, NC, 1983).

[78] J. and J. A. Venn, *Alumni Cantabrigienses. Part I. From the earliest times to 1751* (Cambridge, 1924–7), iv. 349.

[79] BL MS Add. 18220, ff. 11^{r}–13^{r}, 37^{r}–37^{v}.

Nov: 26 1668' and 'Sr H. North Baronet Auto^r^ 1659'.[80] Since no printed work of this title survives, it must be assumed that *Eroclea* was a scribally circulated text—either a collection of poems along the lines of Lovelace's *Lucasta* or a play. Watson seems to have served as a conduit of literary separates in and out of Suffolk, receiving material from his brother Thomas in London and friends at Cambridge, and returning satires, neo-Latin verse and funerary inscriptions by Suffolk and Norfolk writers. The inclusion of the words of anthems and songs, along with the presence of Jenkins as a donor, suggests that the transmission of musical manuscripts may have gone hand in hand with that of literary texts.[81]

Two other viol-playing families have a quite explicit link with the scribal communication of non-musical texts. John Browne as Clerk of Parliaments from 1638 to 1649 and again from 1660 was, during sessions, at the head of the most important scriptorium in England, while Sir Roger L'Estrange served as press-licenser and propagandist for Charles II. Although the story of L'Estrange involuntarily playing in a viol consort before Cromwell is well-known, it is not generally realized that he was also a composer for the instrument.[82] His professional concern was with printed books and pamphlets, yet he thoroughly understood the political influence of scribally circulated texts and twice memorialized Charles II on the need to control them. On the second of these occasions he noted tellingly that 'not one of forty [libels] ever comes to the Presse, and yet by the helpe of Transcripts, they are well nigh as Publique'.[83]

Another kind of link between musical and nonmusical kinds of scribal transmission is suggested by the activities of Sir Nicholas Le Strange (Roger's brother). This enthusiastic viol-player brought to his music-making the skills and enthusiasm of an experienced

[80] Ibid., ff. 25^v^–26^v^.

[81] Composers besides Jenkins mentioned as having set texts in the volume are Benjamin Rogers, Sylvanus Taylour and Thomas Bradbury.

[82] For the compositions, see *Thematic index*. The allegation that he had played for Cromwell led to him being nicknamed 'Noll's fiddler'. His own account of the event is given in his *Truth and loyalty vindicated* (London, 1662), p. 50. Walking in St James's Park, he heard music from John Hingeston's room at Whitehall. Entering, he found some viol players who asked him to join them. While they played, Cromwell entered, listened for a while, and left.

[83] 'Mr L'Estraings Proposition concerning Libells, &c.', 11 Nov. 1675, reproduced in Ch. 2.

textual critic. In the years following his marriage in 1630 he assembled a large body of viol consort music in part books.[84] These were written by four copyists, including Sir Nicholas himself and John Jenkins. (Pamela Willetts has proposed that one of the remaining hands is that of the composer Thomas Brewer who was retained as a house musician.[85]) The filling of the books was itself a labour of many years, but what is equally remarkable is that Le Strange regularly acquired books from other players and, with the help of his amanuenses, carefully collated their versions with his own. A record was made of all differences, including obvious errors, and such details as the order of items in the borrowed volumes. The two largest Le Strange collections, now BL Add. MSS 39550–4 and Royal College of Music MS 1145, contain between them records of twenty-one collated sources identified as Couzens, Sheppy, Pettus, Drury, Dunn, Donne 2[d], Holland, Harman, Couzens Score: B:, Pettus: 2d: coppy, Gibbs, Francklin, Staresmore, Fowler, Ives, Rampley, Barnard score: B:, Mr Fanshaw Score: b:, Bromall, Mr Collins, and Mr Coleman.[86]

The most noteworthy thing about this procedure is that it was possible for Sir Nicholas and his amanuenses to have access to such a large number of manuscripts. If, as Andrew Ashbee suggests, they were borrowed for use at Hunstanton, and this reflected a wider code of trust and generosity among possessors of manuscripts, it could well be that the use made of the single manuscript copy (whether in this or other fields) was far wider than we would expect.[87] But the more significant point is that this vast exercise (reminiscent of the work of editors of parliamentary compilations) was not even necessary. By scoring problematical passages from his partbooks and consulting with his resident professionals, Sir Nicholas would have had little difficulty in finding an acceptable solution for any progression that displeased his ear. The mammoth labour of comparison springs from what is not a musician's but a

[84] Listed in the *Thematic index* under 'The Le Strange manuscripts'.

[85] Willetts, 'Sir Nicholas Le Strange and John Jenkins', p. 40.

[86] Ashbee, 'A further look', p. 28. Willetts, 'Sir Nicholas Le Strange and John Jenkins', pp. 39–40 suggests some identifications. Sir Nicholas also obtained manuscripts from Jenkins's early patrons the Dereham family, from Coprario's friend Richard Ligon, and from the Jacobs family.

[87] Ashbee, 'A further look', p. 28. Sir Robert Cotton's free and easy way with both his own and other people's manuscripts suggests the same.

bibliophile's or philologist's fascination with the vagaries of signification arising from scribal transmission: it reflects a love of the medium quite as much as a love for music.[88] This wider concern with the medium is also evident in his 'Merry passages and jeasts', the manuscript collection of jokes and anecdotes for which he is principally remembered.[89] A further question that arises is to what extent his tastes in music were an outgrowth of the scribal culture to which he belonged rather than representing an autonomous aesthetic preference. (This problem arises again in the relationship between the spread of 'country' political views in the early decades of the century and the tendency of political separates to be concerned with court scandal and imagined conspiracies. Which was giving rise to which?)

Yet another kind of interpenetration of music and scholarship is found in the career of the first Baron Hatton of Kirby, born in 1605. David Pinto has established that the Hatton musical manuscripts formed a substantial part of the collection left to Christ Church, Oxford in 1710 by Dean Aldrich, making them one of the most important family collections of the century. But Hatton was also 'a generall sercher of all antiquityes concerning the whole kingdome, but cheifelye Northamptonshire his own country'. His collection included 'almost a hundred bookes of his owne abstracting, of very choyce antiquityes' in addition to those prepared for him by assistants.[90] In his case major achievements in the collection and transcription of historical records went hand in hand with a concern to secure and copy music. The fate that sent his historical manuscripts to Bodley and the British Library and the musical manuscripts to Christ Church fractured what at Kirby Hall had existed as a unified expression of a preoccupation with the scribally transmitted text.

88 A striking analogy between the activities of the editor and the musician is drawn by Fuller, *Ephemeris parliamentaria*, loc. cit.: 'And may the *Reader* be pleased to take notice that this *Book* is no *Monochord*, or *Instrument* of a *single string*, no nor is it a *single Instrument*; but the exact result of many collections. We have compared *varias lectiones*, or rather *varias auditiones*, the copies as they have been taken by severall *Auditours*.'

89 BL MS Harl. 6395. Edited as *'Merry passages and jeasts': a manuscript jestbook of Sir Nicholas Le Strange (1603–1655)*, ed. H. F. Lippincott (Salzburg, 1974). One use for these anecdotes would have been during the prolonged periods of tuning customary among viol players.

90 Pinto, 'The music of the Hattons', p. 87; draft letter from Sir Symon Archer to Thomas Habington, 27 December 1637 in *The life, diary, and correspondence of Sir William Dugdale*, ed. William Hamper (London, 1827), p. 171 n.

CONCLUSION

In this chapter we have looked at three different products of scribal publication—verse miscellanies, parliamentary compilations and consort music for viols. It is not entirely true that the existing scholarship is narrowly restricted to one or the other field (musicologists and literary scholars have some areas of contact), but it is valid to claim that they have never been acknowledged as separate aspects of a common phenomenon—the publication of texts in handwritten copies within a culture which had developed sophisticated means of generating and transmitting such copies. Not all consumers of scribally published texts will have had verse miscellanies on their bookshelves, parliamentary compilations discretely locked in their cabinets and part books of viol music in their music chests, but some will certainly have done so, and, in any case, these are but three of a multitude of genres of the scribally published sign. It would be a mistake to assume too great a degree of regularity and too high a degree of organization in the procedure by which scribal texts were written, copied and communicated; but that there were such regularities and such organization will already be evident, and it will be one task of this book to explore them. Since the bibliographical aids necessary for a comprehensive survey of primary sources are still largely lacking, the majority of my material will be drawn from already available scholarship but with new research offered where this is necessary and appropriate.

As part of this process, we need first of all to acquire an empirical understanding of the phenomena. Information about scribal practice across the sequence authorship, production and distribution needs to be collected and classified, and new information sought about matters that reveal themselves as significant. Patterns in this information must be recognized and a variety of models considered for the working of each stage of the process of publication. Certainly we will need to look more closely at how far it is valid to extrapolate from one field or genre to another. Is the enormous success of John Jenkins as a scribal author-publisher typical or atypical? How far were his methods similar to or different from those of poets like Donne and King, thinkers like Filmer and Sir Thomas Browne, or historians like Camden and

Cotton? Do Roger North's thousands of pages of manuscript discourses devoted to a wide range of learned enquiries have anything to tell us about the intended social function of the even larger and no less varied body of discourses inscribed by Isaac Newton? But another, no less important kind of understanding will need to be theoretical and interpretative, embracing a broader consideration of the functioning of the scribal medium within seventeenth-century society. We must seek through a process of recontextualization to understand the ways in which scribal publication served to define communities of the like-minded. We must also consider what the scribally published text has to tell us about how information of all kinds was constituted, encountered and encoded by seventeenth-century readers. Beyond these lie other questions (considered in Chapter 4) concerning the ways in which scribal and print media project their respective metaphors of the nature of knowledge, how the reader and the writer are constructed by the scribal text, and how the 'presence' of the writer is projected through the two media. All these things will have a bearing not simply on how we interpret what we find but on what kinds of information it is necessary to look for.

While new research will be required to pursue some of these topics, it must be stressed again how much information about scribal publication is already available under Swanson's category of 'undiscovered public knowledge'. Swanson presents three models for this. The first is the case where evidence that would refute or require the modification of a conjecture has been assembled in ignorance of the original conjecture. The second is where the conclusions '*a* proves *b*' and '*b* proves *c*' have been reached without the bibliographical connections being made that would permit the further hypothesis '*a* proves *c*'. The third is where 'many individually weak tests of a theory can be combined into the equivalent of a much stronger test'.[91] It is this third category, illustrated by Swanson from the early history of investigation into the link between smoking and lung cancer and by Roy Davies from the emergence of Chaos theory in mathematics, which has the most direct relevance to the present

[91] Swanson, pp. 108–13; see also Davies 277–87. Historians will recognize Swanson's third category as the means used to secure the conviction of Strafford in 1641.

enquiry. A passage cited by Davies from James Gleick's *Chaos* could hardly be more pertinent to the problem in hand:

> A mathematical discovery was understood by mathematicians, a physics discovery by physicists, a meteorological discovery by no one. The way ideas spread became as important as the way they originated. Each scientist had a private constellation of intellectual parents. Each had his own picture of the landscape of ideas, and each picture was limited in its own way. Knowledge was imperfect. Scientists were biased by the customs of their disciplines or by the accidental paths of their own educations.[92]

In our case what remains 'undiscovered' is a whole dimension of seventeenth-century culture, one which has been the subject of endless minutely detailed research, and which is everywhere apparent, and yet one which has never been addressed as an entity in its own right.

[92] Davies, p. 283, Gleick, *Chaos: making a new science* (London, 1988), pp. 181–2.

2

'PUBLICATION' IN THE SCRIBAL MEDIUM

CHAPTER 1 introduced some sub-traditions of scribal publication, but postponed the question of how we are to define the term. This will require some finesse. When we speak today of an unpublished manuscript we mean an unprinted manuscript, but we now need to consider how handwritten texts are to be classed as published or unpublished within a culture in which scribal transmission might be chosen without any sense of its being inferior or incomplete.

Although our modern usage of 'publish' excludes the notion of scribal publication, there is no problem about recovering it. There is already a tendency to speak of a sound recording, a video, or computer software as having been published. We do not regard a new poem read during a radio broadcast as having been published on that occasion, but it would not be a contradiction of our other usages if we were to do so. The ancient world accepted the idea of publication by declamation, with a new epic or history being read aloud to an audience prior to its distribution in written form. E. A. J. Honigmann has argued that for Shakespeare 'the theatre gave the primary form of publication'.[1] A corollary of this wider conception was that it became possible for the same text to be published in more than one medium. Francis Beaumont in his commendatory poem printed with the first quarto of Fletcher's *The faithful shepherdess* speaks of the printing of the play as 'This second publication'—performance being the first.[2] A present-day

[1] *The stability of Shakespeare's text* (London, 1965), p. 191.

[2] 'To my friend Maister *John Fletcher* upon his Faithfull Shepheardesse', l. 40, in *The dramatic works in the Beaumont and Fletcher canon*, gen. ed. Fredson Bowers (Cambridge, 1966–), iii. 491; cited Honigmann, loc. cit.

parallel is the notion of a 'pre-publication' text of a scientific paper—in effect one awaiting print publication but freely available in electronic form. No-one would deny that these papers are already published: it is simply that they still await a redundant further publication in a more privileged medium, by which time (such is the pace of science) they may possess only archival interest. Margaret Anne Doody, writing of her novel, *The alchemists*, expresses a literary author's sense of the phenomenon of double publication. Although the book, written between 1965 and 1968, had not been print-published at the time, 'it had been published in an older sense (as it had been read in manuscript by a group of readers)'. Revising it for the press in 1980 she 'felt as if it had been completed, and that in some peculiar sense it was a trespass to return to work begun nearly fifteen years ago'.[3]

The root sense underlying all these usages is of publication as a movement from a private realm of creativity to a public realm of consumption. The problem is to determine whether any given text—in our case a text transmitted through handwritten copies—has made this transition. We will need to recognize both a 'strong' sense in which the text must be shown to have become publicly available and a more inclusive 'weak' sense in which it is enough to show that the text has ceased to be a private possession. A further condition is that scribal publication should be something more than the chrysalis stage of an intended print publication. This would exclude manuscripts circulated for comment and correction prior to printing or in order to attract a sheaf of commendatory verses.[4] However, Pope's circulation among his friends of the *Pastorals* might well be included since the manuscript, like that of its successor, *Windsor forest*, was obviously meant to be enjoyed in its own right as an example of skilled calligraphy.[5]

[3] 'Taking it up again', *London review of books*, 21 March 1991, p. 17.

[4] For the first of these practices we might instance Dryden's circulation of drafts of sections of his translation of the *Aeneid* (*The works of John Dryden*, gen. eds H. T. Swedenberg, jun. and Alan Roper (Los Angeles, 1956–), vi. 868). The second is discussed in Franklin B. Williams, jun., 'Commendatory verses: the rise of the art of puffing', *SB* 19 (1966), 8–9. *Annalia Dvbrensia* (London, 1636; ed. Christopher Whitfield (London, 1962)) employed the same technique to assemble a volume of celebratory poems on Robert Dover's '*Olimpick Games vpon Cotswold-Hills*'.

[5] See *Pastoral poetry and An essay on criticism*, ed. E. Audra and Aubrey Williams (London, 1961), pp. 38–40 and the facsimile edition in Maynard Mack, 'Pope's pastorals', *Scriblerian* 12 (1980), 85–161. Pope has noted the names of the twelve readers of the manuscript. The

Publication in our strong sense is usually equated with the provision of large numbers of copies, and some kinds of scribal publication do fulfil this criterion. Prior to the invention of print there had been entrepreneurial stationers who functioned in a way similar to modern print publishers—obtaining texts, arranging for them to be copied in whatever numbers were needed, and supplying them to public bookshops. In the great cities of the ancient world, *bibliopolae* duplicated texts in scriptoria where slaves copied simultaneously from dictation. In the late middle ages scriptoria producing prayer books, bibles and books of hours developed elaborate routines through which sections of a book could be worked on successively by scribes, artists and illuminators. Medieval universities supported the development of an educational book trade and established collections of manuscripts from which students could make their own copies. Eventually secular stationers emerged who specialized in vernacular manuscripts, an early English example being Lydgate's publisher, John Shirley.[6] 'Scribal editions' of the fifteenth century were sometimes comparable in size with those of the early printers. Marcel Thomas cites an order to a fifteenth-century Flemish scriptorium for 400 copies of a university text, with which we can compare the 250 to 500 copies John Feather estimates as the norm for early printed editions.[7] Texts so issued must be regarded under any criteria as published.

In other cases, the scribally circulated text would have had a much more restricted availability than the average printed text. But is this difference to be regarded as one of kind or merely of

Windsor forest manuscript is praised by Audra and Williams as 'an example of Pope's superb craftsmanship in lettering' (p. 129), while Robert M. Schmitz, *Pope's Windsor forest 1712. A study of the Washington University holograph* (St Louis, Miss., 1952), p. 7, considered that Pope 'had penned the *Pastorals* manuscript as if he had learned the art of lettering in the best scriptorium'. This suggests that Pope saw scribal transmission as having its own integrity, independently of print-publishing; and yet the objection could be made that his calligraphy was directed towards recreating the effect of a *printed* page. In fact he had taught himself his script by imitating typography.

[6] See Cheryl Greenberg, 'John Shirley and the English book trade', *Library*, 6:4 (1982), 369–80. Further information is available in H. S. Bennett, 'The production and dissemination of vernacular manuscripts in the fifteenth century', *Library*, 5:1 (1946–7), 167–78, and the papers gathered in Jeremy Griffiths and Derek Pearsall, eds, *Book production and publishing in Britain 1375–1475* (Cambridge, 1989).

[7] Introduction to Lucien Febvre and Henri-Jean Martin, *L'apparition du livre*, 2nd edn (Paris, 1971), pp. 35–6; Feather, *A history of British publishing* (London, 1988), p. 8.

degree? A book printed in an edition of 500 copies is only available to a maximum of 500 purchasers; moreover, the only potential readers who would be able to take advantage of that availability would be those who had learned of the publication's existence, knew where copies were to be obtained and were interested (and affluent) enough to take advantage of this information between its appearance on the shelves and the return of any unsold copies for pulping. We might assume that a copy of a print-published work would subsequently be obtainable from a library or through the second-hand book trade, but even this is not always the case: a large body of material classified as ephemera or as disposable is not preserved by anyone. Scribal publication, operating at relatively lower volumes and under more restrictive conditions of availability than print publication, was still able to sustain the currency of popular texts for very long periods and bring them to the attention of considerable bodies of readers. The material difference is that it did this through small increments rather than through one explosive provision of copies. Whereas the printed book for which there was no immediate requirement would be ready in a warehouse, new copies of the scribal text only came into existence in response to the desire of prospective readers. So while the survival of a text in a large number of manuscript copies is certainly evidence for its having been published, the fact that it only survives in two or three does not mean that it had not made the crucial transition from private status which would allow us to include it, under our weak sense, in the same category.

This weak sense, in rejecting availability as the primary criterion of published status, invokes an alternative criterion of publication as an activity carried out by a special kind of person called a publisher. In present-day print publication this activity embraces the procurement or commissioning of the book from an author, the editing of the text into a form suitable for production, the contracting out of the printing and binding, the promotion and advertising of the book, the maintaining of stocks of the edition, and its distribution on mutually agreed terms of sale to retailers. The publisher is also required to provide capital for the production stage of the venture and to assume certain responsibilities under the laws relating to copyright, libel and deposit. Even a simple act of desk-top publication, in which the various parties of these transactions may be united in a single individual, will still involve most of the stages described. This definition has the advantage that the 'privately printed' or 'not published' book can be admitted to the category of publications, for there can be no doubt that the defining activities of the publisher have been performed, the only difference being in the method used to secure distribution. Its limitation is that the activities of the modern print-publisher are not a very satisfactory model for those of the seventeenth-century scribal publisher. They also diverge in a number of ways from the activities of the seventeenth-century print-publisher, for whom publishing was still a subsidiary operation to bookselling, printing or binding.

None the less, this freer conception of publication as a social activity is a useful one for our present enquiry. It has always been present in the legal sense of the word as it applies in libel and treason cases. In the case of Oscar Wilde, the publication of a libel was constituted by the act of leaving a card addressed to Wilde at his club.[8] By this ritualized transfer the text of the message was agreed to have moved from the private to the public realm and Wilde was permitted to sue the Marquess of Queensberry. In a wider context, this moment at which a text passes from one to the other domain may be defined as being that at which the initiating agent (who will not necessarily be the author or even acting with the approval of the author) knowingly relinquishes control over the future social use of that text. Once this has happened, the text must be regarded as possessing a potential for wider availability, this potential being realized or not realized according to the subsequent decisions of those to whom power over the text has been transferred. The transmissional history of Donne's *Biathanatos* will help to illustrate this.

Donne wrote his treatise in 1607–8 with no apparent thought of publication through the press. Its argument—that suicide was not in all circumstances to be condemned—made him cautious about who was allowed to see it. In a letter of 1619 to Sir Robert Ker he tells us 'no hand hath passed upon it to copy it, nor many eyes to

[8] Richard Ellmann, *Oscar Wilde* (New York, 1988), p. 438. A relevant treason case is that of Edmund Peacham in 1615 where one of the legal issues considered was whether statements made in notes for an undelivered sermon could be regarded as constituting treason.

read it: onely to some particular friends in both Universities, then when I writ it, I did communicate it'.[9] So, if we are to say that it was published at the time of writing, it was published, like Doody's *The alchemists* or Pope's *Pastorals*, by allowing a series of readers to see a single manuscript. The crucial issue is whether this is to be seen as a private or as a public transaction. Donne's view of the case is clarified by another statement in the same letter when he tells Ker that he is at liberty to show it to 'any that your discretion admits to the sight of it' but that he must observe the condition of warning them that it is a book 'written by *Jack Donne*, and not by *D. Donne*' (p. 22). This constitutes a partial surrender of control over the social use of the text to Ker; however, Donne conditionally envisages a more complete one, saying 'Reserve it for me, if I live, and if I die, I only forbid it the Presse, and the Fire'—in other words, in the event of his death, the text should be treated as published, but only through the scribal medium. In this instance Donne did retrieve the copy, and it was only some years later at the request of the future Lord Herbert of Cherbury that he is known to have allowed another to be made. The process described shows control over the social use of the text being relinquished through a series of separate declarations. The initial circulation among university friends might still, perhaps, be classified as private; however, the letter to Ker involves both an actual and a provisional waiving of control. The later supplying of a copy to Herbert was an outright relinquishing, since Donne had no way of preventing Herbert (or any other person who acquired a copy) from making it available for further copying. While debate is still possible over the precise point at which we should locate the transition from the private to the public realm, the stages by which such a transition could take place are clearly illustrated. This sense of publishing as a surrender of control over the future use of the manuscript constitutes our 'weak' definition, the only additional condition being that the surrender should take place in a context where there was some practical likelihood of the text entering public channels of communication. In a century where the practice

[9] *Letters to severall persons of honour* (London, 1651), p. 21. See also *Biathanatos*, ed. Ernest W. Sullivan II (Newark, NJ, 1984), pp. xli, xlvi–xlvii. Sullivan is too hasty in assuming that the copy circulated by Donne was a holograph: it could have been a scribal copy made under Donne's direction.

of copying was almost universal among the educated this is not a difficult condition to satisfy.

Jonson's 'An epigram to my muse, the Lady Digby, on her husband, Sir Kenelme Digby' illustrates a related process by which a patron or friend might be entrusted with a copy on the explicit understanding that he or she would bring it to wider attention.

> O! what a fame 't will be?
>   What reputation to my lines, and me,
> When hee shall read them at the Treasurers bord,
>   The knowing *Weston*, and that learned Lord
> Allowes them? Then, what copies shall be had,
>   What transcripts begg'd? how cry'd up, and how glad,
> Wilt thou be, *Muse*, when this shall them befall?
>   Being sent to one, they will be read of all.[10]

In this case the author is the publisher in the weak sense in surrendering control over the poems to his friend Digby, who becomes the publisher in the strong sense by reading them to a circle of connoisseurs whose approval will create a demand for transcripts.

The desire to make a piece of writing public, or to keep it private, may also be evident from its own nature. Sir Thomas Browne wrote of the unauthorized 1642 printing of *Religio medici*: 'He that shall peruse that worke, and shall take notice of sundry particularities and personall expressions therein, will easily discerne the intention was not publik: and being a private exercise directed to my selfe, what is delivered therein was rather a memoriall unto me then an example or rule unto any other.'[11] Dudley, Lord North hardly had need to explain that his poems 'were designed, as they tell you, to a domestique confinement, impatient of public view': the only reason that could have led him to print them (albeit in a 'private Edition') was that in the disturbed circumstances of the Civil War they were 'obnoxious to a sodain destruction'.[12] More generally, much as a gentleman or lady was not in a fit state to

[10] *Ben Jonson*, viii. 263.

[11] *Religio medici and other works*, ed. L. C. Martin (Oxford, 1964), p. 1. The work was one which 'being communicated unto one, . . . became common unto many, and was by transcription successively corrupted untill it arrived in a most depraved copy at the presse' (loc. cit.).

[12] *A forest promiscous of several seasons productions* (London, 1659), pp. A2^{r}, 172.

appear out of doors until he or she had been elaborately clothed, so a piece of writing was not ready to appear before readers until it had reached a required state of finish. In private letters, wrote Sprat in 1668, 'the Souls of Men should appear undress'd: And in that negligent habit they may be fit to be seen by one or two in a Chamber, but not to go abroad into the Streets'.[13] Anything lacking the required finish remained a piece of private writing improperly exposed to public view—the argument of Wycherley's poem 'To Sir George Etheridge, on his shewing his verses imperfect':

> Be wise, and ne'er to publick View produce
> Thy undrest Mistress, or unfinisht Muse;
> Since either, by that *Dishabilé*, seem
> To hurt their Beauties in our good Esteem:
> And easier far we kind Impressions make,
> Than we can rooted Prejudices shake.
> From Nature learn, which *Embrio*'s does conceal,
> Thine, till they're perfect, never to reveal.[14]

What is objected to here is not simply the showing round of inferior work but a sense that the rules governing the constitution of a public realm are being violated by an interposing of materials from the private realm (where a sweet disorder in the dress might be attractive rather than otherwise).

This suggests that the dress of texts, in the sense of appearance as well as style, might offer grounds for positing a published status. A finely written manuscript in a large format using good paper invites and may be said to expect readers just as the semi-legible private scrawl (writing in dishabille) indicates an indifference to them. An intention (if no more) to publish might also be suspected when the text in question has adopted a polished public style or employs a recognizably public form of discourse, such as the political satire, the pedagogical treatise or the formal epistle. Criteria such as these can be used to supplement designations based on the proven fact of public accessibility or knowledge, such as that

[13] Preface to his edition of Cowley's *Works*, in *Critical essays of the seventeenth century*, ed. J. E. Spingarn (Oxford, 1957), ii. 137.

[14] *The posthumous works of William Wycherley, Esq.* (London, 1728), p. 182; also in my *Restoration verse* (Harmondsworth, 1968), p. 301. Geoffrey Hiller has drawn my attention to the frequency with which dedications by Elizabethan and Jacobean writers refer to their work being dressed in the livery of the noble dedicatee.

revealed by the history of *Biathanatos*, of the author's transactions with readers. Of course a work intended, like *Religio medici*, for strictly private use might become a public possession against its author's wishes. The same applies to personal letters, generally regarded as unsuitable for print publication, but which were frequently made available for recopying. Sprat, in acting as Cowley's literary executor, would not permit the printing of private correspondence.[15] On the other hand, Hearne's journals show him, in the early decades of the eighteenth century, regularly transcribing letters which had been lent by colleagues and expecting that his own letters would be read and valued by future scholars. Attitudes had undoubtedly changed during the intervening years, but the difference of medium may well have been the crucial one. Even Sprat does not assume that private correspondence was meant solely for the recipient. In any case, once a private letter had begun to be freely copied it became a published text irrespective of the wishes of the recipient, and might even be included in specialized anthologies such as Folger MS V a 321.[16] Such cases reflect the ease with which a text could be introduced to a public, duplication requiring nothing more than a pen and a willingness to use it.

Such a framing of the field of scribal publication still excludes the case of a text communicated within a closed circle of readers on the understanding it is not to be allowed to go beyond the circle. Examples would be documents circulated within a family, like the copies of Dudley North's poems written out by his widow for each of her children, or among tightly knit groups of officials, county neighbours or courtiers.[17] Lawrence Squibb's *A book of all the several officers of the Court of Exchequer*, written in 1642 as a guide to the practice of the court, was recopied many times (sixteen manuscripts are known) and revised on at least two occasions but appears to have circulated only within a small circle of Exchequer officials and politicians with whom they had dealings.[18] Here

[15] Spingarn, ii. 137.

[16] Reproduced in facsimile with facing transcriptions in *A seventeenth-century letter-book*, ed. A. R. Braunmuller (Newark, Del., 1983). The volume is a mixture of formal and personal letters with a few non-epistolary texts.

[17] For the North example, see Randall, *Gentle flame*, pp. 100–2. Cases falling under the other categories are discussed in Ch. 5.

[18] J. D. Alsop, 'A 1721 version of Squibb's 1642 treatise on the Exchequer', *Library*, 6:6

individual control over the social use of the text has been replaced by the control of a community, creating a status delicately balanced between the public and the private. In such cases, and assuming there was no broader transmission of the text concerned, it should be the nature of the community that determined the issue. If it was genuinely closed, and the text could only achieve wider circulation through a violation of trust, private status may be allowed. (An example here would be Marvell's letters to the Corporation of Hull, which contain frequent warnings that they should not be allowed to come to other eyes. An occasion when Marvell felt confidentiality had been breached drew a swift reprimand.[19]) But many communities within which manuscripts circulated were not of this kind: their membership was relatively fluid and a reader sympathetic enough to the aims of a group to be interested in the texts that were circulating within it would probably not find it difficult to be accepted into the network. The analogy in modern print publishing would be that of a learned society or book club whose publications were only available to members but which placed no barriers against gaining membership.

A further difference between scribal and print publication is that, while a printed text is published in a large number of copies on a single occasion, the manuscript text must usually be regarded as republished as often as it is copied. There is an exception to this in the 'scribal editions' of multiple copies of a given exemplar which were sometimes commissioned by commercial dealers; but the mass of surviving manuscripts are the outcome of a discontinuous series of acts of publication in editions of one. In order to mediate between this aspect of scribal publication and the print model, it will be helpful to distinguish between an initiatory and a replicatory act. The first is what happens when a private possessor of a text (who, as mentioned earlier will not necessarily be the author or even acting in accordance with the author's wishes) facilitates its first going forth into the world, while the second is

(1984), 366–9; *A book of all the several officers of the Court of Exchequer*, ed. W. H. Bryson, in *Camden miscellany* 26 (London 1975), pp. 77–136. For the manuscripts and their relationship see Bryson, pp. 80–95.

[19] *The poems and letters of Andrew Marvell*, ed. H. M. Margoliouth, 3rd edn, rev. Pierre Legouis with the collaboration of E. E. Duncan-Jones (Oxford, 1971), ii. 166.

what happens when some individual owner of a subsequent copy permits that copy to be available for recopying. The distinction can be demonstrated through the example of John Hollond's 'The navy ript and ransacked', a treatise of 1660 on the way contractors and shipyard-owners were cheating the crown.[20] Hollond published the work by presenting a single copy to James, Duke of York, in his capacity as Lord Admiral. (This was the initiatory act and deprived the author of control over the future social use of the text.) The Duke passed on the copy to Sir William Coventry who showed it to Pepys. Pepys took a copy for himself and Coventry kept the Duke's copy. However, the three seem to have agreed that it was much too hot to go any further and after only one replicatory act its transmission was brought to an end. It could of course be argued that Hollond's treatise was in the nature of a confidential report—in which case no further circulation might have been envisaged or desired—but neither the text, the writing nor the snappy title suggest this; moreover, Hollond's earlier 'A discourse of the navy' had enjoyed wide circulation in manuscript.[21] The importance of this replicatory power is that it provides us with a scribal counterpart to the notion of 'going out of print'. A text will continue to multiply until interest in it fails and no further replications take place. But this process will be distributed, not centralized, with each copying demanding a separate act of will to continue the life of the text. As we have just seen, the power could also be used in a negative sense to suppress a text by withholding it from any potential future copyists. English law of the time took cognizance of this negative aspect of the replicatory power by insisting that anyone encountering a libel had an obligation to destroy it.[22]

The criteria proposed will have shown how the term 'scribal publication' is to be used in this book and what kinds of manuscripts are covered by it. Naturally, other ways of making

[20] John Hollond, *Two discourses on the navy*, ed. J. R. Tanner (London, 1896), pp. lxix–lxx.

[21] Ibid., pp. lxviii–lxix.

[22] Lord Chief Justice Richardson, in a judgement of June 1632, ruled that 'if it concern a publique person the libell must be shewed to the Kings Councell or some competent judge, but if it concerne anie private person he that findeth it must burne it'. *Reports of cases in the courts of Star Chamber and High Commission*, ed. S. R. Gardiner, Camden Society, NS 39 (London, 1886), p. 152.

the distinction are possible and would lead to a different assignment of published or unpublished status: my aim here has been simply to provide discriminations which would be useful to the task in hand and not in flagrant disregard of our present-day notions of publication. If a greater stress has been laid on the text's potential for wider replication than on its practical availability, this is because that potential was far more easily realized by an intending reader in the manuscript than in the print medium. A text that was of pressing interest, and whose existence had become known through word of mouth, would never lack copyists. It is true that a certain critical population of copies had to be achieved before exemplars would be readily available, much as a certain level is necessary to ensure the survival of a living species. But, once that was done, the process of multiplication would be driven by cultural energies quite as powerful as those which sustained the printed text.

MODES OF PUBLICATION

Having looked at means of distinguishing published from unpublished texts, our next task will be to decide how various kinds of scribal publication are to be distinguished from each other. Here it will be helpful to begin with three predominant categories of manuscript (omitting mixed examples): the authorial holograph, the copy made by a specialist scribe, and the copy made by an individual who wished to possess the text. It is often possible to assign a manuscript to one of these categories on appearance alone. The authorial copy may contain interlinear revisions of a kind which no scribe could have devised. The scribal copy is usually written in a clear, regularly formed hand with consistent page numbering and catchwords on every page. Virtuosic displays of penmanship may also be evident. A copy written in a rapid, untidy hand is probably personal, though not all personal copies are so written, and some private transcribers matched the professionals for the care and beauty of their script. Of course, these distinctions—when they can be made—will not always reveal the mode of publication employed, since, if the scribe was a professional, he or she may still have been working under the author's direction or for someone who wished to possess a copy.

But the classification does suggest the three agents most likely to have performed acts of publication: the author, the stationer or scrivener for whom manuscripts were articles of commerce, and the intending reader.

On this basis I would like to propose that there are three main modes of scribal publication which I will call author publication, entrepreneurial publication and user publication. The first of these is self-explanatory; the second embraces all copying of manuscripts for sale by agents other than the author; the third covers the vast field of non-commercial replication whose most durable outcome was the personal miscellany or volume of 'collections'. The textual tradition of any given work will probably include more than one of these modes. Thus, a seventeenth-century text put into circulation in copies prepared by its author might subsequently be copied for sale or for personal use. Copyists, too, may have found themselves acting in more than one role, as in the case of the privately employed scribe who took a secret extra copy for subsequent sale. But, if we are prepared to ignore some marginal imprecisions, this tripartite distinction will be found to be of service in relating particular instances of scribal publication to the general definitions that were proposed at the beginning of this chapter.

Author publication occurs when the production and distribution of copies takes place under the author's personal direction. Writers from the gentry and aristocracy were particularly likely to publish in this way owing to what J. W. Saunders has called the 'stigma of print' but it must also be regarded as the common way of securing readers for works of which only a small number of copies was required or when a subsequent process of user publication was assumed and perhaps courted.[23] An important criterion for identifying author publication is the presence of signed dedications or epistles to particular persons. Two manuscripts of Sir John Davies's *Nosce teipsum* (first circulated in the early 1590s) contain dedicatory verses to Henry Percy, ninth Earl

[23] J. W. Saunders, 'The stigma of print: a note on the social bases of Tudor poetry', *Essays in criticism* 1 (1951), 139–64. Complementing the 'stigma' was a sense of the higher prestige of the handwritten text. Humfrey Wanley, in describing a book of engravings prepared for Louis XIV, notes 'This Painter ha's gotten the Prints purposely wrought-off for him, without the Words, which are added, for Magnificence-sake, by a fine Pen' (*The diary of Humfrey Wanley 1715–1726*, ed. C. E. Wright and Ruth C. Wright (London, 1966), i. 89.)

of Northumberland, and a not-yet-knighted Edward Coke respectively. All four manuscripts of the complete text contain a verse address to Queen Elizabeth, who must also therefore have received a copy.[24] A second criterion is the presence of passages or corrections in the author's own hand, or those of known amanuenses—the clue that allowed Crum and Hobbs to identify a number of manuscripts as issued under the supervision of Henry King.[25] A third is that the text is correct and accurate, though this is more useful in the negative sense that a text containing frequent obvious errors, or evidence of sophistication, is unlikely to have emanated from the author.[26] Many author-publishers wrote their own copies; but another common method was to have them prepared by an experienced scribe, as when Milton made use of Henry Lawes for the scribal publication of *Comus* following its successful performance in September 1634. Lawes's preface to the 1637 printed text explains that 'Although not openly acknowledg'd by the Author, yet it is a legitimate off-spring, so lovely, and so much desired, that the often copying of it hath tir'd my pen to give my severall friends satisfaction, and brought me to a necessitie of producing it to the publick view'.[27] Lawes here represents the pre-print circulation as a gentlemanly labour on behalf of friends; but hard-working musicians could rarely afford such luxuries and he probably expected a return of gifts from his presentations. An example of an authorially supervised master copy is the manuscript of Sir Arthur Gorges' 'The Olympian Catastrophe' (Huntington

[24] *The poems of Sir John Davies*, ed. Robert Krueger (Oxford, 1975), pp. 3–5; Beal, *IELM*, i/1, 215–16. Author publication is assumed only for the dedication copies, not for subsequent copies that might include the dedications.

[25] Manuscripts produced by scribes working under King's direction are described in *The poems of Henry King*, ed. Margaret Crum (Oxford, 1965), pp. 48–9 and Mary Hobbs, 'The poems of Henry King: another authoritative manuscript', *Library*, 5:31 (1976), 127–35 and 'The Stoughton manuscript', *passim*. Manuscripts of work by other poets in a scribal hand but with authorial revisions are cited in Croft, *Autograph poetry*, i, p. xv.

[26] In cases where authors acted as scribes as well as publishers, they were as likely to make mistakes in transcribing as anyone else: the difference is that they were much more likely to recognize and correct them. For an example of a holograph text containing a large number or corrected transcriptional errors, see Anthony S. G. Edwards, 'The author as scribe: Cavendish's *Metrical visions* and MS Egerton 2402', *Library*, 5:29 (1974), 446–9.

[27] John Milton, *A masque. The earlier versions*, ed. S. E. Sprott (Toronto, 1973), p. 39. Robert K. Root, 'Publication before printing', *PMLA* 28 (1913), 417–31, draws on letters of Petrarch and Boccaccio to illustrate a late-medieval practice in which the work was directed to a patron or dedicatee under the assumption that it would be first revised and then put into circulation by him.

Library MS Ellesmere 1130). Here the scribe, who had originally done his best to produce a clean copy, was required by the author to make 'hundreds of alterations' in the form of superscriptions and paste-ons.[28] The only conceivable use for such a manuscript would be as an exemplar for others.[29]

Some cases of author publication have already been mentioned in Chapter 1, including those of John Jenkins as a composer-publisher and the members of the Caroline parliaments who distributed separates of their speeches. The production of newsletters should also be seen as a specialized form of author publication. Otherwise it is to be found across the entire range of seventeenth-century writing. Important prose texts such as Sir Robert Cotton's *A short view of the long life and reign of Henry the third*; Sir John Davies's *Whether the king of England by his prerogative may set impositions, loans or privy seals without assent of parliament*; Sir Robert Filmer's *Patriarcha*; Halifax's *The character of a trimmer*; Sir John Harington's *A supplie or addicion to the catalogue of bishops*; Sir Thomas Herbert's *Memoirs of the two last years of the reign of King Charles I*; Sir Roger Owen's *Of the antiquity, ampleness, and excellency of the common laws of England*; Raleigh's *A dialogue between a counsellor of state and a justice of the peace*; John Selden's *Table talk* (the 'author' in this case being Richard Milward); Henry Stubbe's *Account of the rise and progress of Mahometanism* and Sir Roger Twysden's *Certain considerations upon the government of England* all appear to have been given to their first readers through author-controlled duplication.[30]

[28] *The poems of Sir Arthur Gorges*, ed. Helen Estabrook Sandison (Oxford, 1953), p. lvii. The alterations are categorized on pp. xlix–lii.

[29] A set of three master-copies from the late-17th-cent. scriptorium studied by W. J. Cameron (Folger MS M. b. 12) also survives in a form heavily reconstructed by excisions and paste-ons. See Cameron 'Scriptorium', *passim*.

[30] For information on the transmissional histories of these texts (the titles of which are often variable), see William A. Jackson, 'Sir Robert Bruce Cotton's *A short view of the long life and raigne of Henry the third*', *Harvard Library bulletin* 4 (1950), 28–37; Beal, *IELM*, i/1, 231–2 (Davies); Peter Laslett, 'Sir Robert Filmer: the man versus the Whig myth', *William and Mary quarterly*, 3:5 (1948), 523–46 and Gordon J. Schochet, 'Sir Robert Filmer: some new bibliographical discoveries', *Library*, 5:26 (1971), 135–60; *The works of George Savile Marquis of Halifax*, ed. Mark N. Brown (Oxford, 1989), i. 343-54 and Beal, *IELM*, ii/1, 507–15 (Halifax); R. H. Miller, 'Sir John Harington's *A supplie or addicion to the catalogue of bishops, to the yeare 1608: composition and text*', *SB* 30 (1977), 145–61; Beal, *IELM*, i/2, 424–7 (Raleigh); Ernest A. Strathmann, 'Ralegh's *Discourse of tenures* and Sir Roger Owen', *HLQ* 20 (1956–7), 219–32; *Table talk of John Selden*, ed. Sir Frederick Pollock (London, 1927), pp. xi–xxiv; James R. Jacob, *Henry Stubbe, radical Protestantism and the early Enlightenment*

Reflecting on the huge body of amateur verse written during the early years of the century, Dennis Kay has written

> Any educated person in the sixty years leading up to the English Civil War is liable to have written verses of some kind. The practice was recommended by educational theorists—some children's verses have survived—and many individuals continued to write, as the occasion struck them, into later life. The survival rate of such exclusively amateur pieces is, inevitably, not high, especially in cases where an author's subsequent career or status required a display of *gravitas* with which a reputation as a poet might appear inconsistent. Even a poet as renowned and as reputedly influential as Sir Edward Dyer is known today only through fragments. Yet new discoveries are constantly made, sometimes of substantial bodies of notable work—Sir Robert Sidney is the most striking recent instance—but more usually of individual pieces.[31]

Dyer was one of the casualties of scribal publication: Robert Sidney a lucky survivor. The great bulk of this verse was distributed by its authors. Among the better-known poets, Alexander Brome, Sir John Davies, Donne, Harington, the two Herberts, King, Marvell and Katherine Philips all seem to have taken a supervisory role in the production and circulation of copies of their works, contrasting in this with Strode, Corbett, Carew, Cotton, Rochester and Dorset, who were more inclined to let circulation take its course.[32] Both groups were sustaining a preference carried over from the reign of Elizabeth when, as Saunders has shown, there was a sharp distinction between the courtier or gentleman poet for whom print publication would have been a social disgrace, and more humbly born aspirants for patronage who turned to the press as a means of self-advertisement.[33] Insofar as this position changed in the early years of the seventeenth century, it was in that the communication of manuscripts became so widespread a practice that the search for

(Cambridge, 1983), pp. 64–5, 76–7, 99, 126, 138, 140–3, 159–62; Frank W. Jessup, *Sir Roger Twysden* (London, 1965), p. 189. Many other widely read texts could be cited.

[31] Dennis Kay, 'Poems by Sir Walter Aston, and a date for the Donne/Goodyer verse epistle "alternis vicibus"', *RES* NS 37 (1986), 198.

[32] Beal's introductions in *IELM*, i and ii indicate when a significant number of surviving manuscripts come from the authors or their amanuenses and contain well-informed judgements about the circumstances of early copying. Otherwise the reader is referred to the standard scholarly editions of these writers.

[33] Saunders, pp. 150–9.

preferment could be pursued through that medium alone. (Massinger, Drayton and Abraham Holland comment abrasively on this phenomenon from the point of view of print-publishing poets.[34])

The most studied case of author-published poetry is that of Donne, who printed very little verse in his lifetime, and always with misgivings. Instead, the poems obtained wide circulation then and for some years after his death in manuscript volumes of which MacColl knew of 'some forty collections of varying size, and over a hundred miscellanies'—a figure since enlarged.[35] These first appeared among a circle of friends and patrons from whom they percolated to a wider readership. The emphasis on large collections is important, as Donne followed the practice of the classical poets in structuring his output into groups determined by genre. MacColl's contention that 'with the exception of verse letters and occasional pieces he rarely gave out copies of single poems' has been disputed by Marotti and Sullivan; but there can be little doubt that, even if not personally responsible, he lent his assistance to the assemblage of the larger, composite groups of satires, elegies, verse letters and ultimately 'works'.[36] It is clear from the history of *Biathanatos*, already considered, and from a letter requesting Sir Henry Goodyer to return a volume of poems, that some of this circulation was regarded by Donne as remaining in the private sphere.[37] But this was partly a reaction of his later life when the poems of his youth were an increasing embarrassment. The extreme rarity of autographs of the poems suggests that he used scribes to produce copies. While there is no evidence that he accepted payment for manuscripts of his verse, there would have been gifts from patrons. Otherwise the circulation of poems

[34] For Massinger, see Peter Beal, 'Massinger at bay: unpublished verses in a war of the theatres', *YES* 10 (1980), 190–203; for Drayton p. 3 above; and for Holland, p. 217 below.

[35] MacColl, p. 29. A new census of sources will be appearing with the Variorum Donne.

[36] MacColl, p. 41; Marotti, p. 15. Helen Gardner's belief that at least one of these collections originated from Donne himself has been questioned by Sullivan who insists that 'no evidence exists that Donne ever successfully collected his poems' (*Dalhousie manuscripts*, p. 10). Ted-Larry Pebworth, 'John Donne, coterie poetry, and the text as performance', *SEL* 29 (1989), 61–75, goes further in presenting a Donne for whom 'once the poetic gesture [had] been made and received' the poem became expendable and might not even be preserved (p. 65). According to this view, the collections are the creation of the coterie, not the author.

[37] *Letters*, p. 197; MacColl, p. 35.

helped to confirm friendships with like-minded contemporaries (several of whom were themselves poets) and to advertise Donne's suitability for advancement in state and church.

Similar methods were also employed by Henry King who used Oxford scribes, including Thomas Manne, the chaplain of his college, Christ Church, to circulate a regularly updated miscellany of poems by himself and friends. At Cambridge during the 1630s, Crashaw also made use of scribes to put his poems into circulation.[38] John Watson's commonplace book, drawing on largely Cambridge material from between the 1640s and the late 1670s, besides confirming that the scribal circulation of verse was still in a flourishing condition, identifies a number of pieces as having been received directly from their authors, those named being Joseph Arrowsmith, Robert Gaton, John Jenkins, Sir Henry North, Matthew Pool, Thomas Townes and Roger Wolverton. Arrowsmith, a fellow of Trinity, had a comedy, *The reformation*, performed by the Duke's Company in 1673. Gaton, Pool and Townes were dons; North, Watson's patron in the country; Jenkins, at that stage, a member of North's household; and Wolverton a physician.

A further issue to be noted under the topic of author publication is its effect on conceptions of the activity of composition. Even among print-publishing writers, then and now, it is not hard to find examples of texts which remain obstinately in process, being revised or updated at each new edition through the writer's lifetime, and after it too as editors wrestle with the multitude of authorial possibilities.[39] While we should be wary of assuming that this is the natural condition of *all* writing (a proportion of authors have always refused to alter any feature of a work once written), it is one that was actively encouraged by the scribal medium, where changes could be made from copy to copy rather than from edition to edition. Sometimes these revisions would be recorded as corrections to a master-manuscript like that of Gorges' *The Olympian catastrophe*. In that case no derived copies survive; but

[38] For King, see n. 25 above. Crashaw's use of scribes is discussed in *The poems English Latin and Greek of Richard Crashaw*, ed. L. C. Martin (Oxford, 1957), pp. xlvi, lv–lvii, lxi–lxii, lxiv and xciii.

[39] The cases of Auden, Graves, Hardy, James, Whitman, Wordsworth and Yeats immediately suggest themselves.

with the Lauderdale translation of the *Aeneid* we possess not only a palimpsestic master copy of book four (Royal Irish Academy MS 12 B2 25) but the author's own notes identifying three scribes by name and the numbers of revised readings introduced at certain transcriptions.[40] The Sidneian psalms, to be considered in the following section, are another case of a text subject to incessant revision, although in this case neither of the two putative master copies survives. The term serial composition is proposed for this phenomenon.

The ideal of creativity revealed in such cases is a gradualistic one. Freed from the print-publishing author's obligation to produce a finalized text suitable for large-scale replication, the scribal author-publisher is able both to polish texts indefinitely and to personalize them to suit the tastes of particular recipients. This practice denies the sharp distinctions which can be drawn for print-published texts between drafts, the 'authorized' first-edition text, and revisions which are fully reflected on and well spaced in time. It also militates against our identifying any particular text as the embodiment of a 'final intention', for while the process of revision may in some instances be one of honing and perfecting, it may equally be one of change for change's sake or of an ongoing adaptation to the expectations of readers. Versions produced in this way do not so much replace as augment each other. In some instances they seem to grow from a lifestyle in which the activity of altering a text was more important than its outcome. Lauderdale's revisions to his *Aeneid*, made during his exile with James II at Saint-Germain, would be hard in many cases to describe as improvements, but seem rather to betray a mind in search of occupation. Roger North's perpetual recasting of the material of his treatises suggests a similar preference not to finalize. Had he been writing for the press, publication would have directed him to new projects and relieved him of the burden of the old; but it would also have deprived him of an activity, which was obviously greatly to his taste, of sitting down with his loved papers and engaging in largely superfluous acts of redrafting. Mary Countess of Pembroke's lifetime of work on the translation of the psalms begun by her

[40] Analysed in Margaret Boddy, 'The manuscripts and printed editions of the translation of Virgil made by Richard Maitland, fourth Earl of Lauderdale, and the connexion with Dryden', *N&Q* 210 (1965), 144–50. The printed editions were posthumous.

brother, Sir Philip Sidney, while stimulated by a sense of family and religious duty, was also the result of an unwillingness to bring an absorbing activity to too precipitate an end. While the later versions are certainly tauter and more polished than the earlier ones, much variation is of the gratuitous kind that could just as well be unmade or further varied. It is a mistake in such cases to assume that revision is the consequence of a Platonic impulse towards the perfected, unalterable text. No doubt in some cases it was, but one should never overlook Ong's insight that this ideal is itself a function of print culture.[41] The model for such revision may well be closer to that of a musican playing variations on a favourite theme.

For the print-published author who wished to employ a scribe-like flexibility, there was the recourse of marking up copies of an edition with handwritten alterations. Two copies of Sir William Killigrew's *Five new plays* (1666) exist in this form, while there are manuscript corrections, believed to be by the author, in almost every copy of the 1651 quarto of D'Avenant's *Gondibert*.[42] A striking example from after our period is the 1739 Dublin *Verses on the death of Dr Swift* in which spaces were left in the notes to be filled in by hand prior to sale, but no surviving copy contains the suppressed text in full.[43]

WOMEN WRITERS AND THE SCRIBAL MEDIUM

The stigma of print bore particularly hard on women writers, as they themselves pointed out. Anne Finch, Countess of Winchilsea, praised Lady Pakington, the reputed author of *The whole duty of man*, as having combined the 'Skill to write' with the 'Modesty to hide'.[44] The alternative to 'hiding' one's work would often be to

[41] Walter J. Ong, *Orality and literacy: the technologizing of the word* (London, 1982), pp. 121–3.

[42] Joseph S. Johnston, jun., 'Sir William Killigrew's revised copy of his *Four new playes*: confirmation of his claim to *The imperial tragedy*', *MP* 74 (1976), 72–4; John Horden, 'Sir William Killigrew's *Four new playes* (1666) with his *Imperial tragedy* (1669): a second annotated copy', *Library*, 6:6 (1984), 271–5; Beal, *IELM*, ii/1, 310–11.

[43] See Clive Probyn, 'Swift's *Verses on the death of Dr. Swift*: the notes', *SB* 39 (1986), 47–61.

[44] 'On the death of the honourable Mr. James Thynne', l. 41 in *The poems of Anne, Countess of Winchilsea*, ed. Myra Reynolds (Chicago, 1903), pp. 56–9.

find a metaphorical equation drawn between an eagerness to appear in print and sexual immorality, as in Lovelace's lines

> Now as her self a Poem she doth dresse,
> And curls a Line as she would do a tresse;
> Powders a Sonnet as she does her hair,
> Then prostitutes them both to publick Aire.[45]

Lady Mary Wroth, after having run into trouble over the print publication in 1621 of her *roman à clef*, *The Countesse of Montgomery's Urania*, kept the second part and a play derived from it in manuscript.[46] Even so pious an undertaking as the Sidneian psalms was never printed.[47] This was not for want of merit: the work was highly admired in its time and sixteen manuscripts survive as a testimony to its wide distribution. Sir John Harington, in an aside in his *Treatise on play*, which itself remained confined to the scribal medium, thought the Countess of Pembroke was being too restrictive:

> seing it is allredy prophecied those precious leaues (those hims that she doth consecrate to Heauen) shall owtlast Wilton walls, meethinke it is pitty they are unpublyshed, but lye still inclosed within those walls lyke prisoners, though many haue made great suyt for theyr liberty.[48]

Whether print publication was what Harington had in mind, or simply a fuller release of the sequence in manuscript is not made clear. (He had sent three of the poems to Lucy Countess of Bedford and left eight among his own papers but may have lacked a

[45] *The poems of Richard Lovelace*, ed. C. H. Wilkinson, corr. repr. (Oxford, 1953), p. 200. Wycherley's lines on Aphra Behn, '*To the* Sappho *of the Age, suppos'd to Ly-In of a* Love-Distemper, *or a* Play', are an even more blatant version (*The complete works of William Wycherley*, ed. Montague Summers (London, 1924), iii. 155–6). For further instances of the accusation, see Jacqueline Pearson, *The prostituted muse: images of women and women dramatists 1642–1737* (Hemel Hempstead, 1988), pp. 6–14.

[46] *The poems of Lady Mary Wroth*, ed. Josephine A. Roberts (Baton Rouge, La., 1983), pp. 28–38.

[47] For the textual history of this work see Mary Sidney, *Triumph of death*, pp. 18–36; *The psalms of Sir Philip Sidney and the Countess of Pembroke*, ed. J. C. A. Rathmell (New York, 1963), pp. xxvii–xxix; and Noel Kinnamon, 'The Sidney psalms: the Penshurst and Tixall manuscripts', *English manuscript studies 1100–1700* 2 (1990), 139–61. Sir Philip's share of the cycle is included in *The poems of Sir Philip Sidney*, ed. William A. Ringler, jun. (Oxford, 1962), pp. 265–337. An *OET* edition is being prepared by Margaret P. Hannay and Kinnamon.

[48] *Nugae antiquae: being a miscellaneous collection of original papers* (London, 1769–75), ii. 6.

complete set.[49]) The work of Noel Kinnamon and the editors of the Sidneian psalms has given us a fairly full picture of the Countess's activity as a writer for and publisher in the scribal medium. At the time of Sir Philip's death in 1586 only forty-three of the 150 psalms had been translated. The Countess proved an inveterate improver both of her brother's work and of her own as it proceeded, the changes showing up as variants between successive manuscripts. Master copies were kept in London as well as at Wilton, with changes made to one not necessarily being transported to the other. The conjectural ancestor *X* which gave rise to ten of the surviving sources is assumed to have been the London master on the grounds that it was there the Countess would have received most requests for copies. The considerable extent to which sources are found to preserve unique authorial readings indicates that the process of publication remained firmly under the writer's control.

Katherine Philips ('Orinda'), the most admired woman poet of the century, built her reputation largely through manuscript transmission, initially within a circle of intimates in Ireland and later on a wider scale. Elaine Hobby lays stress on her status as a published author through the scribal medium:

> In part, the image of Orinda that has come down to us is dependent on the belief that her writing was really a secret and private affair, her poems passed around only in manuscript form to a few trusted friends. This is an anachronistic distortion of the method of 'publication' that she used: circulation of manuscripts was the normal way to make writing public before the widespread use of printed books, and was a method that continued to be popular in court circles throughout the reign of Charles II, at least. Such a description also fails to consider the fact that, as a royalist poet married to a leading parliamentarian, she had positive reasons for avoiding too much public attention during the 1650s, which was when she did most of her writing. Bearing these factors in mind, we find that the evidence suggests that she was actually a well-known writer. . . . The 'public' she was interested in reaching was the coterie of court and leading poets, not the wider world.[50]

[49] See Rathmell, pp. xxvii, xxix. John Davies of Hereford praises the Countess's reticence, along with that of her fellow writers Lucy Countess of Bedford and Elizabeth Lady Cary, commending them in that 'you presse the *Presse* with little you haue made' (*The muse's sacrifice*, in *The complete works of John Davies of Hereford*, ed. Alexander B. Grosart (repr. New York, 1967), ii. 5).

[50] Elaine Hobby, *Virtue of necessity: English women's writing 1649–1688* (London, 1988), p. 129.

Towards the end of Orinda's life collections of her verse were circulating in manuscript, one of these forming the basis of an unauthorized printed edition in 1664 which so greatly distressed her that she tried to have it suppressed. One surviving collection was prepared by a professional scribe after Orinda's death as a gift to her friend Lady Montague (the Mary Aubrey and 'Rosania' of her poems).[51]

The poems themselves yield numerous clues about Orinda's methods as author-publisher. A large group among them is addressed to various members of a circle of English admirers of the French *précieuse* spirit who were known to each other by pastoral names and cultivated 'platonic' friendships. New poems can be assumed to have travelled rapidly through this circle, and some of its members would have built up personal collections of the verse. A second group of poems, printed at the head of the posthumous 1667 edition, is addressed to members of the royal family. The link between the two groups was Sir Charles Cotterell, Master of Ceremonies at the court of Charles II, and, as 'Poliarchus', a leading spirit of the *précieuse* circle. Through Cotterell's advocacy the poems became well known at Whitehall. Roger Boyle, Earl of Orrery, in a verse epistle written during Orinda's lifetime alludes to 'the praises of th'admiring Court' and displays a personal acquaintance with a wide range of her work.[52] A verse address by Orinda to Anne, Duchess of York is evidently meant as the dedicatory poem to a lost manuscript collection of the poems. Through such means Orinda was able to establish herself as a known and noted writer with only one, involuntary appearance in print.

[51] National Library of Wales, Aberystwyth, MS 776–B. Claudia A. Limbert, 'Katherine Philips: another step-father and another sibling, "M^rs^ C: P.", and "Polex:^r^"', *Restoration* 13 (1989), 2–6, has suggested that Sir William Temple (and not Sir Charles Cotterell, as earlier believed) was the compiler of this collection. For a census of the surviving manuscripts, see *The collected works of Katherine Philips*, ed. Patrick Thomas (Stump Cross, 1990–), i. 41–50. The availability of Philips's work in manuscript raises doubts about Allan Pritchard's use of parallels between poems in her 1667 collection and Marvell's 'The garden' to argue for a date of composition in the late 1660s for 'The garden'. It is also possible that Philips had seen 'The garden' in manuscript, reversing the assumed direction of influence. ('Marvell's 'The garden': A Restoration poem?', *SEL* 23 (1983), 371–88.) However, Pritchard's wider plea for scepticism towards the traditional Marvell datings is fully justified.

[52] *Poems by the most deservedly admired Mrs Katherine Philips, the matchless Orinda* (London, 1678), b1^r^–1^v^. The two had met in Dublin in 1662.

Scribal publication, then, provided an avenue for those women poets who either through preference or lack of access eschewed the press. However, literary writings circulated in this way were quantitatively of minor significance besides the texts by women writers dealing with the practical conduct of the household, the preparation of food and clothing and the treatment of illness. Personal collections on these subjects were regarded with great pride by their compilers. The will of Dame Johanna St. John, signed on 7 March 1704, carefully instructs that her 'great Receit Book' was to go to her eldest daughter Anne Cholmondeley, and her 'Book of receits of cookery and Preserves' to her granddaughter, Johanna Soame. But for her other manuscripts she showed no such concern: in leaving her private cabinet to another granddaughter, she specified that she 'would have the papers therein burned first'.[53]

PROFESSIONAL AUTHORSHIP AND THE SCRIBAL MEDIUM

While much of the transmission so far described was of a social or peer-group-bonding nature (a matter to be discussed in Chapter 5), there is evidence that scribal publication, when undertaken in a sufficiently hard-headed spirit, could be more profitable than publication through the press. Print publication offered the writer two chances of income—a payment from the bookseller, and the gift that was expected to follow a dedication; however, booksellers would often jib at any payment at all. The point of view of one representative of the trade, writing in 1624, was that any self-respecting author would not expect it:

> And most of the best Authors are not soe penurious that they looke soe much to theire gaine, as to the good they intend Religion or State. They are too Mercenary that write bookes for Money, and theire couetuousnes makes theire labours fruitles, and disesteemed.[54]

The £5 offered to Milton for the first printing of *Paradise lost* was by the standard of its time a generous payment: it was only the steep rise in the value of literary property which took place from the 1690s that made it seem exploitative. The response of authors

[53] Frank T. Smallwood, 'The will of Dame Johanna St. John', *N&Q* 214 (1969), 346.

[54] BL MS Add. 18648, f. 18^r; cited in Allan Pritchard, 'George Wither's quarrel with the stationers: an anonymous reply to *The schollers purgatory*', *SB* 16 (1963), 37.

to such attitudes was naturally a hostile one. George Wither's *The schollers purgatory* (1624) vigorously presents the case of the aspiring professional. That of the part-time author is hinted at in a *bon mot* recorded by Sir Nicholas Le Strange: 'A Gentleman usd to say of Booke-Sellers, that they were like lice, bredd of the sweat of a Mans Braine, and upon that they live.'[55] Under some agreements the author would not be paid in cash but copies of the book which then had to be turned into money by whatever means presented themselves.[56] Scribal publication offered the resourceful author the chance of higher rewards. Once the charges of copying and paper had been met, the presentation of a work in manuscript to a well-disposed patron could be expected to bring in a sum commensurate with that from the dedicating of a printed book. The presentation could then be repeated to other patrons, as Cosmo Manuche did when he prepared separate dedication copies of *The banished shepherdess* for the Queen Dowager Henrietta Maria and James, third Earl of Northampton, or Daniel when he reassigned his 'Epistle to the Lady Margaret, Countess of Cumberland' to Elizabeth, Lady Hatton.[57] Moreover, once the scribe had been paid, the author was the direct recipient of all benefits, having to surrender nothing to a middleman.

Much author publication was really a form of begging. Giacomo Castelvetro's dedication of his manuscript treatise, *Brieve racconto di tutte le radici, di tutte l'erbe et di tutti i frutti, che crudi o cotti in Italia si mangiano* (1614), to Lucy Countess of Bedford is accompanied by a plea that she should continue the pension he had received from her brother.[58] On 23 November 1660, while searching the room of an impoverished scholar named Robert Gaton who had committed suicide, John Watson discovered the

[55] *Merry passages and jeasts*, p. 141.

[56] One well-documented case of this practice is discussed in my 'Preacher and publisher: Oliver Heywood and Thomas Parkhurst', *SB* 31 (1978), 227–35. Heywood, a victim of the 1662 ejectment of Nonconformists from their livings, obtained a substantial part of editions of his books either as part of his contract or by purchase at a discount. These were distributed to his co-religionists (lists of whose names have been preserved) with 'guilded' copies sometimes provided for influential patrons. While it appears that at least some of these books were distributed gratis by Heywood, it can be assumed that their cost to him was eventually covered by contributions from his 'hearers'.

[57] Williams, 'Castle Ashby manuscripts', pp. 395–8; Arthur Freeman, 'An epistle for two', *Library*, 5:25 (1970), 226–36.

[58] *The fruit, herbs and vegetables of Italy*, trans. Gillian Riley (Harmondsworth, 1989), p. 47.

manuscript of a short poem 'May't please! here is a wearied Bee from hive' which he judged to have been prepared *'pro formâ mendicandi'*.[59] Others were more persistent, or perhaps successful, and the miscellanies of seventeenth-century verse contain many thinly disguised appeals for favour or subvention. The plea did not have to be direct: verse in praise of a patron's house, person or family, a funeral elegy for a relative, or a piece which simply agreed with views the patron was known to hold would produce the same effect, and, when presented in a reasonably dignified way, was an accepted part of the vocation of letters. Neither did the response have to be in cash: houseroom, wine, clothing or assistance in some suit for preferment would be just as welcome.

> Commend this Olio of this Lord, 'tis fit,
> Nay ten to one but you have part of it;
> There is that justice left, since you maintain
> His table, he should counter-feed your brain.
> Then write how well he in his Sack hath droll'd,
> Straight there's a Bottle to your chamber roll'd.
> Or with embroidered words praise his *French* Suit,
> Month hence 'tis yours, with his Mans curse to boot . . .
> Or spin an Elegie on his false hair,
> 'Tis well he cries, but living hair is dear;
> Yet say that out of order ther's one curl,
> And all the hopes of your reward you furl.[60]

Such addresses were part of the machinery of the patron-client relationship—expressions of allegiance to a social superior who in turn was expected to advance the fortunes of the petitioner. None the less, properly handled, and directed to a variety of patrons, they could offer a resourceful writer better returns in money or kind than the sale of the same texts to a print publisher.

One writer, Richard Flecknoe, daringly transposed this practice into print. His numerous books of epigrams (almost an annual event at one stage of his life) are rich in thinly disguised begging poems, many addressed to members of the Cavendish family.[61] The books themselves, of which fourteen out of thirty-two were published 'For the author' and only ten bear the imprint of a

[59] BL MS 18220, f. 4.

[60] Lovelace, 'On *Sanazar*'s being honoured', *Poems*, p. 194.

[61] See my 'Richard Flecknoe as author-publisher', *BSANZ bulletin* 14 (1990), 41–50.

bookseller, were themselves distributed as a form of begging. In one epigram, he frankly confesses that

> To you, from whom I can't so much as look
> For charges of the *binding* of my *Book*;
> Much less the *Printing*, why should I present
> It now? but only out of Compliment?
> And I don't like such Compliments as those,
> When one gets nothing, and is sure to lose.[62]

Flecknoe is a useful because unusually blatant witness to a practice that was already well established in manuscript. But print had the drawback that these machinations were on public display, a matter that must have contributed to the contempt in which Flecknoe was held by Dryden.[63] Flecknoe's readers can hardly have failed to notice that, on the death of patrons, poems written in their honour were sometimes transferred to other recipients—a practice much less risky in manuscript.[64]

The exclusivity of the scribal medium made it ideally suited to another form of the client–patron relationship in which the writer produced numerous pieces specifically tailored to the taste of the patron and his friends. Nashe's claim of 1592—'I haue written in all sorts of humors priuately, I am perswaded, more than any yoong man of my age in England'—appears to refer to light-hearted pieces, now mostly lost, written for the circle of Lord Strange in the early 1590s.[65] The same kind of dependence can be seen in the long series of papers on administrative questions prepared by Sir Robert Cotton for Henry Howard, Earl of Northampton.[66] Shakespeare's sonnets are another outcome of a sustained client–

[62] *Epigrams of all sorts* (London, 1671), p. A4^r. See also Anton Lohr, *Richard Flecknoe. Eine literarische Untersuchung* Leipzig, 1905), p. 104.

[63] Discussed in my 'Shadwell, Flecknoe and the Duke of Newcastle: an impetus for *Mac Flecknoe*', *Papers on language and literature* 21 (1985), 19-27.

[64] For examples see Love, 'Richard Flecknoe', p. 44. Kay, 'Poems by Sir Walter Aston', pp. 206–7 and n. 37 cites parallel cases from manuscript elegies on Prince Henry.

[65] *The works of Thomas Nashe*, ed. R. B. McKerrow, rev. F. P. Wilson (Oxford, 1958), i. 320. For Nashe and Strange see Charles Nicholl, *A cup of news: the life of Thomas Nashe* (London, 1984), pp. 87–98. Nicholl's identification of Strange as the dedicatee of 'The choice of valentines' is confirmed by Folger MS V. a. 399, ff. 53^v–7^r. For the circulation of writings by Nashe in manuscript, see *Works*, v. 136.

[66] Cotton's work for Northampton is described in Kevin Sharpe, *Sir Robert Cotton 1586–1631: history and politics in early modern England* (Oxford, 1979), pp. 114–28 and Linda Levy Peck, *Northampton: patronage and policy at the court of James I* (London, 1982), pp. 103–17. See also below, pp. 83–9.

patron relationship, the earlier decades having an unmistakable status as gifts presented singly or in small groups during the client's regular visits to wait upon the patron.[67] (The opening scene of *Timon of Athens* shows an Athenian version of such a visit.) This would still hold even if the 'story' of the sonnets was a fiction, since it would be a fiction styled around the known conditions of the client's service and the patron's acceptance; moreover, the poems could still have performed the function of a client's gift to a patron who was not the young man presented in them. Moving from the known to the unknown, and from the opening years of the century to the 1670s, it is tempting to see Traherne's industry as a composer of prose meditations (while obviously congenial) as tailored to the tastes of his patron and employer, the elderly Sir Orlando Bridgeman.[68] Not all these cases qualify as examples of scribal publication but they illustrate how an author working in the scribal medium could be just as professional in outlook as his print-orientated counterpart.

Consideration of the links between author publication and the search for patronage leads irresistibly to Andrew Marvell, who made his way during the 1650s to a position which Hilton Kelliher has accurately described as that of Cromwell's own laureate and the 'official verse-propagandist of the new state'.[69] This was done with very little exposure by name in print, though a few texts appeared anonymously. Instead his preference was always to direct poems along precisely calculated paths within networks of patronage. His Latin verse address to Nathaniel Ingelo was composed in order that it should be seen (as it was) by 'the learned Queen Christina, whom it flatters at length', while the 'Horatian ode', although not directly addressed to Cromwell, was very probably meant to reach his hands.[70] Having served these purposes

[67] This is also Arthur F. Marotti's view in 'Shakespeare's sonnets as literary property' in *Soliciting interpretation: literary theory and seventeenth-century English poetry*, ed. Elizabeth Harvey and Katharine Maus (Chicago, 1990), pp. 143–73.

[68] Traherne was chaplain to Bridgeman and his large family. As a famous anecdote concerning Swift records, a chaplain might be required to read meditations aloud to his employer.

[69] *Andrew Marvell poet and politician 1621–78. An exhibition to commemorate the tercentenary of his death* (London, 1978), p. 56.

[70] Kelliher, p. 59. In my reading of the ode, I follow the findings of Denise Cuthbert's meticulous study of the evolution of Marvell's relationship with Cromwell in her Sydney University Ph.D. thesis, 'A re-examination of Andrew Marvell' (1987).

neither poem appears to have circulated further either in print or in manuscript until its appearance in the posthumous *Miscellaneous poems* of 1681, assembled by Mary Palmer. Prior to attaching himself to Cromwell, Marvell had been in the service of another great Puritan leader, Thomas, Lord Fairfax. The hostile references to Cromwell, Fairfax and their cause in the elegy on Lord Francis Villiers (printed anonymously *circa* 1648–9) has led several scholars to reject its somewhat shaky attribution to Marvell; but this is to display a naïve attitude towards the politics of patronage as they affected the scribal medium, especially as Marvell's third major patron was to be Francis Villiers's brother, the second Duke of Buckingham. Over recent decades Marvell scholars have been steadily accumulating evidence for the prior scribal publication of poems from the 1681 collection, but it is only in the case of the post-Restoration satires (mostly excluded from the collection) that this was genuinely extensive.[71] Insofar as a continuing theme can be identified behind Marvell's conduct of his career, it is one of exercising the maximum amount of influence with the minimum amount of visibility. His airy dismissal of Samuel Parker's account of his Cromwellian past was only possible because the 'Horatian ode' and the elegy on the death of Cromwell still remained in manuscript.[72] The second of these seems actually to have been withdrawn at the last moment from the volume of elegies which was to haunt Dryden, Waller and Sprat for the rest of their lives.

Having earlier considered Flecknoe's naturalization into print of the manuscript begging poem, it will be helpful here to consider another area in which print exposed a practice that had previously been earning income for scribal author-publishers. John Jenkins's career as a composer-publisher has already been discussed but not its economic basis. While Jenkins must sometimes have received direct payment or presents in return for manuscripts of his music, Roger North makes clear that his primary support came as a salaried visitor to music-loving houses ('I never heard that he articled with any gentleman where he resided, but accepted what

[71] See Kelliher, *passim*; Pritchard, 'Marvell's "The garden"'; and Margarita Stocker and Timothy Raylor, 'A new Marvell manuscript: Cromwellian patronage and politics', *ELR* 20 (1990), 106–62.

[72] *The rehearsal transpros'd and The rehearsal transpros'd the second part*, ed. D. I. B. Smith (Oxford, 1971), p. 203.

they gave him'), and that such terms were generous enough for Jenkins to be able to leave a number of legacies.[73] This arrangement reflects the conditions of musical life in the country; but in the cities and large towns the professional musician would expect to earn regular income from individual pupils, which would include payment for handwritten tutors and simple 'lessons'.[74] At a later stage the learner would be expected to purchase manuscripts of more advanced compositions, which meant that it was rarely in the composer's interest to publish these in printed form.[75] As late as 1669 it was widely believed that 'no Choice Ayres or Songs are permitted by Authors to come in print'.[76] The price of music so secured was a constant source of complaint. Roger North, for one, had no regrets for an age 'when all passed in MSS, which were not onely hard to get, but often slovenly wrote'.[77]

That having 'lessons' engraved for private sale by the composer could bring even higher returns than the sale of handwritten copies was the discovery of the violin virtuoso Nicola Matteis. North's account of this change is as follows:

> And he found out a way of getting mony which was perfectly new. For seeing his lessons, (which were all *duos*), take with his scollars, and that most gentlemen desired them, he was at some charge to have them graven in copper, and printed in oblong octavos, and this was the beginning of ingraving musick in England. And of these lessons he made books, and presented them, well bound, to most of the lovers, which brought him the 3, 4, and 5 ginnys; and the incouragement was so great, that he made 4 of them.[78]

As in Flecknoe's case, the transition to print illuminates what had previously been buried from sight in manuscript. The musician

[73] North, *Roger North*, p. 344.

[74] A practice already established by the late 15th cent. as is shown by Christopher Page, 'The 15th-century lute: new and neglected sources', *Early music* 9 (1981), 11–21. For a 17th-cent. example, carefully fingered for a novice harpsichordist, see John L. Boston, 'Priscilla Bunbury's virginal book', *Music and letters* 36 (1955), 365–73.

[75] Byrd's 'My lady Nevell's book', superbly written for the composer by the Windsor music scribe, John Baldwin, is one famous example.

[76] *The treasury of musick: containing ayres and dialogues* (London, 1669), p. *A*1^r. John Playford's denial of this proposition is, naturally, a self-interested one.

[77] North, *Roger North*, p. 311 and n. 66.

[78] Ibid. 356. For Matteis's place in the history of music engraving in England (which actually dated from 1613), see D. W. Krummel, *English music printing 1553–1700* (London, 1975), pp. 152–9.

selling individual engraved lessons directly to his pupils or presenting 'books' of these to patrons in return for a 'present' of three, four or five guineas a time would have earned far more than by a sale of his copy to a regular print-publisher supplemented by a single dedication. Moreover, by paying for and retaining the plates he could produce repeated small editions to suit requirements. The good fortune of Matteis lay in his having enough pupils and patrons to be his own print publisher, having graduated to this from scribal publication. It is likely that other manuscripts arising from the teacher–pupil relationship, such as writing-copy-books, dance manuals, devotional works and materials for the study of foreign languages, were sold or 'presented' in the same way, and at the same high prices.

THE AUTHOR PUBLICATION OF PLAY TEXTS

The pre-1641 theatres, always cautious about print publication, tolerated the scribal publication of play-texts, at least from the early 1620s and probably earlier.[79] Humphrey Moseley in his introduction to the 1647 Beaumont and Fletcher folio mentions copies having been made available by actors to their 'private friends', the manuscript of Fletcher's *Bonduca* (BL Add. MS 36758) being one such presentation copy, in the hand of Edward Knight, the King's Men's prompter.[80] A second scribe was responsible for a manuscript of *Beggars' bush* and a royal presentation copy of Suckling's *Aglaura*.[81] The King's Men also made regular use of Ralph Crane's services in order to produce play-manuscripts whose purpose was, in M. A. Buettner's words, 'either to present

[79] W. W. Greg in the *The editorial problem in Shakespeare*, 3rd edn (Oxford, 1954) expressed his position in the following words: 'I am not aware that any private transcript can be dated before 1624, when the scandal over *A Game at Chess* created a sudden demand, but it is quite possible that isolated copies may have been produced earlier' (p. 45). This is a fair assessment of the position as regards surviving manuscripts but has to be questioned on the basis of those lost ones which served as the basis of unauthorized printed editions. John Jowett, 'Jonson's authorization of type in *Sejanus* and other early quartos', *SB* 44 (1991), supports Greg's position on the equally contestable grounds that 'the drama simply did not belong to an élite culture in the sense that metaphysical poetry did' (p. 255).

[80] *Comedies and tragedies written by Francis Beaumont and John Fletcher gentlemen* (London 1647), p. A4^r; W. W. Greg, 'Prompt copies, private transcripts, and the "playhouse scrivener"', *Library*, 4:6 (1926), 148–56; *The dramatic works in the Beaumont and Fletcher canon*, iv. 151.

[81] *Dramatic works*, iii. 227.

to aristocratic patrons or to sell in the marketplace'.[82] Only a handful of Crane's manuscripts survive—the existence of others being inferred from the study of printed texts for which they are believed to have served as copy—but none of these is a working playhouse manuscript; nor would the expensive services of a skilled scribe be wasted on such utilitarian documents as prompt-books, plots and actors' sides.[83] In August 1624 Crane was called on to assist with the scribal publication of Middleton's banned *A game at chess*. Three of the six surviving manuscripts are in his hand, two others being wholly or partly in that of the dramatist. The question whether Crane's copies are to be regarded as examples of author or of entrepreneurial publication is answered by the fact that one of them contains a dedication signed by Middleton to 'the Worthlie-Accomplish'd, Mr: William Hammond'

> This, which nor Stage nor Stationers Stall can Showe,
> (The Common Eye maye wish for, but ne're knowe)
> Comes in it's best Loue, wth the New-yeare forth,
> As a fit Present to the Hand of Worth.[84]

Middleton then was the director of the enterprise: moreover, while undoubtedly expecting a return for his own and Crane's labours, he was keen to preserve the gentlemanly fiction of an exchange of gifts. The practice of presenting plays as new-year-gifts to a patron is also alluded to in Heywood's dedication of the 1633 printed text of *The Jew of Malta* to Thomas Hammon of Gray's Inn, this time with an apology that the donor had no better gift to offer.[85]

[82] *'A game of chess' by Thomas Middleton: a textual edition based on the manuscripts written by Ralph Crane*, ed. Milton Arthur Buettner (Salzburg, 1980), p. 1.

[83] A partial exception is Crane's transcript of *Sir John van Olden Barnavelt*, BL MS Add. 18653, which was marked up by a later hand to serve as a prompt-book. F. P. Wilson, 'Ralph Crane, scrivener to the King's Players', *Library*, 4:7 (1926), points out that the hand of this manuscript is 'less calligraphic' than his other copies and that it is a folio, whereas the private transcripts are quartos (pp. 202–3). For a consideration of the evidence for lost manuscripts, see T. H. Howard-Hill, *Ralph Crane and some Shakespeare first folio comedies* (Charlottesville, Va., 1972).

[84] *'A game of chess'*, p. 44. Crane's transcript of Middleton's *The witch* (Bodleian MS Malone 12) contains a similar dedicatory epistle from the author to Thomas Holmes. However, that of Fletcher's *The humorous lieutenant* as *Demetrius and Enanthe* (Harlech collection) is by Crane himself, indicating entrepreneurial publication.

[85] 'I had no better a New-yeares gift to present you with; receive it therefore as a continuance of that inviolable obliegement, by which, he rests still ingaged; who as he ever hath, shall alwayes remaine, *Tuissimus*' (*The complete works of Christopher Marlowe*, ed.

The 1650s found a large body of play manuscripts in circulation, some of these, no doubt, being survivors from the theatres' own collections but others emanating from a tradition of author publication which acquired new life when playwrights were deprived of their regular livelihood by the closing of the playhouses. Sizeable collections of manuscripts of unprinted pre-1642 plays were assembled by the booksellers Francis Kirkman, Richard Marriott and Humphrey Moseley (the third group being the source of the collection diminished by Warburton's cook).[86] The titles contained in these offer a tantalizing view of the wealth of material then available and the seriousness of the subsequent loss, except insofar as some of the plays may survive in Restoration adaptations.[87] In presenting the Beaumont and Fletcher folio of 1647 to the world, Moseley announced with obvious pride that 'Heretofore when Gentlemen desired but a Copy of any of these *Playes*, the meanest piece here (if any may be called Meane where every one is Best) cost them more then foure times the price you pay for the whole *Volume*'.[88] This would seem to indicate the '3 or 4' guineas mentioned by North as customary for a manuscript presented by its author.

Shakespeare may well have put work into circulation through the agency of scribes. As house dramatist for the King's Men, he was unable to print his plays without the approval of his fellow sharers.[89] Bentley judges that he 'did not himself take to the printer any of the plays he wrote for the Lord Chamberlain-King's company'.

Fredson Bowers (Cambridge 1973–), i. 259). For the earlier history of such presentations, see E. H. Miller, 'New year's day gift books in the sixteenth century', *SB* 15 (1962), 233–41. Wilson (p. 200) records that Ralph Crane made an annual gift of a manuscript to John, Earl of Bridgewater.

[86] The contents of these collections are listed on pp. 292–5 of Alfred Harbage, 'Elizabethan–Restoration palimpsest', *MLR* 35 (1940), 287–319 and in his *Annals of English drama 975–1700*, 3rd edn, rev. S. Schoenbaum and Sylvia Stoler Wagenheim (London, 1989), pp. 212–18. 'Hill's list' appears to represent the Kirkman collection. Manuscripts of already printed plays seem to have been of no interest to the collectors.

[87] The argument of 'Elizabethan–Restoration palimpsest'.

[88] *Comedies and tragedies*, p. A4^{v}. Moseley also complains: 'the *Care & Pains* was wholly mine, which I found to be more then you'l easily imagine, unlesse you knew into how many hands the Originalls were dispersed'. Robert K. Turner discusses the implications of this remark in *Dramatic works*, i. xxx.

[89] See G. E. Bentley, *The profession of dramatist in Shakespeare's time 1590–1642* (Princeton, NJ, 1971), pp. 264–81. The prohibition also applied to his successors Fletcher, Massinger and Brome.

> When his plays were published they appeared without any indication of the author's sponsorship—no dedications, no epistles, no addresses to the reader, no commendatory verses from friends, not even a list of characters, and for most of them neither prologue nor epilogue . . . In whatever manner Shakespeare's several plays may have come into the hands of the printers before 1616 (and the possible methods are various) it is reasonably clear that he himself refrained from ushering them into print . . .[90]

The sale or presentation to a wealthy patron of a manuscript of a favourite play would have offered an opportunity for additional income, and is intrinsically no less improbable than other explanations which have been brought forward for the genesis of the manuscripts which served as copy for the better quarto editions. E. A. J. Honigmann singles out *Troilus and Cressida* and the sonnets, both printed by G. Eld in 1609, as possible outcomes of scribal circulation.[91] The play is described as '*neuer stal'd with the Stage, neuer clapper-clawd with the palmes of the vulger*'[92]; moreover, an attempt at print publication in 1602 had proved abortive—suggesting a certain notoriety. Honigmann's proposal that the play would have been read by contemporaries as an allusion to the fall of Essex would link it with other politically suspect material of the kind that, throughout the century, was restricted to manuscript circulation but often eagerly sought in that form.

In the case of the sonnets, we know from Francis Meres's reference in 1598 to their circulation 'among his priuate friends' and the appearance of two poems in *The passionate pilgrim* (1599) that some elements of the cycle were in circulation during the late 1590s. Other sonnets which survive in manuscript sources may also derive from originals of this period.[93] John Kerrigan, while accepting it as an 'inescapable conclusion' that some of the sonnets were 'quietly made public' through manuscript during the reign of Elizabeth, argues that the final form of the cycle, incorporating 'A

[90] Ibid. 280. Bentley points to the poor condition of the texts as further evidence against the involvement of a writer who 'did take great pains with his text when he published his poems' (loc. cit.).

[91] 'The date and revision of *Troilus and Cressida*' in *Textual criticism and literary interpretation*, ed. Jerome J. McGann (Chicago, 1985), p. 54.

[92] *The famous historie of Troylus and Cresseid* (London, 1609), ¶2 r.

[93] For the manuscripts of the sonnets, see Beal, *IELM*, i/2, 452–4. Twelve sonnets in all are found in manuscript sources, Sonnet 2 occurring twelve times.

lover's complaint' and the more stylistically complex sonnets, was arrived at between 1603 and its appearance in print in 1609.[94] Despite the stress laid by Katharine Duncan-Jones on the solid professional standing of Thomas Thorpe, the 'adventurer' responsible for the 1609 publication, the absence of an authorial dedication and the riddling quality of Thorpe's salute to Mr. W. H. still leave a distinct odour of the intercepted manuscript—which in this case was of high quality but apparently not a holograph.[95] One possibility to be added to the multitude already canvassed is that Mr W. H. was a scribe charged with the production of copies who had made a surreptitious extra copy for sale to Thorpe. His 'begetting' of the text would consist of his having inscribed it—a common metaphor which will be further discussed in Chapter 4. The question is not without its critical implications, both in small matters (a visualizing reader will wish to know whether the image which should accompany 'That in black ink my love may still shine bright' is one of a printed or handwritten page) and in the broader question of the kind of readership to which Shakespeare was addressing the poems, and whether this varied as the cycle evolved through revision.

The Restoration theatre companies, with their repertoires secured by royal edict, had no reason to oppose the print publication of plays. Scribal publication was now reserved for dramatists who maintained a genteel disdain for the press (like Orinda with *Pompey* and Rochester with *Lucina's rape*) or where performance was prevented, as with Dryden's *The state of innocence*. In his preface to the 1677 quarto, Dryden complained of 'many hundred Copies of it being dispers'd, abroad without my knowledge or consent: so that every one gathering new faults, it became at length a Libel against me'. This is undoubtedly an exaggeration, but since seven manuscripts survive it is not implausible that ten times that number may once have existed.[96]

[94] *The sonnets and A lover's complaint* (Harmondsworth, 1986), p. 10. See also pp. 427–33 and the account of the variant texts on pp. 441–54.

[95] Katherine Duncan-Jones, 'Was the 1609 *Shake-speares Sonnets* really unauthorized?', *RES* NS 34 (1983), 151–71. See also Kerrigan, p. 66. The most revealing analysis of the language of the dedication is Donald W. Foster, 'Master W. H., R. I. P.', *PMLA* 102 (1987), 42–54.

[96] *The state of innocence, and fall of man: an opera* (London, 1677), p. b1^r. For the manuscripts see Harbage, *Annals*, p. 309. Five of these are discussed in Marion H. Hamilton,

Tellingly, one of these (Harvard MS Thr. 9) contains corrections in Dryden's own hand, suggesting that the tradition may have arisen from author publication. A manuscript of *The Indian emperour* used as a prompt copy for some country-house theatricals has also been traced back to a source close to the dramatist.[97] Among the poems, *Mac Flecknoe* and the collaborative *Essay upon satire* were consciously intended for scribal circulation though the surviving copies all seem to derive from entrepreneurial, not author, publication. Dryden is also said in one contemporary source to have written lampoons.[98]

PUBLICATION THROUGH ONE COPY

A survey of author publication is the most convenient place to address the apparently paradoxical notion of publication through a single copy, lent or rented. (A case of a manuscript being rented is attested to by Simonds D'Ewes.[99]) Circulation of a single copy to a series of readers has already been documented in the case of *Biathanatos* at the beginning of the period and of Pope's *Pastorals* a century later, and may well have been the mode of transmission of some works which were known prior to their first appearance in print but for which there are no surviving manuscripts. Among a number of documented examples is that of Hobbes's *An historical narration concerning heresie and the punishment thereof*. This was

'The manuscripts of Dryden's *The state of innocence* and the relation of the Harvard MS to the first quarto', *SB* 6 (1954), 237–46.

[97] See Fredson Bowers, 'The 1665 manuscript of Dryden's *Indian emperour*', *SP* 48 (1951), 738–60. The later 'Douai' manuscript is derived from a printed source (*Works*, ix. 382).

[98] For the manuscripts of *Mac Flecknoe*, see *Works*, i. 428–39; David M. Vieth, 'Dryden's *Mac Flecknoe*: the case against editorial confusion', *HLB* 24 (1976), 204–45; and Beal, *IELM*, ii/1, 407–8. Manuscript sources unknown to Vieth are Leeds University Brotherton MS Lt 54, pp. 1–10 and National Library of Ireland MS 2093, pp. 36–55, making 16 in all. For manuscripts of the *Essay*, written with John Sheffield, Earl of Mulgrave, see Beal, *IELM*, ii/1, 396. The accusation that Dryden wrote lampoons is made in Shadwell's 'Upon a late fall'n poet' ('A sad mischance I sing alas'), Yale MS Osborn b 105, p. 330, with reference to Anne Reeves: 'And thô she had Clapt him o're & o're, / Poxt all Wild:House Spanjards, and Forty more, / Yet he lampoon'd those that call'd her Whore' (ll. 37–9). On 23 February 1699 he sent two lampoon separates to Elizabeth Steward with speculations about their authorship (*The letters of John Dryden*, ed. Charles E. Ward (Durham, NC, 1942), p. 133).

[99] *The autobiography and correspondence of Sir Simonds D'Ewes, Bart., during the reigns of James I and Charles I*, ed. James Orchard Halliwell (London, 1845), ii. 39–40. John Shirley had run a lending service for manuscripts as early as the 15th cent.

written in 1666 to deflect a proposed prosecution of *Leviathan* but never printed during his lifetime. A manuscript was available to Charles Blount in 1678 through Hobbes's bookseller and print publisher, William Crooke.[100] Blount himself circulated a single manuscript copy of *A summary account of the Deists' religion.* Writing in 1686 to Thomas Sydenham, he explained: 'The last time I had the happiness of your Company, it was your Request that I would help you to a sight of the Deists Arguments, which I told you, I had sometimes by me, but then had lent them out, they are now return'd me again, and according to my promise I have herewith sent them to you.'[101] Mary Hobbs cites Aubrey's account of Donne's friend, John Hoskins, whose 'booke of poemes, neatly written by one of his clerkes, bigger then Dr Donne's poemes' disappeared after his son lent it to 'he knowes not who, about 1653'.[102] One of Aubrey's own close friends, the deist James Boevey (1622–95), wrote a kind of personal encyclopedia in thirty-nine volumes covering morality, psychology, economics, politics and the skills of negotiation. Aubrey makes clear that it was composed of actual treatises, not just commonplace books, and that it was 'all in his custodie' but available to his friends.[103] Another revealing case is that of George Hakewill, chaplain to Prince Charles, whose lost tract of 1621 dissuading his master from the proposed Spanish marriage brought about not only his own imprisonment but that of those identified as having read the unique manuscript.[104] Celia Fiennes's narrative of her travels through England survives in a partial holograph and a fair copy in the hand of an amanuensis, it being the latter which was the published text, incorporating a preface and a promise that any

[100] In a letter of 1678 sent to Hobbes through Crooke, Blount writes: 'By your Permission, and Mr. *Crook*'s Favour, I have had the Happiness to peruse your incomparable Treatise of Heresie in Manuscript' (*The oracles of reason* (London, 1693), p. 97). Crooke printed the work after Hobbes's death.

[101] Ibid. 87.

[102] John Aubrey, *'Brief lives', chiefly of contemporaries*, ed. Andrew Clark (Oxford, 1898), i. 418.

[103] Ibid., i. 112–14. For Boevey, see Arthur W. Crawley-Boevey, *The 'perverse widow': being passages from the life of Catharina, wife of William Boevey, Esq.* (London, 1898), pp. 24–38. I have traced several manuscripts of treatises by Boevey, but only one (BL Harl. MS 28531) from the list given by Aubrey.

[104] See Arthur Freeman, 'George Hakewill's disgrace and the character of Prince Charles', *N&Q* 215 (1970), 247–9.

errors noted by readers would be corrected in a 'supplement annext to the Book'. The modest statement in the preface that 'it was never designed, soe not likely to fall into the hands of any but my near relations' is called into question by the broadly moralizing tone of what follows; but there is no suggestion that any further copying was envisaged.[105]

Clearly the instances just described inhabit a rather uneasy area between the private and the public. Yet it could be argued that the restriction was not always a chosen one and that some of the authors concerned would have welcomed wider scribal circulation if it were not that they had pressing reasons for confining work to a single copy. The first of these reasons would have been the need to limit knowledge of material that might be judged indecent, heterodox, seditious, or simply too far ahead of its time for a rising statesman, lawyer or cleric. (Borrowers may also have preferred a temporary custody of such perilous writings.) The second reason was the very real danger that a text in uncontrolled circulation would sooner or later be piratically propelled into print. In this connection more credence than is customary should be given to the claims made by authors in the prefaces to printed works that they had been forced to the press by the fear or fact of an unauthorized printing from a corrupt manuscript. Far from being coy attempts to disarm criticism, such pleas identify a real and pressing dilemma for scribally publishing authors. George Wither gave their point of view in 1624 when he complained that if a bookseller 'gett any written Coppy into his powre, likely to be vendible; whether the Author be willing or no, he will publish it; And it shallbe contrived and named alsoe, according to his owne pleasure: which is the reason, so many good Bookes come forth imperfect, and with foolish titles'.[106] Nashe in the 1590s seems to have been acting as an agent for the booksellers Richard Jones and Thomas Newman in obtaining scribally published texts by writers of the Sidney-Pembroke circle for unauthorized print publication.[107]

105 *The journeys of Celia Fiennes*, ed. Christopher Morris (London, 1947), pp. 1–2.

106 *The schollers purgatory, discovered in the stationers common-wealth* (London, 1624), p. 121.

107 Nicholl, pp. 82–5; Christopher R. Wilson, '*Astrophil and Stella*: a tangled editorial web', *Library*, 6:1 (1979), 336–46. Gerald D. Johnson, 'John Busby and the stationers' trade, 1590–1612', *Library*, 6:7 (1985), 1–15, finds a similar pattern in the career of the younger John Busby.

ENTREPRENEURIAL PUBLICATION

Entrepreneurial publication, the second of our three modes, has already been introduced in Chapter 1 through the discussion of professional vendors of parliamentary papers in the reign of Charles I and the operations of the later Starkey and Collins scriptoria in the 1670s. The techniques of production and distribution employed by these agencies are discussed in Chapter 3: our task at the moment is simply to assess the significance of entrepreneurial publication relative to other modes. One important thing to remember is that it was not a new initiative of the seventeenth century but a continuation of established book-trade practice from before the invention of printing. A second is that the skilled manpower required for the scribal publication of separates and manuscript books was amply to hand in the huge number of trained clerks. Throughout the century the work of commerce, the law, the church, the army, the navy and all levels of government was conducted through handwritten documents. Bishops communicated with their parish clergy through written instructions, as did secretaries of state with Lord Lieutenants, Lord Lieutenants with sheriffs, and sheriffs with Justices of the Peace. The business counting house and the attorney's and scrivener's office provided training to young clerks in the skills of the scriptorium which could then be transferred to the book trade. Such training would have covered not simply the production of individual copies but streamlined methods of producing large numbers of copies of a particular text.

Entrepreneurial publication took place when manuscripts were produced and circulated for gain by a scribe or stationer. The term is a little misleading in that not all such copying involved a prior commitment of capital—the cautious trader would produce manuscripts only in response to orders—but it is the best among the available alternatives. ('Commercial publication' would not have distinguished between the activities of authors and those of stationers or entrepreneurial scribes; 'petty commodity publication' while more accurate is too cumbrous.[108]) It was strongly opposed to any notion of authorial control over distribution: such

[108] For an application of this Marxist term to printed books, see N. N. Feltes, *Modes of production of Victorian novels* (Chicago, 1986), pp. 3–10.

manuscripts would be available to anyone who could pay for them and who was trusted by the vendor. The texts copied would always be ones for which there was a strong public demand and for which no competition was expected from the press. The market produced some publishers, such as Robert Julian, who did not maintain bookshops, but much of the trade remained a sideline of established stationers such as Starkey and Collins already mentioned. An important testimony to this is a document by Sir Roger L'Estrange, presented to the House of Lords in 1675, of which a précis is given in a Historical Manuscript Commission Report, but which is here reproduced in full from the original in the House of Lords Record Office:

> The Question of Libells, extends it selfe (I conceive) to manuscripts, as well as Prints; as beeing the more mischievous of the Two: for they are com[m]only so bitter, and dangerous, that not one of forty of them ever comes to ye Presse, and yet by ye help of Transcripts, they are well nigh as Publique.
>
> For the preventing, and suppressing of Printed Libells, I shall only desire such a generall warrant from his Maty: and Councill, as I have formerly had, to support mee in the Execution of my Duty.
>
> And for Libells in Writing, I do humbly offer this to Consideration. That although Copyes of them may passe indifferently from one to another, by other hands, yet some certain Stationers are supposed to bee ye chiefe, and profest dealers in them, as having some Affinity with their Trade.
>
> And when they come to bee detected, the Com[m]on pretence is, *They were left in my shopp*, or *sent in a Letter, I know not by whom*: which may be true in some cases, though but a shift, for ye greater Part.
>
> In the former case, The stationers may be ordered to call a Hall, and administer an Oath to all their members, neither directly, nor Indirectly, to Countenance, dispense, publish, Print or Cause to bee Printed any such Libells.
>
> And secondly, for a Generall Provision; whoever shall receive, and Conceale any such Libell, without giving notice thereof, to some of his Matyes Justices, within a certain space of time after the receipt of it; let him suffer as an Abettour of it, & if he shall not produce ye person of whom he had it, let him suffer as ye Authour of it.[109]

A feature of this report is that much of its phraseology is taken over

[109] 'Mr L'Estraings Proposition concerning Libells, &c.', 11 November 1675, summarized in *HMC, 9th rep., app.*, p. 66b.

from a similar paper of 1662 (PRO SP29/51/10.1), presumably also composed by L'Estrange. This at least confirms that the well-documented popularity of manuscript satires from 1675 onwards was not a novelty, but a continuation of an older practice. A comparable enterprise of the earlier Stuart period would be the production of such a forbidden text as Thomas Scot's *Vox populi*. A spy's report of around 1620 describes a conversation with a scrivener who had received an order from a stationer for twelve copies of the work only to lose it when a rival offered a lower quotation.[110] While each of these examples concerns the sale of forbidden and offensive texts they have implications for the associated trade in less sensational documents. L'Estrange's point about the sale of manuscripts 'having some Affinity' with the stationer's trade would also apply to the copying of perfectly unobjectionable texts which were required in too small numbers to justify printing, or which could be sold more profitably in manuscript than in print.

In other specialist and professional areas we can also assume an involvement by stationers in the entrepreneurial production of manuscripts. Towards the end of the century, the music bookseller John Carr had a 'secretary's office' at his shop at the Middle Temple gate 'for wrighting the theatricall tunes, to accomodate learners and country fidlers'.[111] His better-known contemporary, Henry Playford, regularly included manuscripts in his printed catalogues but may have been only a dealer rather than a scribal publisher.[112] John Bagford sold albums of fragments from medieval manuscripts to a circle of virtuosi who included Pepys, Humfrey Wanley, Hans Sloane and Peter Le Neve.[113] Law booksellers,

110 W. W. Greg, *A companion to Arber* (Oxford, 1967), pp. 176–8. See also pp. 96–7 below.

111 North, *Roger North*, p. 29 n.

112 The presence of manuscripts in Henry Playford's sales catalogues is discussed in D. R. Harvey, 'Henry Playford: a bibliographical study', Victoria University of Wellington Ph.D. thesis, 1985, pp. 133–50. See also Lenore F. Coral, 'Music in English auction sales, 1676–1750', University of London Ph.D. thesis, 1974, pp. 74–80. *A curious collection of musick-books, both vocal and instrumental* (London, 1690) has the 'prick'd' music in pride of place at the head of the catalogue. Up-to-date as well as older music was available in manuscript.

113 See Milton McC. Gatch, 'John Bagford as a collector and disseminator of manuscript fragments', *Library*, 6:7 (1985), 95–114. The practical aim of such collections, whose materials were largely retrieved from old bindings, was to illustrate historically significant hands.

already cited as traders in political separates, also provided treatises and copies of the speeches of eminent judges and counsel. An instance from the beginning of the century illustrates this. Following the union of the crowns of England and Scotland in 1603 there was uncertainty over the rights under the laws of England of Scots born after the union (the *post-nati*). A test case mounted in the Exchequer in 1608 drew on the greatest legal talents of the time, and, although it was known that the material decisions would be printed (the king having issued a patent to that effect to Sir William Woodhouse), reports of speeches by Bacon, Coke, Lord Chancellor Egerton and others were widely circulated as separates and compilations. Egerton complained that 'diuerse vnperfect Reports, and seuerall patches and pieces of my Speech haue bin put in writing, & dispersed into many hands, and some offred to the Presse'. At the request of the king he had to reconstruct his speech from notes and print it together with Coke's detailed report of the judges' arguments, in order 'to preuent the Printing of such mistaken and vnperfect reports of it, as weere already scattered abroad'.[114] The situation described is very similar to that we have already observed in the transmission of parliamentary documents, and, although there is no specific evidence that manuscripts of these actual texts were being commissioned by law stationers in commercial quantities, it perfectly illuminates the circumstances that led to such production. Providers of copies from outside the book trade included industrious secretaries such as Sir Robert Cotton's scribe Flood, who provoked a royal confiscation of the Cottonian library through his trafficking in Sir Robert Dudley's *Propositions delivered to His Majesty*.[115] Likewise, scriveners might market manuscripts on their own account rather than simply copying them for stationers, as Nashe reveals in the preface to *The terrors of the night*:

> A long time since hath it laine suppressed by mee; vntill the vrgent importunitie of a kinde frend of mine (to whom I was sundrie waies beholding) wrested a Coppie from me. That Coppie progressed from one scriueners shop to another, & at length grew so common, that it was readie to bee hung out for one of their signes, like a paire of indentures.

[114] *The speech of the Lord Chancellor of England, touching the post-nati* (London, 1609), A5^v–A6^r; cited in James G. McManaway, 'Privilege to print', *SB* 16 (1963), 202.

[115] D'Ewes, *Autobiography*, ii. 39–42; Sharpe, *Sir Robert Cotton*, pp. 143–4.

Wherevppon I thought it as good for mee to reape the frute of my owne labours, as to let some vnskilfull pen-man or Nouerint-maker startch his ruffe & new spade his beard with the benefite he made of them.[116]

Entrepreneurial publication is to be suspected whenever a text survives in two or more copies in the same non-authorial hand. In the case of manuscript books, as opposed to unbound separates, one would also need to consider the quality of the script. Such bulky items were produced for a relatively restricted clientele who expected a finished and professional product. The third criterion is textual: a text containing errors and sophistications is unlikely to be an outcome of author publication. An indicative case of an entrepreneurially published book is *The discourse of Mr John Selden Esquire*, better known as *Table talk*. This was a collection of sayings noted down by Selden's secretary, Richard Milward. Its first appearance was through author publication by Milward, who can be assumed to have presented copies at least to the book's four joint-dedicatees, Matthew Hale, Edward Heyward, John Vaughan and Rowland Jewkes. This stage of circulation, which can be dated to 1654–60, appears to be represented now only by the Lincoln's Inn manuscript, which has by far the best text. All but one of the eight other surviving manuscripts appear to be the products of a commercial scriptorium or copies of those products, two being in the same professional hand.[117] The outspoken quality of its political judgements would have debarred the work from print publication just as much under Cromwell as under Charles II and James II, but the revolution of 1688 made it a very timely text indeed, especially to the Whigs, who had probably been its most devout readers in manuscript. The circumstances that led to the 1689 edition are described by Harley in a note on one of his two manuscripts.

This Book was given in 168[incomplete] by Charles Erle of Dorset & Middlesex to a Bookseller in Fleet street in order to have it printed; but the Book seller delaying to have it done Mr Tho: Rymer sold a Copy he

[116] *Works*, i. 341.

[117] BL Harl. MS 1315, Sloane MS 2513; Bodleian Add. MS A. 201; House of Lords Record Office, Commons MS 10b; National Library of Scotland Adv. MS 23. 6. 13; Yale MS Osborn b. 102; and a manuscript owned by the author (in the same hand as the Edinburgh manuscript). BL Harl. MS 690, was prepared for Edward Stillingfleet, a friend of Hale and Vaughan, by the same amanuensis who transcribed the medieval chronicle with which it is bound.

procurd to Mr Churchill who printed it as it came out in the year 16[incomplete].[118]

This is typical of the way in which scribally transmitted prose treatises finally reached the press, and is further evidence that the better texts of them are still as a rule to be sought among the manuscripts. The involvement of Dorset is particularly interesting as he was also an author of scribally published satires.[119] In several other cases the printing of a bad manuscript led to the subsequent printing of a better one; but this was not to happen with *Table talk*, which continued to be printed in mutilated form until the publication of the Lincoln's Inn manuscript in 1927. A significant point for the present discussion is that both Rymer and Dorset appear to have known where a manuscript was to be purchased.

Commercial involvement must also be suspected in the case of a large body of anti-court treatises and satires that achieved very wide circulation during the reigns of James I and Charles I. As one consults the catalogues incorporating the manuscripts of such seventeenth-century collectors as Stow, Spelman, Cotton, Selden, Dering, D'Ewes, Wood, Pepys, Stillingfleet, Petyt, Strype and Moore, and their eighteenth-century successors Sloane, Harley, Carte and Rawlinson, titles and authors recur over and over again. The best-known of these texts, *Leicester's commonwealth* (attributed to Robert Parsons), *Tom Tell-truth*, *The forerunner of revenge upon the Duke of Buckingham* (attributed to George Eglisham), and *To the Father Rector at Brussels*, also made appearances in print, but always from unauthorized sources. Today they are chiefly known from such printed archives as Rushworth's *Historical collections*, the *Harleian miscellany* and the Somers *Scarce and interesting tracts* and more modern anthologies dependent on these; but it does not take much investigation to discover that the texts of these printed versions are usually both corrupt and heavily sophisticated, and that they were taken from manuscript copies encountered virtually at random. Characteristically such pieces circulated both as separates and in large retrospective collections of political texts, with entrepreneurial involvement likely at both levels. However,

[118] BL MS Harl. 1315, f. 1^v.

[119] See *IELM*, ii/1, 350–81 and *The poems of Charles Sackville, sixth earl of Dorset*, ed. Brice Harris (New York, 1979), drawing on 118 manuscript sources. Harris, p. xxiv, rejects the early printed collections of Dorset's poems as without authority.

we still await detailed study of the transmissional histories of representative texts of this kind and the larger compilations into which they were recopied.

From the same period, it would be strange if there was no entrepreneurial involvement in the circulation of Nashe's pornographic *The choice of valentines* and Heywood's translation of Ovid's *Art of love*—works whose notoriety suggests they were much more widely available than is indicated by the small number of copies that survives.[120] Rosenbach Museum and Library MS 1083/15, whose contents, composed between 1590 and 1630, are correctly described as 'predominantly satiric and occasionally lubricious', is a miscellany of much the same kind as formed the stock in trade of the Restoration scriptoria.[121] Entrepreneurial copying of lampoons during the Restoration period has already been documented and will be discussed in greater detail in Chapter 6. As with so many aspects of scribal publication, information on these matters is often already in existence but quarantined in studies of particular authors, topics or genres.

USER PUBLICATION

User publication covers a vast area of activity in which, as we have seen, it is not always possible to distinguish between the public and the private. Its most characteristic mode was the edition of one, copied by the writer for private use into a personal miscellany or 'commonplace book'; however, this was never an isolated activity since it always involved a transaction between at least two individuals—the copyist and the provider of the exemplar. It is also a mistake to assume that the copy in a personal miscellany marks the terminus of a chain of acts of publication. In practice, individuals who assembled large numbers of scribally published

[120] For *The choice of valentines*, see Nicholl, *A cup of newes*, pp. 90–4 and Beal, *IELM*, i/2, 356. Nicholl (pp. 93–4) connects both it and Marlowe's translation of Ovid's *Amores* with the circle of Lord Strange. For the 'Art of love', see S. Musgrove, 'Some manuscripts of Heywood's *Art of love*', *Library*, 5:1 (1946–7), 106–12 and Beal, i/2, 220.

[121] See James L. Sanderson, 'An unnoted text of Nashe's "The choise of valentines"', *ELN* 1 (1964), 252–3 and S. A. Tannenbaum, 'Unfamiliar versions of some Elizabethan poems', *PMLA* 45 (1930), 809–21. Marotti, *John Donne*, p. 72 associates the manuscript with the Inns of Court.

documents were also likely to be active transmitters of texts. Where political texts were concerned, the reasons for this will often have been ideological; but it must also have been the case that presenting texts to other collectors, who would reciprocate in kind, was the most efficient way of enlarging a collection. While texts were sometimes copied from book to book, it was more common for them to pass from collector to collector by the medium of separates, which might then be further transmitted in the original or copies. Networks of friends or associates would regularly exchange texts with each other either by a process of chain copying or by a member making copies for the entire group. Individuals might consciously adopt the role of facilitator of the circulation of manuscripts as a means to other kinds of social advantage. The fact that most personal miscellanies rarely record the circumstances of receipt of particular items, and almost never those of further transmission, disguises their dynamic quality as points of transit within networks of copying.

John Watson, as one of those rare collectors who record donors, provides us with an invaluable insight into the sources from which texts arrived first at a Cambridge college and later at a Suffolk parsonage between the 1640s and the 1670s. Having matriculated from Emmanuel College at Easter 1640 he was a fellow of Queens' from 1645 to 1654. In 1661 he became vicar of Mildenhall, holding the post until 1673 which was probably the year of his death. His album, now BL Add. MS 18220, was presented to him in 1667. Its contents are a mixture of new items entered as received and material dating back to the 1640s which was apparently held as separates. He does not indicate when copies of these texts were sent on by himself to other members of his circle of correspondents but there can be little doubt that this happened. In particular, the large number of contributions received from his brother Thomas in London must surely have been matched in kind by texts of Cambridge and Suffolk writers. John Pye, another collector who made notes of receipt and transmission, wrote on one satire 'This was taken vp by one Mr Thwaites man a Gentleman in Leeds Yorks. I had it from Mr Robt Twisse Min^{r}. of ye new Chappell Tothill streete Westm^{r}—Wensday. 4th. Decr. 1666'. His transcript of 'Rochester's farewell' bears the inscription: 'from Mr Ellasby of Chiswick 18th. Septb^{r} 80. Returnd ye originall to him agen 22th

Septb^{r} by ye boy sealed up'.[122] In positing the post as a means of transporting manuscripts it should be remembered that a regular official service only began in 1635 and that even at the close of the century some mail still had to be entrusted to carriers, waggoners and travellers. However, progress in developing the official service was swift: by 1640 one might 'with safetie and securitie send letters into any part of this Kingdome, and receive an answer within five dayes', while from 1680 London had an efficient 'Penny post' which could return answers within a few hours.[123]

Replicatory user copying of this kind, considered on an individual basis, comprises an act of publication in our weak sense. But viewed as a collective enterprise its significance is far greater than this. The author-publisher who presented a short topical text to a small number of chosen readers would do so in the knowledge that copies would multiply by being transmitted through interlocking networks of friends and neighbours. While Sir Thomas Browne regarded the unauthorized copying of *Religio medici* as an uncalled-for and unanticipated violation of privacy, Rochester must by the close of his career have been fully aware that the placing of a poem into circulation at court would eventually lead to its distribution throughout the entire kingdom. During the reign of the 'Temporary Prince' of the Middle Temple Christmas revels of 1636, his 'Court and retinue' were proclaimed in 'transcripts published from hand to hand' which by 16 January were being copied at Oxford.[124] Where such copying was part of an organized programme of promulgation, associates of the writer would be deputed to multiply texts within their own vicinities or circles of correspondents. Writing to Samuel Hartlib on 13 September 1630, Walter Welles apologized for dilatoriness in circulating transcripts of John Dury's *De theoria pacis*, which he had 'thought to have copied out and sent unto B[ishop] of Armath and others'; however, the exemplar, left with a friend who wished to make a personal copy, had been mislaid following the friend's

[122] Yale MS Osborn b 52/1, p. 150; b 52/2 p. 180.

[123] *The humble remonstrance of the grievances of all his Majesties posts of England, together with carriers, waggoners, &c.* (London, n.d. [1642?]), p. 1. Information about postal services in the early 17th cent. can be found in *The inland posts (1392–1672): a calendar of historical documents*, ed. J. W. M. Stone (London, 1987). Letters passing through the official posting system could be opened at will by agents of the secretaries of state.

[124] *The diary of Thomas Crosfield*, ed. Frederick S. Boas (London, 1935), p. 83.

death and only recently retrieved. 'If I had had this last but a fortnight sooner', he continues, 'I had conferred with many friends about it in my late travayles through Northamptonshire and Oxfordshire and Warwickshire and Buck etc. But I undertake it presently to send it to many.'[125]

In some cases user publication might be initiated by some calculated public gesture such as nailing a manuscript to a door, dropping copies of it at court, inscribing it on a wall, tying it to a statue (after the precedent of Pasquino and Marforio in Rome) or leaving it on the table at a tavern or coffee house. A few of hundreds of references that might be cited will illustrate the nature of the practice. On 29 March 1629, following the committal of Sir John Eliot, Selden and five other members of parliament to the tower, the then Bishop Laud noted in his diary that two seditious papers had been found in 'the Dean of Paul's [John Donne] his yard before his house'. A fortnight later a proclamation denouncing the bishops was 'put up upon the Exchange in the day time' and on 17 May two further libels addressed to the king were left at Paul's cross.[126] A later example comes from a letter to Laurence Hyde of 27 October 1676 which mentions a libel against Lord Chancellor Finch as having been fastened to doors at the Rolls and the four Inns of Court.[127] This was in itself an act of publication, but it was also intended to inaugurate a process of user copying. Many satirical epigrams of both the earlier and the later Stuart periods announce themselves as having been given to the world through public posting. Favoured locations were the House of Commons door and those of the king and leading courtiers: others claimed include the 'treason bench' in St James's park and a football found in Spitalfields.[128] It is likely that in many cases the claim was untrue, it being much easier to announce that a satire had been posted in the king's bedchamber than actually to place it

[125] Cited from G. H. Turnbull, *Hartlib, Dury and Comenius: gleanings from Hartlib's papers* (Liverpool, 1947), pp. 135–6. The 'many' were to include only 'assured men'.

[126] *The works of the most reverend father in God, William Laud D. D.* (Oxford, 1847–60), iii. 210; *CSP (Dom.)* 1629, pp. 519, 550–1; John Forster, *Sir John Eliot: a biography 1590–1632* (London, 1864), ii. 473.

[127] *The correspondence of Henry Hyde, Earl of Clarendon, and of his brother Laurence Hyde, Earl of Rochester*, ed. Samuel Weller Singer (London, 1828), i. 2.

[128] Nottingham U. L. MS Pw V 46, p. 282 as 'Trees and Bench' (correctly in other sources); *POAS (Yale)*, v. 485–7.

there. But even the invention of such events acknowledges a method by which the readership of a text could be multiplied, first through public display and then through the incentive to subsequent user publication provided by a catchy title.

In any case, the real interest of this mode of transmission lies not so much in how it was done as by whom, because, whatever user publication is, it is not random and unstructured. Instead, since it usually rests on a personal agreement between the donor and the receiver of the text, there is an overwhelming tendency for the networks that have been mentioned to coincide with social groupings of one kind or another—with families, with groups of individuals linked by common beliefs or interests, with institutions such as the court, the diocese or the college, and with geographical entities such as the county. Since an individual could well be a member of a number of these communities, the passage of a text might be a complex and also a very rapid one. Paths of transmission laid down for one kind of document (e.g. parliamentary speeches) were from then on available for the transmission of others (e.g. antiquarian essays, viol music). These facts are mentioned in order to introduce the notion of the 'scribal community' which will be dealt with in more detail in Chapter 5.

SIR ROBERT COTTON AS SCRIBAL PUBLISHER

A name that has already occurred several times in this book is that of Sir Robert Cotton, and in concluding this chapter it will be helpful to consider how our three modes of scribal publication apply to the rich tradition of copying associated with Cotton as an author and with the famous collection of manuscripts which he assembled. Cotton's life and the main stages in the formation of the library have been knowledgeably described by Kevin Sharpe, and what follows will be largely dependent on his findings.[129] However, the perspective of scribal publication is one that shows Cotton and his cultural mission in a subtly different light from that in which Sharpe sees them. The points I wish to emphasize are that the Cottonian library served as a source of new manuscripts as well as a repository for old ones, and that Cotton himself, while no

[129] Sharpe, *Sir Robert Cotton*.

enemy to the press, assumed an equal and in no way diminished role for the handwritten word.

Born in 1571 Cotton belonged to the third generation of English antiquarians, drawing inspiration from the work of Bale, Parker and Leland in the mid-sixteenth century and direct guidance from the generation of his immediate mentor, William Camden. As a teenager in 1586 he was a founder-member of Camden's Society of Antiquaries which, meeting on a regular basis until 1607 and briefly revived in 1614, brought together a fruitful assemblage of historians, legal men, heralds, collectors and administrators.[130] Papers given to the Society circulated quite widely in manuscript but were kept from the press, not appearing together in printed form until Hearne's *A collection of curious discourses* in 1720. (Leland's writings had a similar history.[131]) Its major concern was always with English rather than classical antiquities, although the two merged enticingly in Camden's *Britannia*, first published in 1586 and later greatly revised with Cotton's assistance. In pursuing these and other historical enquiries, Cotton and his friends made long topographical expeditions to study ruins and inscriptions and to collect artifacts and coins; but their main archival project was the preservation of manuscripts, especially the vulnerable surviviors of the two great disasters which had overtaken the transmission of historical records in the British isles—the advent of the print-communicated new learning of the Renaissance and the dissolution of the monasteries. The famous library, housed at Cotton's house at Westminister, and now part of the British Library's manuscript collection, was not only the finest private archive of its time but, together with the Tower records, the principal support of research into the history of pre-Reformation England. For government officials the library served in Sharpe's words 'as a state paper office and research institute providing a better service than the unsatisfactory official collections and

[130] There is a good, short introduction to the work and personnel of this society in W. R. Gair, 'The politics of scholarship: a dramatic comment on the autocracy of Charles I' in *The Elizabethan theatre III. Papers given at the third international conference on Elizabethan theatre held at the University of Waterloo, Ontario, in July 1970*, ed. David Galloway (Waterloo, Ont., 1973), pp. 100–18. Pauline Croft, 'Annual parliaments and the long parliament', *BIHR* 59 (1986), 155–71, adds the scribally circulated 'Motives to induce an annual parliament' of 1614–21 to the roll of the Society's papers.

[131] See Philip Styles, *Sir Simon Archer 1581–1662* (Oxford, 1946), pp. 5, 25–6.

repositories in the Tower and Exchequer'. Borrowers of Cotton's manuscripts during James's reign comprised 'a *Who's who* of the Jacobean administration'.[132] In this the library differed markedly from the later Harleian collection, whose users, as recorded by Wanley, were primarily committed scholars rather than active statesmen and administrators.[133]

As Sharpe and Gair also show, the antiquarianism of Cotton and his circle was deeply political. Research into the Anglo-Saxon past had originally been inspired by the desire to establish traditions for the English Church which would both prove its original independence of Rome and serve as a defence against Puritan desire for innovation. This project was soon translated to the sphere of national politics with ancient and medieval precedents being sought for the conduct of contemporary affairs. A subject of continuing concern to the Society was the powers and functions of the great officers of the crown, a matter that Cotton himself pursued in papers written for his patron, Henry Howard, Earl of Northampton.[134] This was knowledge with direct bearing on the functioning of government, with Cotton called on more than once to serve as arbiter in demarcation disputes between departments of the administration. In the parliamentary battles of the 1620s antiquarian knowledge had a vital tactical role to play with regard to questions of procedure within the two houses, while also providing precedents to support claims for parliamentary privilege against the exercise of the royal prerogative.[135] During the turbulent 1629 session, Cotton's manuscripts were put to such good use by the opponents of the prerogative that Charles I was driven to a royal confiscation of the library and Cotton himself placed under arrest, an action that reached the stage thinly disguised in Marmion's *The antiquary*.[136] This move was a tacit acknowledgement of the modernity of the king's own ideals of government and the deeply ingrained traditionalism of the 'country' opposition and their common-lawyer allies, albeit their

[132] Sharpe, p. 78.

[133] *The diary of Humfrey Wanley, passim.*

[134] A relationship further explored in Peck, *Northampton*, pp. 103–17.

[135] The role of antiquarian scholarship, largely communicated through manuscript, in one such dispute is illustrated in Colin G. C. Tite, *Impeachment and parliamentary judicature in early Stuart England* (London, 1974), pp. 24–53.

[136] Discussed in Gair, 'The politics of scholarship'.

interpretation of the records of the past had been a very partial one. The sense of the political importance of ancient charters, chronicles and parliamentary records was such that both scholars and men of affairs were keen to make personal copies of them, a work that Cotton actively encouraged. Copying was so extensive that when a section of the library was destroyed by fire in 1731 the texts of many of the lost manuscripts had already been preserved through transcription.[137]

This copying of older records was itself a significant part of the scribal culture of the seventeenth century. At a time when libraries were small and restrictive and cataloguing woefully inadequate, the availability of transcripts in private hands was necessary to make historical research possible.[138] Access to a key text such as Robert of Gloucester's chronicle, which did not appear in print until Hearne's edition of 1724, could only be ensured by the possession of a manuscript.[139] The amount of energy that antiquaries of the time were prepared to commit to such copying is astounding. Sir John Birkenhead, a scholar as well as a journalist, who had begun his career as a scribe in Laud's scriptorium at Lambeth, accumulated transcripts of historical records which were reported to have sold after his death for £900.[140] The correspondence of William Dugdale and the various diaries and journals of Simonds D'Ewes record Herculean programmes of transcription by themselves and amanuenses.[141] (D'Ewes was a close friend of Cotton and drew on materials from his collection.) Christopher first Baron Hatton is said to have outlayed 'an hundred poundes

[137] Sharpe, p. 83. Hearne noted at the time: 'Many transcripts are dispersed up and down, w[ch] now must be looked upon as very valuable' (*Remarks and collections of Thomas Hearne* (Oxford, 1885–1921), xi. 8).

[138] Andrew G. Watson in his introduction to *The library of Sir Simonds D'Ewes* (London, 1966), pp. 40–5 explains the enormous value of such transcripts to 17th cent. scholars.

[139] See Anne Hudson, 'Robert of Gloucester and the antiquaries, 1550–1800', *N&Q* 214 (1969), 322–33.

[140] Aubrey, *Brief lives*, i. 106.

[141] For D'Ewes see *Autobiography and correspondence*; *The journal of Sir Simonds D'Ewes from the first recess of the long parliament to the withdrawal of King Charles from London* (New Haven, Conn., 1942); and *The diary of Sir Simonds D'Ewes (1622–1624), journal d'un étudiant londonien sous le règne de Jacques 1er*, ed. Elisabeth Bourcier (Paris, 1974). Watson pays tribute to D'Ewes 'incredible industry in transcribing records' while noting that 'this could probably be matched by that of contemporaries' (*The library of Sir Simonds D'Ewes*, p. 7). Dugdale's prodigies of transcription can be sampled in his letter of 16 November 1635 to Sir Simon Archer in *Life*, pp. 151–2.

per ann. in abstracting Records', a figure which, if not exaggerated, could have allowed a handsome stipend to two full-time assistants or a more modest wage to three or four.[142] As with many antiquaries, his primary concern was with the antiquities of his own county, Northamptonshire. There was also some commercial copying: D'Ewes accused Starkey of 'base nundination' in offering transcripts of antiquarian manuscripts for sale; but wasted no time following Starkey's death in October 1628 in purchasing his papers, largely composed of transcripts of Tudor and more recent records.[143]

As well as serving as a centre for the transcription of older texts, the library regularly gave birth to new ones, among which were Sir Robert's own writings issued by him as author publisher. Although he assisted fellow historians in a number of large print-publishing projects, his conception of himself was as an author solely for the scribal medium. Cotton died in 1631. The *STC* shows only three works by him as having appeared in print prior to 1641, and it was not until 1651, with the publication by James Howell of *Cottoni posthuma*, that anything like a comprehensive body of his writings was available in print. But in manuscript Cotton is everywhere. His influential anti-Spanish tract of 1627, *The danger wherein the kingdome now standeth, and the remedie*, survives in fifteen copies in the British Library alone and at least twice that number elsewhere. There were also printed editions—two of 1628 (one set from the other), one in *Cottoni posthuma* and one in Rushworth—but none of these derives from an authoritative manuscript.[144] Cotton's *A short view of the long life and reign of King Henry the third*, written for Prince Henry, and *The manner and means how the kings of England have from time to time supported and repaired their estates*, written for James I, are hardly less common, though this has been obscured by vagaries of attribution and title. Composite editions of his tracts also circulated in manuscript. One such collection, believed to have been destroyed by fire in 1937,

[142] Dugdale, *Life*, p. 171 n.

[143] *Autobiography*, i. 294; *The library of Sir Simonds D'Ewes*, pp. 24–6.

[144] The text in *Cottoni posthuma* at least makes sense, though it probably requires emendation in from 20–30 readings. That in Rushworth's *Historical collections* (London, 1659), pp. 471–6 shows signs of heavy editorial reworking. That of the 1628 editions (one of which is the source for the *English experience* reprint) is so corrupt as to be little better than gibberish in places.

consisted of fifteen tracts in chronological order of composition followed by an epicedium.[145] On the other hand the collection in *Cottoni posthuma* does not look particularly authentic. The tracts are not in chronological order, or any kind of order, and four pieces by other authors have crept in.[146] Cotton's most characteristic form of writing was the short essay summarizing the historical precedents relevant to some contemporary administrative question: Sharpe has illuminatingly compared them to the kind of position paper that today might be prepared by a civil servant for a minister. Such pieces, being short, were eminently suited to scribal communication, and also contained the kind of privileged information that would have been carefully guarded from the press. The opportunity to copy Cotton's writings may well have been a bonus to users of the Cottonian library, although it is noteworthy that D'Ewes's greatly-prized copies of three tracts acquired in 1623 are in the hand of Ralph Starkey. These were presumably supplied by Starkey in his capacity as a professional copyist, the price of the three together being thirteen shillings.[147]

One or two glimpses of the day-to-day events of the Cotton household raise the possibility of other kinds of involvement in the transmission of manuscripts. At a dinner attended by Ben Jonson which was later the subject of an official enquiry a manuscript of a poem eulogizing Felton, the assassin of the Duke of Buckingham, was passed round after the meal.[148] The event of 1629 which provided Charles I with his pretext for closing down the library was that a scribe in Cotton's employment was making copies of an outrageously pro-prerogative tract as a means of embarrassing the crown.[149] Incidents such as these, together with Cotton's vigorous

[145] *HMC, 2nd rep.*, p. 90b; *Guide to the location of collections described in the reports and calendars series 1870–1980* (London, 1982), p. 29.

[146] See Dennis Flynn, 'Three unnoticed companion essays to Donne's "An essay of valour"', *BNYPL* 73 (1969), 424–39. Flynn is too hasty in assuming that Howell's source for the collection was Cotton's own papers.

[147] *The library of Sir Simonds D'Ewes*, pp. 238–9.

[148] Sharpe, p. 212. The poem, beginning 'Enjoy thy bondage, make thy prison know' had a long career in manuscript transmission, still being found in some Restoration state poems collections.

[149] See D'Ewes, *Autobiography*, ii. 39–42. D'Ewes was clearly well informed about the circumstances although his account is designed to place Cotton in the most favourable light and to distance him from the actions of his dependants Flood and Richard James. For further sources for the incident, see Sharpe, pp. 143–4.

scribal publication of his own writings, suggest that the library may well have been as important an agency for the circulation of new manuscript texts as it was for the copying of old ones. Such copying can be viewed both as user publication on the part of the transcribers and as a form of non-commercial entrepreneurial publication on Cotton's. This role, and that of the library in the context of his times, has been well portrayed by Sharpe, but a considerable body of bibliographical evidence still remains unexamined. A full critical edition of Cotton's own writings remains the major desideratum—an enormous task but one that would contribute greatly to our understanding of the production and distribution of scribally published texts. Beyond that we have yet to look throroughly at the substantial body of transcripts of both older and more modern texts which derive from the library and which at present are only identifiable when they belong to collections whose historical link with it is known on external grounds.

3

SCRIBAL PRODUCTION

STUDENTS of seventeenth-century print publication are able to assume certain regularities in the processes of production. The extent of these is disputed, but no one would deny that Joseph Moxon's *Mechanick exercises on the whole art of printing* (1683–4) gives as detailed a description of the skills and technology of typefounding, composition and presswork as we could hope for.[1] Over the few matters where Moxon is silent or ambiguous, printers' manuals from later dates and from other countries are available. In addition, patient, empirical studies of specific editions and printeries have built up an enormous amount of data concerning such matters as compositorial 'fingerprints', the re-use of identifiable printing materials, press correction, cancellation and variations in paper stock. The most famous of these studies, Charlton Hinman's *The printing and proof-reading of the first folio of Shakespeare*, presents us with a production-history of an edition so meticulous that it is hard to imagine what might have been added.[2] The organization of production within the printery is less well documented than the work practices of individual craftsmen, but two monumental studies of the records of particular workplaces—D. F. McKenzie's of the Cambridge University Press over the years 1696–1712 and Keith Maslen and John Lancaster's of the Bowyer printery in the early eighteenth century—shed illumination well beyond the sphere of their immediate concern.[3]

By comparison with this well-mapped terrain, the production

[1] ed. Herbert Davis and Harry Carter, 2nd edn (London, 1962).

[2] 2 vols (Oxford, 1963).

[3] D. F. McKenzie, *The Cambridge University Press 1696–1712: a bibliographical study*, 2 vols (Cambridge, 1966); *The Bowyer ledgers*, ed. K. I. D. Maslen and John Lancaster (London, 1991).

practice of scribal publication is largely *terra incognita*. What has been attempted so far in this book is to establish a terminology which can be illustrated from case studies; however, this procedure does not equip us with the means to generalize confidently from the known to the unknown over the wider field of production. The question that now arises is the much more searching one of the representativeness of our existing data, and whether or not it is possible to achieve an assumption of regularities of the kind and to the degree that can be accepted for print publication. In some sections of this chapter the information assembled will inevitably seem slight. This partly reflects limitations of space but also arises from a conviction that areas in which extensive research was not possible within the scope of this project should at least be blocked in, however imperfectly, as an encouragement to those (particularly manuscript librarians and archivists) who are equipped to proceed further. Since our chief concern will be with the work of the paid rather than the amateur scribe, the emphasis will be on entrepreneurial publication and author publication, though some of the findings will also apply to user publication.

In pursuing this aim, knowledge of the conventions of print-production will be vital. The two areas are linked by the fact that their products were designed for a similar, though not identical, social use, and by the involvement in each of booktrade professionals. This does not of itself guarantee that common solutions would have been found to common problems, but does make print practice a fruitful source of hypotheses which can then be tested against the evidence. Besides this, the connection directs our attention to certain methodological problems which have arisen in work on print production, and which would be ignored at our peril.

In the midsummer noon of the McKerrow–Greg–Bowers 'new bibliography', the assumption was too readily made that a printery of the handpress era operated like an efficient modern business overseen by modern managers. Natural human variability and the looser industrial organization of the hand-press era were not allowed for, with the result that the imaginative leap from the data of the page to the activities of the workplace was often made with unjustified confidence. Print bibliographers, and particularly editors, for whom the issue was one of having a basis for textual decision-making, became involved in a process of narrative-building in which the elegance of the narratives was all too often accepted as a badge of their correctness. Or a narrative of some complexity might be constructed which certainly explained the phenomena but was only one of a multitude of ways of doing so. McKenzie's famous 1969 paper, 'Printers of the mind', encouraged a greater realism about the variability of work practices in early printing, but could not wholly prevail against the impulse to assume that physical regularities in the printed book must necessarily correspond to a consistent routine in the process of production.[4] Compositor identification—a much more difficult business than the identification of scribes—remains bedevilled by such assumptions. The lessons which have been learned so painfully by print bibliographers are no less vital for the study of scribal production, in which human variability had even wider scope.

THE RECRUITMENT AND TRAINING OF SCRIBES

Codicologists frequently refer to work as being written in a 'professional' hand. The term does not imply a sharp division into professional and 'amateur' manuscripts, or that the writing of a non-professional would of necessity be less skilled. Some of the most polished and agreeable hands of our period are those of individuals who were not scribes by profession, while paid scribes might write at times in a rapid informal hand. What is implied, rather, is a hand that in its regularity and evenness shows the effects of careful training and long practice, and that remains unvarying over the entire span of the text being copied. It should also be a hand that is well-adapted to the purpose for which the copy was made, which in most cases would mean that it was readily legible. Such a hand might incorporate displays of skill in the use of decorated forms for headings and proper names or in executing intricate flourishes, but it would not project virtuosity as a means of personal expression. Indeed, ideally, it would preserve a certain impersonality, being careful not to intrude on the reader's awareness of the text. In the copying of forbidden texts one will

[4] *SB* 22 (1969), 1–75.

often suspect a deliberate avoidance of idiosyncrasy in order to minimize the danger of identification; in other cases there may be a degree of accommodation to the received style of a particular scriptorium.[5] Such a hand differs as much from that of the cultured gentleman or lady, for whom handwriting, as much as dress or gesture, might be a mode of individuation, as it does from the exhibitionistic displays of another kind of professional, the writing master. The aim then is to enquire what kind of training lay behind the humbler professionalism of the skilled but unvirtuosic craftsman copyist.

Writing as an elementary skill was acquired at home or school, and as a more advanced art might be studied from an engraved copy-book, at a 'writing school' or with a private tutor.[6] The teaching of writing in the 'petty' schools must always have been hindered by the absence of desks. Rosemary O'Day goes as far as to say that it 'was not accepted as one of the skills taught in the elementary school' but this was not true at least of the progressive schoolteachers cited by David Cressy.[7] The 'writing school' taught spelling, arithmetic, the elements of accounting and in some cases shorthand; however, the main emphasis was on training in the customary business hands, and its head was normally an acknowledged writing master.[8] At all levels beyond the elementary, instruction would also cover such matters as the cutting of pens, the mixing of ink, the folding of paper into quires, the ruling of margins, the ensuring of equal lineation, the casting-off of copy,

[5] Such as that of Little Gidding. However, the most striking examples of this second phenomenon are the 'departmental' hands employed in certain areas of the administration and judiciary. L. C. Hector, *The handwriting of English documents*, 2nd edn (London, 1966), pp. 64–8 and 86–97, gives contemporary examples of common-law hand, engrossing hand, Pipe Office hand, Lord Treasurer's Remembrancer's hand, King's Remembrancer's hand and Chancery hand. See also Hilary Jenkinson, *The later court hands in England from the fifteenth to the seventeenth century* (Cambridge, 1927), pp. 68–78.

[6] For further information see Hilary Jenkinson, 'The teaching and practice of handwriting in England', *History* 11 (1926), 130–8, 211–18 and David Cressy, *Literacy and the social order: reading and writing in Tudor and Stuart England* (Cambridge, 1980), pp. 19–41.

[7] *Education and society 1500–1800: the social foundations of education in early modern Britain* (London, 1982), p. 60; Cressy, *Literacy*, pp. 22–7. However, it is significant that most schoolchildren were taught to spell by a vocal method without being allowed to write at the same time (Cressy, pp. 20–1).

[8] A good deal of information about these schools can be gleaned from the biographical section of Ambrose Heal's *The English writing-masters and their copy-books 1570–1800: a biographical dictionary and a biography* (London, 1931).

and the correct placing of catchwords and page numbers. (Page headlines of the kind found in printed books are rare in manuscripts of this period.) An understanding of these matters would be required of anyone seeking employment as a scribe but would not of itself qualify a pupil to perform the work of a clerk or, except under privileged circumstances, that of a secretary—and it is among the ranks of clerks and secretaries that most of our professional copyists are likely to be found. A secretary, as the derivation of the word indicates, was a personal scribe who was privy to his master's secrets. Birth and private recommendation were likely to count as much as skilled penmanship in appointments of this kind, and training would be given directly by the employer. The position of clerk, on the other hand, could not be secured without an initiation into the practices of a particular trade or profession, achieved through a formal apprenticeship or some looser arrangement by which the learner offered unpaid labour in return for instruction.

Evidence has already been presented in this book for the involvement of legal clerks in scribal publication, and it is law writing that best illustrates the nature of scribal training. Edward Chamberlayne suggests that at least a grammar school education was normal for those intending to become 'Clerks to Justices or Lawyers', while fearing that their level of education left them 'longing for Innovations and Changes, and watching for an opportunity to alter the Government both of Church and State'.[9] Legal writing, at whatever level, involved careful drilling in the exact reproduction of standard documents, and some acquaintance with Law French and Latin. In the course of his training, the scribe would be expected to master an engrossing hand as well as a range of hands suitable for correspondence and record keeping, and, since deeds were still frequently written on parchment, he would need to acquire the skills of working with that testing material.

Legal copying not performed by lawyers' clerks was the province of scriveners, whose professional function was one of drawing up contracts, negotiating loans and performing some simpler legal formalities. They also had a statutory responsibility for ensuring the accuracy and authenticity of documents and

[9] *The second part of the present state of England*, 12th edn (London, 1684), pp. 334–6.

preventing forgery. Nashe's identification of scriveners as agents of scribal publication makes them of particular interest to this study.[10] The London scriveners, as the Writers of the Court Letter, first appeared as a separate body in 1373 when they broke away from the Writers of the Text Letter who were later to help found the Stationers' Company. In January 1617 the company, by now plagued with members who were not scriveners by profession, was refounded under new letters patent which are reproduced in full in Francis W. Steer's edition of its early documents.[11] These provided for a period of apprenticeship lasting no less than seven years (an eight-year apprenticeship could be secured more cheaply) and for its commencement to be recorded with the company within six months of the sealing of the indentures. On becoming free of the company, the apprentice was entitled to set up in his own right as a scrivener.

Some of the realities of apprenticeships are betrayed in Francis Kirkman's *The unlucky citizen*, in a chapter whose events, insofar as they draw on personal experience, appear to be set around 1650. His hero is bound apprentice to a scrivener who already has two apprentices but apparently no adult clerks. As the youngest apprentice he is expected to perform numerous 'Petty services' besides his writing:

> I was to make clean the Shooes, carry out the Ashes and Dust, sweep the Shop, cleanse the Sink (and a long nasty one it was) draw the Beer, at washing times to fetch up Coals, and Kettles; these were the within doors employs, and abroad, I was to go of all errands, and carry all burthens . . . and rather than I should want a Burthen, I was to carry earthen Pots and Pans, and Ox Livers, and Bones for the Dog . . . [12]

In all these matters he was under the direction of the kitchen wench who could at any time order him to leave his writing. Having known this would be his lot, he accepted it without grumbling for three years, but by then, having acquired a good suit and his own watch, he began to resent having to carry burdens. A complaint to his father earned him a beating from his master with a '*lusty Bartoon*

[10] See above, pp. 76–7.

[11] *Scriveners' Company common paper 1357–1628 with a continuation to 1678* (London, 1968), pp. 76–113.

[12] Francis Kirkman, *The unlucky citizen: experimentally described in the various misfortunes of an unlucky Londoner* (London, 1673), pp. 35–6.

Cane (the ordinary Weapon with which I was used to be disciplined)' (p. 43). By this time the master's son had become the youngest apprentice, but was naturally free from the menial duties and 'became so insolently proud, as to command me to make clean his Shooes, and do more for him than formerly' (p. 40). The son also took over a clerkship which was the apprentice's main source of fees. In this predicament he undertook the perilous course of covertly undertaking additional legal writing on his own account and hiding it in a trunk.

This part of the citizen's history has introduced us to one potential source of labour for scribal publication, the moonlighting apprentice. The next part leads us to another, the unqualified scrivener. Having absconded from his master, he set up for himself in 'a little *Dog-hole* of a Shop, at the utmost Skirts of *London*' where he wrote letters for sailors' wives and would 'now and then make a Letter of Attorney, or a Deed of Gift . . . or some such Twelve-penny Jobbs' (p. 53). Next, having obtained a release from his former master, he took out indentures with a new one who was a drunkard and needed someone to mind the shop while he spent his days at taverns negotiating loans which were never concluded. With little to do, the apprentice was free to take his first tentative steps in the book trade as translator and print publisher; but he might equally well have been passing his time in copying newsletters or separates.

Kirkman's narrative illustrates some of the circumstances which encouraged young scriveners and their apprentices to undertake copying for the booksellers or for author publishers. A report of 1620 printed in Greg's *A companion to Arber* gives a glimpse of one such transaction:

> Althoughe such bookes as vox populi, and other suche as daylie tooe audaciouslie are dispersed, are forbid[d]en and ought by noe good subiect be intertained or openly divulged, yet (as I am lykewayes crediblie given to vnderstand) there bee dyuers stationers soe soone as they heare of anie such bookes, as haue noe publicke authoritie they indevo^{r} vpon whatsoever condi[ti]on to gett them in theire hands and hopes some younge Fellowes to transcrybe them, & sells them to such Nuefangle persons as will not spare anie charges for acqueiringe such trashe as infatuats the foolishe vulgar wth a misprision of lest-actions, and wth wch they ought not to medle. . . .

To satisfie my selfe more fullie in this particular, I did inquyre of a younge Fellowe a scriviner whoe dwelleth neere to a Stationer who (as I heare) is a man of good meanes whether he had transcrybed anie of the bookes called vox populi to his neighbo[r] the stationer, he did tell mee he had agreed wth him for a dusson, but findinge that he would not wryte them soe cheape as in an other place he could haue them, he had onelie writen one of them, and soe he had taken backe the Copie and putt them out to some other. This stationer as I heare hathe beene before questioned, for ventinge forbiden ware.[13]

Scott's *Vox populi, or news from Spain* was one of the most widely circulated of the anti-Spanish tracts inspired by the proposed match between Prince Charles and the Infanta. Surreptitiously printed copies were available but will have lacked the cachet of the scribally published ones. Having taken his single copy, the scrivener could well have been content to lose the others, as he could now enter production on his own behalf.

The work of the secretary differed considerably from that of the clerk. Where the latter was merely a transcriber, the secretary must be capable, in Angel Day's words, of using 'the *Pen*, the *Wit* and *Inuention* together'.[14] He would need to be within call during most waking hours and might well be, as Donne was with Lord Keeper Egerton and Rowland White with Sir Robert Sidney, on very good personal terms with his employer. Day assures us that 'as hee is in one degree in place of a *servant*, so is he in another degree in place of a *friend*' (p. 106). Polished manners and good connections would be a desideratum. There is a telling picture of the relationship of secretary and employer in III. i of Shirley's *The lady of pleasure* (1635). While the aristocratic master converses wittily with his visitors, the secretary is unobtrusively by his side to take down a letter. Ronald Huebert's modern spelling edition has been cited in order to clarify the stage action:

LORD. [*To Secretary*] Write. 'Madam, where your honour is in danger, my love must not be silent'.

Enter SENTLOVE *and* [ALEXANDER] KICKSHAW

Sentlove and Kickshaw!

ALEXANDER. Your lordship's busy.

[13] *A companion to Arber* (Oxford, 1967), p. 177.

[14] *The English secretary or methods of writing epistles and letters* (London, 1599); facsim. repr. introd. Robert O. Evans (Gainesville, Fla., 1967), p. 129 (second pagination).

LORD. Writing a letter; nay, it sha' not bar any discourse.

SECRETARY.—'Silent'.

LORD. [*Continues dictation.*] 'Though I be no physician, I may prevent a fever in your blood'. [*To* SENTLOVE *and* ALEXANDER] And where have you spent the morning's conversation?

SENTLOVE. Where you would have given the best Barbary in your stable to have met on honourable terms.

LORD. What new beauty? You acquaint yourselves with none but wonders.

SENTLOVE. 'Tis too low a miracle.

LORD. 'Twill require a strong faith.

SECRETARY.— 'Your blood'.

LORD. [*Dictates.*] 'If you be innocent, preserve your fame lest this Decoy madam betray it to your repentance'. By what name is she known?[15]

Shirley deploys the idea for a further thirty lines during which dramatic use is made of the secretary's vocal catchwords to make a punning comment on the action. The point of the scene is to emphasize the linguistic virtuosity, and through this the high intelligence, of the lord, but the secretary shines with reflected light as the chosen servant of such a paragon. When the lords were less gifted, it became the task of secretaries through their 'sufficiencies' to 'give Lustre unto their Masters glorie'.[16]

A secretary of this kind required social as well as scribal skills. One of his tasks in Shirley's play is to control the admission of callers to the Lord's dressing chamber, confirming Day's prescription that 'His office is likewise to entertaine all maner of suters vnto his Lord' (p. 131). His closeness to the lord made him a person of some power: at the conclusion of Shirley's scene, Sentlove, who fancies himself one of the lord's intimates, expresses chagrin that the appointment of the secretary has been made without his advice.[17]

At this social level, the secretary would probably have university or Inns-of-court training and have entered his service as an avenue to greater preferment. But if his master was a writer or a collector of others' writings he would expect to do regular turns at

[15] James Shirley, *The lady of pleasure*, ed. Ronald Huebert (Manchester, 1986), pp. 109–10.

[16] Sir Edward Peyton, 'A discourse of court and courtiers' (1633), BL Harl. MS 364², f. 62ᵛ. The duties of noblemen's secretaries are discussed on ff. 62ᵛ–65ᵛ.

[17] p. 113.

transcription in addition to his other duties, and to serve as a point of relay for documents circulating through author and user publication. Simonds D'Ewes's 'industrious servant' who helped him with his historical research falls into this category as does Lord Herbert of Cherbury's secretary, Rowland Evans, who transcribed his master's *Autobiography*.[18] Another responsibility of a secretary was that he should be able to write a passable imitation of his master's (probably italic) script as well as possessing a well-formed 'secretary' hand.[19] As the century progressed much of the secretary's mystique evaporated—a manual of 1683 translated from Jean Puget de la Serre has the mundane title *The secretary in fashion*—and his ethics declined to the point where he might well become a source by which author-published texts passed into the hands of the entrepreneurs. The same period saw a steady devaluation of his abilities as a penman, for now the aristocracy increasingly wrote their own letters, using a script whose slovenliness proclaimed a modish disdain for the finer arts of the hand.

Women were disqualified from working as scribes both by social custom and by lack of access to education. David Cressy has calculated that only about 10 per cent of seventeenth-century women were literate to the extent of being able to write their names, though the proportion was naturally much higher among the better-off classes and in London.[20] Since it was a fixed article of belief among (male) writing masters that the secretary hand was too difficult for women, they were usually taught only italic. None the less, there is plenty of scattered evidence that as family members they performed the functions of clerks and secretaries. Roger Boyle, first Earl of Orrery is said to have used his daughter Elizabeth as his amanuensis and Edmund Waller his daughter Margaret.[21]

As well as the clerk and the secretary, writing masters are also

[18] D'Ewes, *Autobiography*, i. 409–10; N. W. Bawcutt, 'The manuscripts of Lord Herbert of Cherbury's *Autobiography*', *Library*, 6:12 (1990), 133.

[19] These aspects of the secretary's work are discussed and theorized in Jonathan Goldberg, *Writing matter: from the hands of the English Renaissance* (Stanford, Calif., 1990), pp. 266–73.

[20] *Literacy*, pp. 41, 128–9, 144–9.

[21] *The dramatic works of Roger Boyle, Earl of Orrery*, ed. William Clark Smith II (Cambridge, Mass., 1937), ii. 950. The Waller example was contributed by Peter Beal who has encountered many examples in the Waller family papers of what he suspects is her hand.

likely to have undertaken paid copying, especially at the higher-priced end of the market. By this class we are to understand both the directors of writing schools and private tutors who, like the music and dancing master, would normally give lessons by appointment at the homes of their pupils. Today we are most aware of this class through the activities of virtuosi such as Peter Bales, Martin Billingsley and John Davies of Hereford, but these were simply the high-fliers of a profession whose instruction was normally exercised at a more practical level. Heal's *English writing masters* gives us names and varying degrees of biographical information for a considerable number of these; but many others, especially those working out of London, must have escaped his net. Some are no more than names and addresses from Pepys's 'Alphabetical list of the surviving maister-pen-men of England and more particularly in and about the cities of London and Westminster in the year 1699'—a useful guide to future research.[22] Writing masters had a natural and necessary connection with the small circle of booksellers who published engraved copy-books, usually combining this with the sale of maps and prints to wealthy collectors. It would certainly be no surprise if evidence should emerge to link print-sellers such as John Garrett and John Overton with scribal publication.[23] The training of a writing master was normally acquired by study with another writing master. John Ayres, greatly respected by Pepys, began his working life as a footman, was educated at the expense of his employer, and then studied writing with an older virtuoso, Thomas Topham, who was himself a pupil of Richard Gething. Ayres's income at the height of his career was estimated at an impressive £800 a year.[24]

It remains to mention as a possible agent in scribal publication the mysterious 'printer's scribe' whose existence was revealed by James Binns's investigation into the printing of Latin books in England.[25] The scribe's function was one of rewriting difficult

[22] Discussed in Heal, pp. xi–xii. Pepys, a keen collector of fine writing, gives a total of 77 names and had secured examples of the script of those he most admired.

[23] For these and their predecessors see Leona Rostenberg, *English publishers in the graphic arts 1599–1700* (New York, 1963).

[24] Heal, pp. 7, 10.

[25] '*STC* Latin books: evidence for printing-house practice', *Library*, 5:32 (1977), 5–7. Elkanah Settle blames the errata to his *The conquest of China by the Tartars* (London, 1676) on the transcriber of the press copy.

copy and of making manuscript corrections in printed sheets. While no evidence survives relating to recruitment or training, it is useful to be reminded that printing shops still required the services of a skilled penman. Common-sense would suggest that he was often identical with the proof-reader.

THE PHYSICAL WORK OF THE SCRIBE

As we have just seen, scribes differed from compositors in not being members of a single industry; but all will have had training in certain basic skills of penmanship and in the care and management of the highly refined tools of their vocation. In discussing these tools and the uses to which they were put I draw with gratitude on Michael Finlay's excellent illustrated account in his *Western writing implements in the age of the quill pen* (Wetheral, 1990).

Paper and ink

A consideration of the scribe's equipment should also include the surfaces on which writing was inscribed. 'The Ancients', recalls the English translation of Comenius's *Orbis sensualium pictus*, 'writ in *Tables done over with wax* with a brasan *poitrel*, with the sharp end whereof Letters were engraven, and rubbed out again with the broad end.'[26] The wax-coated table-book was still in use in the seventeenth century, as was that much more durable antique surface, parchment, but the class of writings with which this book is concerned was with negligible exceptions inscribed on paper.

Paper was the product of a technology that was already many centuries old. Its raw material was rags, preferably linen, which for the most part came from discarded clothing: when we turn the pages of an early book, we are actually handling recycled shirts, night attire and underclothes, with perhaps the occasional table cloth. Rags were bought from householders by door-to-door collectors. Delivered to the manufacturer in bales, the cloth was washed, left to rot, sliced and stamped into fragments, and finally reduced to a warmed, aqueous solution of its primary fibres. In this

[26] Joannes Amos Comenius, *Orbis sensualium pictus*, facsim. edn introd. James Bowen (Sydney, 1967), p. 186.

form it became the 'stuff' of papermaking. The sheet was made by dipping a hand-held mould into a vat of stuff, the mould consisting of a rectangular arrangement of wires, with sides in the form of a detachable wooden frame. Lifted from the vat, the mould was shaken to help the fibres knit, and the water allowed to drain away through the wires. The sides were then removed and the deposit laid, 'like a thin *pan-cake*', between pieces of felt to await pressing and drying.[27] Consistency within batches depended on the ability of the vatman to judge just how great a quantity to take into the mould. Colour was determined by that of the rags. To make the paper impermeable, it would later be sized by being dipped in gelatine.[28]

The moulds used in seventeenth-century papermaking were of the 'laid' variety with contiguous thin 'wires' running parallel to the longer side and thicker 'chains' placed at intervals parallel to the shorter side. The pattern of the mould will usually be visible when a leaf is held up to the light and is used by descriptive bibliographers to confirm judgements of format. The watermark was a design in wire attached to the upper surface of the mould. Since moulds were used in pairs, any given book is likely to contain two versions of the watermark. The normal position for the mark was in the middle of one half of the sheet, so orientated as to show vertically in a folio leaf. A countermark is often found in the middle of the other half-sheet. While watermarks had originated as manufacturer's symbols, by our period they had largely become indicators of dimensions and grades of paper, with such standard sizes as pot, foolscap and crown actually named from their customary watermarks.[29] Paper of each dimension was carefully identified by makers as being of the printing or writing variety, with the sheet size of the writing version usually smaller than that

[27] The quoted phrase is Evelyn's from his vivid description of paper-making at Byfleet (*The diary of John Evelyn*, ed. E. S. de Beer (Oxford, 1955), iv. 141).

[28] For a concise account of early papermaking, see Philip Gaskell, *A new introduction to bibliography*, rev. impression (Oxford, 1974), pp. 57–60.

[29] The trade names, dimensions and watermarks of the principal sizes are given in Gaskell, pp. 73–5. A contemporary list which also gives prices is reprinted in R. W. Chapman, 'An inventory of paper, 1674', *Library*, 4:7 (1927), 402–8; however, Edward Heawood, 'Papers used in England after 1600. I. The seventeenth century to *c.* 1680', *Library*, 4:11 (1930), 263–99, questions the accuracy of this source suggesting that 'the samples had been disarranged after the list of sorts had been compiled, but before the marks were described' (p. 264).

of the corresponding printing version. Writing paper was also more heavily gelatinized: indeed, much printing paper could not be written on without blurring. Finlay quotes advice from a writer of 1594 that before entering marginalia in a printed book one should first rub the surface with a bag containing resin and sandarach.[30]

Most writing paper used in England during the seventeenth century was imported from France whose makers were favoured by fast-flowing rivers, an abundant supply of linen, and Huguenot business acumen. Duties that for royal ran as high as a pound a ream (500 sheets) were unable to overcome this superiority, and it was only when protected by embargos on French goods during the reigns of William and Anne that English and Dutch makers were prepared to attempt the finer grades required for writing.[31] Thomas Fuller has left a mid-century user's impression of the the various national papers:

> *Paper* participates in some sort of the *Caracters* of the *Countrymen* which make it, the *Venetian* being *neat, subtile* and *courtlike*, the *French, light, slight* and *slender*, the *Dutch thick, corpulent* and *gross*, not to say sometimes also *charta Bibula, sucking up the Ink with the sponginess thereof.*[32]

The careful writer would clearly prefer the French and Italian writing papers to the Dutch. In the earlier part of the century Norman papers, marketed as 'Caen' and 'Morlaix', dominated the market; however, from around 1660 this preference was challenged by mills from the Angoumois whose product, generically described as Rochelle, was also purchased for re-export by Dutch merchants and often bears Arms of Amsterdam or Vryheyt watermarks.[33]

Duties and the labour-intensive method of production meant that paper represented a significant element in any author or

[30] Finlay, p. 33, citing Sir Hugh Platt, *The jewell house of art and nature* (London, 1594), p. 46.

[31] For an account of the difficulties experienced by British paper-makers in resisting French competition, see D. C. Coleman, *The British paper industry 1495–1860. A study in industrial growth* (Oxford, 1958), pp. 3–23 and Marjorie Plant, *The English book trade. An economic history of the making and sale of books*, 3rd edn (London, 1974), pp. 190–205.

[32] *The history of the worthies of England* (London, 1662), p. 144.

[33] A development discussed in Heawood, 'Paper used in England' and R. P. Thompson, 'English music manuscripts and the fine paper trade, 1648–1688', London University Ph.D. thesis, 1988, i. 31–68.

entrepreneurial publisher's investment. The sample prices assembled by J. E. Thorold Rogers from the records of schools and colleges show the price of a quire (24 or 25 sheets) of writing paper at the beginning of the century as 4*d*. or 5*d*. with ruled and 'singing' paper double that price. This probably represents a durable paper suitable for registers and account books, with the regular price per ream (480–500 sheets) of 5*s*. being for a cheaper grade to be used by students or for printing. By the middle of the century the price per quire had risen by about 1*d*. and that of a ream to 7*s*. (still much cheaper on a cost-per-sheet basis); however, there would simultaneously seem to have been a movement to larger sizes at 1*s*. a quire. The very sparse data for the two closing decades of the century suggests a decline in prices during the 1680s followed by a rise to as much as 8*d*. a quire during the French wars which was sustained into the new century.[34] It is likely that the cost of production remained fairly stable, the price increase being the result of continually rising excise and customs charges.

Paper was acquired in sheets, not single leaves, and normally used in the form of a bifolium formed by folding a whole or half sheet. For somewhat longer texts booklets might be compiled by sewing a number of sheets or leaves through stabholes made a little way in from the fold. William P. Williams found several booklets of this kind among the Castle Ashby manuscripts and Pepys must have had something of the same kind in mind when he recorded under 16 April 1666: 'Up, and set my people, Mercer, W Hewers, Tom, and the girl, at work at ruling and stitching my ruled books for the Muster maisters.'[35] The scarcity and expense of the primary medium of writing meant that it was important to extract the maximum amount of use from it. For scribes, as Germaine Warkentin has demonstrated, this must often have been reflected in difficult, much emended authorial exemplars or uncertainties over order in longer texts still in bifoliar form.[36] Apart from the

[34] *A history of agriculture and prices in England* (Oxford, 1866–1902), vi. 565–9; vii. 451–3. At 8*d*. a quire, and allowing for the fact that the outer, wrapping sheets might not be usable, the cost of paper for a 200-leaf (400-page) folio book would be around 3*s*. The entering of text in a large hand and the leaving of white space conveyed an unmistakable message of conspicuous consumption.

[35] 'The Castle Ashby manuscripts', pp. 395–6; *The diary of Samuel Pepys*, ed. Robert Latham and William Matthews (London, 1970–83), vii. 100.

[36] 'Sidney's *Certain sonnets*: speculations on the evolution of the text', *Library*, 6:2 (1980), 430–44. Cf. Croft, *Autograph poetry*, i. xv.

work of R. P. Thompson on the heavy, high-quality French papers preferred for music copying, the grades and varieties of seventeenth-century writing paper remain largely unstudied. Papers of the same heavy kind were also used for much scribal bookwork and for some separates, though the latter were usually on flimsier paper suitable for folding and pocketing. An important change noted by Thompson is the introduction during the 1660s of the lighter letter papers known as 'Dutch post' and 'Fine horn' (pp. 64–5); but this is just one episode in a story which at present is understood only in the broadest of outlines.

The ink used in scribal bookwork, being a solution of colouring matter in water, required more careful preparation than the crude, oil-based concoction used in printing. Seventeenth-century writers had a choice between the medieval style of ink coloured with a mixture of vegetable tannins (oak galls) and iron sulphate, and the more ancient kind made by dissolving cakes of lampblack compounded with gum. The first of these had the advantage of reacting chemically with the page. The second produced a deeper black but, because there was no reaction with the writing surface, might eventually peel away from it, and was prone to redissolve if exposed to water.[37] Ferro-tannic ink had no such drawbacks and was generally preferred. Careful writers would manufacture their own ink. Moxon, who was a perfectionist about printer's ink, has left us a recipe for writing ink which is typical of the time:

> To a quart of rain-water put 5 ounces of Galls moderately pounded. Stir y^m^ up every day for 14 dayes together. Then put in 2 Ounce & a half of Copperas [ferrous sulphate] and half an Ounce of gum. Do not put in the gum and Copperas till after ye 14 dayes probatum est A little gum gives it a gloss, & boyling makes thick.[38]

The waiting time could be shortened, with some sacrifice of quality, by leaving the mixture in the sun. For those unwilling to

[37] Hector, p. 20; Finlay, p. 26. Recipes by 'E. B.' for both kinds of ink are given in John de Beau Chesne and John Baildon, *A booke containing divers sortes of hands* (London, 1602; facsim. repr. Amsterdam, 1977), p. A2^r^. Printing ink also used lampblack as its colouring agent but dissolved it in oil, not water, and underwent chemical change during drying (Gaskell, pp. 125–6).

[38] Moxon, p. 82; from Bodl. MS. Rawl. D 11 20. Cf. Jonson, prologue to *Volpone*: 'All gall, and coppresse, from his inke, he drayneth, / Onely, a little salt remayneth; / Wherewith, he'll rub your cheeks . . . ' (*Ben Jonson*, v. 24).

take such pains ink was also available from stationers and street hawkers. Refinements on the standard recipes were legion, many writing masters having their own secret formulae.

Once used, ink frequently required to be dried. 'We dry a writing', Comenius explains, 'with *Blotting-paper*, or *Calis-sand* out of a Sand-box'.[39] Early blotting paper was simply unsized brown paper and would not have been as effcient as its present-day descendant. The sand-box, also known as the pounce-pot and the sander, did not contain sand but sandarach, a resin imported from Africa. The practice of rubbing paper with a bag containing this substance or sprinkling it from a sand-box, as well as assisting the writing of marginalia in printed books, was also adopted in order to give a sharper outline to writing. One Italian authority, cited by Finlay, recommended finely crushed egg-shells mixed with powdered incense as a substitute.[40] However, others frowned upon the practice because it slowed the speed of writing.

A matter in which the compositor had an undoubted advantage over the scribe was that of correction: once inscribed, the written mark was hard to remove. If there was no alternative, an erasure might be made by scraping, ideally with a long-handled knife with a leaf-shaped blade specially designed for that purpose.[41] This left the paper noticeably thinner and would have required recourse to the sand-box before the erased section could be overwritten: some scribes preferred to conceal it beneath filagree work. But close acquaintanceship with manuscripts will reveal many other devices for coping with misinscription, the simplest of which was to alter the spelling or even the wording of the text. Words struck through or overwritten, words added interlinearly with a caret, and omitted lines written vertically in margins are found even in careful, high-priced scribal bookwork and seem to have been accepted as an unavoidable feature of the medium.

The pen

The near-universal instrument of writing in our period was the incised feather—cheap, wonderfully light in the hand and able

[39] Comenius, p. 187.
[40] Finlay, p. 33.
[41] Examples are illustrated in Finlay, colour plate II(i), i and m.

with the aid of a penknife to be cut to whatever width or slant was desired. By cutting the quill to an oblique edge, L. C. Hector explains, 'as long as the pen was held naturally and at a constant angle to the writing-surface the strokes it made were thick or thin according to the angle they made with this edge'. For the round hand that established itself towards the end of the century 'the goose-quill was cut to a symmetrically tapered fine point, which needed frequent 'mending' (that is, recutting) by the writer'.[42] A document in which headings were to be in a larger, thicker and more elaborate style than the body letter, or whose scribe made use of decorative flourishes, small marginalia, or words set off in bold or italic, would require the use of several differently sized and cut quills. The shaping of the nib was quite a tricky operation: a minimum of seven cuts was required, all of which called for a good eye and a firm yet steady hand.[43] For those lacking the skill or the patience to cut and mend their nibs, bundles of quills could be purchased ready cut; however, without recutting, the life of these would be short—perhaps no more than a single day's writing. Prodigies of penmanship by which a long manuscript was written with a single quill could only be achieved through continuous, time-consuming resort to the penknife and perhaps some artificial means of hardening the point. Yet the skill of nib-cutting once acquired permitted the writer to shape a quill exactly to the requirements of the text being inscribed, and to complement the choice of ink and paper.

Music paper, while sometimes printed, was more commonly produced with a specialized pen called a rastrum which could produce up to thirty lines simultaneously, divided into staves. Thompson indicates that this was a skilled craft usually executed for stationers rather than by individual musicians, and that 'the life of a rastrum was not very long'.[44] If it was an assemblage of quills this would certainly have been the case; however, as no example survives, one can at present only speculate about its construction.

The need for any further historical account of the quill and its subsidiary implements, the penknife, the ink-horn and the sand-box, is obviated by the existence of Finlay's thorough study.

[42] Hector, p. 19.

[43] Described in Finlay, pp. 10–11 and illustration 29, p. 98.

[44] 'English music manuscripts', p. 82.

Hands

The seventeenth century gave birth to a bewildering variety of hands. There is a widely accepted belief that the overall movement across the period was in this, as in other things (including upper-class dress), one from variety to conformity; but such a view is at best a half-truth. A more accurate model (again as in other things) would be one of of repeated attempts to impose conformity subverted by new assertions of diversity. My view is therefore different from that of L. C. Hector, Anthony G. Petti and Jonathan Goldberg except in recognizing the ultimate triumph of the 'round hand'—but even this was more delayed than is often assumed, and the hand itself less uniform.[45]

In the early years of the century a professional scribe would be expected to write at least two hands, the native secretary and the imported italic. Secretary was a derivative of the fifteenth-century 'gothic' hand of the same name.[46] Those who used it as their regular hand would often use italic for proper names and headings or interpolated passages that required to be distinguished in some way (e.g. letters to be read out in a play). This relationship was rarely if ever reversed: those who wrote italic as their primary hand would simply use another form of italic for such purposes.[47] From its first introduction into England, italic was undoubtedly the hand of greater prestige, being preferred for material to be presented to royal or aristocratic readers; yet the compliment was sometimes a two-edged one. The greater legibility of italic made it suitable for readers whose limited literacy might not have extended to decoding the more complex secretary, which up to the 1620s remained the preferred, everyday hand of the highly educated functionaries who performed the actual work of government. That secretary did not quite so readily yield its

[45] Goldberg, *Writing matter*; Hector, *The handwriting of English documents*; Anthony G. Petti, *English literary hands from Chaucer to Dryden* (London, 1977). Despite my differing on this particular point, I am indebted to all three studies, and make no claim to anything approaching Hector's or Petti's general understanding of the history of written forms, or Goldberg's of the philosophy of inscription. Additional information on hands, along with invaluable specimens and transcripts, will be found in Croft, *Autograph poetry* and W. W. Greg, *English literary autographs, 1550–1650*, 3 vols (London, 1932).

[46] For the origins of the hand, see Petti, pp. 14–20.

[47] Yet it could be argued that the small quotation hand for which Simonds D'Ewes took up his fine-nibbed quill in writing BL Harl. MSS 162–3 has a greater number of secretary features than his larger, much clumsier, text hand.

meaning to a casual glance may have been one of its recommendations for such users: it could also be written much more rapidly than italic.[48]

Italic script developed in early fifteenth-century Florence as an attempt by Humanist scholars to create a hand that would lend clarity and distinction to manuscripts of classical Latin authors. Rejecting the late-medieval hands then current, it turned for inspiration to much earlier models, including ancient inscriptions (for its capitals) and Carolingian miniscule. Initially restricted to a small circle of antiquarians, it gained wider currency when it was taken up by Cosimo de' Medici and then by the Papal chancery, from which it rapidly spread throughout Europe.[49] As its origins suggest, and as Goldberg stresses repeatedly, to write in italic called for a conscious suppression of individuality: the ideal italic was an impersonal hand, indistinguishable from other well-written examples of the script. International circulation of the engraved copy-books of Italian writing masters helped maintain this uniformity. Secretary, conversely, existed in so many regional and personal variants within the British Isles as to be rather a broad family of hands than a single model. Martin Billingsley, betraying a characteristic writing master's dislike of individuality, wrote in 1618: 'To speake of the kindes of *Secretary*, is (in these dayes) no easie matter: for some haue deuised many, and those so strange and disguised; that there is hardly any true straine of a right Secretary in them.'[50] Indeed, it was both desired and expected that one's practice in writing secretary should have an individuating function. When William Bagot in a letter of 1622 to his father apologized for having shown 'a barren invention' in his use of secretary hand, this meant, according to Dawson and Kennedy-Skipton, that his hand 'lacked elegance and individuality'.[51] In fact

[48] As a supplement to the examples in Giles E. Dawson and Laetitia Kennedy-Skipton, *Elizabethan handwriting 1500–1650* (London, 1966), a range of bureaucratic secretary from the early years of the century is conveniently illustrated in Peter Davison, 'King James's Book of bounty: from manuscript to print', *Library*, 5:28 (1973), 26–53. Example Bg (p. 45) is especially remarkable.

[49] The origins of italic are discussed in Stanley Morison, *Politics and script*, ed. Nicholas Barker (Oxford, 1972), pp. 264–78, 290–3 and its later development summarized in Petti, pp. 18–20.

[50] *The pens excellencie* (London, 1618; facsim. repr. Amsterdam, 1977), p. C3^{v}.

[51] *Elizabethan handwriting*, pp. 102–3, 9.

the trouble seems to have been that the younger Bagot was incorporating influences from italic, and that his father saw this as a regrettable abnegation of the proper independence of an English gentleman. The cultural implications of this contrast (further explored in Chapter 4) are of obvious importance.

Italic hand on the Renaissance model is still written today by enthusiasts for well-formed script and poses no difficulty for a modern reader. Secretary on the other hand, even when written with care and precision, requires a constant attentiveness which is not simply an effect of the remoteness of its letter-forms from present-day practice, but arises from the greater complexity of these forms—especially the capitals—and the fact that the same scribe may use several versions of a single letter. Some of its more recondite versions have to be learned virtually as separate scripts if they are to be read with fluency. This variety, while it impedes ready legibility, is one of the factors that makes the script so expressive and visually pleasing. Reading it we become acutely aware of the poverty of the typographer's alphabet and those forms of handwriting which have allowed themselves to be dominated by it. As well as this, secretary's strongly cursive nature gave encouragement to all kinds of flourishes and decoration. Both the problems and the advantages are on display in the section of BL Harleian MS 7368 believed to be in the hand of Shakespeare.[52] Petti comments on the use of two or more forms for single letters, drawing particular attention to 'a', 'b', 'g', 'h', 'p', 's' and 't' (p. 87). The impression may have been even stronger if the writer had not been so sparing in his use of capitals. And yet the graphic expressiveness of the hand, whether or not it is Shakespeare's, cannot be denied. Particularly striking is the tension between the compressed profile of those parts of the letters which fall above the base line of the writing and the daring expeditions made below the line in the form of loops, descenders and redundant ascenders. The graphic virtues of italic, while no less real, are of a chaster and less assertive order.

[52] Ff. 8–9^{v}. This is the hand D section of *The booke of Sir Thomas Moore*, part reproduced with discussion in Stanley Wells and Gary Taylor, *William Shakespeare, a textual companion* (Oxford, 1987), pp. 11, 461–7; Croft, i. 23–4; and Petti, pp. 86–7. F. 9^{r} is reproduced in the Library's *English literary manuscripts*, ed. Hilton Kelliher and Sally Brown (London, 1986), p. 23.

It was the typographer's alphabet as much as the influence of italic which was responsible for the demise of secretary. Regular exposure to the printed roman and italic (the former derived from the original humanistic book hand and the latter from its cursive derivative) encouraged a preference for the related inscribed forms. One minority hand, practised, among others, by Esther Inglis, John North and Alexander Pope, was a close simulacrum of printed lettering. Among the last professional copyists of separates to use a personalized, full-blooded secretary was the 'feathery scribe' active from the 1620s to the 1640s whose work is the subject of research in progress by Hilton Kelliher and Peter Beal (see Plate 1). However, the decline of secretary did not bring any diminution of individualism in handwriting, and can even be said to have enhanced it. To supplant secretary, but also the pure italic, came the so-called 'mixed hand' whose origins lie as far back as the reign of Henry VIII and which was to maintain its dominance until late in the century. This hand was, as its name implies, a blending of italic with secretary forms, but the mixture was never a standardized one. Writers could make their own selection from the two traditions, and also had the freedom of alternating forms of the same letter drawn from each (particularly common with capitals). While aspiring to the greater legibility of italic, the mixed hand still offered the scribe a rich field for choice; so, while much of the intricacy and expressive quality of secretary had to be sacrificed, this did not mean that individual hands ceased to be characteristic and distinguishable.

To the elderly Richard Gething, writing in 1645 as a champion of pure italic, the mixed hand was seen, as many present-day writers prefer to see it, as an unskilled italic 'corruptlie taught, especiallie by Mountebancke and circulatorie professors of impossibillities, to the dishonour of our Nation and abuse of learners in generall'.[53] Jenkinson, approaching the topic from another perspective, presents it as a modification of secretary 'written of a size and with an uniform slope taken from the other hand' into which 'all the *Italic* forms gradually penetrated'.[54] Both

[53] Facsim. in Joyce Irene Whalley, *The pen's excellencie: a pictorial history of Western calligraphy* (New York, 1980), p. 219, from *Chiro-graphia or a book of copies* (London, 1645).

[54] *Later court hands*, p. 65. An example would be Simonds D'Ewes quotation hand mentioned earlier.

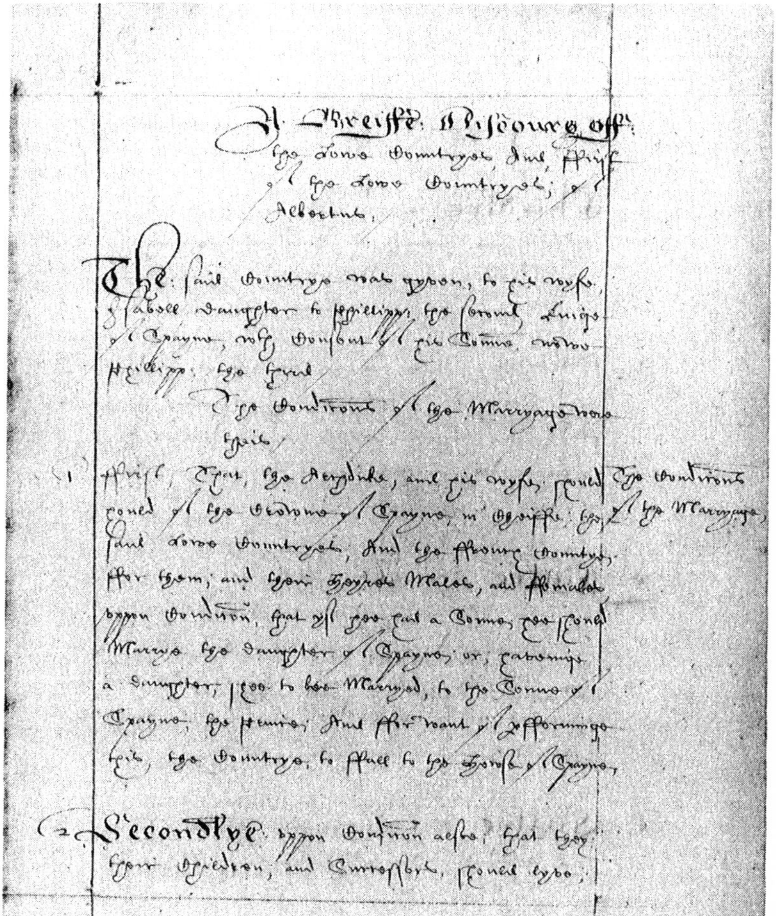

PLATE 1. The 'feathery' scribe.

processes were undoubtedly at work; but the time is long overdue for us to forget its supposedly transitional nature and look at it as a hand, or family of hands, in its own right—one that satisfied through the fecundity of its resources. The truth is that pure italic had always been an exotic flower, and it was the greater liberty of the mixed hand that best answered to the eclectic genius of the mid-century. Petti, while noting that the retroflex secretary 'e' survived even in some eighteenth-century hands, implies that the mixed hand was as good as dead by 1680.[55] Yet National Library of Scotland Adv. MS 19. 3. 4, a collection of *very* modish libertine verse copied no earlier than 1688, is in a hand that still shows a strong secretary influence.

None the less, by the end of the century both the mixed hand and pure italic had yielded to the so-called 'round hand'. Palaeographers differ on the criteria used to distinguish this from the less formal versions of italic. Petti helpfully nominates the hands of Marvell and Dryden as early examples, crediting the former with a 'roundness, clarity, smoothness and cursiveness which look forward to the copperplate of the 19th century' and a harmonious balancing of 'long, oval loops above and below the line'; but these features are not so marked in Dryden's script.[56] To Jenkinson, a perfectionist for whom no hand written after 1350 is wholly satisfactory, the round hand is simply a debased italic, written too rapidly 'with a pen wrongly shaped and wrongly held', while Roger North was reminded of pigs' ribs.[57] The round hand satisfied a need for a cursive that could be written at speed while remaining perfectly legible. By comparison the pure italic had been too slow to write, secretary too slow to read and the mixed hand too confusing in its repertoire of letter forms. Round hand spread independently of the writing virtuosi through such down-to-earth publications as *The a la mode secretarie* (1680), *A set of copies of the round hand now in use* (1685), and *A new coppy book of*

[55] pp. 20, 132.

[56] Petti, p. 119.

[57] *Later court hands*, p. 10; *The life of the right honourable Francis North, Baron of Guilford* (London, 1742), p. 16. Robert Moore, *Of the first invention of writing. An essay* (London, 1716), uses the term 'Bastard Italian' for the round hand, and attributes its popularization to John Ayres (p. 7). The development coincided with a growing preference for more expanded printing types to which Moxon (pp. 22–3) is a witness.

the round hand, as now practis'd (1702).[58] Stanley Morison designates it as 'colourless, thoroughly unromantic, and dull . . . a frankly expeditious script'.[59] Here indeed was a triumph of uniformity, and yet it was of the nature of the round hand with its simple basic forms and ease of mastery that it would be written in a great variety of personal idioms. The division that established itself was that between a standardized version of the hand suitable for public documents and fair copies and a 'running hand' with innumerable variations used for informal correspondence and personal memoranda. Insofar as handwriting sought to emulate the uniformity and the public status of print it would move more and more in the direction of copperplate; but even while this happened new private dialects were establishing themselves.

The professional book hands which are our major concern in this section range across all the major styles discussed, though secretary is largely restricted to the first four decades of the century. Documents written in a self-consciously calligraphic or elaborately decorated hand are in a minority, and there is a paucity of manuscripts of the kind quite common in France of a standard text, such as a prayer book, presented in exquisite calligraphy. A few manuscripts exist from early in the century using a specialized form of italic favoured by writing masters, with clubbed ascenders and descenders. These are likely to be presentation copies for wealthy patrons. Two handsomely written copies of a condensed version of Raleigh's *History of the world*, one in a practised italic and the other in an exceptionally beautiful mixed hand, appear to be survivors from a larger scribal edition which would have been sold or presented, but are unrepresentative of a tradition of copying which aimed above all at the serviceable.[60] Britain certainly had its skilled writing masters, known today through their copy books, but these seem generally to have stood aloof from the hurly-burly

[58] Heal, pp. 150, 157, 165.

[59] Heal, p. xxxiii.

[60] University of North Carolina MS CSWR/A96 (signed in five places by Robert Greville, fourth Lord Brooke) and Emmerson collection, Melbourne (from the library of the Earls of Bute at Aldenham Abbey). A third manuscript was used by Laurence Echard as the basis for his *An abridgement of Sir Walter Raleigh's history* (London, 1698). The Emmerson copy, a small octavo with red-ink margins, containing 402 text leaves plus two of index, is meticulously keyed to the paragraphs of the original. The small-quarto Chapel Hill copy is unruled and lacks the keys.

of scribal publication.[61] A masterpiece like the manuscript of the Sidneian psalms written by John Davies of Hereford for Mary Countess of Pembroke was by its very nature a private commission.[62] The identification of scribes is much more difficult when the relatively invariant italic is used, and some pardonable misattributions have resulted from this.

Generally, professional bookwork and the writing of separates encouraged a hand which created no problems of comprehension, which could be sustained evenly through long documents, and which could be written with some speed. Each of these criteria encouraged the use of the mixed or the round hand. In an important series of anthologies written during the 1690s and the early years of the new century which were identified by W. J. Cameron as having been issued by a single entrepreneurial publisher, the work is all in round hand or a mixed hand not far removed from it. In this case it is evident that the entrepreneur had a clear ideal of the kind of hand he preferred and that the scribes did their best to conform to his wishes. In one sequence of three anthologies written by two scribes, now reduced to one volume as Folger MS M b 12, the care and similarity of the two hands and the disciplined method of presenting the texts both suggest a striving for what Cameron characterizes as 'an impersonal, professional norm'.[63] In two other manuscripts commissioned by the same entrepreneur, Bodleian Eng. poet. 18 and Nottingham University Library Pw V 46, one scribe consciously tries to imitate the hand of the other. On some pages the resemblance is so close as to suggest that both are in the same hand, but on others an accumulation of minor differences indicates that this is not the case. Versatility of this kind was a valued skill in the half-world of political and religious intrigue. Goldberg reports a case from 1594 of an imprisoned priest, John Gerard, who, realizing that a document he was about to write might be used to attribute other papers to him, immediately switched to a hand unlike his usual one (not an easy

[61] Heal, *English writing-masters* includes both a biographical dictionary of the masters and a bibliography of the copy-books. Examples from several of the books are given in Whalley, pp. 216–37. A recognized master could obtain high prices from connoisseurs for relatively small samples of virtuoso script. There may even have been a resistance to writing longer texts which could have been broken up by others for sale to a number of collectors.

[62] Described in Kinnamon, 'The Sidney psalms'.

[63] 'Scriptorium', p. 31.

thing to do without prior training).[64] A similar versatility was noted in August 1678 when Roger L'Estrange wrote to Secretary Williamson concerning Anne Brewster who had been involved in the surreptitious printing of three Whig pamphlets:

> She is in the House of a person formerly an officer under Cromwell: one that writes three or foure very good Hands, and owns to have been employd in Transcribing things for a Counsellor in the Temple. From which Circumstances one may fayrly presume that all those Delicate Copyes, which Brewster carryed to the Presse, were written by Brewsters Land Lord, and Copyd by him, from the Authour.[65]

Here the concern is with the interface between scribal publication and surreptitious printing, but it would be surprising if the varied hands of Brewster's landlord were not also involved in the production of separates and anthologies, especially as he seems to have done work for Andrew Marvell.

The combination of deliberate disguise, skilled imitation of other hands, and a pride in versatility together with the opportunities offered by the mixed hand for varying letter forms means that there will often be no sure way of determining whether two pieces of work are by the same copyist. Pamela Willetts's study of the music script of Stephen Bing may serve as an example of the difficulties that can arise even when there is fair external evidence for an attribution.[66] It is helpful in such cases if, as well as facsimiles (which are indispensable), a technical description of the alphabets used in each document can be given, allowing the reader to go straight to the crucial forms and words. There is a good model for this in the introduction to the Foakes and Rickert edition of Henslowe's diary.[67]

Writing the manuscript

The work of the scribe would begin with the preparation of ink and paper, which in the second case might involve rubbing or dusting with sandarach. Paper would also need to be folded or cut and folded to form leaves which, later in the century, would often

[64] *Writing matter*, pp. 273–4.
[65] PRO SP29/406, f. 49; full document in Kelliher, *Andrew Marvell*, p. 113.
[66] 'Stephen Bing: a forgotten violist', *Chelys* 18 (1989), 3–17.
[67] *Henslowe's diary*, ed. R. A. Foakes and R. T. Rickert (Cambridge, 1961), pp. xliv–l.

be given ruled margins, usually in red. Pepys had paper ruled by 'an old woman in pannier ally'.[68] Sometimes additional folds, rules or lines would be added to guide the writing of columns, or to ensure even lineation. In many manuscripts it is clear that some method, not immediately visible, has been used to direct eye and hand. A technique recommended to children, though perhaps too unsophisticated for adult scribes, was to rule lines lightly with black lead and then rub them out with bread.[69] Otherwise lines could be scratched with a dry point or a temporary impression made with a lute-string.[70] It was possible for the scribe to make use of a ready-bound book, as was done by compilers of private albums and commonplace books; however, it was obviously safer to copy sheet by sheet or quire by quire and bind up afterwards, a practice sometimes betrayed by the presence of an inverted gathering.[71] In any case even new printed books were usually sold unbound at this period. The most common form for the separate was a sheet or half-sheet folded to give two leaves. Three sides were used for text with the fourth left at least half blank to allow for two outer surfaces after further folding, one of which would usually contain the title or an address for delivery. In poetical separates it was usual, and more cost-effective, to fold to a normal folio or quarto gathering for pentameter verse but to a long folio or long quarto for tetrameters.

With ink and paper ready the next concern would be the choice of quill and nib, or of a variety of each. These decisions would be determined by broader considerations regarding design, and would in turn be related to the intended asking price for the product. Moreover, since paper was an even more expensive commodity than it was for printers, careful casting off would be necessary to ensure that a given text was fitted within an agreed number of sheets without any obvious squeezing. Like the compositor, the scribe would choose a standard number of lines

[68] *Diary*, vii. 98.

[69] De Beau Chesne, p. A2^{v}.

[70] For these and other methods of ruling, see Petti, p. 6. The use of a pricking-wheel or pair of dividers to make marks, which then served as a guide for the ruling of lines, was usually restricted to vellum; however, Jayne Ringrose has indicated Cambridge MS Add. 3544 as a paper example.

[71] This should not be confused with the practice of writing in an already bound book from both ends, with the retrograde text upside down.

per page and do his best to maintain a consistent average of words per line. All these matters, corresponding to the printer's choice of measure and fount, would need to be determined before pen was set to paper. The other choice would concern the level of flourish and ornament. Most hands could be written in both plain and decorated versions, the latter, naturally, taking longer to execute and often occupying more space. Here again the choice would be part of an initial decision about the design of the document, which in turn would be a reflection of its purpose and the payment likely to be received for it. Overall the matching of aesthetics to function in a handwritten document was no less deliberate than in a printed one, and usually more so, insofar as here the actual formation of the letters was the responsibility of the workman.

The action of inking the pen is neatly described in 'E. B.'s' line, 'Dip pen, and shake pen, and touch pen for haire'. The 'hair' would be threads from the cloth used to plug the mouth of the inkhorn. Penhold and posture are thus described in the same source:

> Your thombe on your pen as highest bestow,
> The forefinger next, the middle below:
> And holding it thus in most comely wise,
> Your body vpright, stoupe not with your head.
> Your breast from the boord, if that ye be wise,
> Lest that ye take hurt, when ye haue well fed.[72]

The description is supplemented by illustrations of the kind usual in writing manuals of right and wrong versions of the penhold.

The physical needs of the scribe were satisfied by a table and stool, adequate light, a fire in winter, and the modest tools of his trade as they have been described. A chest or cabinet would be desirable for storing paper and written sheets: contemporary illustrations also show papers wedged behind horizontal wooden rails attached to the wall.[73] While most writers' desks appear to be flat, the scholar illustrated in Comenius writes on a small inclined desk resting on a table. Petti regards this as an archaic practice, the new ideal being for the arm to rest directly on the table.[74] Ageing eyes, if unaided by spectacles, might have required the assistance of

[72] De Beau Chesne, p. A2^{r-v}.
[73] Cf. Finlay pp. 72, 73, 107, 152.
[74] *Orbis sensualium pictus*, p. 200; Petti, p. 7.

a prism or magnifying glass. Comenius pays particular attention to illumination. In two illustrations the writer's desk faces an open window.[75] The unpleasant smell of tallow candles is mentioned and wax ones recommended. His suggestion that a screen of green glass be placed in front of the candle reminds us that it would have burned less evenly than its present-day counterpart and that the writer would have had to remain very close to it. Finally, being a night-worker, the writer might well have need of a lanthorn which is pictured in a corner of the study. The scribe's cat was a working animal whose task was to protect paper and especially parchment from mice and rats. Most professional writers would have worked from their homes or from the homes of their masters, the business place that was not also a place of residence being rare at this date. Apprentices normally lived in the master's house.

The editorial work of the scribe

Present-day typesetters are not required to question any detail of their copy, this having been prepared for them by another professional, the copy-editor. Their responsibility is to reproduce what is put before them with complete fidelity, leaving any problems to be dealt with by the back-up professional, the proof-reader. Their seventeenth-century predecessor, while maintaining this as an ideal, would have felt obliged to depart from it in practice:

> *For by the Laws of* Printing, *a* Compositer *is strictly to follow his* Copy, *viz. to observe and do just so much and no more than his* Copy *will bear him out for; so that his* Copy *is to be his Rule and Authority: But the carelesness of some good Authors, and the ignorance of other Authors, has forc'd* Printers *to introduce a Custom, which among them is look'd upon as a task and duty incumbent on the* Compositer, *viz. to discern and amend the bad* Spelling *and* Pointing *of his* Copy, *if it be English . . .*[76]

The compositor, then, had a great deal of latitude in his treatment of the text, including primary responsibility for orthography and punctuation. He was also required to adjust any archaic features to conform to the fashion of the present and to correct obvious errors of sense or grammar. Henry Weber's 1812 edition of Beaumont

[75] pp. 186, 200.
[76] Moxon, p. 192.

and Fletcher records a succession of four well-intentioned miscorrections which took place during resettings of the printed text of *The scornful lady*. The original passage was '*El. Lo.* And say my back was melted when the gods knowes / I keep it at a charge'. Weber's note is:

> It is curious to observe the gradual corruption of this speech. The first quarto reads, 'When the gods knowes.' The second, 'When the God knowes.' The third, 'When God the knowes.' That of 1639, 'When God he knowes.' And the sixth, which is the text-book of the modern editors, 'When Heaven knowes.'[77]

Each of these changes shows a new compositor dutifully trying to make sense out of what appeared to be an error.

Although we have no comparable statement of the responsibilities of the scribe copying a manuscript book or separate, it becomes clear from collating scribally transmitted texts that the same attitude was current. The transcriber no less than the compositor would be expected to impose his own practice with regard to spelling, punctuation and minor points of grammar, to modernize, and to correct solecisms and apparent errors. It was only under exceptional circumstances—most commonly the direct influence of a strong-minded author or patron—that the accidentals of the exemplar would have been regarded as sacrosanct. In addition the scribe would have had to make decisions over the use of the contracted and apocopated forms which were much more widely used than in printing.

Beyond this the scribe must have had a far more acute awareness of the limitations of his exemplar than the compositor. Texts decayed very rapidly in manuscript transmission: by the time Filmer's *Patriarcha* eventually reached the press it was '*so corrupted that it scarce deserved to wear his Name, being not only wretchedly mistranscribed, but strangely mutilated*'.[78] Moreover, there was no public market to which recourse could be had for an ascertained earlier state of the text in question. A professional engagement with the copying of manuscripts cannot but have led to an empirical understanding of the causes of error and the principles of emendation. In cases where the restoration of earlier readings was

[77] *The works of Beaumont and Fletcher* (Edinburgh, 1812), ii. 221.

[78] *Patriarcha*, 2nd edn (London, 1685), p. A3^{r}.

impossible, the scribe, as an educated reader with a contemporary's understanding of the matter in hand, would often have felt obliged to provide a plausible substitute. The traces of such interventions are detectable at every stage of editorial work on texts of the period and provide overwhelming evidence that a majority of scribes regarded themselves as having an editorial as well as a transcriptional responsibility. However, we must always be aware that the intention behind such changes was not the scholarly one of recovering original readings so much as the practical one of offering a presentable text, able to perform its perceived social function. The enemy of the modern editor is not blatant nonsense, which must always have been recognizable for what it was, but the pressing urge to produce at least local sense through speculative emendation.

However, some scribes would rather let an error remain, however gross, than perform any act that would compromise the appearance of the written page, while others may well have been over-conditioned by the legal copyist's awareness that even the most trivial error in transcribing a writ, deed or will could have serious consequences. From time to time, especially in the later years of the century, one encounters manuscripts whose tolerance of nonsense is so remarkable that one is forced to hypothesize either a despairing literalism in transcribing a hopelessly corrupt exemplar, or that the scribe had an imperfect command of English. The latter explanation is given plausibility by the steady immigration, especially from the 1680s, of highly educated Huguenots who would have had difficulty in finding regular work as clerks. Two earlier arrivals, Jean de Beau Chesne and Esther Inglis, were distinguished calligraphers.

Where the scribe differed from the compositor was in a generally greater tolerance of variant practices within the same text. Because printers and booksellers, as members of the same industry, were in constant contact with each other and each other's products, they were encouraged to work towards the standardization of spelling, punctuation and usage, a process that by the first decade of the eighteenth century had led to what is recognizably the forerunner of modern practice. Scribal spellings are nearly always more archaic than contemporary printers' spellings and the notion of there being 'right' and 'wrong' alternatives was much slower in gaining force among writers than among printers. The spelling of any given copy was likely to represent the outcome of a tug-of-war between that of the exemplar and the scribe's personal preferences, and considerable changes might occur when a second copy was made by the same scribe from the same exemplar. Or the scribe might have no particular spelling preferences for some (or many) words but rather a range of possibilities to be alternated at whim or in response to the workings of anticipation and perseveration. In some cases variation arises from a sense of being caught between an older system and a more modern one. The use of double letters for long vowels ('shee', 'wee'), double consonants after short vowels, and the '-ie'/'-y' distinction in forms such as 'easie' and 'wyer' is a hangover from a practice widely observed in the earlier years of the century that the printers abandoned in favour of the less phonetic modern forms. Many writers of the mid-century seem to feel that the phonetically accurate form is the proper one but to be unable to prevent the shorter one slipping in from time to time.

The editorial work of the scribe suffered from generally being done on the basis of what had already been read rather than on a knowledge of what was to come. A grammatical incongruity near the beginning of a long sentence might well provoke an emendation when progressing to the end would have shown that it was justified. Writing further would not necessarily lead to recognition of the earlier miscorrection, since the scribe, transcribing phrase by phrase or at most line by line, could not be expected to retain the overall structure of the sentence firmly in memory. Yet editorial thinking could also be surprisingly lateral. The transcriber of 'The visitt', a satire of the late 1670s preserved in Lincolnshire Archives Office MS Anc 15/B/4, was obviously working from a very corrupt, and perhaps only semi-legible exemplar.[79] Yet he was not a negligent workman: marginal additions in a number of texts he copied show that he proof-read his transcriptions and was not ashamed of revealing his omissions. The problems he had with this particular text can be judged by several errors and obscurities he let pass, most notably the mysterious 'matrix Glances' in

[79] pp. 20–1. The full text of the satire is given in Ch. 6.

> There was obscene Rotchesters Cheife storys
> Of matrix Glances Dildo and Clittoris

but that there was a mind at work behind the neatly inscribing pen is indicated by the lines

> The Taburn was the next resoult, where I
> Quite weary of there Tipling company
> went home a Cursing of this wretched age
> That Couples each old Lady wth. her Page

In the first line it is obvious from context that the poet wrote 'The tavern was the next resort' but it would appear that what the scribe saw, or thought he saw, in his exemplar was 'The Tyburn was the next result'. What we seem to have is a pair of forms, aberrant in themselves, which have been ingeniously devised to exclude neither possibility, leaving the matter to the judgement of the reader.

Multiplication of copies

Author and entrepreneurial publishers would frequently produce 'scribal editions' of works, especially short separates and newsletters but sometimes quite lengthy volumes. Next to nothing is known about the methods used, but where any degree of haste was involved—which was certainly the case with newsletters—there would have been little point in a number of scribes waiting to have their turn at a single exemplar. Copying from dictation would be one solution to this problem, though one for which we so far lack evidence for our period.

The alternative was to make use of some form of progressive copying. This was a system by which scribes used each other's copied sheets as exemplars, and volumes, or extended separates, might be produced which were an indiscriminate mixture of first, second and perhaps more remote copies. The method was first hypothesized as an explanation of inconsistent agreements found in medieval textual traditions.[80] The simplest form would be for scribe A to pass the first sheet copied to scribe B to use as his exemplar. This would also save B the labour of having to duplicate

[80] The medieval form of this practice is analysed in Anne Hudson, 'Middle English' in *Editing medieval texts, English, French, and Latin written in England*, ed. A. G. Rigg (New York, 1977), pp. 45-8.

A's editorial work on the text: he would be able to copy rapidly and mechanically in the knowledge that the version had already been overseen by an experienced professional. If a third scribe was involved in copying, he might well receive sheets from A and B in no particular order representing in one case a first copy and in the other either a first (A's original copy) or a second (B's transcript). The only limiting factor would be that there was a preference for manuscripts to be in the same hand throughout (though there are certainly exceptions to this). Progressive copying should theoretically be detectable by different sections of a given source displaying irreconcilable patterns of agreement, or by one part being rich in unique readings, indicating terminal status, while another lacks such readings, indicating intermediary status. Another conceivable system would see the exemplar divided into separate sections, like medieval *peciae* or cast-off copy in a printing house, which were then passed from scribe to scribe or made the basis of an even more complex form of progressive copying. There is no positive evidence to date that either method was ever actually employed: all that is claimed is that the manufacture of copies would have been a much more prolonged business without it.

The possibility raised in Chapter 1 that the four variant orders of the 1629 *True relation* might have originated within a single agency implies the use of a looser form of shared copying. Here we need to imagine a master text composed of independent units which might have contained alternate versions of some of its elements, or which might have been reconstituted during the course of copying. Once again the claim is not made that this was actually the case, simply that there is nothing implausible in such a proceeding and it should not be overlooked when explanations are sought for the existence of highly variant forms of a composite text.

Scriptoria

Any proven case of progressive copying would indicate that scribes worked in close proximity to each other, if not actually in the same room. There is other evidence that this was often the case. The medieval name for such a room would be a scriptorium, the modern one an office. Defoe, considering in 1712 how he might switch his *Review* from print to scribal production, used neither term but simply spoke of hiring 'some large Hall or Great Room, in the City' and employing 'Thirty or Forty Clarks to write News, Lampoons, Ballads, any Thing in the World besides'.[81] There may be a degree of comic exaggeration in this, and yet in 1683 William Cotton had testified that 'many scores of clerks' were employed by newsletter proprietors, some of whom must have worked in scriptoria similar to those envisaged by Defoe.[82] For our present purposes, 'scriptorium' will be used to designate any communal working space in which the predominant part of the labour performed was that of transcription. In the seventeenth century, when the day-to-day functioning of society was still directed by the handwritten record, government, the law, commerce and the professions all relied on the existence of such working spaces. In many instances scriptoria and their practices stood in an unbroken line of professional descent from medieval forerunners, only the monastic scriptorium having suffered a total extinction of its traditions. The alternative to scriptorial copying was that performed by individuals in their homes or studies. Undoubtedly much production for author and user publication was done in this way, and even entrepreneurial publication may often have involved a farming out of work to individual copyists; but in the writing of newsletters and the large-volume copying of separates there were good reasons why the scriptorial method would be preferred.

Information about the personnel and organization of scriptoria is close to non-existent. The diarist, Thomas Crosfield, records organizing a group of students in Queen's College, Oxford to copy a theological manuscript, but is silent about the actual method employed.[83] The one source which goes into any detail is a report written on 23 October 1674 by Henry Ball on the organization of the scriptorium in the Paper Office at Whitehall in which newsletters were produced for Secretary of State Williamson.[84] In this case (discussed in greater detail in the next

[81] *A review*, viii. 708.

[82] *CSP (Dom.), 1683–4*, p. 54.

[83] On 21 July 1626 he wrote: 'Mr Provost gave me a moderatours place. imposed a taske upon me to rewrite a MS cuiusdam Sorbonistae adversus potestatem summi pontificis disposui inter pueros'. On 26 July he delivered the manuscript 'à multis peractum' (*Diary*, p. 5).

[84] *Letters addressed from London to Sir Joseph Williamson while plenipotentiary at the Congress of Cologne in the years 1673 and 1674*, ed. W. D. Christie (London, 1874), ii. 159–65.

section) four scribes worked under the close supervision of Ball who himself assisted with copying on post-nights. Williamson's scriptorium supplied letters to over a hundred clients many of whom received more than one letter a week. The rival newsletter, operated by Henry Muddiman under the patronage of the other Secretary's office, had at least as large a clientele and must have organized its copying along similar lines. The difference between the two operations was that Muddiman's, despite its official status, was a money-making operation, while Williamson was prepared to trade free copies of his newsletter for information sent in return.[85] The political newsletter-writers of the period of the Exclusion Bill crisis may well have had larger circulations, and John Dyer's scriptorium, dating from 1688, have been the largest of all. Snyder reports that, in the one case when four copies of Dyer's letter survive for the same day, all are in different hands, and, astoundingly, that 'for 1709 and 1710 for which some 300 copies survive, the hands employed must number fifty or more'.[86] Like all journalists, the newsletter producers worked to strict deadlines. Their clients expected their letters to contain fresh news up to and including the post-day.

THE ECONOMICS OF SCRIBAL PUBLISHING

The fields in which scribal publication held an advantage over print publication were firstly the short text copied in limited numbers for immediate use, and secondly the large, retrospective, regularly updated collection, often of prohibited material, written to order for a wealthy clientele. In the rhythm of production, the first kind of text would predominate during periods of heightened activity, such as law terms and parliamentary sessions, while the second might employ the same scribes in quieter times. When scribal publishers competed at the day-by-day level with the print publisher, their advantage lay in their ability to mobilize manpower very rapidly into the transcription of texts of urgent interest. As far as length was concerned, it was the text occupying a single sheet or less that allowed them superiority over their rivals.

[85] Fraser, *Intelligence*, p. 34.

[86] Snyder, pp. 8–9.

The report on the activities of the Starkey and Collins scriptoria shows how effective the methods of scribal publication were at supplying topical documents to a specialized clientele. While both booksellers were dealing with documents that a printer, more vulnerable to reprisal, might have been reluctant to touch, they were also offering a service that for its flexibility in placing new documents into circulation with the minimum of fuss could not have been duplicated by the rival medium with its cumbrous technology and multiple levels of contract.

The fact that bookselling professionals were involved in both kinds of publication encourages us to hypothesize that methods of costing and remuneration may have been similar. At the very least we would expect there to have been some parity between the earning power of the highly skilled craftspeople active in each field. With the aid of data from the Cambridge University Press, Bowyer and Ackers archives, it is possible to gain a clear notion of printers' costing for the 1690s and early eighteenth century.[87] Most journeymen printers, whether compositors or pressmen, were paid by piecework on a daily contract basis. Compositors were paid at a rate per sheet with higher rates for work likely to cause difficulty. The base rate from which others were calculated was given by Samuel Richardson in 1756 as six shillings a sheet for octavos and duodecimos in English type, but with an acknowledgement that it had earlier been 5*s.* or 5*s.* 6*d.* Two shillings was added for each move down to a smaller typeface on the scale pica, small-pica, long primer and brevier.[88] McKenzie's analysis of the Cambridge accounts reveals a standard rate of 5*s.* per sheet for quartos in pica and 7*s.* 6*d.* per sheet for octavos in pica, the latter figure in close agreement with Richardson's.[89] He also reports enhanced rates for setting in type-sizes larger than English (Richardson only having

[87] McKenzie, *Cambridge University Press*; K. I. D. Maslen, 'Masters and men', *Library*, 5:30 (1975), 81–94; D. F. McKenzie and J. C. Ross eds, *A ledger of Charles Ackers: printer of 'The London magazine'* (Oxford, 1968), pp. 12–13; K. I. D. Maslen and John Lancaster, *The Bowyer ledgers.*

[88] Samuel Richardson to William Blackstone, 10 Feb. 1756, in I. G. Philip, *William Blackstone and the reform of the Oxford University Press in the eighteenth century* (Oxford, 1957), pp. 39–42; McKenzie, *Cambridge University Press*, i. 70–80. For the type sizes referred to see Gaskell, pp. 12–16 and Moxon, p. 21.

[89] pp. 78–9. The closest possible approximation to a 'normal standard payment' for composition would be 'almost, but not quite, 4*d.* for 1000 Pica ens of English text in octavo with or without a scatter of notes' (p. 79).

specified smaller ones). Of course these rates were not just for setting but also covered justification, imposition, the correcting of errors discovered by the proof-reader, and the cleaning and distribution of type after use, besides other small tasks which fell to the lot of the compositor. Any comparison made with the output of a scribe would need to take into account that the word once written was in most instances complete. By any calculation it would be possible to produce several times the written word-length in the time it took to prepare the two imposed formes necessary to print a sheet at the press. Moreover, the printery still needed to add the costs of correction, traditionally one-sixth of the composition charge, presswork and the 'master's third', making the written copy even more competitive.[90] Paper was paid for directly by the bookseller and was not a charge to the printer. While it was in the bookseller's interest to seek the lowest possible quotation from the printer, the prices charged for books of specific kinds and sizes, like those for tradesmen's work, were relatively stable, and there would have been a mutual awareness of the range over which negotiation was possible. Binding was not at this period a concern of the printer, and even the bookshops would usually offer new books for sale in sheets, which customers could then send to their own preferred binder. Short pamphlets were sold stab-sewn with two or three quick stitches. It is probable that much scribal production was also sold unbound. The entering of text in bound volumes of blank leaves was more characteristic of the private keeper of commonplace books than of the commercially produced volume.[91]

In the entrepreneurial production of manuscripts, it is likely that the entrepreneur, for reasons of quality control, would follow the practice of the printing trade in supplying the paper, though we have no evidence on this matter. Whether production was arranged by direct agreement with the scribe or through a middleman such as a scrivener would be immaterial with regard to

[90] McKenzie, *Cambridge University Press*, i. 88, shows that both in Cambridge and London presswork was charged around a notional norm of 1*s.* 2*d.* per token of 250 copies, with adjustments for ease or difficulty. For overall costs, see McKenzie and Ross, *Ledger*, pp. 12–13.

[91] The presence of blank leaves at the end of a miscellany is not evidence of private origin since it was a regular practice for the scribes of commercial miscellanies to leave space for future additions.

price since the two would be bidding competitively against each other. The cost of the scribe's labour would depend on whether it was charged on a piecework, hourly or salaried basis. In a scrivener's office, apprentices were theoretically unpaid but in practice appear to have been allowed to earn some fees for piecework, while adult clerks would have worked for a combination of fees and salary. Otherwise, copying would be done by individual craftsmen paid by piecework which might be calculated by the page, the sheet or the whole item. As in printing, there must always have been prior agreement as to the number of sheets to be used in the finished copy, with text cast off to allow for this. (A cast-off master copy in the Osborn collection at Yale of a scribally published satire of 1688 is marked 'six sheets' at the beginning and end and divided by ticks into twenty-four sections.[92]) It is possible that for work using an elaborate decorative script, which as well as requiring exceptional skill would be slower to write, payment by the hour may have been considered, by analogy with the practice of engravers.[93] Alternatively, a premium analagous to that given to compositors and pressmen for working with the larger and smaller typefaces might have been allowed. The vital point is that the entrepreneur working in this way would be dealing with a single craftsman able to perform all stages of the production of the written text.

Numerous contemporary records of payment for manuscripts exist but I know of none for copying as such, which is to say for the bare labour of copying positively distinguished from the cost of paper, the commercial value of the content of what was copied and the premium, profit or fee added by the entrepreneur or master. Prices paid for newsletters are of no help at all as they were primarily in return for information, not the written record, which was often destroyed after reading. The prices we need to discover are those paid for the simple copying of workaday texts for which

[92] In Yale MS Osborn fb 70, the former Phillipps 8301; see *POAS (Yale)*, iv. 351–2, with illustration following p. 190.

[93] Wenceslaus Hollar charged 1*s*. an hour, measuring time with an hour glass which could be stopped when he was interrupted (Richard Pennington, *A descriptive catalogue of the etched work of Wenceslaus Hollar, 1607–1677* (Cambridge, 1982), pp. xlviii–xlix.). Hourly rates were also used at times in printing, especially for presswork and correction. A German illustration of a corrector, reproduced in Moxon, p. 407 (fig. 15) shows him, pipe in mouth, with a double hourglass to the left of his desk.

we can supply an approximate word length. Until a range of such evidence is secured, speculation on piecework rates would be fruitless. While analogies with the practices of print publication are suggestive they can never be conclusive. The contrast is between a centralized, highly disciplined trade operating under the supervision of the Stationers' Company, and a tradition of copying that operated on the margins of a variety of trades concerned with the work of the pen but was central to none of them. Insofar as it relied on piecework, our expectation would be of greater variety in its arrangements than is found in the printing trades.

In cases where copying was salaried rather than done on piecework, we are on slightly firmer ground for estimating the cost of the written product. Scribal publication was too small and specialized an industry to have established its own salary structure, but would have been guided by the expectations of scriveners', attorneys' and merchants' clerks, who enjoyed salaries of at least the level enjoyed by other literate skilled tradesmen, which is to say in the range from 10*s* to £1 per week for a reliable, experienced writer once out of his indentures. In Henry Ball's report of 1674 the wages of the four 'young men' who copied Secretary Williamson's newsletters are given as totalling £120, suggesting an average salary of £30 a year or 11*s*. 6*d*. a week, a sum that compares quite well with the average income of a compositor as recorded by McKenzie.[94] This figure, paid for work which was confidential and carried out at unusual hours, would represent the top of the range for relatively junior employees. Their capacities are thus described:

The 4 clerkes that were in the office (besides myselfe) before Mr. Charles, my Lady Portesmouth's gent. came into it, were Mr. Lawson, Mr. Kelly, Mr. Delamain, and Jo. Keeve, amongst which the above-recited letters were most of them divided (according to the fastness of their writing,

[94] *Letters to Sir Joseph Williamson*, ii. 165; McKenzie, i. 82. Compositors could greatly increase their incomes by taking on additional work at piecework rates, a few being able to average over £1 a week for considerable periods. Likewise, it was standard practice in many departments of the administration for clerks to supplement their salaries by supplying officially permitted copies of documents. Thus clerks in the customs' house enjoyed the privilege of supplying merchants with copies of the daily bills of entry which showed which goods had been received and by which importers. There was considerable chagrin in 1619 when this right was withdrawn to make way for a printed list (John J. McCusker, 'The business press in England before 1775', *Library*, 6:8 (1986), 210, 213 and n.).

which was equall all but Mr. Lawson, who as yett cannot doe as fast as the other), which being alwayes too much for them by reason of the uncertainty of the posts coming in I alwayes helped them doe a share or as many as I could, and had time to spare from the collecting the coppy and lookeing after the business . . .

The actual production of newsletters was done on Tuesdays, Thursdays and Saturdays; on the three other working days two of the clerks went to the Rolls while the other two made summaries of the information received from Williamson's foreign correspondents. The stints on writing days are thus defined:

The number of the letters that each wrote was, on Tuesday, 16 letters, viz. 4 long letters (which are those that contain the whole week's col(lection?) and 12 short (which is 2 dayes newes only); on Thursday, 13 letters, 3 long and 10 short; and on Satturday 7 long, 4 of 4 dayes newes, and 8 short; but now by Mr. Charles not being able to write above 4 letters a day the business will lye much heavyer upon us all.

Despite working under continuous pressure they have made 'the letters long and farr longer then they were before'.[95] Except in the case of Mr Charles, the appointment forced on them by a royal mistress, the expectation was that the production of fourteen long letters, four containing four days' news, and thirty short letters would occupy three days' work and represent a labour cost of a little under six shillings. The standard format of a newsletter, which would have applied for the longer letters, was a single folded sheet with between three and three-and-a-half pages of fairly densely written text. The four-day and short letters were more likely to occupy three pages of a half-sheet. While any calculation of rates can only be guesswork, we will probably not err too badly if we allow for an output equivalent to around twenty-four full sheets per writer per week, or eight a writing-day, which would give a labour cost of about 3*d.* per sheet. By comparison the lowest rate cited by Thomas Powell in 1623 for copying at the Rolls was 2*d.* a sheet for an additional copy of documents which had previously been engrossed at 4*d.* a sheet in the special hand used for this purpose.[96]

[95] *Letters to Sir Joseph Williamson*, pp. 164–5. Evelyn noted in the same year, that Williamson was 'a severe Master to his Servants' (*Diary*, iv. 39).

[96] *The attorney's academy* (London, 1623), pp. 75–7.

The relative cost of scribally and print-published texts

Any notion of a market in manuscripts within which price levels would set themselves as the result of buyer choice and competition between suppliers would be an illusion. As the earlier account of author publication will have demonstrated, many manuscripts were presented in the expectation of a gift or exchange rather than sold for a fixed sum. In the more hard-nosed field of entrepreneurial publication, transactions were of a bespoke nature, with the price a matter of negotiation between the customer and the supplier. None the less there are times when manuscripts appear side by side as items of commerce with printed books and we are able to make direct comparisons between the two kinds of product. Lenore F. Coral cites a catalogue of music issued by Henry Playford in 1698 which contains 'Bassani's Sonata's printed' for 10*s*. and the same 'fairly Prick'd' for £1. 10*s*., and Corelli's op. 1–4 for £2 engraved and £6 in manuscript—suggesting that scribally published music was about three times the price of engraved music.[97] This is not much help in establishing a ratio between the handwritten text and the products of letterpress printing but it does establish that 'fairly Prick'd' music was a luxury product for which Playford's customers were prepared to pay high prices, as for practical performance there could have been little advantage over even fair quality engraving.

In other cases it was the forbidden nature of the texts that justified their high price rather than their being in handwritten form. Yet there must also have been cases where the number of copies needed was so low as to make scribal publication more attractive on economic grounds alone. Leaving aside the privileged position of the scribal publisher with regard to texts which could only be printed with danger, and the various non-commercial motives which could lead to the choice of one or the other avenue, there remained an area of low-volume publication in which he was simply able to offer a cheaper service than the printer. It is true that printers did at times produce what appear to us to be abnormally short runs. In the Ackers ledgers, of a later, slightly higher-priced period, we find fifty copies of Elliston's *Devotional offices* (15.25 sheets) at a unit production cost (rounded to the nearest farthing) of

[97] 'Music in English Auction Sales', p. 76.

3*s* 8$\frac{3}{4}$*d.* per volume; seventy-five three-volume sets of *The journal and proceedings in Georgia* (91.5 sheets octavo) at 14*s* 7$\frac{3}{4}$*d.*, 100 copies of a sermon of two and a half sheets at 3$\frac{1}{4}$*d.*, and 100 of eight sheets of *The devout communicant's companion* at 11*d.*, prices which even after the bookseller's mark-up would have been strongly competitive with handwritten work.[98] Runs of this length are not uneconomic in any absolute sense: it is simply that over a run of thirty to forty copies the cost of composition was still the predominant element, whereas over one of 5000 this would be negligible. Still, below a certain level, it would have become possible to supply a handwritten copy for less than the cost of a printed one. My own view is that even at twenty copies print was still competitive with manuscript, but that below that we enter an area where the advantage would depend on the capacities of individual craftsmen and the nature of the text. Further interrogation of the figures is ruled out by the difficulty of estimating the cost of presswork over very small runs in which the actual pulling of sheets would be a minor item beside the time spent in make ready; but by any calculation the cost of setting and printing ten copies of a printed sheet can hardly have been less than the cost of a week's labour by a scribe.

None the less, in author or entrepreneurial publication, it was probably only on rare occasions that the question of relative cost was the crucial one in a decision to use one rather than the other medium. For the entrepreneurial publisher, the handwritten text was a specialized product to be sold to the well-off at a handsome premium for its rarity or danger, while for the author-publisher it was simply the accustomed way of addressing a particular kind of readership. In user publication, on the other hand, much copying may well have been undertaken because the employment of the writer's own labour made it a cheaper way of acquiring reading matter than the purchase of printed books. This must particularly have been true of the lesser clergy whose educated tastes were poorly served by stipends which were often well below what could be earned by a clerk or compositor in steady employment. Parson Adams's *Aeschylus* in Fielding's *Joseph Andrews* was not copied out by hand from choice but because he was unable to

[98] *Ledger*, pp. 156, 45, 51.

afford a printed edition. Even among the aristocracy, frequently spending well in advance of their receipts, there may well have been a perceived advantage in restricting writings to manuscript.[99]

THE BUILDING OF COMPOSITE COLLECTIONS

The example of the 1629 *Commons debates* enabled us to ask profitable questions about the ways in which larger collections were constructed out of smaller ones. Throughout the century there was an eager demand for collections of related pieces. The bulk of our surviving texts of political material which was originally circulated as separates has come down in this form, and the pattern is repeated in the verse anthologies, the musical part-books, the collections of antiquarian records and other specialized compilations.

Once in circulation, separates of this kind had a strong tendency to cluster. This was because the individual separate usually documented only one part of an ongoing, public process whose records needed to be assembled in much fuller form if they were to be comprehensible. Once related materials had been gathered as bundles of separates, it was often convenient for their owners to copy them into a bound 'paper book', after which the originals might well be abandoned to the kitchen or the privy. The indexed, fair-written volume of satires or political papers, and the set of bound music part-books were in every way easier to use than what they replaced. The entrepreneurial publisher, on the other hand, might well continue to copy from the original bundles, both to economize on labour and so that the resultant collection could be revised and updated at will.

An understanding of the processes by which such collections grew, and varied in growing, is obviously of central importance to any consideration of scribal publication; moreover, it is one that can be obtained to a large extent on the basis of evidence internal to the text. The classic 'rolling archetype' of the scribal publisher is to be considered in a later chapter; but it will be useful here to give examples of the different, because conflationary as well as

[99] For the depleted purchasing power of these two classes of reader, see Plant, pp. 42–6. Lawyers, by contrast, were perceived as an exceptionally wealthy group.

appropriative, procedures that gave rise to the parliamentary compilations. Notestein and Relf in their later publication with Hartley Simpson of the 1621 Commons debates present an analysis of a compilation which they call 'the anonymous journal X', which proves to be particularly revealing in this regard. The document was known to them from five principal sources. Of these, MS 1 and MS 2 represent the work in its finished form as 'a day by day narrative in which various accounts, separates, etc., have been put together to make a detailed record of the proceedings of the Commons'.[100] MS 4 and MS 5 contain excerpts from the longer text, with, in the second case, an interpolation from another source. MS 3, on the other hand, is a document of the kind hypothesized as the foundation of the 1629 *True relation*—a connected narrative of the parliament, though in this case not in finished professional form. Instead, it ranges from a fairly detailed and connected record to 'rough jottings which before they grew cold meant something to the original note-taker' (p. 7). Its importance is that it was one of two diary sources used by the compiler of MS 1. The second source does not survive and its contents must be guessed at from those portions of MS 1 which are not derived from MS 3 or other known sources. It would appear that the second source was more comprehensive, but less well written. Comparing the two, the editors state that 'The unknown diary is labored and the work of a persistent person. MS 3 is the work of an intelligent and penetrating mind who is, however, irregular in recording' (p. 10). Our present interest, though, is in the work of the compiler who unified two diary sources and a body of separates into the fuller record represented by MSS 1 and 2. This compiler's work is at times highly skilled and at others rather stupid—perhaps, the editors suggest, because it had been left to an assistant. But overall:

Depending mainly on MS 3 and the unknown source, the compiler has shown skill in weaving his materials together and in reconstructing a narrative from them. If at times he makes errors, he atones for them by an astonishing accuracy at other times. Not only has he shown ability in placing speeches from two or three different records of a day's

[100] *Commons debates 1621*, ed. Wallace Notestein, Frances Helen Relf and Hartley Simpson (New Haven, Conn., 1935), i. 6.

proceedings but he has sometimes with ingenuity pieced together from the stray offerings of various accounts a substantially complete version of a single speech. MS 3 will have a speech by Sir T. B. in a few brief sentences. In the compilation those sentences will all appear, each put in its proper place in the whole, a fact which can be readily tested from other diaries. . . . The compiler must have had helpful notes from his unknown source, yet he seems to have realized that the notes in MS 3 were better and to have inserted them whenever he could (p. 8).

Something very similar is described by Fuller as the procedure by which he had constructed the texts of his printed *Ephemeris*:

Sometimes one *copie* charitably relieved another, nor was it long before the defects of the same *copie* were supplied out of that other *transcription*. Thus neither is there being for *Books*, nor *living* for *men* in this world, without being mutually beholding one to another; & he who lends to day, may be glad to borrow to morrow.[101]

and by Simonds D'Ewes in his account of how he compiled a manuscript record of the parliaments of Queen Elizabeth:

I had occasion this instant March to pass over some days in discoursing, journeying and visiting: yet did I spend the greater part of it in transcribing some abstracts of Tower records I had borrowed, and in the beginning of a memorable and great work, which I afterwards finished; which, though it were upon the matter, except some few lines here and there, wholly written by an industrious servant I then kept, who wrote a very good secretary and Roman hand, yet it cost me many months' time to direct, compare, and overview, because it was framed up out of many several manuscript materials, with some little helps gathered out of some printed books. This work contained all the journals both of the Upper House and the House of Commons, of all the Parliaments and Sessions of Parliament during all Queen Elizabeth's reign; gathered out of the original journal-books of both the Houses, which I had the most free use of from Henry Elsing, Esq., clerk of the Upper House, and John Wright, Esq., clerk of the House of Commons. Into which, in the due places, (unless in some few particulars where I was fain to guess,) I inserted many speeches and other passages, which I had in other private journals in MS., and in loose papers. I added also many animadversions and elucidations of mine own where occasion served.[102]

Such intricate mosaic-work, indispensable when the materials at

[101] Fuller, *Ephemeris parliamentaria*.
[102] *Autobiography*, i. 409–10.3

hand were independent transcriptions of oral originals, is otherwise encountered only when a scribe or reader had some particular reason to suspect the completeness or accuracy of a scribally transmitted text. But it is valid testimony to a wider practice of agglutinative compilation that characterizes the whole range of scribal publication. At one level, knowledge encountered in fragments, and often further fragmented through the processes of transmission, encouraged a counterpoising activity of reconstitution. At another, new texts of a given kind were added to existing compilations in a process which, once initiated, might well extend to the proportions of a five- or six hundred-page volume. (Examples will be discussed in later chapters.) Whatever else it may be safe to assume about the regularities of scribal publication, there can be no doubt about the strength of this impulse towards the generation of larger and larger forms of the compiled text, a practice that ends only when the upper limit of manageable size is reached, after which, as we will see later, the process becomes one of a simultaneous gaining and shedding of elements. Parliamentary compilations present some of our best, because fullest, evidence of the workings of this process, but will come to be understood, in this as in other respects, only when we are able to study them as part of a much wider practice.

CONCLUSION

Our investigation into the work practices of scribal publishers has revealed a situation not very different after all from that which affects studies of print publication, namely that while the physical work involved in production can be described in some detail, the wider trade context of that work can only be guessed at by inductive reasoning from evidence which is often imperfect and nearly always capable of more than one interpretation. But while a vast and concentrated scholarly enterprise has been directed to assembling the empirical evidence for print publication, that for scribal publication in our period still remains largely unexplored, or, where it has been explored, is dispersed and unintegrated. If the present chapter has not been able to do very much to remedy this situation, it has, I hope, indicated the kinds of evidence we now need to search for and some of the uses to which it might be put.

PART II

SCRIPT AND SOCIETY

4

SOME METAPHORS FOR READING

THE previous chapters have dealt with the production and transmission of scribally published texts. I would now like to enquire how these were perceived by their original readers to differ from printed and oral texts, a topic that will require a more theoretical orientation than has so far been adopted. We will need for a start to consider, drawing on the insights of Walter J. Ong and Jacques Derrida, how the oral, the chirographical and the printed text each presuppose their own distinct modes of knowing. We will then need to test our theoretically derived predictions against a range of figurative formulations of the acts of reading and inscription actually current during the seventeenth century. Lastly I wish to consider the role played by the handwritten text in the constitution of 'fictions of state'—those figurative constructs that were invoked to legitimize the exercise of political authority.

'PRESENCE' AND THE SCRIBAL TEXT

One of the major debates of contemporary literary theory has centred on whether 'presence' is to be accepted as an inherent constituent of discourse. The concept itself is a complex one, having roots both in the psychology of utterance and in theology (God present in all things as the cause of their being). Ong, drawing on a heady synthesis of Thomistic theology, structuralist anthropology and McLuhanite media analysis, argues that presence is an attribute of the oral which becomes dissipated as words are encoded as writing and print.[1] This position is asserted as part of

[1] See his *The presence of the word* (New Haven, Conn., 1967), *Orality and literacy: the technologizing of the word*, and *Fighting for life: contest, sexuality, and consciousness* (Ithaca, NY,

a broader investigation into the ways in which language and thought are conditioned by the circumstances under which texts are encountered in any given culture—whether orally, chirographically, typographically or electronically. Chirographical transmission represents an intermediate stage between oral and typographical transmission in which the values of orality—and the fact of presence—are still strongly felt. The written word is therefore more likely than the printed word to promote a vocal or sub-vocal experience of the text, and a sense of validation through voice. Because it is easier for an author or, indeed, a reader to intervene in the process of transmission, manuscripts remain 'closer to the give-and-take of oral expression' and their readers 'less closed off from the author, less absent, than are the readers of those writing for print'. A manuscript-based culture preserves 'a feeling for the book as a kind of utterance, an occurrence in the course of conversation, rather than as an object', whereas the printed book is 'less like an utterance, and more like a thing'. Print 'situates words in space more relentlessly than writing ever did', thus giving them the status of objects rather than experiences and separating off the apprehension of meaning from an awareness of presence.[2]

Derrida rejects both this priority assumed for speech and the 'reality' of presence. His first formulation of the deconstructive approach to language was directed against the reliance of Western philosophy on a 'metaphysic of presence' through which speech was credited with a capacity to generate self-validating meaning, while writing, viewed as derivative from speech, was denied this

1981). Ong's work also needs to be placed in the context of a broader body of writing on the ways in which cultures and individuals negotiate their way among oral, chirographic, typographic and electronic modes of communication. Of relevance to the present study are Richard Bauman, *Let your words be few: symbolism of speaking and silence among seventeenth-century Quakers* (Cambridge, 1983); David Cressy, *Literacy and the social order*; Ruth Finnegan, *Literacy and orality: studies in the technology of communication* (Oxford, 1988); Jack Goody, *The interface between the written and the oral* (Cambridge, 1987); Alvin Kernan, *Printing technology, letters and Samuel Johnson* (Princeton, NJ, 1987); D. F. McKenzie, *Bibliography and the sociology of texts* (London, 1986) and 'Speech-manuscript-print' in *New directions in textual studies*, ed. Dave Oliphant and Robin Bradford (Austin, Tex., 1990), pp. 87–109; and Marshall McLuhan, *The Gutenberg galaxy: the making of typographic man* (Toronto, 1962). In opposition to Kernan, Ong and McLuhan, Finnegan doubts the existence of 'a clear-cut and non-problematic association between *literacy* or *orality* on the one hand and specific cognitive processes on the other' (p. 150).

[2] Ong, *Orality*, pp. 132, 125, 131, 121. Cf. Pebworth, 'John Donne, coterie poetry, and the text as performance', pp. 65-6.

capacity. The metaphysic is seen to rest on the two assumptions that there is somehow a point where meaning *begins* and that this is to be identified with the moment at which words find spoken or mental utterance. Deconstruction, as is well known, draws with qualifications on the Saussurean view that, since each signified has to be constituted negatively from other signifieds within language viewed as a system of differences, it can never be self-validating or originary. It is this conception of language as the unfinalizable play of signification which Derrida subsumes under the signifier 'writing' and sets in opposition to the metaphysic of presence. The speaker or subject, who under the metaphysic is the source of validation for meaning, now becomes no more than the 'space' within which the play of signification takes place. However, this view does not negate the traditional 'logocentric' project: Derrida's more radical point is that neither can have meaning apart from the tension of its relationship with the other.[3]

Ong, in criticizing this view, reasserts the metaphysic of presence and with it the proposition that the spoken word is more fully human than the written, but sees the distinction drawn by Derrida as a valid report on the way modes of inscription influence our perception of reality.[4] In his stress on the ability of print to empty words of presence, Ong's perception of its function has a superficial similarity to Derrida's of the more general condition of *écriture*, but, whereas Derrida's 'writing' is premised on a perpetual deferment of closure, Ong sees that print both resists *and* demands closure, the latter because it reduces language to the appearance of an exactly replicable object and because print production is crowded into a single, definitive press run. Moreover, not only does it try to insist that the text presented is final and unalterable

[3] The fullest exposition of these views is in Derrida's *Of grammatology*, trans. G. C. Spivak (Baltimore, 1976). There is a lucid summary of his position in Christopher Norris, *Deconstruction: theory and practice* (London, 1982). The papers in which Derrida comes closest to the concerns of the present study are those in which he considers the supposed authenticating power of the written signature as a displaced version of the supposed priority of speech over writing, as in 'Signature, event, context', *Glyph* 1 (1977), 172–97 (also in his *Marges de la philosophie* (Paris, 1972), pp. 365–93). For an acute, deconstructive study of the culture of writing, see Goldberg, *Writing matter*, discussed later in this chapter. Among hostile critiques of deconstruction, particular attention should be given to Anthony Giddens, 'Structuralism, post-structuralism and the production of culture' in *Social theory today*, ed. Anthony Giddens and Jonathan Turner (Cambridge, 1987), pp. 195–223.

[4] Cf. *Orality and literacy*, pp. 101–3.

but it imposes this condition of the text's existence upon its readers as a metaphor of the nature of knowledge, giving rise to what Alvin Kernan describes as 'print's remarkable ability to confer authoritative being and firm truth on its texts'.[5] In this and the other senses discussed, an increase in the perceived objectification of the word through print is to be seen not as a liberation of the possibilities of meaning but as a more rigid form of subjugation. It is the presence-rich chirographic text which becomes the arena of freedom. The freedom offered by typography is narrowly and specifically the freedom *from* presence (Derrida's conception); but it also brings with it a new tyranny arising from the object-like status of the typographic page and the hypostatization of language as possessing a reality independent of specific human acts of utterance and audition.

While the Derridean insight into the constitution of the sign is not an immediate concern of the present discussion, the opposition speech/writing, as formulated by Ong, has obvious bearing on any attempt to theorize the relationship between spoken language and the two kinds of written signifier we are concerned with—the chirographical and the typographical. The notion of 'presence', whether or not regarded as philosophically sustainable, provides us with a method of discriminating between modes of signification as being more or less distanced from a *presumed* source of self-validating meaning. Such a spectrum exists within speech itself to the extent that the capacity of an utterance to invoke the authority of presence is exercised at descending levels of plausibility by the sound of one's own voice, by that of another person addressing one directly, by a voice heard over the telephone, by words heard indistinctly over a public address system in a busy airline terminal, by the raised pitch levels of a diver speaking from within a diving helmet, by the voices of the dead from old recordings, and so on. One might differ over the placing of a particular speech experience on the spectrum but the principle is clear enough. Moreover, there is a point on the spectrum at which certain forms of writing might be regarded as bearing stronger intimations of presence than certain forms of speech. In Chinese tradition such claims are frequently made for calligraphy as against the spoken word, while

[5] *Printing technology*, p. 165.

in the West inscriptions using the writer's blood for ink have always been afforded a highly privileged status, and were generally preferred over vocal attestation in such important matters as pacts with the devil and appointments to the crews of pirate ships. Within the more conventional modes of inscription, a sub-spectrum along the axis chirography–typography–electronography might be formed thus: authorial holograph, scribal transcript, typewritten transcript with manuscript corrections, typewritten transcript without corrections, words printed from copper or steel engraved plates, computer printout, lithographic printing, raised surface printing, baked clay tablets, braille, skywriting with aeroplane, words seen on a TV screen or VDU, neon sign—by each of which the sign is progressively removed from an assumed source of validation in the movement of the author's fingers and relies instead for signifying power on its locus within an autonomous universe of signs.

These concepts need to be applied with some delicacy to writers who persisted in the use of manuscript transmission within a society that was already fully exploiting the possibilities of print; but they also give rise to an expectation that seventeenth-century writers might not only write differently but also adopt different conceptions of the function of writing as they turned from one medium to the other. It is interesting in this respect to note that the major writers of the period tend to display a strong disposition towards one particular medium, and that writers exhibiting these opposed positions often appear chronologically in pairs. Thus, against Spenser as a print-fixated poet, we might set Donne as one committed to manuscript. For Spenser, that *The faerie queene* should be print-published and circulated to as wide a readership as possible was an indispensable premise of its strident nationalism, its Puritan didacticism and its claim to stand as a worthy continuation of the great tradition of European epic.[6] But equally to the point is the look of the poem on the page, its magisterial succession of stanzas, each grounded on the concluding Alexandrine, progressing past with the air of a fleet in full sail—a design that, despite its

[6] One could argue, of course, that this is an immense confidence trick on the part of a narrative whose aim is, in Jonathan Goldberg's words, to 'induce frustration [and] . . . deny closure' (*Endlesse worke. Spenser and the structures of discourse* (Baltimore, 1981), p. xii); and one would have to answer that it does this too.

Italian and Chaucerian forerunners, seems so perfectly adjusted to the strengths of Renaissance typography. Donne, on the other hand, the leading non-dramatic poet of the next generation, not only rejected print but does not even look particularly distinguished in print. Whereas the typographical designer's art is based on the repetition of standardized visual patterns, whether they be type-pieces, fleurons, or stanzas, within a harmoniously balanced page, Donne's art leads to bizarrely shaped and constantly varied stanzas—even in some cases within the same poem. His stanza pattern for any given poem is determined by the requirements of the thought, without consideration for visual effect, and as the thought is invariably knotty and intricate, so are the stanzas, in a great many instances, straggly and gnarled. In this, in Donne's concentration as a writer on private experience, and in his uncompromising intellectuality, he was consciously opposing the values of the open market and the promiscuously purchasable page created by print.

Shakespeare and Jonson form another such pair, this time contemporaneous. Rejecting Shakespeare's disdain, as a dramatist, for the typographical medium (discussed in Chapter 3), Jonson took extraordinary care over the printing of his plays and in the 1616 folio produced one of the great typographical monuments of his age. In the 1605 quarto of *Sejanus*, as Philip Ayres has pointed out, the very look of the page, with its severe columns of verse flanked by marginal scholia and with the proclamations set in the style of a Roman lapidary inscription with medial stops between each word, was meant as an iconographic expression of its subject.[7] With Dryden and Rochester, to whom we will be returning shortly, the distinction occurs in an exceptionally revealing form. Rochester, the courtier, subscribed to an aesthetic of improvisation in writing as in everything else, being valued as much for his witty conversation as for his verse. He wrote for a small circle of friends, who saw the poems in manuscript, and seems to have had no interest in their future fate. Dryden, 'saturnine' and reserved in

[7] 'The iconography of Jonson's *Sejanus*, 1605: copy-text for the Revels edition', in *Editing texts: papers from a conference at the Humanities Research Centre*, ed. J. C. Eade (Canberra, 1985), pp. 47–53. John Jowett, 'Jonson's authorization of type in *Sejanus*', pp. 254–65, argues for the typography of the edition permitting a manuscript-like immediacy of access to the author; however, this was lost in the folio where the play was stripped of its Roman dress to fit the overall design of the volume.

company, found self-expression through the polished period and the balanced couplet, carefully and professionally working up the effects which to Rochester were a matter of spontaneity. His audience was a public not a private one, ranging in size from the 'town' to the nation, and was addressed as a matter of course through print.

Specialists in one medium would sometimes make revealing excursions into the other. Dryden took a holiday from print to write *Mac Flecknoe* which, withheld from the press, circulated alongside Rochester's verse in scribally published miscellanies, and which might well be read as a demonstration to Rochester, who in 'An allusion to Horace' had reproved Dryden for lack of conversational brilliance, of how well a skilled professional could recreate his own manner. *Mac Flecknoe* differs from every other known poem written by Dryden to that date in being vituperative, scatological and riddlingly allusive. But in this Dryden was simply accepting the decorum of the alternative medium with the same skill with which he adapted to any other decorum. By contrast, his other known scribally published work, the collaborative 'Essay on satire', is a polished literary piece which makes no flagrant departure from print decorums. Donne made the transition in the other direction in a small number of highly reluctant appearances in print. These reveal no attempt whatsoever to write down to a wider public. If anything, in the two *Anniversaries*, written in return for the patronage of Sir Robert Drury, and the elegy on the death of Prince Henry, he produced work of exceptional difficulty, even for him. In the opening lines of the elegy he comes close to self-parody in his determination to show that as a scribally publishing poet he was going to make no concessions at all to print.

Too few writers published extensively in both media to permit any more searching analysis of the effects of moving from one to another. If such a study were to be attempted, the best subjects might well be proselytizing writers on social, theological and scientific subjects such as Samuel Hartlib and Henry Oldenburg, who moved freely between the printed pamphlet, the scribal separate and the personal letter as each was found appropriate to the task in hand. Yet, Ong's distinctions would lead us to expect that a preference for the scribal medium would be accompanied by other preferences. Such writing would be more vocal and less visual; it would address a more intimate community of readers with a strong sense of immediacy; it would prefer freer, speech-like rhythms rather than arithmetically regulated metre, and organic notions of form rather than those reliant on a visually inspired symmetry; it would invite the reader to become a writer by annotating, extending or writing an 'answer' to the text presented. The literary comparisons just made suggest that these expectations are often fulfilled, though there are other cases—the pairing of Cowley and Carew would be an example—which appear, at least on first sight, to reverse them.[8] So while the precise working of these predispositions with regard to one and the other medium is something that must be considered on a case-by-case basis, it will do no harm to approach the next stage of our investigation with a sense of certain opposed tendencies in the two media which, while not always followed through, can fairly be regarded as innate. In applying this insight to political thought, our concern will be to demonstrate how attempts to legitimize the exercise of power demand the prior assertion of a point of origin for meaning within one or other of the realms of voice, script and, latterly, print.

METAPHORS OF INSCRIPTION

These general metaphors for the nature of knowledge projected by script and print undoubtedly influenced the attitudes of individual writers and readers towards the two media; but our distinctions need to be refined by reference to the associations between inscription and life actually made by contemporaries. As my point of departure for an examination of these historically contingent associations, it will be convenient to take a series of metaphors for the act of reading which are discussed in the fifth chapter of Ann and John Thompson's *Shakespeare: meaning and metaphor.*[9]

[8] Carew, the scribally publishing poet, exhibits a restraint and elegance which is missing from the self-consciously libertarian Cowley with his love of extreme metaphors and cultivation of the unmeasured pindaric form. However, the evidence assembled by Beal (*IELM*, ii/1, 240–1) suggests that Cowley might better be viewed as a scribal author-publisher who suffered from his work being ruthlessly pirated by booksellers. John Kerrigan writes sensitively on Carew's engagement with the scribal medium in his 'Thomas Carew', *PBA* 74 (1988), 311–50.

[9] (Brighton, 1987), pp. 163–206.

Although the Thompsons' concern with this material is cognitive rather than cultural, they cast valuable light on associations which seem to have been habitual to the period and which, by virtue of their presence in writers as influential as Shakespeare and Jonson, were continually being reinforced.

We begin with a very powerful and deep-rooted metaphor which sexualized the material of writing, paper, as female and the acts of reading and writing as displaced versions of sexual domination of the female by the male. The 'procreative' pen has already made its appearance in a quotation from Thomas Fuller.[10] The metaphor of the woman as page finds one of its most familiar expressions in Valentine's 'mad' speech to Angelica in Act IV of Congreve's *Love for love* (1695):

ANGELICA. Do you know me, *Valentine*?
VALENTINE. Oh very well.
ANGELICA. Who am I?
VALENTINE. You're a Woman,—One to whom Heav'n gave Beauty, when it grafted Roses on a Briar. You are the reflection of Heav'n in a Pond, and he that leaps at you is sunk. You are all white, a sheet of lovely spotless Paper, when you first are Born; but you are to be scrawl'd and blotted by every Goose's Quill.[11]

Despite the fashionable Lockean overtones of this passage, the underlying force of the metaphor arises from an equivalence between writing and sex, found very widely in seventeenth-century poetry and drama. Shakespeare's internalization of it is explored by the Thompsons in these terms:

in *Much Ado About Nothing* Leonato misreads Hero's appearance (presumably her blushes) as evidence of her sexual guilt: 'Could she here deny / The story that is printed in her blood?' (4. 1. 121–2). Othello looks for similarly readable signs in Desdemona: 'Was this fair paper, this most goodly book, / Made to write 'whore' upon?' (*Othello*, 4. 2. 71–2). Here the face is not specified and Desdemona as a whole seems to be paper or book. Another instance where the body as a whole is readable occurs in *Measure for Measure* when Claudio acknowledges that Juliet is visibly

[10] p. 17.

[11] IV.i. 631–46 in *The complete plays of William Congreve*, ed. Herbert Davis (Chicago, 1967). Another version of the image is found at the close of the act: 'She is harder to be understood than a Piece of *Ægyptian* Antiquity, or an *Irish* Manuscript; you may pore till you spoil your Eyes, and not improve your Knowledge' (IV. i. 801–3).

pregnant by remarking, 'The stealth of our most mutual entertainment / With character too gross is writ on Juliet' (1. 2. 154–5). It is striking how regularly when a woman's face or person is in question, it is her sexual guilt or innocence that is to be read from it. The general tendency is for women to be seen as the books or papers which are to be read by men—having been written or printed upon by other men.[12]

The wider currency of images of women as '"blank pages" waiting to be inscribed by the male pen/penis' (as the Thompsons put it) has been noted by Susan Gubar, for whom 'women have had to experience cultural scripts in their lives by suffering them in their bodies'.[13] A related image is that of the blot as a sign of sexual stigma, as in Fauconbridge's description of himself to his mother as 'The sonne that blotteth you with wedlocks breach' in *The troublesome reign of John, King of England*, Part 1.[14] Drayton's 'The epistle of Rosamond to King Henry the second' offers a concatenation of such imagery:

> This scribbled Paper which I send to thee,
> If noted rightly, doth resemble mee:
> As this pure Ground, whereon these Letters stand,
> So pure was I, ere stayned by thy Hand;
> Ere I was blotted with this foule Offence,
> So cleere and spotlesse was mine Innocence:
> Now, like these Markes which taint this hatefull Scroule,
> Such the blacke sinnes which spot my leprous Soule.[15]

But there is a no less telling absence: the male writer of love poetry may image himself as either the writer or the reader, but will rarely present himself as the surface being inscribed, this being metaphor-

[12] Op. cit., p. 177. Further examples from early drama of this analogy are given in Louis Charles Stagg, *The figurative language of the tragedies of Shakespeare's chief 17th-century contemporaries: an index*, 3rd edn (New York, 1982) and *The figurative language of the tragedies of Shakespeare's chief 16th-century contemporaries: an index* (New York, 1984). R. W. van Fossen in his edition of Thomas Heywood's *A woman killed with kindness* (London, 1961) refers to it as a 'favourite idea' of the dramatist (p. 35n.).

[13] Op. cit., p. 177; Susan Gubar, '"The blank page" and the issues of female creativity', in Elizabeth Abel, ed., *Writing and sexual difference* (Brighton, 1982), p. 81. The Renaissance notion of the body as directly inscribed by metaphorical meanings found wider expression in icon books, allegorical drama, the Quaker practice of public metaphorical acts (discussed in Bauman, *Let your words be few*, pp. 84–94) and the practice of branding felons with a sign indicating their crime (discussed by the Thompsons, p. 109).

[14] *Troublesome reign*, facsim. ed. J. S. Farmer (Edinburgh, 1911), B4^r.

[15] *Works*, ii. 133.

ically assigned as the female role.[16] By the same logic, for a woman to wield the pen is a metaphorical emasculation:

> How would thy masc'line Spirit, Father *Ben*,
> Sweat to behold basely deposed men,
> Justled from the Prerog'tive of their Bed,
> Whilst *wives* are per'wig'd with their *husbands head*.
> Each snatches the male quill from his faint hand
> And must both nobler write and understand,
> He to her fury the soft plume doth bow,
> O Pen, nere truely justly slit till now![17]

Here the metaphor is one of the male being deprived of his penis by the writing woman, with the last line punning on 'slit' in the sense of vagina.[18]

Jonathan Goldberg views the sexualization of writing from a more complex perspective according to which the emphasis in instruction books on 'the softness and malleability' of the hand that holds the phallic pen 'suggests feminization even as it founds the privileged male subject'. As regards women writers, a series of *double entendres* in Dekker's *Westward ho!* arising from an attempt at seduction by a bogus writing master is read by him as an initiation into 'fornication, fellatio and masturbation'.[19] Gubar's darker view that women's writing is 'not an ejaculation of pleasure but a reaction to rending' is closer to the expressed Renaissance perception (p. 86).

A related topos is what is described by the Thompsons as the 'sex-as-printing' metaphor. One version of this is present in Fuller's 'Indeed the Press, at first a *Virgin*, then a *chast Wife*, is since turned *Common*, as to prostitute her self to all Scurrilous Pamphlets'.[20] However, the aspect of the printing press that most vividly imposed itself on the Renaissance masculine imagination was its ability to produce an endless succession of identical copies of

[16] An exception needs to be made for the conceit of the image of the beloved being transferred into the eyes or heart, as in Donne's 'The dampe', l. 4.

[17] 'On *Sanazar*'s being honoured', Lovelace, *Poems*, p. 200.

[18] As in the following couplet from a satire on Nell Gwynn ('I sing the story of a scoundrel lass'): 'To Thee I doe resigne my Youth and Witt / Then dear be kind, and gently broach my slit' (Ohio State University MS Eng. 15, p. 225).

[19] Goldberg, *Writing matter*, pp. 99–100.

[20] *History of the worthies*, p. 30.

the type-page. In its metaphorical transformation this becomes an image of patriarchally legitimized procreation. The characteristic form of the topos is one which presents the woman as a means whereby a man is able to produce an exact simulacrum of himself ('Your Mother was most true to Wedlock, Prince, / For she did print your Royall Father off, / Conceiuing you'[21]). In the various forms given to this metaphor the woman may be presented as the press, as the sheet of paper 'pressed' by the man, or simply as a text over which the man possesses copyright—but the recurring theme is the precise exactness of the resulting copy. Through this image of a mechanized, unvarying reproduction of a patriarchal exemplum, printing is posited as the agency by which women are reduced to a state of total passivity. This in turn leads us to two other common metaphors, those of the woman as wax which receives an impression from the male ('She caru'd thee for her seale, and ment therby, / Thou shouldst print more, not let that coppy die'[22]) and as the metal which is cast into the form of a medal or coin, these earlier forms of the concept having a typographical analogue in the punchcutter's 'matrix'. Examples of all three metaphors are given by the Thompsons, but a reader familiar with the drama and poetry of the period should have no trouble in recalling further examples.

In yet another transformation, used by Donne in his Latin verses to Richard Andrewes, the press, as woman, shares in the sin of Eve, bringing forth offspring in pain who are destined for death.

Parturiunt madido quae nixu praela, recepta,
  Sed quae scripta manu, sunt veneranda magis.

. . . .

Qui liber in pluteos, blattis cinerique relictos,
  Si modo sit praeli sanguine tinctus, abit;
Accedat calamo scriptus, reverenter habetur,
  Involat et veterum scrinia summa Patrum.[23]

[21] *The winter's tale*, ll. 2576–9, in *William Shakespeare. The complete works*, ed. Stanley Wells and Gary Taylor (Oxford, 1986), p. 1294; discussed with similar passages in Thompson and Thompson, pp. 177–83.

[22] Sonnet 11, in *Works*, p. 850.

[23] *The poems of John Donne*, ed. H. J. C. Grierson (Oxford, 1912), i. 397, which should, however, be read in the light of H. W. Garrod, 'The Latin poem addressed by Donne to Dr Andrews', *RES* 21 (1945), 38–42. I am in debt to Hilton Kelliher for the identity of the poem's addressee.

These lines are normally quoted in Edmund Blunden's English verse translation which suppresses the metaphors of the original.[24] A more accurate translation would be: 'What presses give birth to with sodden pangs is acceptable, but manuscripts are more venerated. A book dyed with the blood of the press departs to an open shelf where it is exposed to moths and ashes; but one written by the pen is held in reverence and flies to the privileged shelf reserved for the ancient fathers.' Here the surface on which the text was inscribed has ceased to be an element in the metaphor and the contrast is between the patriarchal pen and the press imaged as a woman in perpetual labour.

The figuring of the press in these terms implies a contrasting position for the scribal text—still patriarchal in its mode of inscription, but free from the suggestion of a controlled, iterative procreation of unvarying simulacra. Certainly the handwritten copy could never serve, as the printed one does, as an icon of marital fidelity: the fact that a given copy may contain the inscription of several hands, and might expect to be reinscribed by successive owners, points towards the implications latent in Congreve's scribbled page of a threateningly catholic sexuality. The woman who has allowed herself to be scrawled and blotted by every goose's quill is hardly going to offer any assurance of paternity in her children. (History has provided an appropriate exemplum in the eighteenth-century countess of Oxford whose variously fathered offspring were known as the 'Harleian miscellany'.) In other words, the modes of reproduction characteristic of print and script pointed, at the level of metaphor, towards a socially approved and a socially disapproved mode of procreation. Viewed in this way, script emerges as the seductive, untrustworthy medium whose texts, replicating themselves by suspect means, must always elude possession.

THE VIOLENCE OF THE PEN

However, other metaphorical equivalences are found for both the handwritten and the printed text. John Davies of Hereford in 'The

[24] 'Some seventeenth-century Latin poems by English writers', *University of Toronto quarterly* 25 (1955–6), 11.

muse's sacrifice' (1612) puns on pressing as a form of judicial torture.

> But *Poesie* (dismall *Poesie*) thou art
> most subiect to this sou'raigne *Sottishnesse*;
> So, there's good Cause thou shouldst be out of heart,
> sith all, almost, now put thee under *Presse*.[25]

Goldberg in *Writing matter* has built a cultural interpretation of considerable scope on the equation which he finds in early writing manuals between inscription and violence. Starting from a metaphorical description of quills as weapons in Vives' Latin dialogue 'Scriptio', he moves on to discuss the prominence given in accounts of the technology of inscription to the penknife, and the way in which the sharpened quill is itself frequently figured as a knife or dagger.[26] A penknife could in fact be an effective weapon—in the last act of *The changeling* De Flores kills himself with one. But the violence Goldberg is concerned with is the institutionalized violence of the Renaissance state, issuing in the form of racism, sexism and colonial exploitation.

> Writing is wielded as a weapon through a series of social positions. The knife works: to produce the quill, to produce the writer. The scene of writing, we could assume after Derrida, is always associated with violence; here, with the very materials of his craft, scenes of mutual violence are staged, openings and enclosures that extend and contain the activity of writing. In Vives or Bales, we can see the paths that are taken once the writer has his weapons to hand. But these scenes can be read too on the pages of the writing manuals, in their descriptions of the instruments, in their demarcations of the spheres in which the writer's hand moves.[27]

In introducing Goldberg we have switched from consideration of the relatively simple figurative transformations actually acknowledged by men and women of the time to the imposed constructions of the twentieth-century theorist. The same kind of

[25] *Works*, ii, 'The muse's sacrifice', p. 5.

[26] Goldberg, *Writing matter*, pp. 60–107. Goldberg's deconstructionist argument is too complex to be summarized here. I have done no more than to abstract a few themes with direct bearing on my own concerns.

[27] Ibid. 69. A full explication of this passage would need to return to Derrida's critique of Lévi-Strauss in *Of grammatology*, discussed by Goldberg on pp. 16–55.

post hoc structuring lies behind a number of Goldberg's more extravagant conceits, such as the suggestion that writing on vellum with the sharpened pen is a re-enactment of the slaughtering of the animal whose skin provides the surface, or that the image of the pen as plough shows how 'colonial activity extends from the agricultural metaphor that extends from the writing surface'.[28] He also sees a figuration of violence in the dismembered hands that are used to illustrate penholds (synecdoche as the trope of mutilation), and interprets the violence committed by the penknife upon the pen as a metaphorical self-wounding (see his reference p. 99 to the 'castrative economy' of the penhold). None the less, the image his study presents of the 'armed' scribe who wrote with a knife in one hand, for support and erasure, and the pen in the other is an appropriate one for a century which produced Montrose's 'I'll write thy epitaph in blood and wounds', and Marvell's:

> When the sword glitters o'er the judge's head,
> And fear has coward churchmen silenced,
> Then is the poet's time, 'tis then he draws,
> And single fights forsaken virtue's cause.[29]

But otherwise, Goldberg's account of metaphors for writing credits it with a role in instilling submission to established power that conflicts strongly with the view proposed earlier of script as the medium of freedom, intimacy and individuality, and of the scribal text's essential evasiveness and indeterminacy. In fact, both views can claim historical justification. The apparent contradiction arises chiefly from Goldberg's primary concern being with the invariant international hand of the Renaissance, the italic, rather than the bewilderingly diverse local and individual hands. He is also, in a book that misleadingly claims to be a study of handwriting, almost exclusively concerned with engraved and

[28] Ibid. 73; see also p. 64. However, something like the first of these metaphors does occur at least once in a seventeenth-century poem, Alexander Radcliffe's 'The swords farewell, upon the approach of a Michaelmas-Term':

> Farewel (dear Sword) thour't prov'd, and laid aside;
> Thy youngest Brother, *Penknife*, must be try'd;
> That thou art best, needs but a thin dispute,
> Thou woundest skin of *Man*, he skin of *Brute*.
> (*The ramble: an anti-heroick poem* (London, 1682), p. 119)

[29] 'Tom May's death', ll. 63–6.

woodcut images of handwriting, i.e. with printed simulacra. In a passage quoted by Goldberg from a letter of Erasmus, Guillaume Budé is reproved for using so individualistic a hand that Erasmus had to transcribe it before he could read it. Goldberg reads this episode as evidence of a 'disciplinary submission' on the part of humanistic pedagogy to power conceived in Foucaultian terms as totalized and superinstitutional.[30] But it is equally a testimony that writing could be a conscious expression of individualism and a rejection of rather than a submission to the values of the unifying nation state or the universal church. This was certainly the view of writers of English secretary hand, for whom, as we saw in Chapter 3, the forming of a writing style was a conscious mode of self-fashioning. The copy book and the standardized hand were objects of admiration only to those who had an untroubled faith in the goodness of popes, princes and courts, or those who found it politic to pretend they did.

The rich variety of actual practice can be seen at a glance by turning from the specimens of copy-book hands in Joyce Whalley's *The pen's excellencie* to actual contemporary manuscripts.[31] To a modern eye even the mixed secretary-italic and the succeeding round hand often show marked variation from individual to individual. Just as striking is the way in which the hand of the same individual can vary, even over short periods of time, suggesting an impatience with the idea of submission to a single unvarying paradigm. The exact replication of the writing master's forms, which Goldberg treats as the norm of pedagogy, would be rejected by the Bagots as sterile; and there must surely have been masters whose aim was to encourage creative invention in the same way as tailors and fencing masters encouraged their pupils to aim at a distinguishing individual excellence. A musical analogy would be the addition of ornaments or divisions to a plain melody, which, again, was meant to be an expression of the performer's individualism and never to be done the same way twice. Guy Miege wrote towards the end of the century:

As to the . . . *Roman*, *Italian* and *Round Hands*, there are few Men that

[30] Goldberg, pp. 114–15.

[31] For representative reproductions of hands of the period, see the collections by Dawson and Kennedy-Skipton, Petti, Croft and Greg cited in Ch. 3.

> write them exactly, according to the Models prescribed by Writing Masters. But every one writes as he fancies, and as his Genius leads him. Insomuch that one may truly say, there are as many Hands as there be individual Writers, it being as hard to find an absolute Likeness between two Persons Writings, as it is to find two Faces or two Voices alike. So wisely Nature has provided against the Confusion which must necessarily arise from an universal Likeness.[32]

The uniformizing tendency attributed by Goldberg to writing certainly existed, and finds a representation in metaphor; but, despite the relentless self-advertisement of writing masters, of which his book gives copious documentation, it was strongly opposed in England by the champions of variety. Goldberg takes the writing masters too much at their own valuation when they claim that the whole of humanist culture is grounded in their craft. Similar claims were made by music masters, dancing masters, fencing-masters, cookery instructors (as in *The staple of news*) and self-advertising pedants of all persuasions. When a common hand did in the end establish itself, it was the flexible, utilitarian hand of the business world, not the courtly template of the pedagogues.

SCRIPT AND THE STATE

Apart from its figurative resonances, script had a number of practical functions, *vis à vis* speech and print, as an agent in the exercise of political authority. The New Historicism (of which Goldberg must count as a maverick adherent) has accustomed students of the literature of the period to read texts in the light of a wider social narrative relating to the acquisition of power by the centralizing state at the expense of older, more dispersed forms of authority.[33] This will be one of the issues to be considered later in the present chapter. However, my immediate aim is the more restricted one of taking the system of power as it was then understood and looking at the roles assigned within it to speech, writing and print respectively. Having done this we will be in a better position to consider the more general question of how

[32] *The English grammar*, 2nd edn (London, 1691), p. 119.

[33] Two already classical examples of this kind of analysis will be found in Stephen Greenblatt's essays 'Shakespeare and the exorcists' and 'Martial law in the land of Cockaigne', in his *Shakespearean negotiations* (Oxford, 1988), pp. 94–128, 129–63.

modes of communication contributed to the framing of myths of legitimacy. My concern will be with what speech-act theorists call the 'performative' role of utterance, and with the circumstances under which something analogous to that role can be attributed to script and print.[34] In mixed acts (e.g. a speech read from a written copy), the dominant medium is taken as that in which the authority of the text is seen to be grounded.

During the periods of effective Stuart rule, power was seen as vested in three agencies, the sovereign, the parliament and the courts of law. In the terms of one widely accepted (though not uncontested) myth of legitimation, the authority of the second and third of these was derived from the king but secured by the king's accepting an obligation to maintain the laws of the kingdom. This was a view elastic enough to be acceptable both to James I in his speech to parliament on 21 March 1610 and Pym in pressing for the impeachment of Strafford on 25 November 1640.[35] In each case power could be exercised through utterance, writing or the use of seals, some actions being satisfied by one of these, but others requiring a combination. In the day-to-day exercise of authority, voice remained the dominant medium. On deliberative occasions, the king was counselled through the spoken advice of his ministers and issued his own conclusions vocally to his advisers and parliament, which he would often address in person. When a message was sent to parliament it was usually a spoken message delivered by a royal officer. Otherwise, the king's agreement to policies was to be gained through the spoken persuasion of favourites. In the other main areas of authority, the law and parliament, power was again exercised through utterance. The two houses of parliament enacted their measures through spoken debate and votes. Although each house employed a clerk to record its decisions and communicate its wishes in writing, the director of its proceedings was, appropriately, a 'speaker', though only known by that name in the Commons. The decisions of the law were delivered in a spoken verdict, and the power to influence

[34] As defined in J. L Austin, *How to do things with words*, 2nd edn (Oxford, 1975), a performative utterance is one which accomplishes what it refers to: e.g. 'I sentence you to death'.

[35] See J. P. Kenyon, ed., *The Stuart constitution 1603–1688*, 2nd edn (Cambridge, 1986), pp. 11–13, 191–3.

those decisions was exercised in most instances through the spoken arguments of counsel. (The famous exception to this rule was the court of Star Chamber whose deliberations, though conducted orally, were largely concerned with written presentations.)

In this context of deliberation, writing was secondary to voice in the sense that it rarely possessed a performative function. However, directions for the execution of spoken commands, whether they were those of the king, the courts or the parliament, had always to be in the form of a written instruction. The king's word might be law but his warrant was required before action could be undertaken by his servants. These documents were written not printed, and were validated by signatures and seals. On occasions, one of which is defined by the scrivener in *Richard III*, they needed to be read aloud in order to have legal force. Here the written document possessed a latent authority awaiting release by utterance, rather than one initiated by utterance.

> Here is the indictment of the good Lord Hastings,
> Which in a set hand fairely is engrosst,
> That it may be to day read ouer in Paules:
> And marke how well the sequele hangs together,
> Eleuen houres I haue spent to wryte it ouer . . .
> And yet within these fiue houres Hastings liued,
> Vntaynted, vnexamined, free, at liberty:
> Heeres a good world, the while. (ll. 1977–86)

Writing was also a source of authority where it served as a record of speech uttered on former occasions. Both parliament and the law were deeply reliant on precedents, and a great deal of energy went into unearthing these from old manuscripts. But this knowledge, important as it was, only became actualized as power when it was translated back into voice within the appropriate forum.

Where writing emerged as of at least equal power to speech was through its use for contractual agreements under the law, including transactions relating to the ownership of property. This also applied to contracts between subjects and the crown, whether individual or, in the case of Magna Charta, collective. Agreements between sovereign states were also performed through the signing of written documents. In some of these cases the document can still be regarded as a substitute for an absent voice; but this could not be the case when the signing of a document was, as frequently happened, an application of closure to the rights of voice, or when negotiations were conducted entirely in the written medium. A parliamentary bill still required to be read on three occasions before it could be passed, but a legal writ existed entirely as a written formulation and would never be uttered in words. Indeed it might be composed in Latin or a long-obsolete version of Norman French, this death of speech being the birth of writing in its modern conception as transcending presence. It was the authority attributed to writing as contract that constituted the most effective counter to the exercise of power through voice. Printing, however great its capacity to sway public opinion, was of minimal importance to the institutional exercise of power, even a printed warrant requiring a validating signature or seal.

FICTIONS OF AUTHORITY

At this point in our discussion the discussion of political practice shades over into the discussion of political fictions, particularly those fundamental legitimizing fictions to which any institutional exercise of power must ultimately appeal. Auden's reply to 'the lie of Authority' was to assert 'There is no such thing as the State'.[36] If there is indeed no such thing as the state (which is unquestionably the case), then when we speak of the state we are speaking of a fiction—a construct of the imagination—and if this is so, all other formulations on which the claim to exercise power is based must equally be fictional. This insight is far from being a new one. To Hobbes the state was 'but an Artificiall Man' in whom '*Soveraignty* is an Artificiall *Soul*', the artifice concerned being of the same order as that displayed by 'Engines that move themselves by springs and wheeles as doth a watch'.[37] To Halifax, a political 'Fundamental' was no more than 'a general unintelligible Notion'.

Every Party, when they find a Maxim for their turn, they presently call it

[36] W. H. Auden, *Another time* (London, 1940), p. 114.

[37] *Leviathan*, ed. C. B. Macpherson (Harmondsworth, 1968), p. 81. More generally, advocates of social-contract theories of government have never been in a position to demonstrate that the contracts they assumed had ever taken place.

a Fundamental, they think they nail it with a Peg of Iron, whereas in truth they only tie it with a wisp of Straw. . . . Every thing that is created is Mortal, *ergo* all Fundamentals of human Creation will die.[38]

Machiavelli provided a recipe book from which new fictions could be generated.

This nominalist view of power makes it necessary that, if we are to discuss legitimizing codes, we should do so in their nature as fictions, using the tools employed for the analysis of literary fictions, and, in recent years, also for the law as an authored system. For our present purposes these tools can be regarded as narratology and tropology. Fictions of authority are to be understood as topoi or combinations of topoi organized in relationship to themselves and the world by means of figures. 'Figures' here embraces all the verbal devices of classical rhetoric but particularly the master tropes of metaphor, metonymy, synecdoche and irony, both in their local use as devices of style and their extended use as complex tropes and ideological master narratives. Such fictions may be acknowledged as such without losing their societal utility; but their motivating force is usually stronger if they are accepted as possessing a 'real' existence (in the case of abstract nouns) or comprising a true description of events (in the case of originary narratives).

The relative status accorded to voice, script and print within the political structure will be considered first in relationship to the key social fiction that located the origin of all secular power in the king's person.[39] That power might then be actualized either through the royal touch or the royal voice. Touch was exercised directly in the ceremony of ennoblement and indirectly through writing and the use of seals, these representing different degrees of displacement from the validating body. Touch differed from voice in its being part of a chain of legitimation which reached back into the remote past: in the ceremony of coronation, the king was confirmed in his status by the touch of bishops whose own act of

[38] *The works of George Savile Marquess of Halifax*, ed. Mark N. Brown (Oxford, 1989), ii. 220.

[39] Rationalizing contemporary versions of this are given by Barclay, Hobbes and Filmer; however, in its purest form, as expounded and accepted by James I, the theory maintained that the king's power devolved immediately from God. The point must be made that, expressed in this form, it was still a relatively recent theory. Both the view that power

ordination linked them directly with the touch of Christ and the apostles. Touch, therefore, was metonymic, extending through contiguity rather than resemblance. Voice, on the other hand, communicable only through the vibrations of air and fading as soon as heard, could claim no such metonymic force and was a purer example of the ability of the royal person to generate new meanings. Here the operative figure is metaphor—each such act being a re-enactment through resemblance of the world-creating logos. In its extreme form, as embraced in practice if not quite in theory by Charles I, the royal utterance was seen as the source not just of self-validating meaning but of all meaning, since that king presumed upon a moral right not simply to temporize but to lie, i.e. to be a legitimizer of contingent as well as originary fictions. Prudently, parliament chose in the end to deprive him of the organs of utterance.

A corollary to what has been said is that any challenge to the accepted hierarchy of modes of communication was also a challenge to the current legitimizing fiction. In the case of Puritan opposition to the crown in the earlier part of the century, this took the initial form of a reorientation of the authority of voice away from the signification-generating monarch to the inspired preacher; yet, the Puritan preacher's inspiration still came from his internalization of the printed Bible; so, despite the great stress laid on vocal attestation, it was the press that provided Puritanism with its locus of validation.[40] Laudian Anglicanism reacted by replacing the pulpit with the altar as the central focus of worship, in effect an attempt to privilege sight over hearing. The other principal challenge was that of the Common Lawyers who appealed from the authority of voice to the authority of script by assembling a vast body of medieval precedents to buttress their case for the political authority of the judiciary and parliament, which for their purposes counted as a court. 'Between 1603 and 1660', David Douglas notes, 'this literature had grown to a vast size, and claims such as those of Edward Coke that the laws of England had remained unchanged through the five successive ages of the

derived from the people and the Cokean view that power was assigned by and under the law were of greater antiquity.

[40] Puritan anxiety over the relative merits of preaching and reading is discussed in McKenzie, 'Speech-manuscript-print', pp. 91, 100–1 and *passim*.

Britons, Romans, Saxons, Danes, and Normans, won a wide acceptance even from well informed men, as did the similar assertions contained in Selden's *History of tithes*'.[41] To Coke, like Hooker, there was no 'intelligible sense in which law could be said to be made'.[42] Inherited from remote antiquity, grounded in ancient written records, and incarnate in its various courts with their assigned jurisdictions, the common law of England was the source from which both king and parliament received their powers and to which they must answer when those powers were extended beyond their permitted limits. This represents yet another case of the logocentric search for legitimation through a fiction of origin, and one that, in this case, is still encountered today in the form of the related Blackstonean conception of the common law, though Blackstone's appeal was to the rationality of the law rather than its antiquity.[43] Today that origin is sited within the print and electronic media. In Coke's time it was to be sought principally among written records, but increasingly *through* the medium of printed commentaries and reports (including his own). However, this transporting of legal doctrine and data from script into print was nearly always undertaken with reluctance, partly because it involved a sacrifice of control over power-conferring knowledge and partly because printed law took on a fixed, unnegotiable quality.[44] When the constitutional break with the authority of the crown was made in 1642 it was on the basis foreshadowed by the Common Lawyers rather than the Puritan theocrats.

The rejection of the royal authority by the parliament disposed for the time being of the fiction of a single, signification-conferring voice as the source of political authority, and initially must have seemed to open the way to a babble of mutually competing voices. In this crisis, recourse was had to relegitimation through writing in the form of the personal subscriptions demanded to the Protestation Oath of 1641, the Vow and Covenant of 1643 and the

[41] David Douglas, *English scholars 1660–1730*, 2nd edn (London, 1951), p. 119.

[42] George H. Sabine, *A history of political theory*, 4th edn, rev. T. L. Thorson (Hinsdale, 1973), p. 419.

[43] The collapse of Coke's view and its replacement by Blackstone's is discussed in Robert Willman, 'Blackstone and the 'theoretical perfection' of English law in the reign of Charles II', *Historical journal* 26 (1983), 39–70.

[44] For evidence on this matter see McKenzie, 'Speech-manuscript-print', pp. 97–9.

Solemn League and Covenant of 1644.[45] In testimony to this reinstatement of the authority of writing, the Cromwellian state saw marked advances towards the creation of a civil service of the modern kind in which administrative decisions were based on the study of written reports. The exhaustive private record-keeping of officials of a later date like Pepys, William Petyt and Sir Daniel Fleming was the effect of attitudes imbibed during this period. The legitimizing voice having been at least temporarily silenced, it was important to fill the vacuum with huge bodies of script.

With the coronation of Charles II in 1660 a fiction of authority based on the originary power of the royal utterance was again in place, but it was a fiction that made little attempt to disguise its fictive nature. This was certainly Dryden's view in 'Annus mirabilis'. In recounting a royal visit to the dockyards, he confronts us with a disconcertingly human Charles II:

> Our careful Monarch stands in Person by,
> His new-cast Canons firmness to explore:
> The strength of big-corn'd powder loves to try,
> And Ball and Cartrage sorts for every bore.

Here the royal touch, severed from its sanctifying metonymies, is totally demystified. But elsewhere Dryden's recourse is to a divinizing Mannerist iconography adapted from that applied to Charles I as the royal martyr, and grotesquely inapplicable to his son:

> Mean time he sadly suffers in their grief,
> Out-weeps an Hermite, and out-prays a Saint:
> All the long night he studies their relief,
> How they may be suppli'd, and he may want.[46]

It was not a matter of concern that the two perceptions were irreconcilable. To Dryden at this time the real danger was that fictions that carried too great a charge of conviction could mislead those who relied on them over the real extent of their power. It was enough in this new world if they were expressed with elegance and bravura.

[45] Discussed from the point of view of the history of literacy in Cressy, *Literacy and the social order*, pp. 65–91. Subscription to these by signature or mark was sought, on a parish by parish basis, from all adult males, with those refusing to subscribe being reported to parliament.

[46] *Annus mirabilis: the year of wonders, 1666*, ll. 593–6, 1041–4, in *Works*, i. 82, 98.

THE FRAGILITY OF VOICE

The special value of literary texts to this kind of historical enquiry is that writers, as specialists in the use of figurative language, will often possess a privileged understanding of the figurative nature of belief systems, and be able to engage in a very direct and revealing way with the master narratives of their culture. In the present case, a text of 1595, Shakespeare's *Richard II*, is of great help in understanding the rivalry between the fiction that linked legitimacy with voice and that which sought to found legitimacy in writing.

The opening scenes of the play present us with the workings of a political culture organized round the sovereign authority of the royal utterance. The fact that the power of that utterance is used capriciously in no way detracts from its performative force. The shortening of Bullingbrooke's exile brings the acknowledgement

> How long a time lies in one little word,
> Foure lagging winters and foure wanton springes,
> End in a word, such is the breath of Kinges. (ll. 485–7)

Voice is figured throughout as breath, its validating power here lying not in its metaphorical recapitulation of the *logos* but in its being an emanation of the *pneuma*. Gaunt's attempts to check Richard's irresponsible exercise of the prerogative of voice fail, among other reasons, because he lacks breath (l. 644). The seizure of Gaunt's property is achieved by a single performative utterance:

> Towards our assistance we doe seaze to vs:
> The plate, coine, reuenewes, and moueables
> Whereof our Vnckle Gaunt did stand possest. (ll. 775–7)

Although the decision has to be reiterated for York's benefit, the second version

> Thinke what you wil, we cease into our hands
> His plate, his goods, his money and his landes. (ll. 824–5)

is redundant. The appropriation has already been made by the act of speaking it.

Richard's misfortune lies in being a king who has failed to realize that the logocentric idealization on which his power rests is no more than a fiction: indeed it is not clear that he ever arrives at that realization. This leaves him defenceless against those who are prepared to challenge the fiction of the primacy of voice with an alternative fiction based on the primacy of writing. Gaunt is the first to speak of this power when he laments that England 'leasde out . . . / Like to a tenement or pelting Farme / . . . is now bound in with shame, / With inckie blots, and rotten parchment bonds' (ll. 673–8). Writing as such is not identified specifically with Bullingbrooke, although it is his 'letters pattents' (l. 1194) that provide the justification for his return and other letters and warrants attend his progress; rather it is a force that Richard himself has unwisely tolerated and which, first in the form of the parchment bonds and later in that of the written agreement by the plotters against Bullingbrooke, is to bring about his ruin.

The deposition scene confounds the figurative basis of the authority of voice by showing that Richard's fiction is untenable even in its own terms. The problem is one encountered in even sharper form in a later play, Nathaniel Lee's *The tragedy of Nero*, where the emperor performs an act of autoapotheosis through a performative utterance:

> Great Julius and Augustus you adore;
> And why not me who have their very pow'r?
> To them you daily offer Sacrifice:
> I am a GOD; my self I Canonize.[47]

The problem here is that the authority assumed by the first part of the final line is not conferred until the second. (Descartes' 'cogito ergo sum', which may have helped suggest Lee's line, labours under the same difficulty.) In confuting its originary status even as it claims it, the line reveals what deconstruction would claim as the condition of all utterance, and which is certainly the case of all fictions of authority. Richard's position, however, is the reverse one: trapped within his fiction he must find a way of divesting himself of the authority of voice through the exercise of that authority. The process begins with a dismantling through voice of the subsidiary authority conferred by touch:

> Now, marke me how I will vndoe my selfe.
> I giue this heauie Weight from off my Head,

[47] I. ii. 24–7 in *The works of Nathaniel Lee*, ed. Thomas B. Stroup and Arthur L. Cooke (New Brunswick, NJ, 1954), i. 32.

And this vnwieldie Scepter from my Hand,
The pride of Kingly sway from out my Heart
With mine owne Teares I wash away my Balme,
With mine owne Hands I giue away my Crowne,
With mine owne Tongue denie my Sacred State,
With mine owne Breath release all dutious Oathes;
All Pompe and Maiestie I doe forsweare:
My Manors, Rents, Reuenues, I forgoe;
My Acts, Decrees, and Statutes I denie:
God pardon all Oathes that are broke to mee,
God keepe all Vowes vnbroke are made to thee. . . .
(ll. 2025–37)

Although the words are accompanied by gestures it is the words which give the gestures their performative status. The dismantling of that which cannot be dismantled, because to do so would destroy the power by which the act must be performed, leaves Richard with an identity crisis so severe that he asks for a mirror in order to reassure himself of his own existence—an existence which must now be reconstituted through sight not sound.

Northumberland, as advocate for a competing fiction by which authority is grounded in writing, now demands that Richard read a document specifying

These Accusations, and these grieuous Crymes,
Committed by your Person, and your followers,
Against the State, and Profit of this Land:
That by confessing them, the Soules of men
May deeme, that you are worthily depos'd. (ll. 2045–9)

The purpose of this is not simply to reassure those who are not present to hear Richard's speech-act, but to indicate that the authority of voice is now subservient to the authority of script. However, Richard indignantly refuses to read. Whether or not he can be regarded as having divested himself of the authority of voice, he has said or done nothing that indicates he rejects the primacy of voice over writing. All his abdication has achieved is to create a situation in which the authority predicated under that particular fiction is placed in limbo. Northumberland again presses his paper, arguing that the commons (sharers now in the allocation of power) will not be satisfied unless it is read, but is neatly evaded by Richard:

They shall be satisfy'd: Ile reade enough,
When I doe see the very Booke indeede,
Where all my sinnes are writ, and that's my selfe.
Giue me that Glasse, and therein will I reade. (ll. 2095–8)

Here Richard picks up the metaphor, more usually applied by Shakespeare to women, of the face as a paper written on by experience. However, the concession is only a brief one—moments later the mirror lies shattered, and Richard in effect rejects any other than a physical submission to Bullingbrooke, a decision that must now inevitably lead to the stopping of that breath that can not help but utter power.

The crucial point that emerges as Richard is led away to the tower is that, while he has been deposed, the fiction that all lawful authority emanates from the person of the sovereign remains intact (as it does, in an otiose sense, in Britain today). What has changed in the play is that it must now be perceived as a fiction rather than as a truth, a fact that neither Richard nor Bullingbrooke will ever be able to alter. Bullingbrooke's assumption of kingship as Henry IV is not accomplished by a performative utterance but by a simple statement of intention: 'In Gods name Ile ascend the regall throne' (l. 1936). He will reign as a king whose power has no originary basis—an *ironic* king whose rule (like that of Claudius in *Hamlet*) has to be reconstituted at every turn through negotiation. This is also to define him as a Machiavellian king, one who must constantly manufacture fictions fitted to compel the obedience of others without being permitted to have any belief in them himself. In a tetralogy of plays already written Shakespeare had chronicled the dire consequences this conception of the rhetoric of statecraft was to have for Henry's successors. The ideal, clearly, was one of a more prudent Richard II. His portrait of that king represented a powerful plea from the stage, an institution whose own rationale lay in the power to enforce belief in fictions uttered through voice, for a monarchy that would restore the same authority to the heart of politics. James I and Charles I were daringly but imperfectly, to oblige.

In the terms in which it has just been approached, Shakespeare's play casts a sharp analytic light on the fictions of authority that were used to confer legitimacy upon Stuart kingship. While it was Elizabeth who was heard to sigh 'I am Richard II', it was the personal rule of Charles I which in both its conduct and its conclusion offered the closest parallel to the events of the play. Charles's great innovation in the cultural poetics of kingship was his conferring a primacy on the royal voice over the written record which (despite Shakespeare) probably had no real parallel in previous English history—even the Conqueror had grounded his administration on a book. Charles's seizure in 1629 of the collections of state papers made by Sir Robert Cotton and John Stanesby and in 1635 of Coke's papers may be regarded as a kind of *coup d'état* against the authority of script.[48] Puritanism was as successful and as unsuccessful as Northumberland and Henry in reversing this priority: removing the man, it could never finally extirpate the fiction.

In contrast to Shakespeare's plea for a politics grounded in the authority of voice, Donne asserted the primacy of script. In matters of religion he certainly saw the authority of writing as the higher of the two. Winfried Schleiner sees this as arising from a conviction, shared with Augustine, that sight is 'so much the Noblest of all the senses, as that it is all the senses'.[49] He concludes that 'Although there are some impressive passages stressing the idea of the sacramental power of the word, Donne holds that God's first language addressed itself to the eye'.[50] In the course of a sermon preached in 1623 or 1624 he used an astonishing metaphor in which an originary 'writing' is presented as the master trope of spiritual obligation:

Beloved, the death of Christ is given to us, as a *Hand-writing*; for, when Christ naild that *Chirographum*, that first hand-writing, that had passed between the Devill and us, to his Crosse, he did not leave us out of debt, nor absolutely discharged, but he laid another *Chirographum* upon us, another Obligation arising out of his death. His death is delivered to us, as

[48] Stanesby had collected 'sundry manuscripts, journals, and other passages of Parliament, with divers other notes and papers of several natures to the number of about 300 quires of paper, together with some small printed books'. In November 1629 they were seized in his absence by Thomas Meautys one of the clerks of council. On petitioning the council in 1631 he was told 'that he should have none of his papers about the Parliament, as they intended to suppress such kinds of collections' (*HMC, 4th rep.*, p. 54a).

[49] *The sermons of John Donne*, ed. Evelyn M. Simpson and George R. Potter (Los Angeles, 1953–62), viii. 221.

[50] Winfried Schleiner, *The imagery of John Donne's sermons* (Providence, 1970), p. 153. With this should be contrasted the Puritan and anti-Laudian distrust of the visual.

a *writing*, but not a writing onely in the nature of a peece of *Evidence*, to plead our inheritance by, but a writing in the nature of a Copy, to learne by; It is not onely given us to reade, but to write over, and practise; Not onely to tell us *what he* did, but *how we* should do so too.[51]

Here the use of copying from a copy-book as a metaphor for religious duty parallels the ideal documented by Goldberg of the training of the hand as forming an induction into civil obedience. The companion metaphor of the fall and redemption as written contracts or mortgages is a logical extension of Coke's vision of the common law as the most ancient of all systems of power. In a reversal of the Derridean priority, chirocentrism replaces logocentrism, and speech, not writing, becomes the medium of *différance* in politics as well as theology. Remembering Donne's long connection with the law, first as a student at Lincoln's Inn, then as secretary to Lord Keeper Egerton, and latterly as divinity reader at Lincoln's Inn, it is hardly surprising that his God should have become a scrivener. But he is also a scribal publisher! Jeremiah, Donne goes on to tell us, 'when the hand of God had been upon him . . . published Gods hand-writing: not onely to his owne conscience, by acknowledging that all these afflictions were for his sins, but by acknowledging to the world, that God had laid such and such afflictions upon him'.[52] Scribal publication (Donne's own preferred medium for his verse) is here not simply a metaphor for the origin of power, but the model for how its demands are to be both internalized and externalized by the governed.

A different sense of lives lived under the constraint of writing is vividly conveyed by a play from the very end of the century, Congreve's *The way of the world*, whose action involves a complex attempt to contravene the effect of wills, deeds, entails and marriage settlements. Through one of these Lady Wishfort has gained control over part of Millamant's inheritance. Through another, Fainall thinks he has control of his wife's money. Through yet another, Mirabell possesses the whole of Mrs Fainall's estate in trust, thus negating Fainall's document. By Act v there is also a contract 'in Writing' between Mirabell and Millamant. Finally there is the bogus Sir Rowland's 'black box' which Lady

[51] *Sermons*, x. 196. I am grateful to Mark Allinson for drawing my attention to this remarkable passage.

[52] *Sermons*, x. 200.

Wishfort believes gives him the power to reduce Mirabell to poverty. Within the constraints imposed on action by the handwritten word, the rights of voice are fragile. Conversation must always be guarded—the celebrated verbal wit of the play is predominantly a mode of self-disguise.[53] Only in the famous proviso scene, in effect a spoken, extra-judicial addendum to the written marriage contract, is speech allowed to stand as a source of authority in its own right. The shrinking of the role of voice in private life reflects a sense of its wider decline in the nation in the reaction against Stuart logocentrism.

Neither *Richard II* nor *The way of the world* is concerned with the relative status of print and script within this process. For as long as print was seen as institutionally subordinate to both voice and script, its function could be relegated to that of conveying the decisions of authority to the governed. This was certainly the ideal the Stuart monarchs strove to impose through their close supervision of the printing and bookselling trades. But twice in the century the press became an agency of power in its own right. It did this not through acquiring a performative role within the accepted institutionalization of power (though we will see in Chapter 7 that it was in the process of doing this) but through its ability to promulgate new, subversive fictions with an irresistible force and rapidity. The first of these periods was 1641–9 and the second 1677–82, the fiction in each case being a variant on the old theme of anti-Popery.[54]

By the time Dryden came to write *Absalom and Achitophel*, defending Charles II against the second of these crises, he had seen the ingenious inventions of Titus Oates's printed *A true narrative of the horrid plot and conspiracy of the Popish party against the life of His Sacred Majesty* acquire a greater power over the minds of his countrymen than the utterance of a discredited king.[55] Oates's incredibly circumstantial accounts of imaginary papist intrigues bombarded its readers with a whole new construction of reality, richly metonymic and virtually unfalsifiable insofar as anyone

[53] The language of the play is considered from this point of view in my *Congreve* (Oxford, 1974), pp. 85–107. For a wider-ranging consideration of the transactional basis of Restoration wit, see D. R. M. Wilkinson, *The comedy of habit* (Leiden, 1964).

[54] Discussed in Peter Lake, 'Anti-popery: the structure of a prejudice' in *Conflict in early Stuart England*, ed. Richard Cust and Anne Hughes (London, 1989), pp. 72–106.

[55] (London, 1679). Dryden's poem appeared in 1682.

challenging the existence of the plot must *ipso facto* be one of the plotters.[56] Indeed, the study of literary realism in English might more profitably commence with the *Narrative* and its imitations than with *Robinson Crusoe*, which surely learned many techniques from it. Oates's fabrications are not in themselves fictions of authority since they do not aspire to a performative force: his title still accepts the sovereign's person as the source of legitimate power. But they do in a number of indirect ways withdraw credibility from voice and script in order to confer it on their own preferred medium of print. The world of Jesuit intrigue as Oates, William Bedloe and the tribe of informers present it is a world of whispers, covert meetings, overheard conversations and secretly transmitted letters and commissions, all directed towards a horrific overthrow of social order. With voice and script branded as the media of concealment and dissimulation, the witnesses can be credited with the heroic, Promethean act of having transferred this concealed information into print where it was available to all and could be properly assessed. This done, the innate power of print-logic could be exploited along the lines suggested by Ong and Kernan. The well-financed managers of their campaign made sure that their various narratives were given to the public in handsome, physically ample folios with engraved portraits and parliamentary imprimaturs. In this way they were able to appeal directly to the power of the printed page to confer objectivity and impersonality upon the texts it presented and to repress any aspiration to dialogue on the part of the reader, releasing language from the grounding in presence which still attended script and voice. The visual suggestiveness of the printed page was able to achieve a tacit displacement of the phonocentric ideal of authority even while the printed text continued to give it lip service.

Dryden in *Absalom and Achitophel* undertook the task of reasserting the validity of the phonocentric ideal under circumstances that were less than ideal. His presentation of Charles as a divine-right monarch at the close of the poem was one way of doing this:

> Thus from his Royal Throne by Heav'n inspir'd,
> The God-like *David* spoke: with awfull fear

[56] Cf. *Absalom and Achitophel*, ll. 664–71.

His Train their Maker in their Master hear. (ll. 936–8; *Works*, ii. 33)

Here and in the speech that follows, the grand originary fiction of the royal utterance as an emanation of the logos was being revived with something like its former force for the last time in English history. Metaphor had, for the moment, triumphed over metonymy. But this revival was by now beyond the power of kings to secure for themselves; instead, crucially, it demanded the services of skilled wordsmiths, working in the medium of print. The service that Oates had performed for the Whigs, Dryden now had to perform for the Tories. The responsibility for sustaining fictions of authority had been passed to the professional makers of fictions, a fact that was soon to lead to a vast increase in their remuneration.

What both Shakespeare and Dryden were eventually led to was a view of power very different from Donne's or Foucault's, or that implied by Goldberg's interpretation of the politics of the hand. For them power was neither autonomous nor originary but something immediate and provisional that required to be recreated at every turn through the arts of language. Wise kings—Henry IV, Claudius and Charles II—were always conscious of this fact: foolish ones—Richard II and Charles I—forgot it. Strangely, though, the foolish kings are also the flamboyant performers—royal actors who press the fictive authority of utterance to its extreme, and nowhere more dazzlingly than in the loss of power. But, fatally for themselves, they are actors who have forgotten that legitimacy has no reality beyond their own projection of an originary fiction.

CONCLUSION

What has been said so far in this chapter will have suggested a number of roles for the handwritten text in the exercise of power so defined, and it is now time to summarize the consequence of these for our understanding of scribal publication. The first role was an executive one exercised through warrants, memos and official letters. This was generally little more than a means to allow the prerogative of voice to operate at a distance, and it was, in any case, rare for such documents to enter wider channels of scribal publication. They are to be regarded as bearers of power only by delegation, whether from voice or from other writings.

A second and much more important role was as written contract and legal record—the body of statutes, deeds, charters and written precedents that set the limiting conditions for the actions of both king and parliament. The Stuart monarchs, aided by compliant judges, did their best to push back these limits; but for a sovereign to override, say, the written law of inheritance would be to undermine the very legitimacy of the crown—a Cokean point that Dryden was careful to stress in *Absalom and Achitophel* (ll. 777–80). From the subject's point of view the defence of ancient rights (especially during the 1620s and 1670s) was most effectively pursued by the searching out of ancient documents which purported to guarantee these rights. The circulation of these older records and their supplementation with current ones (e.g. legal judgements and parliamentary proceedings) provided a significant proportion of scribally published texts throughout the century. It is through these that the scribal medium was most valuably a conduit of power.

The role of the scribally published satire or treatise in its relationship to the exercise of power was usually either the illocutionary one of raising issues which would eventually be debated vocally at the heart of the decision-making process or that of reporting back on the functioning of that process. Where this kind of scribally published text comes closest to possessing a perlocutionary function which is not delegated by print or voice is in the essay or poem addressed directly and personally to a powerful individual. Marvell's 'A Horatian ode upon Cromwell's return from Ireland' is interesting here because of the uncanny accuracy with which it foreshadowed policies which for the historical Cromwell still lay some way in the future.[57] A good deal of this writing (in verse as well as prose) filled a function similar to that of a report or position paper circulating in a modern government department—that is as a means of formulating policies for the consideration of the decision-makers. The writers might well themselves be civil servants, either in form, like Sir Robert Cotton, or on a salaried basis, as in the cases of Marvell and

[57] Cuthbert, 'A re-examination of Andrew Marvell', pp. 172–255.

Dryden. In other cases, the perspective is closer to that of the modern journalist advising and criticizing from outside the political system, but often being able to modify and at times to initiate policies. The chief difference between the seventeenth century and ourselves in this respect was that there was nothing corresponding to our sharp professional divide between the executive, the civil service and the press. A wealthy gentleman, like Cotton, attending regularly at court, could be called on for written advice by both the king and leading nobles without ever holding a formal position in the apparatus of state. In the same way a squire who was not a regular attender at court, like Sir Robert Filmer, could circulate political advice in the form of scribally published essays with a fair hope of it reaching the oral decision-makers.

The last and in some ways most fascinating function of the scribal text was that represented by the sceptical philosophizing of Rochester and the pornopolitics of the lampoon. The function of much oppositional satire, both before and after the Civil War, was explicitly that of neutralizing or evacuating the dominant fictions of state without any serious intention of replacing them with new fictions. Rochester's position—worked out in some detail in his adaptation of Fletcher's *Valentinian*—was that while a literal belief in fictions of authority was necessary for the governed it was a severe impediment to governors. Valentinian was hardly to be condemned (by the standards of the 1670s) for his frank summing up of the noble, patriotic Aecius:

> The honesty of this Æcius
> Who is indeed ye Bullworke of my Empire
> Is to bee cherish't for ye good it brings
> Not vallu'd as a merit in the owner
> As Princes are Slaves bound up by Gratitude
> And duty has noe claime beyond acknowledgement
> Which I'le pay Æcius whome I still have found
> Dull, faithfull, humble, Violent, & Brave,
> Talents as I could wish 'em for my Slave

but errs fatally when he treats his own divinity as if it has a factual rather than a fictive basis:

> Did not my Will ye Worlds most sacred Law
> Doome thee to dye

And darest thou in Rebellion bee a live
Is death more frightfull grown then disobedience[58]

The presentation of Charles II as a priapic buffoon in Rochester's 'In the isle of Great Britain' and the darker deconstruction of the mysteries of state in the closing stanzas of 'Upon nothing' are variations on the same theme. The important thing, after the disaster of 1649, was that kings and their ministers should never be allowed to place any excessive trust in the power promised by legitimating fictions. The volumes of the lampooners were mirrors in which rulers could read the truth that their authority, however constituted, rested on ingeniously figured lies, and then, if they wished, break the glass.

The other major function of the scribally transmitted text was that of providing physical and ideological definition for class and interest groups within the state. As this requires a different conceptual approach it will be considered a separate chapter.

[58] BL MS Add. 28,692, ff. 14^{r-v}, 64^{r}. Only the first couplet of the first passage is by Fletcher.

5

THE SOCIAL USES OF THE SCRIBALLY PUBLISHED TEXT

HAVING investigated the position of the handwritten text within the cultural symbologies of the time, I would now like to transfer attention to its societal functions. At a very simple level it was one of several means of acquiring and transmitting information, to be chosen in preference to other media according to the audience addressed but also because this was usually privileged information, not meant to be available to all enquirers. A second function which was of great importance was that of bonding groups of like-minded individuals into a community, sect or political faction, with the exchange of texts in manuscript serving to nourish a shared set of values and to enrich personal allegiances. (A modern counterpart would be a group of researchers exchanging results and draft papers by electronic mail.) However, the function with which I would like to begin is that of scribal publication as a means by which ideologically charged texts could be distributed through the governing class, or various interest-groups within that class, without their coming to the knowledge of the governed. Clearly this falls far short of accounting for all occasions on which texts were published scribally; but it does provide our best explanation for the vigour of the institution and the care taken to maintain it even when its existence posed a threat to entrenched interests.

The positing of a distinct 'governing class' is something of a simplification, though one that has precedent in the usage of historians. For our present purpose this class is to be seen as constituting the court and its officials, the aristocracy with their families and clients, the gentry, merchants concerned in the financing of state enterprises, and the upper hierarchical levels of the law, medicine, the church, the army and the navy. To these we should add young aspirants to such positions, which would include university and Inns-of-Court students. Apart from peers and, from 1611, baronets, whose status descended by inheritance, membership of the class was still relatively fluid: the acquisition of land would secure admittance, at least to the lower levels, while the loss of it soon led to exclusion.[1] Yet, while there might well be debate over marginal cases, there was a clear sense in the minds of such contemporaries as Gregory King and Edward Chamberlayne that there was such a class and that its members could be numbered.[2] Stuart monarchs, militarily and administratively weaker than their continental counterparts, were forced to rule through a mixture of bluff and negotiation, which meant that their relations with the governing class, or factions within it, were often conducted as a process of dialogue in which the scribally published text played a very significant role.

The internal structure of the governing class was sustained by two forms of exclusion, one operating vertically and the other horizontally. The vertical form was that of social subordination manifest through elaborate codes of deference and the practice of claiming or yielding precedence in a wide range of everyday encounters. Even so simple a matter as walking along a narrow street, taking one's place at a dinner table or going into church would involve continual decisions about whether to domineer or defer. Individuals soon acquired a very sharp sense of their own place and that of others in a hierarchically ordered society, and, while they might compete fiercely for precedence within their own stratum of the hierarchy, would do so out of a belief in the inherent value of precedence as a principle of social organization. The Civil Wars brought only a partial and temporary relaxation of this attitude. The horizontal exclusion was that set up by allegiances claimed and given within specific chains of lordship or patronage which in some cases were still of a recognizably feudal

[1] Cf. J. P. Kenyon, *Stuart England*, 2nd edn (Harmondsworth, 1985), pp. 23–7; Peter Laslett, *The world we have lost: further explored* (London, 1983), pp. 238–45.

[2] See Gregory King, *Natural and political observations and conclusions upon the state and condition of England* (London, 1696) and the tabular analysis of his estimates in Laslett, *The world we have lost*, pp. 30–4. Chamberlayne's more particularized account of administrative and social hierarchies can be found in the annual editions of his *Angliae notitiae, or the present state of England* (from 1669).

nature, and which only gradually began to be subsumed under the wider allegiances of party. Such relationships replicated hierarchy within their own vertical structure but distinguished between individuals of similar status by reference to their allegiances upward and downward.

The paths taken by the scribally transmitted text from reader to reader were affected by both kinds of exclusion. In relationships of patronage and dependence, the client would present manuscripts upwards, either as a bid for reward or an expression of gratitude, and would dutifully copy texts transmitted downwards, especially if they were composed or approved of by the patron. The Donne Dalhousie manuscripts illustrate the first of these processes, consisting of texts presented to the Essex family by a variety of writers who sought or enjoyed their patronage; John Watson's transcriptions of writings by Sir Henry North the second process.[3] Exchanges of texts between individuals who belonged to the same stratum of the hierarchy were likely to be an extension of other kinds of mutual sociability. Matthew Locke's widely copied 'Consort of two parts for several friends' exemplifies this relationship among near equals, the title indicating its status as a gift rather than a plea for patronage.[4] However, circulation might follow oblique or erratic paths arising out of shared enthusiasms (antiquarianism, viol-playing, astrology, sedition). An outbreak of oblique transmission might be an indication that long-accepted exclusions were under strain, pointing to stratigraphical stress within the system. Certainly, the impetus to initiate an exchange of texts within a community (or to create a new community out of the exchange of texts) would frequently have a motive that was either reformist or reactionary. A perception of crisis might lead to the near-simultaneous birth of opposed groups, like the Whig and Yorkist circles of scribally publishing poets of the late 1670s.

By its nature scribal publication could hardly proceed at random. Instead, since it usually rested on a personal agreement between the supplier of the text and the copyist, or copyist and recipient, there was a strong tendency for patterns of transmission

[3] Sullivan, *Dalhousie manuscripts*, pp. 4–7; BL Add. MS 18220, ff. 9^{r}, 13^{r}, 24^{r}–25^{r}, 25^{v}–26^{v}, 43^{r}–44^{r}, 63^{v}–64^{r}, 68^{r}–69^{v}.

[4] For the sources, and hints at the identities of some of the friends, see Robert Thompson, 'The sources of Locke's consort "For seaverall friends"', *Chelys* 19 (1990), 16–43.

to coincide with pre-existing communities—the court, the diocese, the college, the county, the circle of friends (*vide* John Chamberlain), neighbours or colleagues, the extended family, the sect or faction. For groups such as these, bonded by the exchange of manuscripts, the term 'scribal community' is proposed. The notion of such a community is illustrated by two papers written in the 1940s by Peter Laslett, in which he argues that the gentry of Kent prior to the Civil War constituted an entity of this kind, regularly composing and circulating handwritten treatises on matters of urgent concern to themselves as a group.[5] A circle of the same period, centred in the midlands, which supported the antiquarian research of William Dugdale, is described by David Douglas and Philip Styles.[6] J. S. Morrill characterizes the Cheshire squire, William Davenport, as 'one of a reading circle who received [scribal] pamphlets and then passed them on'.[7] In these cases, and no doubt others, the scribal community coincided with what historians describe as the 'county community', although not all county communities would have been scribal communities in our sense.[8] Craig Monson's *Voices and viols in England, 1600–1650: the sources and the music* adopts a wider geographical perspective, tracing the regional workings of a tradition that was heavily dependent on scribal publication. Other active and substantial communities are described in Kevin Sharpe's account of the circle of political antiquaries centred on the Cottonian library in the reigns of James I and Charles I, and G. H. Turnbull's group biography of the mid-century Hartlib circle.[9] Author and user

[5] Peter Laslett, 'The gentry of Kent in 1640', *Cambridge historical journal* 9 (1947–9), 148–64, and 'Sir Robert Filmer: the man versus the Whig myth', 523–46. In the first of these papers (p. 149) and again in *The world we have lost*, p. 226, he goes as far as to characterize the Kent gentry of the time as a 'dispersed university'.

[6] Douglas, *English scholars*, pp. 31–2; Styles, *Sir Simon Archer*, pp. 27–30.

[7] 'William Davenport and the 'silent majority' of early Stuart England', *Journal of the Chester Archaeological Society* 18 (1975), 121.

[8] For county communities, see in particular Alan Everitt, *The local community and the Great Rebellion* (London, 1969) and *The community of Kent and the Great Rebellion 1640–60* (Leicester, 1966); Clive Holmes, 'The county community in Stuart historiography', *Journal of British studies* 19 (1980), 54–73; and Laslett, *The world we have lost*, pp. 223–8. Historians are divided over how far the example of Kent can be extrapolated to other counties.

[9] Sharpe, *Sir Robert Cotton* (see pp. 83–9 above); Turnbull, *Hartlib, Dury and Comenius*. The Great Tew circle of Lucius Cary, second Viscount Falkland read early work by Hobbes in manuscript and preserved Falkland's own *Discourse on the infallibility of the church*. There is a sympathetic account of the circle and its influence in Hugh Trevor-Roper, *Catholics, Anglicans and Puritans* (London, 1987), p. 174.

publication, in such cases, was often a mode of social bonding whose aim was to nourish and articulate a corporate ideology.

Testimony to this sense of the scribally circulated text as a group possession is given by the changes that will often be made to the contents of collections when they pass through user copying from their original communities into new ones. An exemplary demonstration is given by Mary Hobbs in her study of the anthologies copied by Christ Church scribes for Henry King as author publisher, though also including work by other poets he admired. These were first recopied in other Oxford colleges, representing distinct but closely related scribal communities. They then passed into circulation in London among two very different communities—the Inns of Court and the musicians (who plundered them for song texts). Their passage from community to community was marked by deletions and interpolations to suit the tastes of their new readerships. Thus, the parallel Oxford collections, while repeating most of the Christ Church material, also contain 'turgid elegies on men of other colleges'.[10]

The findings of these scholars point to the advances in our understanding of scribal publication that would accrue from further systematic study of individual communities, such as is currently being undertaken at the University of Sheffield for the Hartlib group. This approach would be particularly illuminating for the four Inns of Court—Gray's Inn, Lincoln's Inn and the Inner and Middle Temple—each of which had its own intellectual traditions, and which, with their unlimited access to legal copyists, were among the most important centres for the circulation of literary and political separates.[11] Laslett's papers, although light on detail, present a plausible picture of the scribal community as a cultural agency, besides explaining why manuscript treatises of a certain kind should have begun to circulate among the gentry of a particular county in the 1620s. Hobbs's and Monson's work complements this by demonstrating how individual collections of texts can be analysed as communal constructs. Sharpe's study of the

[10] Hobbs, 'Stoughton manuscript', p. 155.

[11] A start to this has been made by Marotti, *John Donne* (Lincoln's Inn); Philip J. Finkelpearl, *John Marston of the Middle Temple: an Elizabethan dramatist in his social setting* (Cambridge, Mass., 1969), and Sandra A. Burner, *James Shirley: a study of literary coteries and patronage in seventeenth-century England* (Lanham, 1988), pp. 41–84 (Gray's Inn); however, the concerns of all three remain rather narrowly literary.

Cotton circle shows how a community could coalesce around a single active individual, but one who himself was formed by an earlier community—Camden's society of antiquaries. The instances of Hartlib and later Henry Oldenburg illustrate how a newcomer with no such advantages could become the hub of an active scribal community through diligent performance of a secretarial role in sustaining the circulation of correspondence and manuscript treatises. Oldenburg's function became institutionalized and partially conveyed into the print medium with the foundation in 1662 of the Royal Society, but Hartlib's primary affiliation remained with the scribally orientated world of reserved knowledge. Illuminating with regard to the tendency of scribal reading circles to seek a closer corporate identity is a formal agreement signed in 1642 by John Dury, Comenius, Hartlib and William Hamilton to govern the conduct of their joint research.[12]

Print could also be used to define communities, and we will need to consider how these differed from scribal communities. Lois Potter has shown how Cavalier writers of the interregnum developed a subtle set of interpretative codes which allowed the public text to be read in a factional way, the community as such being defined by its awareness of and willingness to impose those codes.[13] From subsequent decades, we might consider the role the press played for clergy ejected from their livings under the Commonwealth or the 1662 Act of Uniformity or for refusal to take the oaths of allegiance to William and Mary. Denied the pulpit, some turned to the printed tract as a substitute for the spoken sermon, circulating copies gratis to those who could not afford to pay for them, and using the presentation of specially bound copies to wealthy sympathizers as a form of fund raising.[14] For non-jurors the writing and presentation of substantial works of antiquarian scholarship seems to have served a similar function.[15]

[12] Turnbull, pp. 459–60.

[13] Lois Potter, *Secret rites and secret writing: royalist literature, 1641–1660* (Cambridge, 1989). For a more theoretical consideration of the stylistics of indirection, see Annabel Patterson, *Censorship and interpretation: the conditions of writing and reading in early modern England* (Madison, Wis., 1984).

[14] This was particularly so of the 1662 ejectees. One well-documented case, that of Oliver Heywood, is discussed in Love, 'Preacher and publisher'.

[15] The careers of George Hickes and Thomas Hearne both suggest this pattern, the difference being that Hickes concentrated on a single large work, his *Linguarum veterum septentrionalium thesaurus* (London, 1703–5), whereas Hearne issued a long succession of

In all these cases we can speak of printed texts as giving rise to 'communities of the book'. The advent of the subscription list late in the century made these communities publicly visible while strengthening the political dimension of book purchase. In an age when the bookseller was also the publisher, the clientele of a particular shop might form a community in its own right, cemented by common tastes and regular meetings at the source of supply. Beyond this, much knowledge about and possession of printed texts would pass by a series of personal transactions among individuals and families: it was only those key texts whose aim was the defence or overthrow of the political *status quo*, and for which every effort was made to ensure indiscriminate circulation, that could be regarded as wholly transcending any particular pre-existing community of sympathizers.

Yet there remain significant differences between the kinds of community formed by the exchange of manuscripts and those formed around identification with the printed text. The most important is that the printed text, being available as an article of commerce, had no easy way of excluding readers. Inherent in the choice of scribal publication—including the more reserved forms of entrepreneurial publication—was the idea that the power to be gained from the text was dependent on possession of it being denied to others. Thus the quadripartite contract of 1642 between Hartlib, Comenius, Dury and Hamilton contained a confidentiality clause concerning the divulging of their productions.[16] The political aspect of this exclusion is laid bare in the introductory epistle to the printed text of *Arcana aulica* (London, 1652), one of a number of English adaptations of Eustace du Refuge's *Traité de la cour*:

It is some years since I first met with it in a Manuscript, and in a Foraign Language . . . I have since that time found it published in *Latine*, but still as nameless as at our first acquaintance. The divulging of it, seriously, I did

editions of medieval chronicles. In each case, the help given to their research by their many supporters (which in Hickes's case included physical concealment) had a strong political colouring.

[16] 'Visum autem est, et datâ fide spondemus, pacta haec foederis nostri . . . non vulgare ad alios, nisi communi consensu: atque id iis solis, quos ejusdem foederis socios fore idoneos confidamus: . . . Nisi forsan et Patronis ac promotoribus, quos suscitabit Deus, eadem haec patere opus videatur, ad intentionis nostrae integritatem demonstrandam' (Turnbull, p. 460).

much lament, and that for a twofold Reason; One was, to see it come abroad so lamely, and so much injured; another was, to finde it divulged at all: For surely, it is a Tract not intended for the unskilful palate of the vulgar. . . . [17]

Du Refuge's exposé of court skulduggery might encourage 'unskilful' readers to imitate what they should abhor; but even abhorring had its dangers when respect for the English court (whether Stuart or Cromwellian) might be threatened. The extreme case of scribally withheld knowledge was the vast individual databases assembled by men such as Simonds D'Ewes, Daniel Fleming, Pepys, Petyt, Newton and Roger North. Print publication implied the opposed view of a community being formed by the public sharing of knowledge. In this sense the printed text was as likely to be directed at the fracturing of existing communities as the formation of new ones. Its function was Promethean: knowledge exposed in print was knowledge which was no longer reserved for the advantage of the few but retailed for the use of the many. Titus Oates in revealing the imaginary secrets communicated in clandestine meetings and covert manuscripts by largely imaginary Jesuits was specifically claiming this heroic status. Print-based communities were characterized by an openness and flexibility that contrasted with the coherence and inward-turned autonomy of the scribal reading circle. However, in rejecting that autonomy, they also sacrificed the ability to distribute kinds of knowledge of which the state did not approve. The printed text was, with a few high-risk exceptions, a censored and controlled text; the scribal text, a free one.

CENSORSHIP AND THE SCRIBAL TEXT

From the notion of scribal publication as a vehicle for ideological debate within the governing class, we would expect to find it at its greatest vigour in the periods preceding the outbreak of national crises rather than during the actual crisis itself. Once the extremity of the situation had become generally acknowledged, the press should logically become the preferred medium for debate as

[17] *Arcana aulica: or Walsingham's manual of prudential maxims for the states-man and the courtier* (London, 1652), pp. A5^r–A5^v; discussed in W. Lee Ustick, 'The courtier and the bookseller: some vagaries of seventeenth-century publishing', *RES* 5 (1929), 143–4.

struggling factions looked outside their own class for support and the underclasses took advantage of slackening control. The truth of this hypothesis cannot be tested quantitatively since only the level of print production, and not that of scribal publication, is amenable to accurate measurement; but it is clear enough that the choice of scribal over print publication was often made through a desire to evade censorship, whether it was imposed by the state or was a self-censorship accepted by writers who did not wish to compromise the façade of governing-class solidarity.[18]

It was thus the case that many who would dearly have preferred to have their works appear in print were forced to choose scribal publication by default. Unable to provide a printed text of the Kentish Petition of 1644, George Thomason obtained a separate for his collection, annotating it 'All wch was Receivd wth much thoughtfulness; but m^r^ Rushworth durst not license it to print'. Aware of the dangers of print, governments of all complexions did their best, when it lay within their power, to control it, the goal of this control, as spelled out in a Star Chamber edict of 1637, being that a printed book should contain nothing 'that is contrary to Christian Faith, and the Doctrine and Discipline of the Church of *England*, nor against the State or Gouerment, nor contrary to good life, or good manners, or otherwise, as the nature and subiect of the work shall require'.[19] There was already a natural tendency for scribally published texts to be oppositional, since, where a text supported the position of those who controlled the apparatus of suppression, there would not only be no barrier to its print publication but probably great benefit to be gained from a public declaration of the writer's allegiances. Oppositional texts would find their way to the press in periods when censorship was weak but withhold themselves when it was strong or particularly unsympathetic to the writer's point of view. The history of the print publication of parliamentary proceedings is one example of this: in periods of relative harmony between the crown and parliament both sides were content to accept the traditional

[18] Patterson, *Censorship and interpretation*, p. 7, describes such self-censorship as 'a joint project, a cultural bargain between writers and political leaders'. However, the bargain was one that only applied to print.

[19] *A decree of Starre-chamber, concerning printing, made the eleventh day of July last past* (London, 1637), C1^r^–C1^v^.

convention against it; but in times of crisis—notably the 1640s and the early 1680s—parliament waived the rule so its own case could be put to the people. The 1680 vote on this issue was justified publicly as being 'for the benefit of the clerks who supply the whole kingdom with news', confirming the existence of an established system of scribal publication of political information.[20]

One example of a text neatly suspended between the media is Francis Osborne's *Advice to a son*, a deeply disillusioned piece of 'courtesy' literature which could probably only have made its way to the press under the relatively unconstrained circumstances that prevailed towards the end of the interregnum. Its marginal status is confirmed by the fact that, after its first part had appeared in print without hindrance in 1656, the work was twice the subject of attempts at suppression, firstly in 1658 by the Vice Chancellor of Oxford and again in 1676 by the House of Lords. The second section of the *Advice*, 'Love and marriage', which is described as '*a result of more juvenile yeares*' and only included because the author feared '*if let alone, it might hereafter creepe abroad from under a false impression, and one more scandalous to that sexe, than becomes my Complexion or Obligation*', would seem to be a revision of a scribally published forerunner, though I know of no surviving manuscript.[21] There can be no doubt that Osborne's decision to print the book in 1656 was a deliberate one, if possibly opportunistic. But both the genre and the ruthless realism of his paternal advice link it with scribal tradition: it is difficult to think of it as a work conceived from the start for print publication. The *Advice* may be taken as representing a limiting case of what was legally publishable while the press remained controlled, and of preserving, even when circulated in print, much of the character of a subversive kind of wisdom literature which was usually reserved for manuscript. Halifax, Osborne's most distinguished successor in this genre, never intended the *Advice to a daughter* for the press and did his best to prevent the unauthorized edition of 1688.[22]

Censorship was at its most effective during the periods of unchallenged Stuart rule. In the reigns of James I and Charles I, it

[20] *HMC, 12th rep., app., vii*, p. 173.

[21] Francis Osborne, *Advice to a son: or directions for your better conduct* (Oxford, 1656), p. 46. For a sympathetic account of the book, see Wilkinson, *The comedy of habit*, pp. 26–43.

[22] *Works of George Savile*, ed. Brown, iii. 355, 357n.

was exercised in the first instance through the Stationers' Company, which had a responsibility under its charter for preventing the publication of offensive writings. In addition, books touching on matters of faith were supposed to be submitted to ecclesiastical licensers.[23] The method of censorship was reviewed in 1643, when parliament replaced the old ecclesiastical licensing arrangement with a new one under which all works intended for the press had to be approved by licensers appointed by itself—the system attacked by Milton in *Areopagitica.* This initiative did not have its intended effect, and soon ceased to be observed with any strictness. Under the Licensing Act of 1662, Charles II provided for a full-time official licenser with powers of investigation and seizure, a post filled with great energy by Roger L'Estrange; however, the act was allowed to lapse from 27 May 1679 to 24 June 1685 and finally dropped for good in 1695.[24] The practical effectiveness of these official attempts at control over the press varied greatly. The Civil War and the Exclusion crisis saw them flouted with impunity by writers of all political persuasions and came closer than any other period to a modern conception of open public debate.

It should be noted that even the existence of Draconian punishments for involvement in the print-publishing of heterodox or treasonable books was not sufficient to prevent the production of dissident texts, either by courageous, ideologically committed printers and booksellers or for under-the-counter sale at a high mark-up by the trade at large. In both cases, the effectiveness of whatever controls were in place at any time depended on the co-operation in enforcing them of the Stationers' Company. This was always a questionable matter since the stationers felt a conflict of interest between the need to appease the government (which protected them from competition and secured the market in copyrights) and the temptation to profit from the strong demand for dissident religious and political texts. During much of the reign of Charles II the printing of banned Nonconformist tracts was organized by a ring of powerful booksellers within the Company

[23] There is a convenient account of the workings of this system in W. W. Greg, *Licensers for the press, &c. to 1640* (Oxford, 1962), pp. 1–4.

[24] For a fuller account of this intricate matter, see F. S. Siebert, *Freedom of the press in England, 1476–1776* (Urbana, Ill., 1965).

whose position protected them from action by their fellows and usually from the exasperated L'Estrange. Licensed printers were blackmailed into working on such texts by the threat of losing their regular work for the booksellers concerned and interlopers shielded from suppression for as long as they co-operated in the plans of the company.[25] Another tactic was for the company to seize sheets printed by unlicensed printers and then assign them to favoured stationers for surreptitious sale.

Once a book had appeared in print, either legally or illegally, powerful means of suppression were available. Punishments of great ferocity were inflicted on authors, printers and booksellers under the laws against treason, libel and *scandalum magnatum* (the libelling of peers), and seizures could be organized in sufficiently disciplined communities. The discovery in 1622 that a standard work of Biblical explication, David Pareus's *In divinam ad Romanos Sancti Pauli epistolam commentarius* (Heidelberg, 1613), gave support to the proposition that 'subordinate magistrates may rise against their Prince if he interfere with religion' led to extraordinary scenes at the universities in which 'every schollar [was] sent for into ye Publick Hall, & ye Keys of theyre studyes demand^{d} & theyre studyes search't while they stayd there'.[26] This was followed by epistles from Cambridge declaring 'the books of Dr. Pareus Bucanus condemned to eternal infamy, and forbidden to be read' and from Oxford 'not doubting that all contagion of his doctrine is purged from the University'. All this served as a magnificent advertisement for the book: within days of a solemn burning at Paul's Cross an Oxford student was warning a correspondent: 'Pareus' book must be sent safely wrapped up for fear of discovery.'[27] In another case, discussed by Patterson, the suppression of a printed preface led immediately to its circulation in manuscript.[28]

All this meant that oppositional texts were frequently circulated

[25] The workings of this trade are discussed in John Hetet, 'A literary underground in Restoration England: printers and dissenters in the context of constraints, 1660–1689', Cambridge University Ph.D. thesis, 1987.

[26] *CSP (Dom.) 1619–23*, p. 396; Bodleian MS Wood D 18, 45^{v}.

[27] *CSP (Dom.) 1619–23*, pp. 426, 421. The particular sensitivity felt about this text arose from the fact that James I was even then engaged in supporting a rising by the Protestants of France against their lawful prince, Louis XIII.

[28] *Censorship and interpretation*, p. 44.

scribally only for lack of opportunity to appear in print. The question here is, once again, whether the manner and content of the work may still have been conditioned by this, albeit involuntary, choice of medium. There are many suggestions that it was. The author torn between the possibilities of script and print publication, but having decided in the end on one medium, would then have to accept the decorum and the genres appropriate to it. The ruling decorum of print was essentially that which governed the public utterances of gentlemen. A certain level of formality was expected; and while opinions could be expressed with brutal vigour they would appear in the dress suitable to the hierarchical status of the author, who would refrain from language that would cause him to lose caste in the eyes of his social inferiors. Scribal publication, since it would not normally come to the eyes of these inferiors and was in most cases anonymous, offered much more latitude. Indeed, the fact that texts so circulated were expected to be oppositional, and that the liberty was available, whether or not accepted, of using language of a frankness and familiarity that would not have been appropriate in print, encouraged the presence of these features even when they were not required. It must have been hard for the writer of a lampoon intended for scribal circulation not to be obscene and not to traduce the great—this was, after all, what readers expected of such texts. A rhetorically aware writer might even feel an aesthetic obligation arising from the doctrine of the three styles to adopt the language of the brothel in such compositions.

One kind of evidence for this is the many cases of scribally circulated texts tidied up and bowdlerized for later appearances in print; a better one might be the conversion downwards for manuscript circulation of a text originally presented in print—though I know of no actual example. However, the shortened text of Marvell's 'To his coy mistress' found in the miscellany of his parliamentary colleague Sir William Haward could conceivably represent a related process by which a poem written for scribal circulation in more refined times was reworked by its author to suit the coarser tastes of the Restoration court.[29] One is also tempted to enlist the malicious scribal circulation in 1603 of a

[29] Bodleian MS Don. b 8, pp. 283–4; facsimile in Kelliher, *Andrew Marvell*, p. 53.

speech by an atheist from the printed play, *The first part of the tragicall raigne of Selimus* (London, 1594) under the title 'Certaine hellish verses devysed by that Atheist and traitor Ralegh'.[30] Here the words remained more or less unchanged but the new title and medium gave them a much more subversive significance.

This sense of the scribally published text as intrinsically prone to be oppositional has important implications for any assessment of its role in national politics. While the needs of individual scribal communities would partly have been satisfied from within those communities and by material filtering osmotically from intersecting networks, it is also easy to demonstrate a supplementary process, particularly evident in the cases of parliamentary news and accounts of court scandal, of radial distribution from London. Any consideration of the spread of anti-court attitudes in the decades prior to both the Civil War and the Exclusion crisis must concern itself with the constant stream of political separates dispatched by the newsletter writers of the metropolis to such readers as William Davenport, which then entered local reading networks. While this activity was not an organized one in the sense the term can be used of the trade in printed books, it was still the work of an identifiable group of professionals who, whatever their individual political views or desire to conform to those of their customers, would have understood that court scandal was the hottest and most saleable form of news. But the possibility can not be dismissed that the writers collectively did tend towards an anti-court position. Nathaniel Thompson, writing in 1683, was in no doubt that 'the generality of News-writers about Town are Factious', a judgement endorsed by Peter Fraser.[31] The reason is simple enough: a court sympathizer would not be likely to become involved professionally in the circulation of information which the court desired should remain concealed.

J. S. Morrill, having noted that the material copied out by Davenport between 1613 and 1650 'was (until 1641) consistently anti-government and particularly anti-Court', then wants to

[30] Text in Jean Jacquot, 'Ralegh's 'Hellish verses' and the 'Tragicall raigne of Selimus'', *MLR* 48 (1953), 1–9. For another widely circulated piece of scribally published Raleighana of the same year, see Franklin B. Williams, jun., 'Thomas Rogers on Raleigh's atheism', *N&Q* 213 (1968), 368–70. This was, of course, the year of Raleigh's conviction for treason.

[31] *Loyal protestant and true domestic intelligencer*, no. 239, 1 March 1682/3, p. 2; Fraser, *Intelligence of the secretaries of state*, pp. 127–32.

conclude that 'the selection of these particular types of material rather than others . . . reveals something of his political views'.[32] Yet as far as Davenport's political *actions* were concerned, he seems to have been a man without strong views, inclining if anything to a moderate royalism. One is moved in this case to ask whether there really had been any process of selection at work, or whether Davenport was simply accepting what was brought to him by a medium which was inherently adversarial to authority but which he could not ignore because it was the only source available to him for certain valuable kinds of information. Certainly we can make no judgements concerning the extent of selectivity when we have no information about the range of options from which the selection was made. If we had that information it might well appear that the medium was very much part of the message and that the message of the London scribal journalists and traders in separates was a 'country' one. Moreover, exposure to such material can hardly have failed to have a radicalizing effect when there was no way of testing such confident assertions as Eglisham's that Buckingham had poisoned James I.

While censorship was an important factor in the continuing vitality of scribal publication, it should not be forgotten that, because of the 'stigma of print' or a level of demand that would never have justified printing, many scribally published texts would not have reached the press at any period. Many others—as we have seen—were designed from the start for circulation within a particular circle or coterie within the governing class and drew their political character from this fact. Their power and influence would be in inverse proportion to the extent of their circulation. These factors confirm that a healthy tradition of scribal publication would have existed even had there been no censorship.

SCRIPT AS A MEDIUM OF INFORMATION

So far in this chapter we have looked first at the role of scribal publication in defining communities of the like-minded, and then at the ways in which the choice of medium was influenced by censorship. However, a full understanding of the societal functions of scribal publication can only be achieved through a consideration

[32] 'William Davenport', pp. 119, 121.

of how information of all kinds was transmitted within those classes most concerned with the conduct of affairs.[33] This will also be an opportunity to cast some new light on Jürgen Habermas's contention, first advanced in 1962, that late-seventeenth-century England saw the creation of the modern 'public sphere' and to illustrate the contribution made by scribal publication to this development.[34]

A young man of parts and some education wishing to rise in the world during the Stuart period had a choice between two main avenues of advancement. The first of these, already discussed, was the system by which one placed one's talents at the service of a patron (secular or ecclesiastical) who was usually also involved in the search for advancement at a higher level. Most patrons were male, but in the earlier part of the century a number of aristocratic women performed the role with distinction, while after 1660 the leading royal concubines were courted quite as much as leading ministers. The second avenue was commerce, to which the normal point of entry was an apprenticeship to a trade, although a person already possessing some capital might skip this hurdle. Success in both paths depended vitally on the ability to predict the future—to know whose star was rising and whose declining at court and how commodities were likely to perform on the exchange. Moreover, that knowledge had to be possessed if possible before and certainly no later than the rest of one's community.

For an élite to which information was so vital, there were remarkably few printed media through which one could learn of current happenings. Printed corantos made sporadic appearances from the 1620s and flourished for a time during the Civil War and Commonwealth years; but non-official newspapers, especially those dealing with domestic news, were not to enjoy a regular, unthreatened existence until the 1690s.[35] Governments, when they were powerful enough, imposed the severest restrictions on the

[33] A matter more fully considered in F. J. Levy, 'How information spread among the gentry, 1550–1640', *Journal of British studies* 21 (1982), 11–34 and Richard Cust, 'News and politics in early seventeenth-century England', *P&P* 112 (Aug., 1986), 60–90.

[34] *The structural transformation of the public sphere: an inquiry into a category of bourgeois society*, trans. Thomas Burger with the assistance of Frederick Lawrence (Cambridge, Mass., 1989), 57–67.

[35] The official *London gazette* of the post-Restoration years restricted itself to foreign news, while the newspapers of the later years of Charles II were unreliable (see Fraser, *Intelligence of the secretaries of state*, p. 122) and subject to official harrassment.

printing of news, as part of a wider policy of securing a monopoly of information to themselves. Behind this attitude lay not only a conviction that such information should be reserved to those actually concerned in political decision making, but a practical awareness that private information could be traded for new information—a technique brought to its highest point of refinement by Joseph Williamson in the years following the Restoration.

Certainly, for the first few decades of the century, news was still primarily an oral commodity, and its emporium the nave of St Paul's cathedral. Here in the reign of James I, as Francis Osborne recalled,

> It was the fashion of those times, and did so continue 'till these (wherein not only the Mother but her Daughters are ruined) for the principall Gentry, Lords, Courtiers and men of all professions not meerely Mechanick, to meet in *Pauls Church* by eleven, and walk in the middle Ile till twelve, and after dinner from three, to six; during which time some discoursed of Businesse, others of Newes. Now, in regard of the universall commerce, there happened little that did not first or last arrive here: And I being young, and wanting a more advantagious imployment, did, during my aboad in London, which was three fourth parts of the yeare, associate my selfe at those houres with the choycest company I could pick out, amongst such as I found most inquisitive after affaires of State; who being then my selfe in a daily attendance upon a hope (though a rotten one) of a future Preferment, I appeared the more considerable, being as ready to satisfy, according to my weak abilities, their Curiosity, as they were mine:[36]

Another frequenter recorded: 'The Noyse in it, is like that of Bees, a strange hum[m]ing or Buzz; mixt of walking Tonges and feet; it, is a kind of still roare, or Loud whisper.'[37] News of this kind passed with no reliance on writing except insofar as letters may have brought information from the country and other letters returned it again. The nave of the church was no venue for reading.

The decline of 'Paul's walking' has never been properly chronicled. The destruction of the old building by fire in 1666 marked its certain end; but one imagines that it had been in

[36] Francis Osborne, *Traditionall memoyres on the raigne of King Iames* (London, 1658), pp. 64–6.

[37] John Earle, *The autograph manuscript of Microcosmographie* (Leeds, 1966), p. 143.

abeyance since the disestablishment of the cathedral under the Commonwealth. Between the Restoration and the fire, Pepys was a frequent visitor to neighbouring bookshops but not it would seem to the old 'walk'. His own oral information-gathering was done at the Royal Exchange and taverns. Into this vacuum, which was eventually to be satisfied by the printed newspaper, came the manuscript newspaper and separate, no longer just a means of retailing news from a predominantly oral culture, but increasingly valuable in their own right as a means by which that information was to be gained and interpreted.

Habermas's notion of the 'public sphere' is specifically associated with the coffee-house culture of the later seventeenth century.[38] Yet it can hardly be denied that, viewed as a medium of oral communication, this culture represented a radical fracturing of the vast information exchange of Paul's into a multitude of separate, more specialized exchanges through which orally transmitted information would have passed more slowly and with less efficiency. (An analogy would be the difference between a series of computer terminals receiving information from and returning it to a large central processor, and a network of PC users who only ever communicated on an informal one-to-one basis.) This new arrangement satisfied one requirement of the new economic order symbolized by the founding in 1694 of the Bank of England by encouraging a more intense communication between those sharing common interests (e.g. insurers at Lloyds) while helping to ensure that certain especially sensitive kinds of information were kept from wider knowledge; but it was still essential for the proper functioning of the system that knowledge of general significance should pass through it rapidly. The fact that this *did* happen was a puzzle even to contemporaries: Mr Spectator could only explain it by positing that the possession of a new piece of news would compel demented individuals to rush from coffee house to coffee house for the prestige of being the first to announce (or whisper) it.[39] But this is purely fanciful. The truth of the matter lies rather in the burlesque diary of no. 154 with its engaging picture of the coffee house as a site of reading in which the customer vainly tries

[38] *Structural transformation*, pp. 32–3, 59.

[39] See the accounts of Peter Hush (no. 457; Addison and Pope) and Thomas Quid-nunc (no. 625; Tickell) in *The spectator*, ed. Donald F. Bond (Oxford, 1965), iv. 111–14, v. 136–7.

to discover whether or not the Grand Vizier has been strangled. That no attempt was made to restore the old grand exchange for oral news, and that it was the new system that sustained the modernizing tendencies in London's intellectual and commercial cultures, would suggest that written and printed information had more than compensated for the loss in efficiency in the circulation of oral news, and was serving, in effect, as the central processor. It is therefore in the sphere of inscription—the printed pamphlet and the scribal separate—rather than that of voice that we should be looking for the architecture of the public sphere.

This new public culture created by writing needs to be further analysed in terms of four phases: production, distribution, consumption and social use. Here production indicates the printing of topical pamphlets (entirely professionalized) and the copying of scribal texts (still largely in the hands of authors and readers). Distribution covers the processes by which short printed texts were made available to buyers (principally through mercury women and hawkers) and scribal texts to their readers (professionally by bespoke sale but otherwise by personal exchange). Consumption embraces the various ways in which a text of either kind could be read (a variety of relationships depending not only on the material form of the text but the physical circumstances under which the reading took place). Finally, social use covers the consequences that followed from the reading (decision on a course of action, oral dissemination of data, debate with other readers, the production of another piece of writing). Since to deal satisfactorily with these matters would require a book rather than a chapter, simplification is essential. In this case it will take the form of describing a number of the subordinate spaces in which the reading of scribal texts took place, and the kinds of production, distribution, consumption and social action that were privileged by those spaces.

SITES FOR READING

On the opening page of *If on a winter's night a traveller*, Italo Calvino presents an inventory of the ways in which reading, as a physical activity, might be undertaken by an Italian of the late 1970s.

> Find the most comfortable position: seated, stretched out, curled up, or lying flat. Flat on your back, on your side, on your stomach. In an easy chair, on the sofa, in the rocker, the deck chair, on the hassock. In the hammock, if you have a hammock. On top of your bed, of course, or in the bed. You can even stand on your hands, head down, in the yoga position. With the book upside down, naturally. . . . Stretch your legs, go ahead and put your feet on a cushion, on two cushions, on the arms of the sofa, on the wings of the chair, on the coffee table, on the desk, on the piano, on the globe. Take your shoes off first. If you want to, put your feet up; if not, put them back.[40]

This is reading in the privileged private space of the home; but as the fiction progresses other possibilities are canvassed: listening in a university office to someone's extemporized translation, reading in the context of a seminar, reading from a pile of photocopies in a publisher's office, reading in a café while waiting for someone, reading on a deckchair on the terrace of a chalet, reading on a rocky ledge in the mountains, reading while flying, disembarking and passing through customs, and so on until we finally arrive in a library whose users describe their highly divergent subjective experiences of the text.

There are a number of omissions from this inventory. No one reads in the bath, on the lavatory, in a laundromat, on a bus or train, under the desk during school lessons, or behind a screen of agenda papers at boring meetings. Incomprehensibly to an Australian, no-one lies on the beach reading at intervals between dips in the surf. But on the whole, Calvino offers much valuable data (along with a few postmodern red herrings) to future historians of late-twentieth-century reading. For the seventeenth century we possess no such inventories and must draw on casually encountered information whose representativeness can rarely be ascertained. Some travellers were able to read in a coach, but how easy was it to read in sedan chairs or boats on the river? It was certainly possible to read in the newer churches, since Protestant architects laid great stress on the ability to see in their buildings, but may not have been in medieval survivors. Reading in bed seems to have been regarded as anti-social and a fire-risk. Reading while walking seems to have been common—or is that simply an illusion

[40] *If on a winter's night a traveller*, trans Wiliam Weaver (London, 1982), p. 9.

created by representations of reading in plays?[41] Yet Margaret Clifford, Countess of Cumberland, would walk in the woods with her Bible, depositing it 'in some faire tree' when she wished to meditate on a passage; while the Earl of Essex, confined to his home in 1600, would often walk 'upon his open leades, and in his garden, with his wiffe; now he, now she, reading one to the other'.[42] The practice of browsing in booksellers' shops was well established and would have compensated for the severe lack of public libraries. Did readers read as much as we do, or as quickly? How much more retentive were their highly trained memories than ours? Indeed, how far did the desire to memorize structure the practice of reading? In an age where literacy itself was far less widespread than in the West today, how much reading was communal rather than solitary? Basic questions such as these are often more difficult to answer than that of how seventeenth-century readers used to interpret the texts they read, a matter for which we have no shortage of evidence.[43]

The problem is particularly acute for the reading of the handwritten text. There are many pictorial representations of the act of reading but they rarely allow us to determine whether it is a printed book or a manuscript which is being read. Our evidence, then, must be the messages conveyed by the physical records themselves, drawing in this on the insights of McKenzie and Ong, and our knowledge of the places where reading took place. In the remainder of this chapter I wish to consider four of these sites for reading which were of special importance for the scribally published text—the country house, the coffee house, the court, and the main sites of learned reading, the Inns of Court and universities.

The country house

Outside London and the large towns, the reading of scribally published texts is chiefly associated with the houses of the

[41] Cf. Ford, *The broken heart*, I. iii; Shakespeare, *Hamlet*, sc. 7, ll. 1098 ff. and *Richard III*, sc. 15, ll. 2085–8; Webster, *The duchess of Malfi*, v. v.

[42] Aemilia Lanyer, 'The description of Cooke-ham', ll. 83–4 in *Kissing the rod: an anthology of seventeenth-century women's verse*, ed. Germaine Greer *et al.* (London, 1988), p. 48; Rowland White to Sir Robert Sidney, 12 Apr. 1600, cited in Margaret P. Hannay, *Philip's phoenix: Mary Sidney, Countess of Pembroke* (Oxford, 1990), p. 155.

[43] The problem is of course how far methods taught in textbooks of interpretation actually applied in everyday reading. For one point of view on this, see Eugene R. Kintgen, 'Reconstructing Elizabethan reading', *SEL* 30 (1990), 1–18.

aristocracy and the gentry. While some members of these classes could afford to employ secretaries or stewards to do their writing for them, it was common for the lesser landowner to be his own scribe and record keeper. The facility at writing so developed was frequently put to work in user or author publication, and was reflected in a habit of reading that was serious, attentive and solitary.

By the seventeenth century it had become usual for landed families to preserve large bodies of handwritten records. Even the semi-literate and uncultured would still need to retain a considerable amount of documentation relating to the sale and purchase of items relating to the estate. One also encounters an intense concern with family genealogies and the history of land ownership—matters endlessly productive of research. Commenting on one such investigation, Philip Styles notes that 'in that age of transition a certain amount of antiquarian knowledge was necessary to make feudal tenures profitable': in Sir Simon Archer's case one sees 'how easily the lord of the manor merged into the feudal historian'.[44] Where the hereditary landowner was also a justice he might have custody of judicial records of some complexity. If his interests were unintellectual, the collection of manuscripts might stop there; but the squire of the seventeenth century was often far removed from the stereotype of 'a rough unsophisticated countryman who was interested only in the state of his rent-roll and the pleasures of the chase', as J. T. Cliffe puts it. Indeed, in Yorkshire, remote from the traditional centres of education, 247 out of 679 heads of gentry families identifiable in 1642 had spent time at a university, an Inn of Court or a Catholic college, and 93 at both a university and an Inn.[45] Lacking profound learning, the squire might still be a dogged autodidact, like Sir John Newdigate who compiled thematic commonplace books devoted to theology, law, history and husbandry, and aspired to devote between eight and ten hours a day to study.[46] It would also be common for him to have a passionate interest in matters of religion and to be deeply read in

[44] *Sir Simon Archer*, pp. 20, 22. The investigation is described on pp. 15–23.

[45] *The Yorkshire gentry from the Reformation to the Civil War* (London, 1969), pp. 81, 73. See also O'Day, *Education and society*, pp. 88–99.

[46] Vivienne Larminie, *The godly magistrate: the private philosophy and public life of Sir John Newdigate, 1571–1610* (Oxford, 1982), pp. 7–8.

controversial literature. From a man of this type—and they formed at least a significant minority—we would expect not only a keenness to obtain scribally published texts, but a habit of integrating these into a private database, largely written in his own hand.

A description of one such landowner is given in Alan Macfarlane's *The justice and mare's ale*. Sir Daniel Fleming of Rydal Hall, Westmorland, born in 1633, inherited the paternal estate at the age of 19 after brief stays at Oxford and one of the Inns of Court. Of his industriousness as a scribe, Macfarlane gives the following account:

> His voluminous personal papers show him to be a truly remarkable man. He combined great intelligence, vast erudition, immense curiosity and great energy, with a love of documents. When his papers were deposited in the Cumbria Record Office in the 1960s they comprised about seventy manilla boxes. There were also roughly 6,000 letters to and from him. There are copies of love letters, books of jokes, series of grocers' bills, payments to harvest workers and many other items. Just the letters concerning the education of his children, when published, filled three bulky volumes. His immense energy and organization is shown in an account book he kept which, if fully published, would run to many volumes. His legal learning is illustrated by his letters and book purchases, but one particularly strong indication is the annotated copy of the *Statutes of the peace* which he kept with him in his judicial business. The first 286 pages are a printed abstract of the legal position in relation to alphabetically arranged subjects such as 'Alehouses', 'Archery', 'Arrests'. These first pages are densely annotated with added topics, modifications, amplifications from all the current legal writers. Not content with this, Fleming then proceeded to fill a further 482 pages in his tiny handwriting with annotations and explanations, with the forms of writs and warrants, with the statutes concerning taxation and the poor, and numerous other topics.[47]

We cannot know to what extent this (to us) prodigious industry at penmanship was typical of Fleming's class at this time; but my own guess would be that it represented a wide social practice, excessive, if at all, only in quantity not kind. Fleming belonged to a

[47] Alan Macfarlane in collaboration with Sarah Harrison, *The justice and the mare's ale: law and disorder in seventeenth-century England* (Oxford, 1981), p. 42. For the Fleming MSS, see *HMC, 12th rep., app., pt. vii.*

generation trained by the new bureaucrats of the interregnum in the importance of meticulous documentation, and which also still respected the medieval view of copying as a work of virtue to be instilled in the young to preserve them from debauched courses (an attitude intensified rather than otherwise by Puritanism).

From earlier in the century the autobiographical writings of another learned squire, Simonds D'Ewes, reveal a similar delight in the activities of ordering, filing and transcribing, joined with an often declared conviction of guilt in not keeping up to the targets he set himself. His account of the compilation of his massive scribal edition of the parliamentary papers of Elizabeth's reign has already been quoted in Chapter 3: in this case it was the editorial work that was performed by D'Ewes while the actual copying was done by 'an industrious servant'; however, at the same time D'Ewes himself was also engaged in a transcription of the medieval commentary on the laws of England known as the *Fleta*, switching between editorial work on one project and actual copying in the second. 'The ensuing month of August', runs a typical account from the autobiography, 'was almost wholly spent in transcribing Fleta out of a copy I had of it, and in directing my servant in the penning of the parliamentary journals of Queen Elizabeth's time.'[48] Unlike Fleming, D'Ewes was a professed antiquary, one of a large community of gentleman-scholars; but he shared with the Cumbrian justice an almost fetishistic delight in manuscripts and a passion for transcribing that exceeded any immediate practical need. James Boevey from the age of 14 'had a candle burning by him all night, with pen, inke, and paper, to write downe thoughts as they came into his head; that so he might not loose a thought'.[49]

What is described here is not scribal publication as such but the wider culture of transcription from which it grew. For Fleming, D'Ewes, Boevey and many like them a significant pleasure of reading was that it should be an encounter with their own script—a matter partly narcissistic, partly a reflection of a spirituality turned in upon private experience, and partly a comforting reminder of prodigies of godly labour. But it was also a new and powerful mode of social control, and one which in this case broke with Ong's notion of the residual orality of the chirographic text.

48 *Autobiography*, i. 409, 435.
49 Aubrey, *Brief lives*, i. 113.

Ong sees oral culture as 'homeostatic' in its readiness to shed or reconstitute the past whenever the past ceases to serve the needs of the present.[50] In doing so it sacrifices the possibility of controlling the future through the past. These immensely patient labours of transcription, whether it was Fleming's desire to preserve records of his own family and community, Archer's to trace the history of Warwickshire tenures, D'Ewes's to have access to ancient parliamentary and administrative precedents, or Roger North's to preserve his deliberations on an encyclopaediac range of subjects, were a way of capturing the past for future service. D'Ewes put his historical database at the service of parliaments in which he served, while Fleming used his records in pursuing a notorious band of lawbreakers. This pursuit, the subject of Macfarlane's study, was only successful because of Fleming's power to integrate information within his personal archive. But power, once again, resided in the data remaining private—if available in printed form it would have deprived the owner and his allies of a vital advantage. The same clearly applies to the encylopaedia of 'active philosophy' composed by Boevey after he had 'retired to a countrey life', which handled 'all the Arts and Tricks practised in Negotiation, and how they were to be ballanced by counter-prudentiall rules'.[51] Once again there was knowledge to be shared and knowledge to be reserved.

This kind of country-house reader would have been a writer prior to his being a reader, and with a preference for the products of his own pen. His reading would have been solitary, with a 'closet' away from the bustle of the household set up for writing and where documents could be concealed from prying eyes. (Women readers would have had to be of high social standing before they acquired this privilege, though the example of Dame Sara Cowper (1644–1720) shows that they could be just as industrious as men in assembling large private collections of manuscripts.) The utilitarian nature of much reading, nourished in turn by patient study of the Bible and devotional books, would have encouraged high levels of concentration. Striking thoughts would be abstracted for preservation in a commonplace book. Among scribally published texts most likely to have passed before

[50] Ong, *Orality*, pp. 46–9.
[51] Aubrey, i. 112.

his eyes would have been newsletters and separates sent from town, and essays and epistles from other educated squires of his district, echoing the practice observed by Laslett in Kent and also evident in the Fleming MSS and the collections of William Davenport.[52] The habits of filing and ordering made necessary by his functions as landlord and justice would also have encouraged the rereading of important manuscripts. A class of writing that would be preserved with especial care was the advices and treatises prepared by parents for the guidance of their children, an important sub-genre that would occasionally break into wider circulation but mostly remained within the extended family.[53] As far as we can judge, the reading of the scribally published text within such a household would be a careful and attentive business, always likely to provoke the complementary activity of writing. What held good for the squire might equally be true of the vicar in his parsonage, whom the squire had frequently appointed.

The cultural ideal of the learned squire is preserved for us in the political genre, common to both the scribal and print media, of the political tract or verse epistle in the form of a 'Letter to a gentleman in the country'. The gentleman in these cases represents a judge to whom the competing innovators of the metropolis submit their causes for censure confident that he will lend his weight to their own side. He is assumed to be deeply versed in history and the constitution (which in a sense he embodies). His political understanding has been nourished by an early study of the classics, and his judgement of human nature by his experience on the bench, but his understanding of the political traditions of the nation is one that has been gained through a first-hand

[52] Fleming corresponded frequently on political matters with his neighbours (*HMC, 12th rep., app., vii*, pp. iii–iv), as well as receiving regular newsletters from the Secretary of State's office. For Davenport see Morrill, 'William Davenport', pp. 115–29 and Cust, 'News and politics', pp. 80–3.

[53] Examples already discussed include Osborne's 'Advice to a son' and Halifax's 'Advice to a daughter'. Dame Sara Cowper preserved shorter epistles of this kind to two of her children (Hertfordshire Record Office MS D/Ep F37, pp. 49–55). The well-known letter from Lord Burghley to Robert Cecil, material from which was appropriated by Dame Sara, is available in facsimile in Braunmuller, *A seventeenth-century letter-book*, pp. 276–87. Daniel Fleming's advice to his son, reprinted in Cumberland and Westmorland Antiquarian and Archaeological Society, tract series no. xi (Kendal, 1928), pp. 92–9, is another version of the Burleigh letter, as is the widely circulated 'Admonition of the Earl of Essex to his son'. For the genre at large, see *Advice to a son: precepts of Lord Burghley, Sir Walter Raleigh, and Francis Osborne*, ed. Louis B. Wright (Ithaca, NY, 1962), pp. ix–xxvi.

acquaintance with ancient records. Removed from the factions and hurly burly of the town, he has room in his life for scholarship and reflection. The ideal was realized in men such as D'Ewes, Fleming and Walter Yonge, and for many others it was a construction to be identified with to the limit of their capacities.[54] The reading that informed such a life would be directed towards the past rather than the present, shunning novelty in order to search out time-sanctioned verities. That such a paragon should be addressed in a letter (even if it was a printed one) was a tacit acknowledgement that his concern would be with the products of the pen quite as much as with those of the press. But, as the emergence of this construction was a response to political needs, so was its decline inevitable once the urgency of those needs was no longer felt. Steele's mockery of Sir Roger's devotion to Dyer's letter ('our Authentick Intelligence, our *Aristotle* in Politicks'[55]) was a sign that both the role and the medium were becoming irrelevant.

The coffee house

Habermas's 'public sphere' is most immediately observable in the coffee houses of London. With the decline of Paul's and the Exchange as centralized sources for the dissemination of oral information within the capital, their place was taken by the newcomers, the indiscriminate public space giving way to a variety of more restricted and intimate ones. First known in the early 1650s, coffee houses spread widely in England during the 1660s and 1670s and were the chosen meeting place for men of business as well as men of leisure. From an early period they became highly specialized in terms of clientele, many performing the role of semi-private clubs for patrons of varying trades, faiths or political views. They could also be semi-public places of business, providing an office address for the advertisers of services. At the universities they were seen as disruptive influences. Roger North gives an informed if somewhat jaundiced view of their effect on Cambridge over the decades following the Restoration:

[54] For Yonge, see V. L. and M. L. Pearl, 'Richard Corbett's 'Against the opposing of the Duke in parliament, 1628' and the anonymous rejoinder, 'An answere to the same, lyne for lyne': the earliest dated manuscript copies', *RES* NS 42 (1991), 32 and the sources there cited.

[55] *Spectator*, i. 182–3.

> At that time and long after there was but one, kept by one Kirk. The trade of news also was scarce set up, for they had only the public gazette, till Kirk got a written newsletter circulated by one Muddiman. But now the case is much altered, for it is become a custom after chapel to repair to one or other of the coffee-houses (for there are divers), where hours are spent in talking, and less profitable reading of newspapers, of which swarms are continually supplied from London. And the scholars generally as so entête after news (which is none of their business) that they neglect all for it. And it is become very rare for any of them to go directly to his chamber after prayers without first doing his suit at the coffee-house, which is a vast loss of time grown out of a pure novelty. For who can apply close to a subject with his head full of the din of a coffee-house?[56]

The replacement of the public concourse by the coffee house as the primary venue for the exchange of information had an inevitable effect on the way in which that information was communicated. The confidentiality of coffee-house discussion encouraged a new frankness, much as the brew itself probably encouraged increased mental acuity among drinkers whose nervous systems had not been habituated to caffeine since childhood. Mr Spectator speaks of thrusting his head 'into a Round of Politicians at *Will*'s, and listning with great Attention to the Narratives that are made in those little Circular Audiences'—a description that accords perfectly with Habermas's vision of 'private people come together as a public'.[57] But, as indicated under our earlier informational model, the retreat towards intimacy—and professional specialism—also reduced the quantity and variety of the oral information that entered the place of exchange. For this reason the coffee house had to become a site for reading as well as conversation: early illustrations nearly always show reading matter scattered on the tables. Newspapers, when available, were provided by the proprietor; but newspapers were of dubious value for an understanding of the world—strictly censored during those periods when censorship was possible and unreliable in those periods when it was not. Most vitally, the information they presented was available to hundreds of others

[56] Roger North, 'Life of Dr John North', in *General preface and life of Dr John North*, ed. Peter Millard (Toronto, 1984), p. 115. For a very similar attitude towards the impact of the coffee-drinking culture on Oxford, see *The life and times of Anthony Wood*, ed. Andrew Clark (Oxford, 1891–5), ii. 300 and 429.

[57] *Spectator*, i. 3; Habermas, p. 27.

who might be relied upon to be drawing the same conclusions from it.

The role of the coffee houses as centres for the dissemination of newsletters and separates has already been touched upon. They had become dangerous enough by the winter of 1675–6 in their circulation of forbidden documents to provoke an attempt at suppression.[58] Dyer the coffee house man whose inflammatory 1688 newsletter so annoyed L'Estrange was only one of a number of proprietors who were actively engaged in scribal journalism. Will Urwin, of the Will's just mentioned, whose customers included Dryden and the Covent Garden wits, issued a newsletter in 1678 which was delivered by 'a little tapster boy' from his coffee house.[59] Coffee houses were the ideal place to inject new texts into circulation. Being common to both the City and the West End, the coffee-house culture could transfer texts rapidly between milieux which had little other direct contact. A report on radical Nonconformists, apparently dating from the late 1660s, connects them both with coffee houses and the transmission of lampoons:

> The Independents and Anabaptists with some of the fiercer Presbyterians are proud and censorious; Quaker like they will denounce Judgments both upon King & Kingdome upon any pretended Miscariages they doe but heare of.
>
> They are great Frequenters of Coffeehouses and great Improvers of any little matters that is but whispered against the Court or the Government.
>
> These with some hipocriticall Loyalists take paines to divulge any thing that may cast a reproach upon the King, and to disperse any scandalous Verses of which many have been abroad of late.[60]

In an age when many men took delivery of their mail at their coffee house, and where the owner might have his own service for delivering letters, they were an obvious recourse for the aspiring scribal publisher. Within their walls, the newsletter and separate served both as reading matter and as a currency of exchange

[58] Further discussed in Ch. 6, pp. 240–2.

[59] *HMC, 11th rep., app., vii*, p. 20. Further information on the nexus between coffee houses and the writing and circulation of newsletters is given in Bryant Lillywhite, *London coffee houses: a reference book of coffee houses of the seventeenth, eighteenth and nineteenth centuries* (London, 1963), pp. 19–20, under the years 1679, 1683 and 1688, and Fraser, *Intelligence*, pp. 114–21.

[60] 'The state of the non-conformists in England soon after the Restoration. From a MS in the possession of Thomas Astle Esq', BL MS Stowe 185, ff. 175^{r-v}.

between customers. For information, if it was of real value, was always to be traded, not given. Men's clothes had changed by 1660 from the earlier doublet and hose with the cloak for outward protection to the shirt and breeches beneath a knee-length coat with capacious pockets. These pockets were the perfect receptacle for separates. Rochester is known to have carried manuscripts in this way, as does Mr Friendall his daily wad of love letters in Southerne's *The wives' excuse*.[61] In the economy of the coffee house the scribal texts supplied by the proprietor were supplemented by those traded for oral news or other reserved writings by their information-hungry patrons.

In their semi-secretive, semi-public character the newsletters and lampoons exactly mimicked the institutions that played host to them. But our concern now is not with their social function as such but the way in which the nature of the space provided helps identify and define particular kinds of reading. A text might be read aloud by one member of a party to his table-fellows, and perhaps inadvertently to the entire room. In a coffee-house scene in a comedy of 1667 the coffee-master brings a *Gazette* to a table, which, at the suggestion 'Pray let one read for all', is read out while the reader's companions interpolate their questions and comments.[62] Steele, writing in 1711 as 'Abraham Froth', described how it was the custom at Sir Roger de Coverley's in the country 'upon the coming in of the Post to sit about a Pot of Coffee, and hear the old Knight read *Dyer*'s Letter, which he does with his Spectacles upon his Nose, and in an audible Voice, smiling very often at those little strokes of Satyr which are so frequent in the Writings of that Author'.[63] This while not a description of a coffee house may be accepted as a coffee-house custom transposed to the shires. Reading might equally be silent, but it was a silence within the ambience of communion. The solitary kind of reading was necessary to the pursuit of whatever shared goal had brought the patrons of the house together, but what was divined from it still

[61] It was from a pocket that Rochester produced the copy of 'In the isle of Great Britain' that he inadvertently gave to Charles II. Cf. also his 'Timon a satyr', ll. 13–16: 'He takes me in his coach and as we go / Pulls out a libel of a sheet or two . . .'. For Mr Friendall see, *The wives' excuse*, v. ii. 52–65 in *The works of Thomas Southerne*, ed. Robert Jordan and Harold Love (Oxford, 1988), i. 330.

[62] Sir Thomas St Serfe, *Tarugo's wiles: or the coffee house* (London, 1667), p. 24.

[63] *Spectator*, ii. 4–5.

needed to be handled with a degree of reserve in that these fellow patrons might also be spies or competitors. The coffee-house reader was both of and not of his particular scene of aspiration, retaining the detachment famously captured in Pope's '*Coffee*, (which makes the Politician wise, / And see thro' all things with his half shut Eyes)'.[64] The reading was a necessary preparative to engaging in conversation—the other rationale of the house—but even the conversation, as Alexander Radcliffe noted, was of a different kind from the bonhomie of the tavern.

> A Pox 'o these Fellows contriving,
> They've spoilt our pleasant design;
> We were once in a way of true living,
> Improving Discourse by good Wine.
> But now Conversation grows tedeous,
> O'er Coffee they still confer Notes;
> 'Stead of Authors both learn'd and facetious,
> They quote onely *Dugdale* and *Oats*.[65]

It is likely enough that the Nonconformists' tendency to 'denounce Judgments' and to be 'great Improvers of any little matters' represents the tone of such conversation quite accurately. It easily slid back into writing in the form of the lampoon or the scribally-circulated essay.

The court

The court as a site of writing has been much studied but is more difficult to focus on as a site of reading. To begin with we need to distinguish the court as the royal household from the court as the centre of the national administration, which was still technically conducted from within the household and to some degree by the same officers. In its first function it was the scene of ceremonies to which any person of suitable social standing could attach themselves under the guise of 'waiting', and which were an excellent opportunity for an exchange of manuscripts. But the

[64] iii. 117–18, in *The rape of the lock and other poems*, ed. Geoffrey Tillotson (London, 1962), p. 130. Charles A. Knight writes: 'By serving as the forum where readership moved into conversation, the coffee-house played a role for the periodical essay at least equal to that later played for the novel by the circulating library' ('The literary periodical in the early eighteenth century', *Library*, 6:8 (1986), 242).

[65] 'To the Tune of *Per fas per nefas*', *The ramble*, p. 34.

court was also a community of individuals living in close proximity. At the palace of Whitehall favoured courtiers, concubines, high officers of state and hundreds of servants and officials had apartments or humbler spaces which became their homes, at least for the period when the monarch was in residence. A writer of 1642 has left us a lament for a Whitehall suddenly deserted:

There is no presse at the Wine-Sellor Dores and Windowes, no gaping noise amongst the angry Cookes in the Kitchings, no wayting for the opening of the Posterne-dore to take water at the Stayres, no racket nor balling in the Tenis Court, no throng nor rumbling of Coaches before the Court Gates, but all in a dumbe silence, as the Pallace stood not neere a well peopled City, but as it were the decay'd buildings of ruin'd *Troy*, where scarce a passenger is known to tread once in twenty yeares.[66]

Rochester, writing in the early 1670s, compared life at court to being 'shutt up in a Drumme, you can thinke of nothing but the noise is made about you'.[67] Graham Parry has stressed the self-absorbed quality of the Caroline court in terms that also apply to its Restoration successor, describing it as 'excessively distracted by sophisticated game-playing, insufficiently aware of its dangerous isolation, and indifferent to the growing bitterness in the world outside'.[68]

Within this bustling, self-contained community, it was possible to take meals, to attend plays or worship, to gamble for high stakes at the Groom Porter's, to conduct love affairs, to call on the purveyors of an amazing range of products and services, and to hear and generate gossip. What was difficult to find was any more purposive activity: the 'work' of the courtier was in most cases simply to be physically present in the presence chamber. Sensibly noting that 'men cannot bee allwayes discowrcing, nor women always pricking in clowts', Sir John Harington thought it was 'not amisse to play at some sociable game (at which more than ii may

[66] *A deep sigh breath'd through the lodgings at White-hall, deploring the absence of the covrt, and the miseries of the palace* (London, 1642), A3^{v}.

[67] *The letters of John Wilmot, Earl of Rochester*, ed. Jeremy Treglown (Oxford, 1980), p. 93.

[68] *The seventeenth century. The intellectual and cultural context of English literature, 1603–1700* (Harlow, 1989), p. 35. The court's self-image is elegantly explored in his *The golden age restor'd. The culture of the Stuart court, 1603–42* (Manchester, 1981).

play) wherby the attendawnce may seem the lesse tedious to the players, and the rest that looke on may in a sort intertayn themselvs with the beholding it'.[69] Another way of combating the tedium of such occasions was through the composition and circulation of subversive writings, which must have gained a special piquancy when the victims were also present in the chamber.

The circulation of written texts, then, was part of the everyday current of life in the palace. Most of these were highly topical and quickly rendered out of date by the flow of events. They could also be ruthlessly frank about the real rationale of court life, which was incessant conflict for wealth and influence, with closeness to the sovereign the recognized way of securing this.[70] That most of these texts remained in manuscript was a concession that this rationale should be concealed as far as possible from the governed; however, the existence of networks of scribal publication at the centre of power was a standing invitation to outsiders to seek to obtain manuscripts from these networks and to insert writings into them that promoted their own interests. The rapidity with which material relating to the Somerset scandal (and others) in the reign of James I spread through the kingdom reflects the first of these phenomena, and the penetration achieved by Whig satires of the late 1670s the second. Few of these texts were in any way taxing. 'The court aristocracy of the seventeenth century', Habermas notes, speaking here on a European scale, 'was not really a reading public. To be sure, it kept men of letters as it kept servants, but literary production based on patronage was more a matter of a kind of conspicuous consumption than of serious reading by an interested public.'[71] The scholar courtiers of Elizabeth's reign were supplanted under the Stuarts by men of very different attainments. Attention might still be sought through writing as through dress, sexual attractiveness, polished manners or conversational wit, but not necessarily to more effect.

[69] *Nugae antiquae*, ii. 14. He goes on to complain about the hardness of the court chairs and benches.

[70] The rules of this conflict are exposed in Kevin Sharpe's 'Crown, parliament and locality: government and communication in early Stuart England' in his *Politics and ideas in early Stuart England: essays and studies* (London, 1989), pp. 75–100, and in his own and Neil Cuddy's contributions to *The English court from the wars of the roses to the Civil War*, ed. David Starkey (London, 1987), pp. 173–260.

[71] Habermas, p. 38.

The court then was not a place for deep or serious reading. The majority of texts in circulation were short and uncomplicated enough to be produced from pockets in idle intervals of wearisome ceremonies, or as a source of sociable amusement. Pepys, on a hot summer's day in 1666 while on the grass by the canal in St James's Park, found himself 'thinking of a Lampoone which hath run in my head this week, to make upon the late fight at sea and the miscarriages there—but other businesses put it out of my head'.[72] And yet court life did encourage one kind of reading skill, which was that by which texts circulating in the form of separates were interrogated for clues to the current and future configurations of influence. Satire in particular had an important role as a means of undermining the standing of rivals: the malice of court lampooners, whether of Suckling's generation or Rochester's, is rarely if ever gratuitous but needs to be tracked back to the interests of a particular patron or faction. Apart from this, the levity of court reading reflects its function as an escape valve for an institution otherwise characterized by a rigid formality. Where texts of a more seriously informative or monitory kind are encountered which endeavour to address policy issues otherwise than in terms of personalities, it is likely that their intended readership was among the administrators rather then the courtiers (insofar as any sharp division can be made between the two).

Above all, scribally transmitted court writing was an insiders' writing, reflecting the values of an institution that was devoted to the manufacture and maintenance of an image in which it could hardly itself be expected to believe. As such it stands in an antithetical relationship to the idealization of the court in the masques of Jonson, Carew, D'Avenant and Crowne, performed for the benefit of outsiders rather than inmates and subsequently promulgated through the print medium. The frankness, indeed cynicism, of these scribally circulated writings can often be disconcerting when comparison is made with work presented by the same writer in more public forums. Harington's *A supplie or addicion to the catalogue of bishops to the year 1608* is one text whose ambivalences and apparent self-contradictions only make sense when it is firmly seen as the work of one insider writing to another

[72] *Diary*, vii. 207.

insider (Prince Henry) about still other insiders (the bishops) whose status as leaders of the church must not be allowed to become confused with their status as fellow-courtiers.[73] What was true of the king's court was equally true of its tributaries. 'Every great courtier', R. Malcolm Smuts points out, 'maintained his own household near Whitehall, each a miniature court in its own right which functioned as the nerve center for its owner's affinity.'[74] In the case of Harington's *Supplie*, it is important to remember that Prince Henry had his own court, distinct from those of his father, mother and siblings, and that this possessed its own political and cultural programme. The levees of great commoners like Somerset and Buckingham were hardly less splendid than those of the king.

The Haward miscellany

One of our best guides to the kinds of texts circulated at the Stuart court is the bulky (721 written pages plus blanks) miscellany assembled between the late 1660s and circa 1682 by Sir William Haward of Tandridge, and now Bodleian MS don. b 8. A note on the manuscript by a later owner, Peter le Neve, identifies Sir William as 'K$^{nt.}$ of the Privy Chamber to King Cha: y^{e} 1st. Cha: 2^{d}. and King James the second' and as having enjoyed an apartment in Scotland Yard, the area adjacent to the court, formerly reserved for the use of visiting Scottish monarchs. He was knighted in 1643.[75] His post at court, which he acquired in 1641 and still retained in 1689, was one of forty-eight Gentlemen of the Privy Chamber in Ordinary. Of these Chamberlayne writes:

> Their Office is Twelve every Quarter to wait on the Kings Person within doors and without, so long as His Majesty is on foot; and when the King eats in the Privy-Chamber, they wait at the Table, and bring in His Meet. They wait also at the Reception of Ambassadors; and every night two of them lye in the Kings Privy-Chamber.[76]

[73] Ed. R. H. Miller (Potomac, 1981). The first printed edition did not appear until 1653. For the manuscripts, see Beal, *IELM*, i/2, pp. 154–5. The importance of appreciating 'the innerness of many of Harington's allusions' is brought out in Patrick Collinson's review, *Library*, 6:4 (1982), 198–200.

[74] *Court culture and the origins of the royalist tradition in early Stuart England* (Philadelphia, 1987), p. 55.

[75] There is a short biographical account of Sir William in W. Paley Baildon, *The Hawardes of Tandridge co. Surrey* (London, 1894), pp. 23–31 which records that he sold his estate at Tandridge in 1681 and that his wife, Martha, died in 1689.

[76] *Angliae notitia: or, the present state of England. The first part*, 10th edn (London, 1677), p.

The privy chamber was intermediate between the presence chamber and the bedchamber, placing its officers closer to the sovereign than the general run of courtiers but not in the inner circle of his intimates. Sir William was also MP for Bletchingley and later Reigate in the pension parliament. A satirical account dated 1670 of the court supporters in that parliament, copied by him into his book, describes him as 'a privy-Chamber-man, & Commission^er^ for sale of Fee-farme Rents' (p. 256). He was therefore a courtier in the three senses of one who held office within the royal household, of one who supported the crown in parliament, and of one who lived for periods of the year within the royal precinct in Whitehall. (Presumably he would return to his country estate during the summer.) To claim him as a 'typical' courtier would be to go beyond our present knowledge, but the range of interests revealed by his book, covering scandal, politics, poetry, heraldry, constitutional history, law, antiquarianism, geography, but not much religion, is what we would expect of the court of Charles II.[77] His book may therefore be regarded as a kind of net held out to catch whatever scribally published documents came into circulation at Whitehall.

Although the book is composed of transcriptions of material originally encountered as separates, it is not clear how soon after acquisition texts were entered. While the overall tendency of the items is chronological, this could well be the result of one or many *post hoc* reorderings of documents rather than conscientious entering in order of receipt. (Certainly, the position of a text in the volume should only be used with caution in determining its date of composition.[78]) One oddity is that pp. 1–68 were originally left blank and thus contain the last material to be entered, a matter confirmed by handwriting as well as dates. Haward gives no information concerning the subsequent fate of the separates from which he copied, or whether his own book served as an exemplar

159. See also Nicholas Carlisle, *An inquiry into the place and quality of the gentlemen of His Majesty's most honourable privy chamber* (London, 1829).

[77] However, Sir William was at least on good terms with princes of the Church: on 14 Nov. 1685 Evelyn encountered him at dinner with several prelates at Lambeth Palace, noting that 'The Dinner was for cheere extraordinary' (*Diary*, iv. 489).

[78] Paul Hammond, 'The dating of three poems by Rochester from the evidence of Bodleian MS Don. b 8', *Bodleian Library record* 11 (1982–5), 58–9 seems to assume copying in order of receipt; but this can be no more than a hypothesis.

for user publication. Given that separates were a kind of currency around the court and could be used to confirm alliances and attract favour, it is quite likely that the volume was meant as a source book for further transcription as well as a personal record. Nor is there much information about the individuals from whom documents were received. Poems by court authors are often in good texts and correctly ascribed, suggesting they may have been received via author publication; however, Rochester's 'Artemisa to Chloe' bears the uncertain annotation 'This poeme is supposed to bee made by ye Earle of Rochester, or Mr Wolseley' (p. 494). An account of a diplomatic incident involving the British resident at Venice (pp. 60–8) was passed on by John Grenville, Earl of Bath, and a narrative of the naval attack on Bergen by Sir Gilbert Talbot.[79] We must assume that these were connections on which Haward particularly prided himself. On another occasion he may well have seen the original of an epigram placed on the door of the royal bedchamber, since it occurred during his term of waiting and the finder was known to him.[80] But the important point is that, although the names of sources are suppressed, the entire contents of his book had come from donation, exchange or purchase. Behind its carefully inscribed pages lie possibly hundreds of individual transactions.

What prospect of the range of court reading are we given by this volume? To begin with there is a very substantial body of satirical verse, partly written by courtiers about other courtiers, partly drawn from the broader 'state poems' tradition, and partly belonging to an older, more genial tradition of social verse. Overall there are 180 verse items ranging from two-line epigrams to lengthy satires. That there should be a good representation of writing by Rochester (eight items plus some dubia) and the wits of the Buckingham circle is hardly surprising. What is unexpected is the very full coverage of oppositional satire directed at the crown and its policies, especially from what will be described in the next chapter as the 'Marvellian' tradition, centring on the various

[79] 'This paper was written by ye Com[m]and of Sr Gilbert Talbott for me, & giuen mee by his owne hand on Saturday in ye Euening, being y^e^. 21th. of January. 1676/7' (p. 66). A poem by Talbot, 'The Hermite to his Citty Freind' is given on pp. 648–50.

[80] 'About nyne of ye Clocke at night on Friday being y^e^. 26th. of November, 1675. This ensueing Distick was found put ouer ye Doore of ye Kings new Bedchamber, & taken downe by Francis Rogers page of ye Bedchamber' (p. 539).

'Advice to a painter poems'. In particular, Haward was diligent in his recording of satires, some of considerable grossness, on the king and members of the royal family.[81] Encountered without knowledge of its provenance one would assume this to be the miscellany of either a Whig sympathiser or an extreme Yorkist rather than a faithful servant of the reigning monarch. Haward sometimes tries to cover himself by using disapproving titles, as with 'An horrid Anagram on the Motto of y[e] Kings Armes' (p. 539), 'A detestable Libell' (p. 554) and 'A damn'd Ballad of this is the Tyme' (p. 568) as well as a number of items signalled as 'base', but otherwise seems to have been remarkably detached about the undoubtedly treasonable nature of much of his material. (Cognitive dissonance of another kind is suggested when Rochester's(?) pornographic 'Seigneur Dildoe' is followed by 'On the Bible A Pindarique Ode' ('Haile Holy thinge', pp. 478–80) and that in turn by additional stanzas to 'Seigneur Dildoe'.)

As a member of parliament it would be expected that Haward would collect parliamentary separates. These include brief notes on the session commencing 22 November 1669 (pp. 446–7), a committee paper and the famous speech of Lord Lucas against the Subsidy Bill from February 1671 (pp. 198–201, 202–4); an extended parliamentary compilation, of the kind discussed in Chapter 1, for the session commencing 19 February 1673 which saw the passing of the Test Act (pp. 384–409), a journal for the session commencing 20 October 1673 (pp. 467–75), and a scattering of papers, petitions and speeches from other sessions (pp. 156–68, 293–5, 302, 446, 686, 704–6). There are no complete compilations of pre-1660 parliaments, but Haward did transcribe a

[81] These include 'To her Ma[tie] upon her dancing' ('Reforme, deare Queene, y[e] errours of your youth'), the two satires on the killing of a beadle by a gang led by the Duke of Monmouth ('Neare Holborne lyes a parke of great renowne', and 'Assist mee, some auspicious Muse, to tell'), several attacks on the Duchesses of Cleveland and Portsmouth, and a gallery of unflattering portraits of the king. Charles, as well as being addressed in several virulent epigrams, is the subject of the longer satires, 'The Chronicle' ('Chast, pious, prudent Charles y[e] Second'), 'Another base songe' ('I am a senceless thing wth a hye')', 'A base Copy' (Rochester's 'I'th' Isle of great Britaine'), 'The Kings Farewell to Danby' ('Farewell, my deare Danby, my pimpe, & my Cheate'), 'An historicall Poeme' ('Of a tall Stature, & of sable Hue'), 'On Madam Lawson' ('Mee-thinkes I see our Mighty Monarch stand'), besides other pieces attacking his policies rather than his person. Those satires whose first lines have been given will all be found in *POAS (Yale)* i and ii together with page-references to their MS sources; however, the titles and first-lines are as Haward gives them and vary in some instances from those of the Yale editors.

number of parliamentary and administrative separates from the reigns of Elizabeth, James I and Charles I, among them a collection of speeches relating to the Earl of Essex (pp. 75–83), a speech of James I (pp. 169–74), and a list of propositions made by the commons in 1610 concerning the abolition of knights' services (pp. 361–7). Supplementing these are a number of political pieces of an extra-parliamentary kind, including several by or concerned with Shaftesbury at various stages of his career (pp. 370–2, 448–9, 501–2, 523–4, 555–7, 702–3, 713–17). Lauderdale's administration of Scotland is attacked in a discourse dated 1675 on pp. 541–54. Anne, Duchess of York's reasons for embracing the Roman Catholic faith (pp. 562–3) are balanced at pp. 457–63 by her father's letter dissuading her from this course, and at 606–10 by a transcript of a printed narrative of the Pope-burning of 17 November 1679. Pages 661–80 contain two lengthy papers on the king's supposed mariage to Lucy Walters—actually Whig diatribes against the Duke of York. There is also the inevitable linked group of attacks on Buckingham *père* (pp. 108–17).

While not an antiquary in the severe sense of Cotton or D'Ewes, Sir William did have interests in this direction that were strong enough to draw recognition from Evelyn who described him in 1671 as 'a greate pretender to English antiquities &c'.[82] At p. 502 he provides a copy of an inscription found at Beverley minister. The early pages of the volume, which were the last to be written, include exchequer and tower records concerning the office of Constable of the Tower, the patent of creation of Thomas Howard, Earl of Surrey to be Duke of Norfolk in the reign of Henry VIII, an 'An Act concerning y[e] Title, Name, & Dignity of Earle of Arundell' and an account of the funeral of Richard, Duke of York, the father of Edward IV (pp. 36–42, 49–54). An interest in heraldry reveals itself in pieces on the arms of Gresham (pp. 279–80) and Wriothesley (pp. 420–22) and a report prepared by Haward together with Sir William Dugdale and Walter Chetwind on Wycherley's father Daniel's right to arms (pp. 60–3). 'A Roll of the Peeres of y[e] Kingdome of Englande' dated 4 February 1673 is given at pp. 373–8 and a transcript of Monck's commission as Captain General of Charles II's armies at pp. 43–9. Diplomatic

[82] *Diary*, iii. 598. The Pepysian copy of Robert of Gloucester's chronicle was originally written for Haward.

interests are reflected in some papers from the British ambassador at the Imperial court at Vienna (pp. 33–6) and a narrative by the British resident at Venice of an affront done to him by the Duke of Mantua's gondoliers (pp. 66–8). Haward also transcribed the lengthy charter of the East India Company in the form confirmed by Charles II in 1660 (pp. 310–41) and a treatise by Sir Harry Sheeres on the Mediterranean Sea and the Straits of Gibraltar (pp. 1–22).

Although, as mentioned, there is little evidence in this particular collection of any deep concern with religion, Haward did have a keen interest in prophecies. The prophecy was a genre of scribal publication which knew no boundaries of class or institution and would well for this reason reward specialized study.[83] Texts of this nature in Haward's volume are a versified extract from Nostradamus ('The bloud oth' Just Londons firme doome shall fix', p. 217), 'A Prognostication of ye Westphalian Boore, named Michell Rochells, of the yeare. 1672' (pp. 262–4), 'A prophecy, or Merlins Riddle' (p. 456); 'A Prophecy pretended, to be made many yeares agone' (p. 540); 'Merlin reuiu'd' (p. 660), and the long Fifth-monarchist prophetic allegory, *The panther*, copied in April 1681 (pp. 689–95). My summary passes over a number of legal speeches, letters (real and bogus), administrative position papers, political pieces and facetiae of various kinds, but gives a fair sense both of the range of Haward's interests and the richness of the traditions of scribal publication on which he was able to draw from his rooms in Scotland Yard.

This very richness creates difficulties of interpretation of a kind which have already been raised with regard to Harington's *A supplie*. Granted that Haward shows a lively interest in contemporary poetry, has carefully preserved a number of important parliamentary records, was well supplied with political and legal separates, and was interested enough to copy a few documents of an antiquarian and geographical nature, one remains puzzled as to what his point of view was towards the texts he inscribed. It is

[83] A useful starting point would be Keith Thomas's chapter on 'Ancient prophecies', in *Religion and the decline of magic* (New York, 1971), pp. 389-432. During the Second World War, Goebbels encouraged the circulation of a doctored version of the prophecies of Nostradamus by what we would call scribal user publication, arguing that this would be more influential than an appearance in print.

likely enough that having become involved in a culture based on barter, he found it prudent to take whatever it delivered to him, but this would not require that material held as separates always had to be copied into his private miscellany. If we could assume that his interest was the undiscriminating one of the collector, and that virtually any well-penned separate was grist to his mill, the question would disappear but only to be replaced by that of what point of view is *not* revealed by this remarkably catholic assemblage of material. The interesting fact that he was consulted on a matter of ducal nomenclature after the Revolution supports the suspicion of Whiggish sympathies; but might indicate no more than that he was an experienced survivor.[84] The temptation is to assume either a Halifax-like cynicism towards all creeds and parties combined with a fascination with the machinery by which they operate, or a Harington-like ability to accommodate contradictory views of the same institution or individual.[85] Yet our most important clue regarding Sir William is that he should have chosen to preserve this topical, evanescent material with such devoted care, providing an ark for much that would otherwise have been lost. Here there is a striking similarity to Pepys in his capacity as a collector of naval records and specimens of fine contemporary handwriting. Relishing the written ephemera of the past, both men could see a need to lay down new stores for the future.

The universities

And yee who with more secrecie did write
Lines which you thought too precious for the light,
In reseru'd Manuscripts, for shame giue o're
Your hard-strain'd numbers, and disperse no more
Your heauy Rimes, which see[n]e by quicker Eie
Would make one quite abiure all Poetrie,
And studie *Stow* and *Hollinshed*, and make
Tractates of Trauells, or an Almanake . . . [86]

[84] See his letter to Viscount Hatton of 23 Mar. 1689 written from Scotland Yard (BL Add. MS 29563, ff. 453–4). The hand is that of the commonplace book.

[85] Collinson cites Harington's 'half-apology to the ghost of Bishop Aylmer, "whom in mine own perticuler I loued very well, and yet . . . I shall shew perhaps no great signe of it"' (*A supplie*, p. 46). Overall *A supplie* reveals an effortless accommodation of respect for the episcopacy with a profound disrespect for many of its representatives.

[86] Davies of Hereford, *Works*, ii. 81.

These lines from Abraham Holland's *A continued inquisition against paper-persecutors* (1624/5) offer one unsurprising contemporary perception of scribally published verse—that it was a secret medium, and that it was crabbed and difficult in its style. While a fair range of such verse from the earlier years of the century might be held to fit this description, Holland's criticism would seem to be directed primarily at the Inns-of-Court and university wits who wrote in what we call the Metaphysical style, and, like their master Donne, actively preferred manuscript to print.

To find writing and reading of this nature pursued within these institutions is hardly surprising. They were for a start devoted to the training of readers, writers and speakers—the future clergymen, lawyers and administrators. Beyond this they possessed a rich corporate culture, centred in the universities on the college and in the Inns of Court on the individual Inn. Much of the poetry there circulated in manuscript copies was innocent of Holland's charges, being light-hearted social verse, written for recitation on convivial occasions. (Swift in eighteenth-century Dublin belonged to a belated culture of this kind which had its origins in his student days at Trinity College.) Other pieces, especially the ubiquitous elegies and epitaphs, belong to the rites of passage of the institution and are the texts that testify most directly to its enduring ethos. These tend to marry a virtuosity in expression to thoroughly conventional subject matter. But the genuinely 'hard-strain'd' pieces reflect another aspect of university and Inns-of-Court verse, an insistent intellectuality, nourished by years of training in the arts of philosophical disputation and forensic argument. Much university verse was still written in Latin. Circulated as separates and carefully recorded in commonplace books, these texts represent an important but as yet little-studied creative initiative.[87]

Colleges and the Inns were also places where alliances between groups of the rising young could be formed which might persist through an entire lifetime or professional career. Indeed, many young men from aristocratic and gentry families attended for a year or two partly for that reason. On arrival, the novice student

[87] J. W. Binns's *Intellectual culture in Elizabethan and Jacobean England: the Latin writings of the age* (Leeds, 1990) presents an admirably thorough conspectus of the printed writings but gives only cursory attention to manuscript sources and hardly any to commonplace books and personal miscellanies.

would have been exposed to a series of partly authoritarian and partly peer-group pressures designed to instill a new sense of personal identity constructed round membership of both the immediate academic community (college or Inn) and the wider one (the university or profession). Yet, at a later stage it might well have become vital to resist these pressures by creating new communities within the community—a function in which writing and its controlled circulation might perform a central role. The membership of one such group is suggested by John Hoskins' 'Convivium philosophicum' in which the names of thirteen of the author's friends who attended a drinking party at the Mitre are given as Latin puns: Donne becomes 'Factus', Christopher Brooke 'Torrens' and Hugh Holland 'Hugo Inferior-Germanus'.[88] King at Oxford and Crashaw at Cambridge were each involved in active transcriptional cultures, while Oxford in the Laudian era also held the more convivial circle of Corbett and Strode. Later in the century Oxford gave birth to the 'invisible college' whose interest lay in experiments rather than epigrams, but which was equally the child of a process by which the larger institutions were continually giving birth to smaller more specialized ones involving the circulation of 'reserved' writings in manuscript. The reading of these texts could sometimes be a communal experience, as was often the case with printed texts. One widely attested practice was for members of a group to take turns in reading a text aloud with pauses for explication and discussion.

At this period, all areas of formal university scholarship—classical and scriptural languages, rhetoric, logic, theology, Aristotelian science, law, mathematics, medicine and music—were still reliant to a significant degree on the handwritten text transmitted from scholar to scholar and teacher to student. Rosemary O'Day cites several cases of tutors preparing manuscript materials for their students. In one instance from the first decade of the century we find Daniel Featley of Corpus Christi, Oxford worried that 'the many notes and directions' he had given his pupils might fall into the hands of other tutors whom he regarded as rivals.[89] Richard Holdsworth, fellow of Emmanuel, Cambridge, whose *Directions for a student in the universities* was

[88] Text in Aubrey, *Brief lives*, ii. 50–3.

[89] O'Day, *Education and society*, p. 116.

itself intended to be copied by his pupils, considered scribal textbooks to be more valuable than printed ones in the earlier stages of study. Of introductory works on logic he wrote:

This first Systeme may either be a printed one the shortest and exactest one that can be gott or else a written one of your Tutors own collecting: & for some reasons I should rather preferre the latter. First because those that are printed are most of them rather fitted to riper judgments, then for the capacitie & convenience of a young beginners containing many things either too difficult, or lesse necessary for such an one. An other reason is because it is found by experience, that a teacher is more carefull & earnest to inculcate his own notions thã an others, as best understanding why, & to what end every thing there is sayd & bec: there every thing fully agrees with his own judgment wch will scarce happen in an other's works. A third reason may be this, that a Scholar by writing it over shall have gott some knowledge of it, before his Tutor come to read, and explain it to him, w^ch: will make him understand it a great deale better, than if he had not looked over it at all.[90]

The user and entrepreneurial transmission of volumes of lecture summaries, already long established, was to prove one of the most enduring traditions of scribal publication, surviving in British and European universities until the late nineteenth century, and in the case of certain distinguished teachers (Saussure in linguistics; Wittgenstein in philosophy) even longer.[91] Outside curricular studies a shared interest in matters as varied as alchemy, astrology, heraldry, antiquarianism, topography, chronology, modern languages or the more arcane forms of hunting could easily lead to the exchange of epistles, separates or handwritten treatises. One strong incentive to devote time to the composition and reading of these pieces was that the two university cities were rather boring places. Another, more important one was that printed books were

[90] In Harris Francis Fletcher, *The intellectual development of John Milton* (Urbana, Ill., 1961), ii. 634.

[91] In 19th-cent. medical schools a lecturer might give the same lecture for an entire career, or even purchase those of his predecessor and deliver them. But what was actually spoken would not necessarily be the text as such (which students were assumed to have acquired by copying the notes of *their* predecessors) but a series of comments on and digressions around it, incorporating current clinical findings. One example of this is discussed in my *James Edward Neild: Victorian virtuoso* (Melbourne, 1989), p. 286. Among major scientific texts reconstructed with the aid of scribally published lecture notes was Joseph Black's *Lectures on the elements of chemistry*, 2 vols (Edinburgh, 1803).

not always easy to come by. Most instruction was still oral, and university and college libraries were open only to graduates. For the many students prevented by poverty from purchasing their own copies, standard texts could only be acquired through transcription.[92] John North, entering Jesus College, Cambridge, as a fellow-commoner in 1661, was 'early sensible of a great disadvantage to him in his studies by the not having a good library in his reach' and, like many others, ventured beyond his means in building his personal collection. Roger North deplored that 'the most pregnant lads, sons of ministers and others not able to buy for themselves, are lost for want of a little early access to books'.[93] When Henry Peacham counselled the newly-arrived student to seek out learned men 'whose conference and company may bee . . . a liuing and a mouing Library', it was in the understanding that he was unlikely to have access to real libraries.[94]

University reading of scribally published, as of print-published texts was ideally a serious and attentive pursuit. James Howell, writing in 1627 to a cousin at Oxford, is one of a number of writers who use the ancient metaphor of the digestion of food to describe the necessary stages of scholarly reading:

> So in feeding your soul with Science, you must first assume and suck in the matter into your apprehension, then must the memory retain and keep it in, afterwards by disputation, discours, and meditation, it must be well concocted; then must it be agglutinated and converted to nutriment; All this may be reduc'd to these two heads, *tenere fideliter*, & *uti foeliciter*, which are two of the happiest properties in a student . . . [95]

The great emphasis laid on the strengthening of memory led to a pleasure in texts that exploited this capacity by being richly allusive and intricately structured. The study of classical rhetoric and

[92] Cf. O'Day, p. 124.

[93] *General preface and life*, pp. 105, 179. North's remark illustrates O'Day's point that universities were 'socially segregated communities' (p. 90). Up to half the students at some colleges at our period came from aristocratic or gentry families and had no intention of completing their degrees. The intending cleric who did actually complete his BA was usually from a 'plebeian' family.

[94] *The compleat gentleman* (London, 1622), p. 39. The few exceptions were fragile: one of Thomas Crosfield's first acts as librarian of the Queen's College was to ban scholars from the library on penalty of a shilling fine, and to purchase a new lock and keys (*Diary*, p. 46).

[95] James Howell, *Epistolae Ho-Elianae. Familiar letters domestic and forren* (London, 1655), ii. 206.

constant exposure to the sermons organized round the methodical 'division' of the text encouraged an acute sense of the relationship of part to whole within discourses of all kind. (Attendance at sermons, which was compulsory for undergraduates, might be followed by a demand to reconstitute their substance from memory.) Training in Aristotelian logic—the core subject of the seventeenth-century syllabus—made the ingenious manipulation of its procedures in Donne and the Metaphysicals a source of pleasure rather than difficulty. Since this was reading conducted within a community of readers that met corporately several times a day, it would both supply and receive matter from conversation; yet this conversation would itself be of a formal kind, often conducted in Latin, and influenced by the adversarial model of the formal disputation, which O'Day describes as 'the ordinary means of scholarly communication in the Elizabethan and Early Stuart period'. 'Students who intended to take the BA degree', she notes, 'could not evade this part of the course as they could the requirement to attend university lectures. Student notebooks are dominated by work for the disputations.'[96] Tim Yellowhammer in IV. i of Middleton's *A chaste maid in Cheapside* (1613) is ridiculed for disputing in Latin with his tutor, but is doing no more than would have been expected of him within the walls of his college. So disciplined a culture also lent itself to riotous festive inversion of revered methods, as in the speeches of the Oxford Terrae-filii, but even burlesque required its own kind of learned virtuosity.

The university reader was nearly always a writer, at least at the humble level of making notes of what was read or annotating the the margins of his text. '*The Study*', writes Comenius, 'is a place where *a Student*, a part from men, sitteth alone, addicted to his *Studies*, whilst he readeth *Books*, which being within his reach, he layeth open upon *a Desk* and picketh all the best things out of them into his own *Manual*, or marketh them in them with a dash, or *a little star*, in the *Margent*.'[97] The 'manual' was usually a common-place book in which material was entered under subject headings,

[96] p. 112.

[97] *Orbis sensualium pictus*, pp. 200–1: '*Muséum* est locus, ubi studiosus, secretus ab hominibus, solus sedet, *Studiis* deditus, dum lectitat *Libros*, quos penes se super *Pluteum* exponit, & ex illis in *Manuale* suum optima quaeque excerpit, aut in illis *Liturâ*, vel ad *marginem Asterico*, notat'. Cf. Holdsworth in Fletcher, ii. 638.

but John North 'noted as he went along, . . . not in the common way by commonplace, but every book severally, setting down whatever he found worthily to be observed in that book'.[98] Holdsworth was also sceptical about 'the toyle & the interuption it must needs creat to theyr studies, to rise evry foot to a great Folio book, & toss it and turn it for evry little passage y^{t} is to be writt downe', preferring indexed 'bookes of Collections'.[99] The need to participate in the wider culture of writing within the university meant that texts were often assembled for their value as models. The don who might himself be called on to provide an elegy, an oration, a grace or a memorial inscription would be sure to have personal copies of work by admired practitioners. Writing of this kind was an advertisement for the wit of the donor community and the excellence of its Latinity, with rival authors competing in the display of their linguistic endowments.[100] In reading too, attention to style must sometimes have predominated over attention to matter, especially as fates and fortunes were not so intimately bound up as in the metropolis with the accurate prediction of future events.

Academic miscellanies, while invaluable, are unlikely to reveal the full range of what was read in scribal form because they do not generally include what we might think of as 'professional' texts as recorded in evanescent 'paper books' kept by students. But they do give us valuable insight into the shared culture that linked scholars of all ages and disciplines. The gift of a blank album to a student was a common practice: its pages would then be filled up with a greater or lesser degree of enthusiasm depending on the tastes of the recipient. Some from each generation of students would remain in the university to become fellows, sustaining the writing culture they had encountered in their student years and drawing contributions of texts from the wider world to which their contemporaries had dispersed. Advanced at last to church livings, they continued to serve as representatives of both formal and informal academic culture and as staging points for the transmission of manuscripts.

98 North, *General preface and life*, p. 107.

99 Fletcher, ii. 651. Earlier Holdsworth had given advice and models for note taking (pp. 635–6).

100 For a socio-cultural analysis of this phenomenon, see Ong, *Fighting for life*. Holdsworth (p. 645) insists on the need to record 'quaint & handsome expressions' from

The most studied of university readers, Gabriel Harvey (1550–1630), is only vestigially of our period.[101] His vigorous faith in the political mission of humanist learning was one shared by the generation of his patrons Sidney and Leicester but, paradoxically, was not to survive the accession of the scholar-king James I, having already been called into question when Oxford's Henry Cuffe incited Essex to rebellion by the exposition of a passage from Lucan's *Pharsalia*. None the less, the practices noted by Lisa Jardine and Anthony Grafton in their study of Harvey's classical reading are worthy of note insofar as some will undoubtedly have been handed on to the academic generation of Donne and Marston.[102] For a start Harvey's readings are communal, both in the sense of often being conducted in the company of a patron or academic colleague, and in the wider sense of being offered to future readers through his copious marginalia. Secondly we should notice their synoptic nature: favourite texts were characteristically read in combination with a range of related texts, with many annotations specifically aimed at clarifying these connections. This latter aspect of Harvey's reading was encouraged by the culture of print with its capacity to provide the scholar with a wide range of learned writings and commentaries, but the resultant marginalia were a scribal phenomenon that might sometimes even be copied from volume to volume, though this is not known to have happened in his case. The next stage in the process was for the marginal commentary to be integrated into a scribally circulated abridgement, or a review essay of the kind represented by Filmer's *Quaestio quodlibetica*.[103]

The Inns of Court

The atmosphere of the Inns of Court, intermediate in position between the city and Westminster, was less solemn than that of the universities, especially since some students entered in order to gain experience of the metropolis rather than with any serious intention

Latin authors for use in the student's own writing and disputations.

[101] See *Gabriel Harvey's marginalia*, ed. G. C. Moore Smith (Stratford-upon-Avon, 1913) and Virginia F. Stern, *Gabriel Harvey. His life, marginalia and library* (Oxford, 1979).

[102] 'How Gabriel Harvey read his Livy', *P&P* 129 (Nov., 1990), 30–78.

[103] A commentary on Roger Fenton's *A treatise of usury*. For its circulation, see Laslett, 'Sir Robert Filmer', p. 528.

of preparing for a legal career.[104] But the fact that many students came from at least a year or two at the universities, and that the transition required an intitiation into a new institutional culture, meant that the forming of cliques and circles linked by the exchange of manuscripts was no less common. Moreover, these students were generally older now, and therefore closer to the choice to be made among the various careers offered by the great centre of patronage. If that choice was for the law, the Inn might remain their lifelong professional base, a matter that ensured that documents, as well as circulating among peer groups, also had a chance of surviving to new generations. The fact that the practice of the law was centred on the handwritten record, and that professional copyists existed to assist with the transcription of these records, was an encouragement to the scribal publication of non-legal texts. For those with an interest in literature (and it is remarkable how many poets and dramatists spent time at one of the Inns), the soliciting, exchanging or purchasing of separates of new poetry would be the counterpart of a student today becoming involved in the University literary magazine.

Reading in the Inns of Court would have been much more varied in its nature than University reading. Not only were the readers more mature and under laxer discipline, but they must have made a much sharper distinction between professional reading—the process of familiarizing themselves with a vast, imperfectly co-ordinated body of legal precedents—and reading for the purpose of intellectual development, self-cultivation or enjoyment. Reading of this first kind needed to be patient, industrious and, once again, responsive to the ways in which knowledge could be structured for memorization; however, it could also be more selective than, say, reading in science or theology. A very large part of the wording of legal documents has always been conventional and repetitive. Attention characteristically would be directed towards those relatively localized formulations within the conventionalized document that might provide the basis for a legal argument and could be filed for future use in the pages of a commonplace book. Roger North in the course of a

[104] For the Inns at this time, see W. R. Prest, *The Inns of Court under Elizabeth I and the early Stuarts 1590–1640* (London, 1972); David Lemmings, 'The student body of the Inns of Court under the later Stuarts', *BIHR* 58 (1985), 149–66; and O'Day, pp. 154–6.

valuable account of the reading habits of his brother, the future Lord Keeper, locates the skill of this activity in 'the judicious, but very contracted, Note of the Matter'. Francis North, like his other brother John, rejected the conventional method of ordering his materials under alphabetically arranged headings:

> It was his Lordship's constant Practice to commonplace as he read. He had no bad Memory, but was diffident, and would not trust it. He acquired a very small but legible Hand; for, where contracting is the main Business, it is not well to write, as the Fashion now is, uncial or semiuncial Letters, to look like Pigs Ribs. His writing in his Commonplaces was not by way of *Index*, but *Epitome*; because, as he used to say, the looking over the Commonplace Book on any Occasion, gave him a sort of Survey of what he had read about Matters not then inquisited, which refreshed them somewhat in his Memory: And that had not been obtained in a way of mere what and where, as the Style of most *Indexes* runs.[105]

Roger North regarded a commonplace book as 'of little Use to any but to him that made it. For the Law is inculcated by reading the long Arguments to be found in the Books, where Reasons are given *pro* and *con*, and not by any Extracts, however curiously made' (pp. 18–19) and thought that even such celebrated abridgements as Coke upon Littleton should not be put into the hands of students. Students predictably disagreed, sustaining a huge scribal circulation of abridgements and epitomes—many of the best-known text books of the century coming into print only after extensive copying, and often against their compilers' wishes. McKenzie observes: 'Of the hundreds of seventeenth-century editions of law books, many are wrongly attributed and only a few have reliable texts', the main reasons being 'the immense variety of manuscript sources, their wide textual divergence, and the reluctance of the best legal minds to accept that the law should be fixed in public print'.[106]

As was also the case at the universities, students were encouraged to 'digest' their reading through meditation, disputation (in the form of putting cases and mooting) and mutual discussion. Roger North, who held that 'Reading goes off with some Cloud, but Discourse makes all Notions limpid and just', thought that even

[105] *Life of Francis North*, pp. 6–17.
[106] 'Speech–manuscript–print', p. 98.

solitary speech could be of value 'for, in speaking, a Man is his own Auditor (if he had no others at Hand) to correct himself' (p. 16). His brother, being 'most sensible of the Benefit of Discourse' and having discovered that something well talked over never departed from his memory, made a point of making his day's reading the topic of 'his Night's Congress with his Friends, either at Commons or over a Chop' (p. 19). Francis North's regular programme was to spend the morning commonplacing from reports, and then at about noon to turn to 'institutionary' reading in general law books as well as 'some of the Antiquarian Books' which called for little note-taking. Besides these 'the Day afforded him Room for a little History, especially of *England*, modern Books, and Controversy in Print', though these 'Excursions into Humanity and Arts' were not to be regarded as 'suitable to the Genius of every young Student in the Law' (pp. 18–19). Similar programmes are recorded for Simonds D'Ewes and Edward Waterhouse.[107] Such disciplined study was important to the young student as there was no counterpart in the Inns to the tutorial system of the universities.

Despite Roger North's misgivings about his brother's 'Excursions', the study of the common law, for those who embraced it with enthusiasm, would almost invariably encourage an enlargement of interests in the area of English history and antiquities, matters that had little representation in the University curriculum. Working in a profession that made daily use of manuscripts led naturally to the study and transcription of manuscripts of the past, many of which were still of professional value. Simonds D'Ewes must have been among the most industrious of these reader/transcribers but should be seen as just one representative of a deeply historicist intellectual culture centred on the Inns. William Crashawe, the father of the poet, regarded them as 'the most comfortable and delightfull company for a scholler, that (out of the Universities) this kingdome yeelds'.[108] Legal training could also, especially when reinforcing university training in logic and theology, encourage the intense intellectuality that characterizes the work of such Inns-of-Court poets as Donne and Sir John Davies. The reading of such texts not only satisfied tastes formed

[107] O'Day, pp. 159–60.

[108] *Romish forgeries and falsifications* (London, 1606), P3[r]; cited in R. M. Fisher, 'William Crashawe's library at the Temple 1605–1615', *Library*, 5:30 (1975), 117.

by earlier education, but was a mark of the mental qualities by which law students liked to see themselves as distinguished from their contemporaries at court, with whom they were in constant rivalry. (Following a playhouse scuffle in July 1673, it was noted that 'the Inns of Court men rayle horribly at the actions of the Court, and draw themselves into partyes to affront the courtiers anywhere'.[109])

None the less, it must be conceded that the intellectual seriousness of Inns-of-Court literary writing declined significantly in the later decades of the century. If a kind of poetry unique to the Inns still survived in the 1670s it was in the work of William Wycherley and Alexander Radcliffe. Wycherley's verse, though not published in print until the collections of 1704 and 1728, is clearly in many cases of much earlier date. Most of it professedly belongs to a genre of scribally published *vers de société* addressed to friends and acquaintances on the occasion of some event affecting them or some opinion they had uttered. The printed texts conceal the identities of most of these individuals; but poems addressed to Buckingham, Sedley, Etherege, Shadwell and Aphra Behn place themselves firmly within the Buckingham circle of the 1670s, and it is likely that much of the other verse also circulated there. For good reasons this verse remains little read even by those who admire Wycherley's plays. Its faults—merciless logic chopping and excessive length—are legal faults. Legal too is the insistently agonistic tone of the many poems which either contest an opinion delivered by another or defend one of the writer's against criticism. There is little of the ease, the realism or the brevity that characterizes the verse of his courtier friends, and when such qualities are encountered it may well be because they have been supplied by Pope who did a great deal of rewriting prior to eventual print publication.

Wycherley's contemporary, the Gray's Inn wit Alexander Radcliffe, also wrote initially for scribal circulation. The dedication to his printed collection, *The ramble: an anti-heroick poem* (London, 1682) refers to the prior circulation of some pieces 'in single Sheets',[110] and three pieces, 'The ramble', 'A call to the guard

[109] *Letters addressed . . . to Sir Joseph Williamson*, i. 87. Donne's fourth satire is an earlier testimony to this antagonism.

[110] p. (A3^{r-v}).

by a drum' and 'Upon a bowl of punch' are found in scribal miscellanies among work by court libertine poets. In this his verse reflects a situation in which the corporate intellectual life of the Inns had weakened under pressure from an evolving 'town' culture with its headquarters in the theatres, bookshops and coffee-houses of the Covent Garden area: two later Inns-of-Court writers, Southerne and Congreve, show virtually no impress from their legal training. As a token of this capitulation the Inns' elaborately theatrical Christmas rituals quietly fell into disuse to be replaced by mundane drinking and gambling. However, Radcliffe's 'Upon the Memory of Mr. John Sprat, late Steward of Grayes-Inn', a witty mock-epitaph, was clearly meant for readers within his Inn, and can not have made very much sense outside it.[111] Accompanying it at the end of his 1682 volume are a few other pieces of light comic verse written for legal, not courtly readers.

As a site of reading, then, the Inns changed considerably. In the early decades of the century they nourished a confident, highly intellectualized alternative to the literary culture of the court; but by the end of the century their only cultural distinctiveness was that directly imposed by the professional work of the law and a continuing concern with antiquarian research. At both periods scribal publication of new work was the norm, but by the latter the legal community had largely ceased to be a source of texts and styles and was content to become a transmitter. This process coincided with a decline in the social status of students entering the Inns which may in turn have brought a more narrow concentration on preparation for a career in the law.[112]

CONCLUSION

The attempt to distinguish sites for reading and to identify styles of reading likely to have been carried out within those sites has several problematic aspects. One is its frankly *a priori* quality; another is the very obvious point that a single individual, like Calvino's hero, could easily move from one site to another, and presumably, as we

[111] Ibid. 126–7.

[112] The lowered status is documented in Lemmings, 'The student body'. He attributes to the increased inability of the home counties gentry to afford legal training for their sons.

do ourselves, from one style of reading to another. The prophecy of the Westphalian boor, which was transcribed by both Haward and John Watson, must have had one kind of significance read at court by the worldly Sir William and quite another read by Watson at his quiet vicarage in the country, but it is difficult to imagine what the difference would have been had the reader been a common acquaintance with access to both collections.

We are on safer ground when we direct our attention to the ways in which conditions imposed by the site would have determined the nature of the collections assembled within it and through this the possibilities of interpretation open to the reader of the individual item. Clearly a Pindaric ode on the bible means one thing read as part of a collection of godly verse and quite another wedged between two segments of 'Seigneur Dildoe': equally clearly it would not be within all communities of readers that such a juxtaposition would have been possible. Probably about two thirds of the contents of the Haward and Watson miscellanies exists in other manuscript sources—a few of them in thirty or more copies. Currently available bibliographical aids are too imperfect to permit more than a partial reconstruction of these connections, but it is likely that hundreds of other scribal collections, whether they were compiled by individuals or by professionals trying to anticipate the tides of fashion, share at least one item in common with them. Each of these collections can be read both centripetally as providing a unique context of interpretation for the individual item and centrifugally as a trace-bearing artefact of a site or community. To apply one set of results to the elucidation of the other would require great delicacy, since each would be derived from the same data, but need not be an impossible project so long as we were prepared to tread the circle warily. If we were also prepared to range comparatively over the widest practicable spread of collections, the prize to be won would be an understanding of reading as an activity that was always communal as well as individual, and through this a new way of understanding both individuals and communities of the Stuart century.

6

RESTORATION SCRIPTORIAL SATIRE

PROBABLY the best documented tradition of scribal publication is that of the 'state poems' and libertine verse circulated during the last four decades of the century. With the work of David M. Vieth and Keith Walker on the text and canon of Rochester, of W. J. Cameron on an important scriptorium of the 1690s, and of the editors (including Cameron) of the Yale *Poems on affairs of state* series having already identified a large body of manuscript anthologies and separates, Peter Beal's entries for Dorset, Etherege, Marvell and Rochester in the *Index of English literary manuscripts* must have brought us close to a complete knowledge of the surviving sources.[1] Brice Harris's findings as the biographer and editor of Dorset, John Harold Wilson's studies of the court satirists, and Paul Hammond's detailed account of the 'Robinson' miscellany illustrate various aspects of the cultures of authorship and production.[2] That an important collection of this material is housed in the Beinecke Library at Yale is due to the enthusiasm of a collector, the late James M. Osborn, who was also an encourager of the *POAS* project. The other major concentrations are at the British and Bodleian libraries and the University of Nottingham library—the last of these the fruit of a Duke of Portland's interest in the career of an ancestor.

[1] See Vieth, *Attribution*, and *Complete poems*, and Vieth and Bror Danielsson, eds, *The Gyldenstolpe manuscript miscellany of poems by John Wilmot, Earl of Rochester, and other Restoration authors* (Stockholm, 1967), *POAS (Yale)*, vols i–vii, and Cameron, 'Scriptorium'.

[2] Brice Harris, *Charles Sackville, sixth earl of Dorset, patron and poet of the Restoration* (Urbana, Ill., 1940) and *The poems of Charles Sackville*; John Harold Wilson, *The court wits of the Restoration* (Princeton, NJ, 1948) and *Court satires of the Restoration* (Columbus, Oh., 1976); Paul Hammond, 'The Robinson manuscript miscellany of Restoration verse in the Brotherton Collection Leeds', *Proceedings of the Leeds Philosophical and Literary Society*, Literary and historical section, 18/3 (1982), 277–324.

While a few more miscellanies will no doubt be discovered, it is unlikely that they will challenge the picture we already possess of this active and highly professionalized tradition. This makes the satire ideally suited to serve as a detailed case study of the practical workings of scribal publication. The term 'scriptorial satire' has been chosen because so many of the surviving examples were produced as part of scribal editions; however, the notion of the 'scriptorium' is once again used loosely. While some copying probably did take place in spaces organized for that purpose by scriveners or booksellers, much may equally well have been performed by scribes working on piecework in their own homes.

A marked feature of this material is its coherence as a canon of writing. The miscellanies in which it survives restrict themselves, for the most part, to three categories of material. The first of these is what has been referred to as the 'state poems' tradition—satires on politicians and politics. The second comprises satire directed at courtiers and court ladies, and the third erotic, sometimes pornographic, verse mostly written *by* courtiers—these last two categories comprising the 'court libertine' tradition. There are overlaps in subject matter between all three categories; and yet distinctions in tone and approach mean that there is rarely any real difficulty in distinguishing between a 'state' and a 'libertine' satire. The principal form encountered is the lampoon, a satirical attack on a group of victims, who are first addressed in general terms and then picked off one by one. This was in one sub-tradition a folk-form, deriving from much older models of improvised satirical balladry, and in another a pseudo-learned one, whose origin is to be found in Jacobean experiments at the naturalization of classical satire.[3]

Lampoons of the folk-derived class are stanzaic, usually written to a broadside ballad, country dance or playhouse tune. A Star

[3] For the folk aspects of the tradition, see in particular C. J. Sisson, *Lost plays of Shakespeare's age* (Cambridge, 1936), pp. 186–203. On p. 198 Sisson cites a Nottingham example of 1617 where the lampoon was sung to an accompaniment of candlesticks, tongs and basins, indicating its relationship to the 'rough music' of the skimmington. The Jacobean experiments of Hall, Marston and Donne are discussed in O. J. Campbell, *Comicall satyre and Shakespeare's 'Troilus and Cressida'* (San Marino, 1938); John Peter, *Complaint and satire in early English literature* (Oxford, 1956); Anthony Caputi, *John Marston, satirist* (Ithaca, NY, 1961); and Alvin Kernan, *The cankered muse: satire of the English renaissance* (New Haven, Conn., 1959).

Chamber bill of 1622 preserves a fragment of a 'naïve' lampoon directed at a Leicester couple Henry and Jane Skipwith:

John Pilkington did in the moneth of Aprill nowe last past most malitiously frame and contrive an vntrue scandelous and most infamous Libell in wrytinge ag^t. Yo^r said Subiecte and his said wife in theis words followinge (vizt) Henrie Skipwith his wife him Wippeth, because he Married a Twanger, Hee married her a riche Whoare, and hath made her full poore, and paies her olde debtes for anger.[4]

Pilkington sung the piece at various taverns and gatherings around Leicester. The rhythm is recognizable in literary examples such as this of 1667

Good people, draw near
If a ballad you'd hear,
  It will teach you the new way of thriving.
Ne'er trouble your heads
With your books or your beads;
  The world's ruled by cheating and swiving.[5]

or this of 1688

  The talk up and down
  In country and town
Has been long of a parliament's sitting,
  But we'll make it clear
  Ne'er a month in the year
Is proper for such a meeting.[6]

Only the last of these specifies its tune, 'Cold and raw, the north did blow', a version of a much earlier drinking song known as 'Stingo, or oil of barley'. Purcell's use of the piece as the ground bass of a movement in his 1692 birthday ode for Queen Mary has been

[4] PRO STAC8 261/25. For a similar sung text of 1632, see Gardiner, *Reports*, pp. 148–53.

[5] 'A ballad', Wilson, *Court satires*, p. 10.

[6] 'The statesman's almanac', *POAS (Yale)*, iv. 279. For the persistence of the form, compare the following stanza from a poem about the Collingwood Football Club, published in the Melbourne *Age*, 21 September 1990, p. 2:

If the AFL's smart,
They'll give the Magpies a start
Each time that they enter the ring.
It may create some gladness
And help ease the sadness
That comes with the wobbles of spring.

explained by her once having called for it in preference to his own songs; but its history as a lampoon melody suggests a more subversive explanation.[7]

Although it has not been customary for scholars to treat the stanzaic lampoon as a sung form, and the manuscript sources frequently neglect to identify the tune, musical performance will often give cogency to an otherwise nondescript text, besides solving problems of metre and accentuation. To hear Rochester's(?) 'Signior Dildo' sung to its original tune of 'Peggy's gone over sea with the soldier' locates it socially as an improvisatorial drinking song in a way that gives point to what on the page is a rather tedious repetition of a rudimentary joke.[8] One very common stanza form of three iambic tetrameter lines followed by a refrain usually implies a version of the melody known to us as 'Greensleeves'. A nine-line stanza in triple metre with lines five and six half the length of the others infallibly indicates 'Packington's pound'. These and other well-known ballad tunes could be heard daily in the streets and would be recognized by contemporary readers even when not specified in a title. The numerous lampoons using the 'litany' format may well have been chanted in a mock-ecclesiastical way with all present joining in the response (usually 'Libera nos domine').

The other lampoon mode is that which uses heroic couplets to suggest an alliance with the emerging tradition of classically derived satire. But the relationship is more one of show than of substance: if there is a classical influence at work it is the epigrams of Martial rather than the satires of Horace and Juvenal.[9] The usual pattern is for a perfunctory introduction to be followed by a series

[7] For the story see Claude M. Simpson's invaluable *The British broadside ballad and its music* (New Brunswick, NJ, 1966), p. 692.

[8] The tune is identified in Bodl. MS don. b 8, pp. 477–8, 480–2, the only text that survives from close to the time of composition. For the melody see Simpson, p. 572. Stanzaic lampoon tunes not found in Simpson should be sought in the six volumes of Thomas D'Urfey's *Songs compleat, pleasant and divertive* (London, 1719–20)—better known as *Pills to purge melancholy*—and *The complete country dance tunes from Playford's dancing master (1651–ca. 1728)*, ed. Jeremy Barlow (London, 1985). The attribution to Rochester does not seem to have been made until the 1690s.

[9] The influence is discussed in my 'Rochester and the traditions of satire' in my *Restoration literature: critical approaches* (London, 1972), pp. 145–75, drawing on Peter's discussion (*Complaint and satire*, pp. 155–6) of the influence of the classical epigram on the formal experiments of the Jacobean satirists.

of epigram-like attacks on a list of victims. The introduction often does little more than characterize the speaker of the satire as a plain-spoken enemy of cant, and sometimes even this can be dispensed with:

> This way of writing I observe by some
> Is introduced by an exordium,
> But I will leave to make all that ado,
> And in plain English tell you who fucks who.[10]

In other poems, particularly those using the 'ghost', 'dream', 'farewell' or 'advice' conventions, the exordium may be more sustained, but all comes in the end to the parade of personal attacks and it is rare to find a formal conclusion, a couplet or two normally sufficing to terminate the slaughter. Dorset's 'A faithful catalogue of our most eminent ninnies' (1688)—the longest and most vituperative essay in the genre—ends in mid-flight with a brusque 'Cetera desunt'. Alongside the two styles of lampoon, we encounter translations, songs (serious and 'mock'), a few true formal verse satires after classical and contemporary French models, and the occasional more serious political reflection, often using dialogue form. A few short prose satires also occur, usually employing the mock-auction-catalogue, mock-oration or mock-petition formula.

The victims of the satire are drawn from a world largely bounded by the court, the parliament, the Inns of Court, the theatres, and fashionable taverns and coffee houses. While scribally published satires were unquestionably read in the city there are not many cases of citizens being addressed as the primary audience. The writers adopt a tone of familiarity with the great and near-great which, while no doubt often bogus, has the appearance of allowing the reader vicarious entry to a select circle of all-knowing wits. The scribally published text had always attracted through its promise of revealing concealed knowledge, and when such knowledge was not actually available it would be manufactured. (No statement made in a lampoon should be accepted as a historical fact without supporting evidence.) Language is direct, colloquial, and frequently indecent. Names of writers appear more frequently

[10] 'Satire', Wilson, *Court satires*, p. 81.

than one would expect with such compromising works but must be regarded with the same scepticism as their substance. Most are probably speculative, and it is not exceptional for the same poem to appear in different sources attributed to two or three different authors. The editor of the 1704 edition of the second Duke of Buckingham's *Works* warns:

I might add, That several Copies of Verses in this Edition are now restored to their proper Authors, which were attributed before to Persons, to whom they [n]ever belong'd, the Transcribers of the last Age, as well as those of the former, either following common Report, which is often mistaken, or else setting any plausible Names before their Copies, (no matter with what justice this was done) provided it would but promote the value of their Manuscript.[11]

The practice is one that has already been noted in connection with early Stuart parliamentary separates: in this case the attempt to remedy it leads to several new errors. A sub-genre of lampoons satirizing lampooners is a useful source for names of minor poets active in the field, but should be used with caution in assigning authors to particular items.[12] More valuably for our present enquiry, authors of lampoons will frequently identify the scribal publisher who put the work into circulation—Robert Julian, Lenthal Warcup, John Somerton and Henry Heveningham being four so named.[13]

Satire of this kind had already been current during the reigns of James I and Charles I and the interregnum. It is to be regretted in this respect that Yale University Press have never thought to supplement their *Poems on affairs of state 1660–1714* with a preliminary series running from the accession of James I. The

[11] *Miscellaneous works, written by his grace George, late Duke of Buckingham*, 2nd edn (London, 1704), i. A4[r].

[12] Four examples conveniently available in Wilson, *Court satires* are 'The King, Duke and state' (pp. 92–6), 'Dear Julian, twice or thrice a year' (pp. 131–7), 'Mine and the poets' plague consume you all' (pp. 138–40) and 'Here take this, Warcup, spread this up and down' (pp. 159–65). To these should be added Buckingham's 'Thou common shore of this poetic town' (*POAS (Yale)*, i. 387–91), and 'On Monmouth, John Howe, and Lord Mulgrave' (*POAS (Yale)*, v. 4–6). Two lampooners, Roger Martin and John Howe, ingeniously work their names into the concluding couplet of poems (Wilson, pp. 119, 256).

[13] For Julian, Warcup and Somerton see below. Heveningham is the addressee of a prefatory letter to 'The divorce' (1691), quoted in *POAS (Yale)*, v. 534. For his literary career see W. J. Cameron, 'John Dryden and Henry Heveningham', *N&Q* 202 (June–Dec. 1957), 199–203.

events covered would have yielded nothing in interest, and, leaving Dryden and Marvell aside, the talents involved would, on the whole, have been mightier ones. The assassination of the first Duke of Buckingham in 1628 provoked a particularly rich harvest of oppositional verse, some of which occurs as linked groups in manuscript collections of that period.[14] After Milton's friend, Alexander Gill, had drawn attention to himself by claiming that 'if there were a hell and devil surely the Duke was there', a search was made of the 'chamber, study, and pockets' of his friend William Pickering, 'wherein they found divers libels and letters written by Alexander Gill and others, all of them touching on the late Duke of Buckingham'.[15] Bodleian MS Douce 357, acquired as a blank book by one 'A. P.' in 1642, is important for including political verse from both before and after the Restoration. The fifty-six items from the earlier period include linked groups of five poems on the death of Buckingham and nine on the execution of Strafford (including Cleveland's 'Here lies wise and valiant dust'). The 121 post-Restoration satires, written in a different hand, range in date of composition from the mid-1660s to the early 1690s, but are presented in no particular sequence. The collection appears to be unique among the larger anthologies in combining substantial bodies of verse from both the earlier and later seventeenth century.[16] It is possible that the later factors in lampoons no longer had access to the archives of their predecessors. The great fire of 1666, with the attendant destruction of the booksellers' stocks in the vaults under Saint Paul's, could well have been responsible for this. But it is also possible that the tradition of anti-court satire itself became dormant for some years, reviving only towards the end of

[14] Reprinted in *Poems and songs relating to George Villiers, Duke of Buckingham*, ed. F. W. Fairholt (London, 1850) and J. A. Taylor, 'Two unpublished poems on the Duke of Buckingham', *RES*, NS 40 (1989), 232–40. The second of the poems printed by Taylor, William Hemminge's 'Heere lyes thy vrne, O what A little blowe', passed as part of a linked group of three into the archive of the 'Cameron' scriptorium of the 1690s. See also V. L. and M. L. Pearl, 'Richard Corbett's "Against the opposing of the duke in parliament"', pp. 32–9.

[15] *CSP (Dom.) 1628–9*, pp. 338–9.

[16] The other examples known to me are the personal miscellanies, Society of Antiquaries MS 330, compiled by an unidentified Oxford don, BL Add. MS 18220, compiled by the Cambridge don and Sussex vicar, John Watson, and Yale MS Osborn b 52/1–2, compiled by John Pye. Such collections were written piecemeal over many years, whereas Douce 357 appears to have been produced in two or three concentrated acts of copying.

the decade. That tradition will now be considered under its main phases from its beginnings to the accession of Queen Anne in 1703.

'MARVELLIAN' SATIRE 1667–1678

Referring to the years immediately following the Restoration, George deF. Lord notes, not without reason, that 'except for one or two inferior squibs on the plight of the Cavaliers, who were bitter about the Restoration settlement . . . not a breath of criticism survives among all the commendatory verses on the royal family, on Lord Chancellor Hyde, or on Charles' reigning mistress, the Countess of Castlemaine'.[17] Even the savage anti-Dissenter measures of the early 1660s brought no evident reaction in the form of scribally circulated satire. The provocation that led to a revival of the earlier tradition was a printed poem, Waller's *Instructions to a painter*, which presented a flattering portrait of the behaviour of the Duke of York in the Battle of Lowestoft fought on 3 June 1665. This gave rise to a series of three further 'Advice to a painter' poems (1666–7), known as the second, third, and fourth Advices, which were followed by a 'Fifth advice', 'The last instructions to a painter' (both 1667) and 'Further advice to a painter' (1671).[18] Of these the 'Last instructions' (part of which is found in adapted form as 'The loyal Scot') is definitely by Marvell and one or more of the others could well be. A number of other satires of the late 1660s and early 1670s were also attributed to him, though often not until many years later. These are 'Clarendon's housewarming' (When Clarendon had discern'd beforehand'), 'The King's vows' ('When the plate was at pawn and the fob at low ebb'), 'A ballad called the Haymarket hectors' ('I sing a woeful ditty'), 'Upon His Majesty's being made free of the city' ('The Londoners gent'), 'On the statue erected by Sir Robert Viner' ('As cities that to the fierce conquerors yield') and 'The statue at Charing Cross' ('What can be the mystery why Charing Cross').[19]

[17] *POAS (Yale)*, i. 20.

[18] The genre continued to be a productive one until well into the nineteenth century. For its history see Mary Tom Osborne, *Advice-to-a-painter poems, 1633–1856* (Austin, 1949) and *POAS (Yale), passim*.

[19] Annotated texts of these poems will be found in *POAS (Yale)*, i. 20–273 *passim*. The two extreme positions are those of Lord in *POAS (Yale)*, i, who attributes the second and third advices, 'Clarendon's housewarming', the 'Last instructions', 'Further advice to a painter', 'Upon Blood's attempt to steal the crown', 'Upon his Majesty being made free of

Although some of these poems were surreptitiously printed, their initial circulation was in manuscript. Together with such widely circulated satires as 'The downfall of the Chancellor' ('Pride, lust, ambition and the people's hate') and 'On the prorogation' ('Prorogu'd on prorogation—damn'd rogues and whores'), they constituted the core of a widely-read body of oppositional satire, which was soon consolidated into linked groups and sub-collections.

The early history of this 'Marvellian' tradition, can to some extent be reconstructed from its later copyings. Pepys is a witness to the role of user publication in this process. On 14 December 1666, he acquired a copy of what was evidently the 'Second advice', 'sealed up, from Sir H. Cholmly'. This suggests a folded separate rather than the surreptitiously printed broadside that was also in circulation. On 20 January 1667 John Brisbane, another naval official, showed him a copy of the 'Third advice', which he took home in order to copy it, 'having the former—being also mightily pleased with it'. On 1 July, while he was travelling from Rochester to London with John Creed, they 'fell to reading of the several *Advices to a Painter*, which made us good sport'—however, this may have been a printed collection.[20] The second, third and fourth advices are found together in a number of manuscripts in the company of other poems from the tradition. Several of these collections are of interest because the 'Marvellian' material occurs as an apparently self-contained unit within a larger structure. In Princeton MS Taylor 1 and its twin BL Harley 7315 (first compilation) it forms the opening items of a commercial anthology of state poems to 1680 whose other contents seem to have been drawn in no particular order from an assemblage of separates. (The satire immediately following, 'I sing the praise of a worthy wight', dates from the late 1670s.) In Harvard Eng. Misc. e 586, a private miscellany, the group is immediately followed by transcriptions from the 1680 Rochester *Poems on several occasions*

the city', 'On the statue erected by Sir Robert Viner' and 'The statue at Charing Cross' to Marvell, and that of Elizabeth Story Donno, in *Andrew Marvell, the complete poems* (Harmondsworth, 1972), who will allow him only 'The last instructions', with 'Blood and the crown' listed as of uncertain attribution. For discussion of the ascriptions see Donno, pp. 217–18 and Kelliher, *Andrew Marvell*, pp. 97–104.

[20] *Diary*, vii. 407; viii. 21, 313. See also *POAS (Yale)*, i, pp. xxxix–xli. Surreptitious printed editions, all dated 1667, survive of the second advice, the second and third advice

and those in turn by notes on legal cases. Harvard MS Eng. 624 and Society of Antiquaries MS 330 present alternative versions of an anti-Clarendon linked group, the first instance occurring at the beginning of a carelessly-written copy of an anthology compiled circa 1680 and the second in an anthology with both English and Latin sections commenced in 1671 by an Oxford don.

Bodleian MS Eng. poet. d 49 stands apart from the other sources in being a printed book, Marvell's posthumous *Miscellaneous poems* (London, 1681), with extensive manuscript additions. This volume has always been a problem to Marvell scholars since some of the additions are obviously derived from sources very close to Marvell (perhaps even his own copies), while others are satires that are not commonly accepted into the canon. The general assumption has been that they draw on Marvell's own archive of texts and that this included a mixture of his own and others' writing. It is also claimed that the hand of the additions is that of his nephew, William Popple. While there is nothing improbable about these claims, they fail to allow for the possibility that the volume was a publisher's made-up collection that may once have existed in more than one copy. An analogy might be drawn with an appendix of manuscript verse, discussed below, which was sold with some copies of the Rochester *Poems on several occasions* first published in the previous year.

What has been described so far has been an oppositional tradition; but as it evolved through the late 1670s it was increasingly a Whig, Exclusionist tradition. 'Loyal' satirists existed but it was not until the early years of the next decade that they commanded assured networks of entrepreneurial publication. The most telling testimony to the impact of the lampoonists was the attempt made in the new year of 1676 to close down the coffee houses. The author of 'The king, duke and state' (in yet another set of words to the ubiquitous 'stingo') was in no doubt that the lampooners were to blame for the banning.

> I must needs confesse,
> The King could doe no lesse,
> To stop the mouth of Coffee poet,
> No great man or grave

together, and advices two to five with 'Clarendon's housewarming'. For these see *POAS (Yale)*, i. 447–8.

Could be dull fool or knave,
But straight all ye Citty must know it.[21]

The original proclamation of 29 December 1675 does not refer specifically to the availability of seditious manuscripts, merely objecting to 'the great resort of Idle and disaffected persons' including 'many Tradesmen and others' and that 'in such Houses, and by occasion of the meetings of such persons therein, divers False, Malitious and Scandalous Reports are devised and spread abroad, to the Defamation of His Majesties Government, and to the Disturbance of the Peace and Quiet of the Realm'.[22] But the coffee-house proclamation was followed on 7 January 1676 by another which indicates the government's real concern:

Whereas divers malicious and disaffected persons do daily devise and publish, as well by Writing, as Printing, sundry false, infamous, and scandalous Libells, endeavouring thereby, not only to traduce and reproach the Ecclesiastical and Temporal Government of this Kingdom, and the publick Ministers of the same, but also to stir up and dispose the minds of His Majesties Subjects to Sedition and Rebellion; For the discovery of such wicked Offenders, and to the intent that they may receive the severest Punishments which by the Laws of this Kingdom may be inflicted upon them, His Majesty (with the advice of His Privy Council) doth by this Royal Proclamation Publish and Declare, That if any person or persons shall discover and make known . . . the person or persons to whom any such Libell, at any time since the last Act of General Pardon, hath been, or shall hereafter be brought, and by him or them received, in order to Print or transcribe the same; Or the Place where such Libell shall be printing or transcribing, whereby the same shall happen to be seized; Or the person or persons by whom any such Libell at any time since the said Act hath been, or shall hereafter be printed or transcribed; Or shall discover and make known . . . any private Printing-Press . . . He or they making every such discovery, shall have and receive, as a reward from His Majesty, the sum of Twenty pounds.[23]

The proclamation has been carefully drafted to apply to both scribally published and print-published libels and to scriptoria as well as clandestine presses. If enforced with the firmness envisaged

[21] All Souls College, Oxford MS 116, ff. 44^r. There is a second text in Bodleian MS don. b 8, p. 556.

[22] *A proclamation for the suppression of coffee-houses* (London, 1675), p. 1.

[23] *A proclamation for the better discovery of seditious libellers* (London, 1676), p. 1.

by Roger L'Estrange in his 'Proposition concerning Libells' it might have done much to halt the flow of anti-court propaganda; but it is doubtful if this was regarded as practical, its true purpose being to create a means of controlling the coffee-houses short of actual suppression. On the day following the proclamation just quoted *An additional proclamation concerning coffee-houses* was issued which withdrew the earlier demand for abolition, replacing it with another by which each coffee-house proprietor was to take the oaths of allegiance and supremacy and enter into a recognizance of £500 to 'use his utmost endeavour to prevent and hinder all Scandalous Papers, Books or Libels concerning the Government, or the Publick Ministers thereof, from being brought into his House, or to be there read, Perus'd or Divulg'd'. From the outbreak of the Exclusion Bill crisis in 1678 parliament took care to remove what constraints remained on the free flow of both printed and scribal comment, refusing to renew the Licensing Act and encouraging the penny-post as an alternative method of conveying mail, and therefore libels, speedily and cheaply through the London area. By the early 1680s professionally written anthologies of oppositional satire, of the kind represented by BL Add. MS 34362, Harl. MS 7315[1] and Princeton MS Taylor 1, were already available.[24]

COURT LIBERTINE SATIRE OF THE 1670S

The restored court of 1660 was quick to claim its old responsibility for the patronage and supervision of literature. During the early years of Charles's reign, the elderly Duke of Newcastle reassumed the role of Maecenas he had held before the Civil War. Then, Jonson, D'Avenant and Shirley had come under his care. Under the new dispensation, an attempt to enlist Dryden came unstuck over the question of which of the two was to have the credit for *Sir Martin Mar-all*; but Shadwell was delighted to take up the vacancy, while Richard Flecknoe was a regular house guest with the Duke

[24] For the latter two see below. The first is a wide-ranging anthology of state verse compiled in 1682. The inscription on the title-page, 'Sam[ll] Danvers. 1664' seems to be a red herring: the most likely explanation is that the scribe was utilizing a blank book that had been so signed by Danvers.

and members of his very extended family.[25] Newcastle stood for an older concept of patronage but had not fallen too far behind in his tastes. In his championing of Ben Jonson against Shakespeare as the model of comic excellence and in his preference for an improvisatorial ideal of poetic wit, drawing its inspiration from courtly conversation, he was at one with the younger court poets of his time.[26] They in turn seem to have entertained an affectionate respect for both himself and his duchess.[27]

However, most of these younger writers preferred to attach themselves to a younger mentor in the person of George Villiers, second Duke of Buckingham (1628–87), whose wavering loyalties during the interregnum did not prevent him from wielding great influence at court, especially following the fall of Clarendon, which he helped engineer. The extraordinary excesses of Buckingham's private life, remembered through Dryden's portrait of him as 'Zimri' in *Absalom and Achitophel*, have blinded posterity to his very considerable political achievements.[28] A skilled intriguer, a malicious wit, and a man of real if erratic personal charm, he became the acknowledged leader of the group of court wits whose other prominent members were Rochester, Dorset, John, Lord Vaughan (later Earl of Carbery), Sir Charles Sedley, Etherege, Shadwell, Wycherley, Henry Savile and Fleetwood Sheppard. On 6 February 1668, Dorset, Sedley, Etherege and Buckingham sat together in the pit at the first performance of Etherege's *She would if she could*.[29] In 1670 Dorset and Sedley accompanied Buckingham, then at the height of his influence, on an embassy to Louis

[25] For these relationships, see my 'Shadwell, Flecknoe and the Duke of Newcastle' and 'Richard Flecknoe as author-publisher'.

[26] For Cavendish's life, see Geoffrey Trease, *Portrait of a cavalier: William Cavendish, first Duke of Newcastle* (London, 1979). His aesthetic ideals are explained by Douglas Grant in his introduction to *The phanseys of William Cavendish, Marquis of Newcastle* (London, 1956). The influence of the conversational ideal is discussed with reference to Restoration comedy in Robert Markley, *Two-edg'd weapons. Style and ideology in the comedies of Etherege, Wycherley, and Congreve* (Oxford, 1988).

[27] Evident in Etherege's 'To her Excellence the Marchioness of Newcastle after the reading of her incomparable poems', *The poems of Sir George Etherege*, ed. James Thorpe (Princeton, NJ, 1963), pp. 14–15.

[28] Buckingham's life is described in Hester Chapman's *Great Villiers* (London, 1949) and John Harold Wilson's *A rake and his times: George Villiers, second Duke of Buckingham* (New York, 1954). Of these Chapman gets closer to the man and Wilson is more reliable concerning the career.

[29] Pepys, *Diary*, ix. 54.

XIV. Sir Robert Howard should also be mentioned, for, although he and his brother Edward were butts of the wits' satire, he collaborated on *The country gentleman* with Buckingham and on a play about the Manchu conquest of China with Rochester, and was a political organizer for Buckingham in the House of Commons. Buckingham's witty client, Martin Clifford, and even wittier chaplain, Thomas Sprat (both coadjutors in *The rehearsal*), were also close to the circle, though never actual members.[30] Among the established living poets Waller and Butler had close links, while D'Avenant and Dryden were less respected, despite the latter's attempts to ingratiate himself. On Buckingham's departure from office in January 1674 most of the circle followed him into opposition.

But in the first decade following the Restoration, loyalty to the crown presented no problems. Dorset (then known as Lord Buckhurst) came to court aged seventeen in 1660 and began to establish himself as a writer from 1663 when he took part with a group that also included Waller and Sedley in a translation of Corneille's *La mort de Pompée* and engaged in a scribally circulated verse correspondence with Etherege.[31] Whereas the state lampoon took some years to regain its former vigour, the court lampoon was reportedly reinstated by early in the same year when an attempt by the Earl of Chesterfield to protect his wife from the attentions of the Duke of York by hurrying her off to the country set off an outburst of satirical balladry.[32] Anthony Hamilton remembered Dorset, Sedley, Etherege and Rochester as having been contributors, though the latter was actually still absent on the grand tour. Rochester arrived at court at Christmas 1664, immediately following his return from Europe. The period at

[30] Sprat's desertion to the Tories at the time of the Exclusion crisis must have severed his relationship with Buckingham, but letters discussed in Harris, *Charles Sackville*, pp. 137–40 show that after the Revolution he was quick to capitalize on an earlier friendship with Dorset. Clifford seems to have been the source of the greatly expanded version of Buckingham's 'commonplace book' preserved in Hertfordshire CRO MS D/EP F37.

[31] Harris, *Charles Sackville*, pp. 26–7 and 103–5. For the correspondence, see Dorset, *Poems*, ed. Harris, pp. 105–17 and Etherege, *Poems*, pp. 35–45.

[32] Anthony Hamilton, *Mémoires du chevalier de Gramont*, ed. Claire-Éliane Engel (Monaco, 1958), pp. 217–18. A surviving lampoon from 1663, 'Cary's face is not the best' (Wilson, *Court satires*, pp. 3–9), ignores the episode in presenting appraisals of the sexual potential of 18 leading women of the court, but shows all the features of the later misogynist lampoon.

which he began to establish himself as a writer is not clear. If the lyric 'This Bee alone of all his race', attributed to him in National Library of Ireland MS 2093, is authentic, it must have been written prior to the marriage of Lady Mary Stuart to Lord Richard Butler which had taken place by 16 March 1667; but otherwise, apart from three short pieces supposedly written as a schoolboy, no poem currently accepted into the Rochester canon can be confidently given a date earlier than 1670.[33] Testimony to his absorption into the Buckingham circle is given by the choice of Buckhurst (representing the king) and Sedley as godfathers at the christening of his son Charles on 2 January 1671 and the affectionate letter written by Buckhurst on that occasion.[34] The surviving letters from Buckingham himself to Rochester belong to 1676–7 but display an ease and informality that implies long friendship.

The earliest surviving group enterprise of the Buckingham circle was the series of mock-commendatory poems written in response to the publication during Easter term 1669 of Edward Howard's narrative poem, *The British princes*. The responses were probably assembled during the following summer by the time-honoured method of circulating the growing file from writer to writer.[35] It belongs to a tradition whose most notable prior landmarks were the printed collections inspired by *Coryate's crudities* in 1611 and Davenant's *Gondibert* in 1651, and the satires on Samuel Austin the younger collected in *Naps upon Parnassus* in 1658. In the fullest version, that of Bodleian MS Eng. poet. e 4, a private miscellany assembled by an Oxford man, the collection is as follows. Titles, first lines and ascriptions are all given as they appear in the original:

On Mr Edward Howards New Utopia. ('Thou damn'd Antipodes to common Sense,') Charles L. Buckhurst [pp. 188–9]

[33] 'This bee alone' is addressed to Lady Mary under her maiden name. For the marriage, see Pepys, *Diary*, vi. 168n. The lines published under Rochester's name in *Britannia rediviva* (Oxford, 1660) and *Epicedia academiae Oxoniensis* (Oxford, 1660) were believed by Anthony à Wood to be the work of Robert Whitehall (*Athenae Oxonienses*, ed. Philip Bliss (London, 1813–20), iii. 1232).

[34] *Letters*, pp. 60–1.

[35] For the method, see Williams, 'Commendatory verses', pp. 8–9, and for the contributors A. J. Bull, 'Thomas Shadwell's satire on Edward Howard', *RES* 6 (1930), 312–15.

1 [*sic*]. To Mr Edward Howard on his British Princes. ('Come on, you Criticks, find one fault who dare;') Charles B. Buckhurst, now E. Dorsett [p. 190]
2. To the Honourable Ed. Howard Esq. upon his Incomparable, Incomprehensible Poem of the British Princes. ('Sir/ You have[36] oblig'd the British Nation more,') Edmund Waller [pp. 191–2]
3. On the British Princes. ('Your Book our old Knight Errants fame revives,') Th. Spratt [p. 192]
4. An Heroick Poem on the Names and Com[m]anders of England, Rome, and Gaul, or forty six Verses on forty six hundred. ('Our Bard most bravely draws up his Militia,') J. D. [pp. 193–4]
[Annotation to lines 5–6 of previous:] Two Verses left out in the Impression of the Poem. ('A Vest as wondrous Vortiger had on,') [p. 194]
[5.] On the British Princes ('With Envy (Criticks) you'l this Poem read,') Mart. Clifford [p. 194]
6. In Imitation of his most excellent Style ('Of all great Nature *fated* unto witt,') Tho. Shadwell [pp. 195–6]
7. On the same. ('Wonder not, Sir, that praises ne're yet due') L. Vaughan [p. 196]
8. On the British Princes ('As when a Bully draws his sword,')
E[dmund] A[shton] [p. 197]
9. On these two Verses of Mr Howards. But Fame had sent forth all her nimble spies, / To blaze this Match, and lend to Fate some eyes. ('But wherefore all this pother about Fame') Buckingham [pp. 197–8]
On the humour in Mr Howards Play, where Mr Kinaston disputes his staying in, or going out of Town, as he is pulling on his Boots. In Imitation of the Earle of Orrerey. ('How hath my Passion made me Cupids scoff!') G. D Buckingham. [pp. 198–9]

This is actually a later recension of the series which has been augmented with poems by Dorset and Buckingham directed at Howard's play *The new Utopia*, published and, as far as is known, first performed in 1671. Buckingham's second contribution appears in variant form in III. ii of *The rehearsal*, written with the assistance of Sprat, Clifford and Butler and first performed in December 1671, and may even have been the germ of that work. The Howard linked-group adds the shadowy Edmund Ashton to our roll-call of the Buckingham circle, but omits Sedley, who could, however, well lurk behind the provocative initials 'J. D.'. (Dryden as Howard's brother-in-law would hardly have associ-

[36] Corrected in MS to 'Y'have'.

ated himself with such a project.) Rochester is also missing, probably because of his absence in Paris during the spring and early summer of 1669. Despite the Howard satires having been circulated as a lengthy linked group, there is no evidence at this date of substantial anthologies of the verse of the circle being in circulation. It seems likely that for many years poems were transmitted only as separates and linked groups, and that only author and user publication were undertaken.

But Rochester, while continuing as late as 'An allusion to Horace' (1675–6) to argue the superiority of the intimate coterie audience, was finding a growing readership through user publication. In part this was purposive: poems written to wound enemies or to further his position at court would have failed in their aim if they had never spread beyond his own intimates.[37] He is known to have carried separates in his coat pockets and on one occasion late in 1673 or early in 1674 to have reached into the wrong pocket and handed the king a copy of 'I'th' isle of Great Britain', in which Charles was very roughly handled. In this case the desire to find a readership for his lampoons proved disastrous, but in others it was a necessary concomitant of writing. Two possible methods of spreading a lampoon are suggested in the anonymous 'Satyr unmuzzled' (1680) which speaks of 'lewd libels . . . / Which are i'th'streets by porters dropp'd and hurl'd; / Or else by Julian 'mongst the bullies spread—'.[38] It seems unlikely that handwritten lampoons would have been thrown around in the streets; and yet few compositions of this kind were ever printed.[39] Spreading amongst the bullies is well documented, and it is also known that poems were posted on doors and walls, inscribed as

[37] In his conversations with Burnet, he confirms that his lampoons were intended not merely to amuse his friends but to mortify his victims, something which could only happen if they were made generally available at Whitehall (*Some passages of the life and death of the Right Honourable John Earl of Rochester* (London, 1680), pp. 25–6).

[38] *POAS (Yale)*, ii. 209.

[39] However, H. J. Chaytor, *From script to print: an introduction to medieval vernacular literature* (Cambridge, 1945), p. 131 refers to 'dropping lampoons in public or private places, or fastening them up on walls' as common medieval practices. Proculus in Fletcher's *Valentinian*, IV. i. 84 produces a compromising letter which has been 'Scatterd belike i'th Court' (*Dramatic works*, iv. 338). Evelyn notes under 2 April 1668: 'Amongst other Libertine Libells, there was now printed & thrown about a bold Petition of the poore Whores, to the Lady *Castlemaine* &c:' (*Diary*, iii. 507). This was a printed version of a scribally published satire which continued to be widely copied independently of its printed transmission.

graffiti and strategically inveigled into the apartments of leading courtiers.[40] Once spoken of at Whitehall they would have been eagerly sought for private copying.

Moreover, by 1673 verse by Rochester was also circulating at those hotbeds of scribal publication, the Inns of Court. The young Theophilus, seventh Earl of Huntingdon, marooned at his family seat at Donnington Park, Leicestershire, was supplied with new lampoons by his town correspondent, Godfrey Thacker of Gray's Inn. By March of that year Thacker had already sent 'A ramble in St James's Park', 'Too long the wise commons' and an imperfectly memorized version of lines from 'I rise at eleven'. On 15 April Thacker wrote: 'I have been in quest of some more of my L[d] Rochesters ingenuitie but cannot as yet accomplish my desires, but in the meanetime I present you with a coppy that is stolne from one to another a bout towne and fortunately this morning came to my hands'.[41] The poem enclosed ('Betwixt Father Patrick and's Highness of late') is probably not by Rochester, but the image of texts stealing 'from one to another' is a revealing one and suggests that other work beside that mentioned had already escaped into the wider possession of the town. A letter from Henry Ball to Sir Joseph Williamson of the same year is another piece of evidence for widening interest in the lampoons of the Buckingham circle:

> But all men feare our officers of this army are not well pickt out, for the most of them debaucht profane persons and publique atheists which they say openly they learne of the Duke of Buckingham, one yesterday publickly in company I am told saying he believed neither Heaven nor Hell. These kinds of reports make the Town full of malicious libells. I am

[40] Examples given by the well-placed Sir William Haward and preserved in Bodl. MS don. b 8 are 'Haec Carmina in limine thalami Regis a quo, nescio, Nebulone, scripta reperiebantur' ('Bella fugis, Bellas sequeris, Belloque repugnas'), p. 183; 'Ouer the priuy Stayres att Whitehall found written wth a black-Lead-pen' ('Hobbs his Religion, Hyde his Moralls gaue'), p. 183; 'Written ouer Nell Gwins doore' ('These Lodgings are ready lett, & appoynted'), p. 212; the couplet, referred to in Ch. 5, which was found over the door of the king's bedchamber on 26 November 1675 ('In vaine for Ayde to yo[ur]. old Freinds you call'), p. 539; 'The Inscription put ouer y[e] Gate att Marchant-Taylers Hall, when y[e] Duke dined there, die Martis. 21°. Octobr. 1679', p. 597; and two short poems fixed to the House of Commons door on 26 January and 15 April 1680 respectively, p. 644.

[41] Cited in Lucyle Hook, 'Something more about Rochester', *MLN* 75 (1960), 482. Lady Campden in 1682 was less fortunate. A letter of 20 April complains that new lampoons (not of course by Rochester) had appeared attacking the ladies but she was unable to get a copy of them (Wilson, *Court satires*, p. 81).

told of severall, and promised the copyes of some which I dare not venture by the Post.[42]

Ball's combination of horror at the libertinism of the circle with eagerness to obtain the manuscripts in which its blasphemies were expounded is a familiar one, albeit that, as an active scribal journalist and government spy, he was obliged to keep informed about such matters.

The transition from a limited to a more intense form of author and user publication and from that to entrepreneurial publication probably resulted from recourse to professional scribes to assist in the copying of lampoons for distribution at court. Rochester's household in 1675 apparently included at least one skilled scribe in the person of Thomas Alcock who later composed a narrative of an episode of 1675–6 in which Rochester set up as a mountebank under the name of Alexander Bendo.[43] But by this date Rochester may well have been in touch with the period's best-known scribal publisher, Robert Julian. Julian, a naval clerk, had previously been secretary to Admiral Sir Edward Spragge.[44] During engagements against the Dutch and the Algerines his place would have been by Spragge's side on the quarterdeck in order to take down messages (Nelson's secretary was killed at Trafalgar while performing this duty). Dorset and Rochester who, on different occasions, both served under Spragge's command, would have shared this perilous eminence and have had the responsibility of delivering some of the messages.[45] Following Spragge's death in action on 11 August

[42] *Letters addressed to Sir Joseph Williamson*, i. 67.

[43] Thomas Alcock and Rochester, *The famous pathologist or the noble mountebank*, ed. V. de Sola Pinto (Nottingham, 1961). Pinto asserts that the manuscript is in Alcock's own hand, which may well be the case, although the signatures reproduced on p. 9 can hardly be regarded as confirmation.

[44] For Julian see Brice Harris, 'Captain Robert Julian, secretary to the muses', *ELH* 10 (1943), 294–309; Mary Claire Randolph, '"Mr Julian, secretary of the muses": Pasquil in London', *N&Q* 184 (Jan.–June 1943), 2–6; and Judith Slater, 'The early career of Captain Robert Julian, secretary to the muses', *N&Q* 211 (June–Dec. 1966), 260–2. The accounts indicate that he was fond of the bottle and heavily scarred. In 1685 he was described as 'an ancient man and almost blind' (*CTB*, viii, 1685–9, p. 231). A letter written by him in 1670 (PRO SP29/281A/226) asks for a message to be sent to his wife. Assuming a birth date *c.*1620–5, he may have been the Robert Julian who married Mary Blewitt at Saint Peter's upon Cornhill on 29 Apr. 1647 (*A register of all the christninges, burialles and weddinges within the parish of Saint Peeters upon Cornhill*, ed. G. W. G. Leveson Gower (London, 1877), p. 258).

[45] During the Four Days Battle of June 1666, Rochester carried a dispatch from Spragge under fire in a small boat. It was presumably written by Julian.

1673, Julian's post disappeared and he was imprisoned for debt. Among those to whom he applied for relief was Dorset, who is addressed in an undated letter as Earl of Middlesex, the title by which he was known between 4 April 1675 and 27 August 1677.[46] Julian speaks in this letter of having already received support from certain 'Persons of Honor', conceivably including Rochester, who is spoken of elsewhere as being linked with him in 'mutuall friendship'.[47] Another could well have been Pepys, to whom Julian had introduced himself in a finely penned letter of 30 June 1667 (see Plate 2) and who was a collector of the work of writing masters.[48] Dorset kept Julian's letter and seems subsequently to have been his principal patron. Certainly, by 1677 Julian was well recognized as a professional factor of lampoons, and Dorset's own poems were listed among his wares. A hypothesis which would account both for this and for the emergence of the poems of the court wits of the Buckingham circle into wider circulation during the mid-1670s is that he was initially employed by members of the group as a scribe in author publication, and moved by stages into the entrepreneurial publication first of separates and then of larger compilations.[49] The circle may also have helped supply the high-level protection that he must undoubtedly have possessed in order to continue as long as he did in his scandalous and highly illegal trade. For in the earlier years, at least, of his activities, Julian's primary affiliation was with the anti-Yorkist opposition.

Both the political and the literary ideals of the Buckingham circle are on display in Rochester's 'An allusion to Horace' written during the winter of 1675–6. The literary ideals (foreshadowed in Buckingham's own *The rehearsal*) include an emphasis on sense and plainness, hostility towards the heroic play and its chief proponent, Dryden, and an aristocratic belief in the supremacy of impromptu,

[46] Printed in Harris, *Charles Sackville*, pp. 178–9. The original was not able to be traced among the Sackville papers at the Kent CRO.

[47] 'Rochester's ghost addressing it self to the secretary of the muses' ('From the deep-vaulted Den of endless Night'), l. 9, *Poems on affairs of state, from the reign of K. James the first, to this present year 1703* (London, 1703), p. 128.

[48] PRO SP29/207/119, f. 181r.

[49] Satirical accounts of Julian make frequent reference to his 'books' (for examples, see Harris 'Captain Robert Julian' and Randolph, 'Mr Julian'); however, no surviving anthology appears to contain his hand. Julian's script is represented in numerous documents of 1667–73 in the Public Record Office written as Spragge's secretary, some signed with his own name and some with Spragge's.

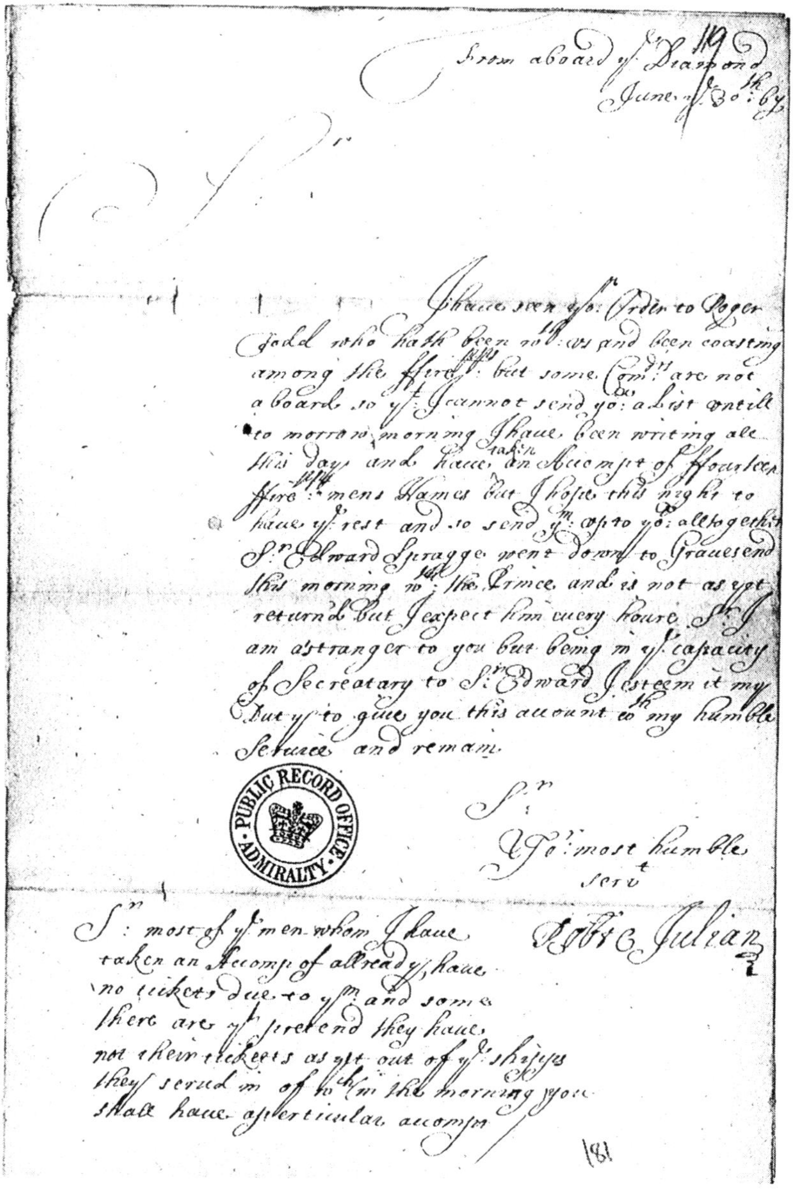

119

From aboard ye Diamond
June ye 30th: 67

Sr

I have seen yor: Order to Roger Codd who hath been wth: us and been coasting among the ffireshipps: but some Comdrs are not aboard so yt I cannot send yo: a List untill to morrow morning I have been writing all this day and have taken an Accompt of ffourteen ffireshipp: mens Names but I hope this night to have ye rest and so send ym up to yo: altogether Sr Edward Spragge went down to Gravesend this morning wth the Prince and is not as yet return'd but I expect him every houre Sr I am a stranger to you but being in ye capacity of Secretary to Sr Edward I esteem it my Duty to give you this account wth my humble Service and remain

Sr
Yor: most humble
servt
Robt Julian

Sr: most of ye men whom I have taken an Accompt of already ye have no tickets due to ym and some there are yt pretend they have not their tickets as yet out of ye shipps they served in of wch in the morning you shall have a perticular accompt

181

PLATE 2. Robert Julian to Samuel Pepys, 30 June 1667.

quasi-conversational wit over the laboured products of the professional pensmith. The circle shared Newcastle's preference for the Jonsonian style in comedy, and supported his protégé, Shadwell, who dedicated several times to its members. It also lent its assistance to Etherege and Wycherley, the two masters of the earlier phase of Restoration comedy of manners. The membership of the group as it stood in the mid-1670s is defined in the closing lines of the 'Allusion':

> I loath the Rabble, 'tis enough for me,
> If Sidley, Shadwell, Shepherd, Witcherley,
> Godolphin, Buttler, Buckhurst, Buckingham,
> And some few more, whom I omit to name
> Approve my Sense, I count their Censure Fame.[50]

The inclusion of the Tory, Godolphin, and the elderly Samuel Butler (if he is the individual intended) indicates that this is rather a list of Rochester's primary readership as an author-publisher than of the Buckingham faction per se; but otherwise the fit is exact. However, it still points to a political entity. While Wycherley and Etherege, for their own reasons, were to move into the Yorkist camp, Buckingham, Dorset, Sedley, Sheppard and Shadwell were all in separate ways to play a significant part in bringing about the great change of 1688, though Buckingham did not live to see it.

Buckingham had always been close to Marvell, his wife's former tutor, and, while a Francophile in his personal tastes, shared Shaftesbury's suspicion of the king's Catholic brother and heir, James Duke of York. By the crucial year of 1677 the position of Buckingham and his clients was one of Whig placemen in a Tory court, sceptical in religion but anti-Catholic in politics, French in culture but by now pro-Dutch in foreign policy, boon companions of the king yet resentful of the power of those unconstitutional ministers of state, his mistresses. They had been important to Charles as a counterpoise to the partisans of his brother, but by 1677 they were losing their usefulness through their association with Shaftesbury's anti-Yorkist extremism. Poetry, along with sceptical philosophy and practical debauchery, was the bonding agent of a group whose ultimate rationale was political—the

[50] Quoted in Walker's text (*Poems*, p. 102).

heterodox, Erastian wing of the Whig alliance. Rochester's cultivation during 1679–80 of the latitudinarian Protestant and Whig ideologue, Gilbert Burnet, is to be seen as a conscious political self-distancing from a Catholicizing court.

The concluding lines of the 'Allusion' suggest something of the closed, defensive position of the circle in the late 1670s within a court whose policies it was opposing in parliament and for whose leaders, if Rochester's letters are any guide, it had profound contempt. But the poem as a whole, although it argues for the priority of satire written for an intimate audience of cognoscenti, was also through the boldness of its cultural critique and its cultivation of a Horatian 'public' voice, addressing itself to an audience beyond these confines. One might even argue that it was presenting the values of frankness and clarity cultivated within the closed circle as the model for a critical public discourse that would address itself to matters of state as well as of taste. In this respect Rochester seems to accept even as he condemns the wider audience of opinion makers to which his work was now being brought by professional copyists.

ROBERT JULIAN AS SCRIBAL PUBLISHER

Whatever Julian's earlier relationship with his authors may have been, the close of the 1670s saw him well established as an entrepreneurial marketer of lampoons. Keeping no shop, his model for distribution was that adopted by other purveyors of luxury items of personal sale at the levees of the rich and powerful.[51] The increasing reliance of courtly authors on commercial factors of manuscripts inevitably brought its strains. In Julian's case it seems to have led to a temporary breakdown of trust over the scribe's mixing of work from the Buckingham circle with that of their Tory opponents.

Much of our knowledge of Julian comes from a considerable body of satires addressed to him by name.[52] Some of these also

[51] A practice well documented in Restoration comedy. Cf. Etherege, *The man of mode* (1676), I. i (oranges, shoes) and Vanbrugh, *The relapse* (1696), I. iii (clothes, shoes, stockings, wigs).

[52] Listed in Hugh Macdonald, *John Dryden, a bibliography of early editions and of Drydeniana* (Oxford, 1939), pp. 214–15. See also Harris, 'Captain Robert Julian' and Randolph, 'Mr Julian'.

claim to have been sent to him as a scribal publisher for circulation, as in the opening lines of the 'Letter to Julian' (1684):

> Dear Julian, twice or thrice a year
> I write to help thee in some gear;
> For thou by nonsense liv'st, not wit,
> As carps thrive best where cattle shit.[53]

The truth of such claims would be possible to accept if we could assume that he was reasonably thick-skinned and regarded the opportunity for advertisement as more important than the evidence the addresses provided of his involvement in an illegal trade. But there is one address that displays a vituperativeness towards Julian that makes it unlikely that he would have wished to publish it. This is 'A familiar epistle to Mr Julian secretary to the muses', apparently written before August 1677 (Dorset is still Middlesex) and attributable with reasonable certainty to Buckingham himself. Its opening lines will indicate the general tone of the piece, and also how active Julian had now become as a scribal publisher.

> Thou common shore of this poetic town,
> Where all our excrements of wit are thrown—
> For sonnet, satire, bawdry, blasphemy
> Are empti'd and disburden'd all on thee:
> The choleric wight, untrussing in a rage,
> Finds thee and leaves his load upon thy page—
> Thou Julian, O thou wise Vespasian, rather,
> Dost from this dung thy well-pick'd guineas gather.
> All mischief's thine; transcribing, thou dost stoop
> From lofty Middlesex to lowly Scroope.[54]

So far the references to Julian may be accepted as heavy-handed banter, but as the poem progresses it becomes clear that it is not only an address to Julian but an attack on him, and that his crime has been his association with the (then) Tory satirist, Sir Carr Scroope, who is the second target of the lampooner.

> This is the man ordain'd to do thee good,

[53] Wilson, *Court satires*, p. 131. Cf. also ll. 1–2 of 'A letter to Julian from Tunbridge' (ibid. 141): 'Dear friend, I fain would try once more / To help thee clear thy brandy score'.

[54] *POAS (Yale)*, i. 388–91, ll. 1–10.

The pelican to feed thee with his blood,
Thy wit, thy poet, nay thy friend! for he
Is fit to be a friend to none but thee. (ll. 87–90)

The rift between the Buckingham circle and Scroope had begun with an obscene parody by Rochester of Scoope's lyric, 'I cannot change as others do', and an attack on Rochester by Scroope in his widely copied 'In defence of satire' (1677). Rochester replied to this in 'On the supposed author of a late poem 'In defence of satire"; Scroope retorted in 'The author's reply' and Rochester delivered the *coup de grâce* in 'On poet Ninny'. The first three of these circulated as a linked group, but the fourth somehow became attached to another Rochester linked group directed at John Sheffield, Earl of Mulgrave.[55] More to the point is that Scroope was at least a temporary member of a rival group of Tory poets which had been formed in 1676 by Mulgrave, and which had Dryden as its principal professional luminary.[56]

The impetus to this new scribal community arose from the increasingly oppositional position of the Buckingham group and the consequent need to create a Yorkist centre of patronage. The formation of the group was made manifest in print by the publication of Lee's *The rival queens* in 1677 with a dedication to Mulgrave, a commendatory poem by Dryden and a prologue by Scroope, and confirmed by the 1680 *Ovid's epistles translated* whose contributors are a virtual roll-call of the Tory poets. In manuscript, the satirical scrapping with Scroope was parallelled in Rochester's poetical assaults on Mulgrave and Mulgrave's return of fire, with assistance from Dryden, in a long lampoon of 1679, 'An essay upon satire', whose targets are the wits of the Buckingham circle and their new political ally Halifax.[57] Dryden's attack on Shadwell in *Mac Flecknoe*, datable to mid-1676–77 though not appearing in

[55] For the poems and their sources, see *POAS (Yale)*, i. 364–75 and *Poems*, ed. Walker, pp. 109–10, 114–16 and notes. Aspects of the Rochester-Scroope imbroglio are discussed in Vieth, *Attribution*, pp. 137–63, 231–8 and 322–52.

[56] For the Mulgrave circle, see Vieth, *Attribution*, pp. 322–52 and *passim*. In March 1676 Scroope had still been close enough to the Buckingham circle to be entrusted with the prologue to Etherege's *The man of mode*. A snap at him in ll. 53–6 of Mulgrave and Dryden's 'An essay on satire' was probably prompted by his return to the Whig fold at the time of the Exclusion crisis. He is attacked as a Whig in 'A rambling satyr' ('Shall the world be thus abused and I sett still'), Lincolnshire Archives Office MS Anc 15/B/4, pp. 104–5.

[57] Text in *POAS (Yale)*, i. 396–413.

print until 1682 and surviving in sixteen manuscript copies independent of the printed text, represented a gauntlet thrown down by the leading professional of one faction to the leading professional of the other.[58] 'Advice to Apollo', for which a date late in 1677 would be plausible, praises Rochester and Dorset but is tart in its references to Scroope, Mulgrave and Dryden.[59] There is a tacit assumption in all these widely circulated poems that readers will be familiar with other writings allusively referred to and their putative authors, confirming that circulation had advanced beyond the simple passing of separates from friend to friend.

Julian's crime, and the cause of Buckingham's annoyance in his 'Epistle', was that he had begun to circulate work by both factions. Having been honoured with the opportunity to publish poems by Middlesex, he had intermingled them with the excremental outpourings of Scroope. Buckingham is thus justified in branding him as a 'poor apostate' (l. 20), though the allusion was a predictable one. We can also safely allow for a degree of aristocratic outrage that the choice sprouts of his own and his friends' wit had become objects of commerce: the poem takes care to indicate that it is Scroope's wares which are the proper ones for such a purpose. The caution seems to have been sufficient to put an end to Julian's truancy. A monologue put into his mouth in a satire of 1685, when the Tory ascendancy had removed his political protection, not only presents him as a Whig pensioner but contains a specific quotation of Buckingham's words of eight years earlier:

> Was't not hard measure, say, my Whiggish peers,
> Vending your nonsense to expose my ears?
> My pocket stuffed with scandal long has been
> The house of office to vend out your spleen,
> The common sink o'th' town, wherein you shit

[58] For the manuscripts see Beal, *IELM*, ii/1, 407–8. The sixteenth copy is in National Library of Ireland MS 2093, knowledge of which I owe to Dr Beal. Shadwell replied in the scribally published 'Upon a late fallen poet' ('A sad mischance I sing alas') and the printed *The medal of John Bayes* (London, 1682).

[59] Text in *POAS (Yale)*, i. 392–5. For a hypothesis regarding the origin of the poem, see Wilson, *Court wits*, p. 195. However, Wilson's belief that this was the group lampoon referred to in a letter of 1 Nov. 1677 from Henry Savile to Rochester is not reflected in any apparent stylistic feature. If permitted to guess at an author, I would suggest Sedley. A parting shot at Fleetwood Sheppard, a friend of both Buckingham and Dorset, indicates that none of these three was responsible.

To carry off your excrements of wit.
Such gallantry has not of late been shown;
To save your ears, poor Julian lost his own;
But if you ever catch me at that strain—
To vend your scurrilous scoundrel stuff again—
May infamy and scandal be my bane.[60]

Among the names of Julian's writers that follow are those of Rochester's protégé, John Grubham Howe, at that time as extreme a Whig as he was later to be a Tory, Etherege, and Julian's 'great Maecenas', Dorset, who is praised as having paid 'double fees for what himself had writ'. The appearance in the list of the most un-Whiggish Mulgrave and Dryden confirms that at the period of their collaboration they had been numbered, albeit briefly, among Julian's stable of authors.

A valuable picture of Julian in action is given in a rare Tory satire of 1679–80, 'The visitt', here given complete from the apparently unique source, Lincolnshire Archives Office MS Anc 15/B/4, with the warning that the text shows signs of corruption:[61]

Pox on the Rhiming Fops that Plague the Town
with Libelling the Court and Rayling at the Gown
A man can make no visitt now but his Caresse
Is a Lewd Satyr shewn which Pray S^{r}. Guess
whose still [style?] it is: good Faith S^{r}. I dont care
For truly I read none that Treasons are
Then hee Replys Lord tis the wittyest thing
Tis smart on Nelly Portsmouth, and the King[62]
Just as he speakes comes Julian Passing by
His Pocketts stuft wth: scarrilous Poetry
my Freind Crys hee and adds to that a Bow
Thou slaue to th' muses, whats the newest now

[60] Wilson, *Court satires*, pp. 138–9. Julian is also included in the anti-Whig, 'A rambling satyr' (see n. 56).

[61] The manuscript, formerly in the possession of a John Brownloe, is a professionally prepared anthology of satires from the period 1679–82, possibly written as a series of separates rather than an integral volume. It is related textually to BL Harl. MS 6913 and Nottingham UL MS Pw V 38. The text is reproduced with the permission of the Trustees of the Grimsthorpe and Drummond Castle Trust.

[62] Satires that would qualify here are Rochester's 'When to the King I bid good Morrow', 1676 (*Poems*, ed. Walker, pp. 102–3) and Lacy's 'Preserved by wonder in the oak, O Charles', 1677 (*POAS (Yale)*, i. 425–8). It cannot be Mulgrave and Dryden's 'An essay upon satire' (ibid. 396–413) which is enquired for later in the poem.

S'Blood S^{r}. says he you're sicke oth old Disease
you want new Papers, dam mee where's my Fees
Of Guineys tost with Julian you're a Rogue
we'are straight Presented with whats new in vogue
There was obscene Rotchesters Cheife storys
of matrix Glances Dildo and Clittoris
With Dorsetts Tawdry Nonsense drest For sale
This motto on't Braue Buckhurst nere Faile
Gods Blood and wounds Crys Julian thats grown stale
I scarce can Put it off For nants and Ale
The next was smoothly writ by squinting Carr
Of Pembrooks drunken tricks, his Bull and Beare[63]
Behen was there with Bawdry in a vaile
But swearing Bloodily as in a Goale
Mulgraue appear'd with his base Borrowed witt
And Dryden at his heeles a owning it
There was Lewd Buckinghams slimb Poetry
But stufft so full of horrid Blasphemy
made Julian doubt there was no diety
Feirce Drydens satyr wee desir'd to veiw
For wee had heard he mourn'd in Black and Blew
Hee search'd for it but twas not to be Found
Twas Put ith Garett for a hundred Pound
The Taburn was the next resoult, where I
Quite weary of there Tipling company
went home a Cursing of this wretched age
That Couples each old Lady wth. her Page
And whores the Chastest virgin wth. her dog
And Calls the best of Kings a senceless Log[64]

The ambiguous use of 'he' in line 9 should not be allowed to obscure the fact that it is Julian, not the friend, who is doing the selling. The payment of guineas leads to his producing his wares

[63] Pembroke's menagerie is mentioned by Aubrey (*Brief lives*, ed. Andrew Clark (Oxford, 1898), i. 317). Sir Carr Scroope appears to refer to Pembroke, but not his beasts, in 'In defense of satire', ll. 32–5, *POAS (Yale)*, i. 365 and n. 35.

[64] Citing an Aesopian allusion in a satire of 1680, 'The rabble' ('The rabble hates, the gentry fear'), l. 17; text in *POAS (Yale)*, ii. 342–3, also found in the cited manuscript, p. 115, with an attribution to Fleetwood Sheppard: 'England is Betwixt Thee and Yorke / The Fabble of the Frogg / Hee is the feirce devouring storke / And thou the Lumpish Logg.' Cf. also 'The history of insipids' (1674), ll. 163–8: 'Then farewell, sacred Majesty, / Let's pull all brutish tyrants down! . . . / Mankind, like miserable frogs, / Is wretched, king'd by storks or logs.' (*POAS (Yale)*, i. 251)

from his pockets. The writers mentioned were those popular at the close of the decade, all being represented in Yale MS Osborn b 105, the scribal sibling of the 1680 Rochester *Poems*. The poem must date from not long after the incident of 18 December 1679 when Dryden was attacked in Rose Alley, supposedly because of his share in 'An essay on satire'. The customers are keen to see a copy of the 'Essay' but learn that it has been suppressed by Julian in return for a bribe (and no doubt other kinds of pressure).

THE 1680 COMPILATIONS AND THEIR SCRIPTORIA

1680 sees the beginning of a new stage in the scribal publication of lampoons, characterized by the writing of substantial miscellanies. In part this simply indicates that a large enough body of poems was in circulation to permit the preparation of such collections, but it was also influenced by demand for work by Rochester in the year of his illness and death. The decision of parliament on 30 October to permit the printing of votes and transactions may also have contributed by closing down a busy area of scribal production.

Until this time the entrepreneurially published anthology of court-libertine (as of Marvellian) verse had been a rarity. Of surviving compilations only Harvard MS Eng. 636F, Princeton MS 14401 and BL MS Harl. 7312 appear to antedate 1680.[65] The raw materials for the new compilations were the separates and linked groups which had been circulated by Julian and whatever others had joined him in his trade. The work of these publishers seems always to have been uncoordinated, except insofar as they drew from time to time on each other's separates. It was also of brief duration with most ceasing to produce anthologies of court-libertine verse after the appearance of the printed Rochester *Poems on several occasions*, itself based on a scribally published anthology, late in 1680. There is no sense of the situation of the 1690s where a single agency was supplying most of the book-trade's requirement for scribally published satire. Since a number of these, admittedly scandalous, 1680 volumes survive with pages excised or poems and passages scribbled over, it is likely that the loss rate has been exceptionally high.

[65] MS Eng. 636F is considered below. Harl. 7312, an important source of libertine and pornographic verse, dates from 1678–9.

The fact that each anthologist was drawing on a restricted repertoire of separates and linked groups results in striking similarities in contents and sometimes order. The detailed collations presented in Keith Walker's edition of Rochester permit genealogical analysis of the textual interrelationships of several of the most widely copied poems. These have been supplemented, in my own case, by repetition and extension of some of Walker's collations, and selective collation of a number of other popular copied texts. The claim that any given pair of anthologies is the work of different compilers rather than representing varied selections from a body of separates held by a single scriptorium is based on this work, with a necessary acknowledgement of its incomplete character. A thorough investigation of these highly complex textual relationships would be a labour of many years. The archives so far identified and their surviving products are listed below.

(a) The 'Hansen' archive. The archive of this short-lived scriptorium was the source for at least four manuscripts, of which two survive, a third is known from a later scribal copy, and a fourth served as copy for the 1680 Rochester *Poems*.[66] Its most celebrated product is the important, though mutilated Rochester source, Yale MS Osborn b 105. The name 'Hansen' inscribed on its title page must surely refer to the diplomat, Friedrich Augustus Hansen, who visited England briefly in September 1680 in the entourage of Charles, the electoral prince Palatine.[67] It is a professional production which draws on excellent sources within the Buckingham circle and presents good texts and authoritative attributions. The collateral printed collection omits eleven poems which are present in the manuscript, of which four can be associated directly or by implication with the Mulgrave circle. These are Mulgrave's own 'Since now my Silvia, is as kind as faire', Dryden's *Mac Flecknoe*, and two vicious attacks on Buckingham, 'A new ballad to an old tune call'd Sage leafe' and the 'D: of B: letany'. The effect of these absences is to make the printed

[66] The relationship between the manuscript and the printed edition is exhaustively investigated in Vieth, *Attribution* pp. 56–100.

[67] For the evidence for this see Love, 'Scribal texts and literary communities: the Rochester circle and Osborn b. 105', *SB* 42 (1989), 232–3.

collection much more narrowly aligned with the Buckingham group, with its remaining adversarial poems (all by Scroope) embedded in linked groups where they are neutralized by answers. It is not at present clear whether this is the result of pruning—presumably by the print-publisher—or whether the manuscript copy for the printed text represented an earlier stage of the compilation which was subsequently augmented.[68] Whatever the case, that the collection was compiled in full awareness of the controversy is shown by the choice of Rochester's 'Epistolary essay' to Mulgrave as its opening item. The printed *Poems* has been stripped of attributions, presumably so as to suggest that its contents were entirely by Rochester.

The ready availability of this collection in its printed form led to some recopying of items into manuscript collections. However, the wider importance of Osborn b 105 for the history of scriptorial satire is that its writer was also concerned in the production of a companion volume of state poems which has survived in two copies. The first of these, Princeton MS Taylor 1, was written in the same hand as Osborn b 105 at almost exactly the same date and contains political satires from the Marvellian tradition, including four of the 'Advice to a painter poems', 'The downfall of the chancellor', 'Britannia and Raleigh' ('Ah! Raleigh, when thy breath thou didst resign'), 'The history of insipids' ('Chaste, pious, prudent Charles the Second') and 'A dialogue between the two horses' ('We read in profane and sacred records'). Only the two anti-Buckingham poems, 'The D: of B: letany' and 'A new ballad to an old tune call'd Sage leafe' are common to both collections. Another copy of the state-poems collection, lacking one item, is the first of two manuscript anthologies in the same hand bound as BL MS Harl. 7315, the second being a product of the later 'Cameron' scriptorium. The two 1680 compilations, the political and the libertine, define the scriptorial archive of a professional trader in manuscripts briefly active during that year but not apparently after it. They also make clear that, as with the 'Cameron' scriptorium, the publisher acknowledged a demand for

[68] There is a suggestion, explored in my 'Scribal texts', pp. 227–8, that any such compiler may have been associated with Gray's Inn. This is strengthened by Godfrey Thacker's activity there as a collector of Rochesterian verse.

two different kinds of product—witty, sexually explicit court satire and outspoken comment on the wider field of public events.

(b) The Gyldenstolpe archive. This has been named from an important anthology discovered by Bror Danielsson in the Riks-Bibliotheket, Stockholm (MS Vu. 69) and published in facsimile in 1967 by him and Vieth as *The Gyldenstolpe manuscript miscellany*. It belongs to a group of anthologies (not all of them textually related) which commence with Edmund Ashton's 'Gentle reproofs have long been tried in vain', apparently as an advertisement that the reproofs in what followed were going to be the reverse of gentle.[69] Its contents, predominantly from the court libertine tradition, contain a high degree of overlap with Osborn b 105, but, where the matter has been tested, there is no consistent textual affiliation. The collection must therefore be viewed as an independent garnering from the same corpus of material circulating as separates and linked groups. There is, however, an intermingling of recently written political satires, together with one or two earlier ones not usually associated with the Marvellian group. The *terminus ad quem* for compilation was set by Vieth as the 'late summer of 1680'.[70]

Here again we have a guide, though in this case not a complete one, to the scriptorial archive of a professional trader in manuscripts. A small collection of lampoons which was bound by Pepys with his copy of the 1680 *Poems* is revealed unmistakably by its variants to be drawn from the same archive.[71] Nottingham University Library MS Portland Pw V 32 is a very similar small collection from the same source, in this case explicitly titled *A supplement to some of my Lord Rochester's poems*. A third sub-collection, closely related in both order and contents to Pw V 32, provided the opening element of a later compilation, Princeton MS Taylor 3. It is likely that small collections of this kind were commissioned for sale with the printed 1680 collection. Nottingham University Library MS Portland Pw V 40 draws on

[69] Other anthologies having this as their first item are BL Add. MS 21094, BL Harl. MSS 6913 and 7312, Pepysian Library, Magdalene College Cambridge MS appendix to Rochester *Poems on several occasions* (1680), Nottingham UL MSS Pw V 32 and 38, and Princeton MS Taylor 3. The poem also appears in the Danchin manuscript (see below).

[70] *Gyldenstolpe miscellany*, p. xxiv.

[71] Richard Luckett, Pepysian Librarian, Magdalene College, has identified the handwriting as that of Pepys's secretary, Paul Lorrain.

another product of the scriptorium, intermingling poems from this source (identifiable by both stemmatological evidence and sequence) with others transcribed from the 'Pforzheimer' edition of the 1680 *Poems*—another case in which the work of the scriptorium is associated with the 1680 printed text.[72] Suggestive similarities in order plus a tendency to contiguity in stemmas also suggest a relationship with the Leeds 'Robinson' anthology; but in this case it is likely that the derivation was not direct but by the absorption of a sub-collection or a body of separates issued from the original 'Gyldenstolpe' scriptorium.

The scriptorium, then, was an apparently short-lived operation of 1680–1. There must be a high probability that it was run by a bookseller who also handled copies of the 1680 Rochester *Poems*.

(c) Harvard University Library MS Eng. 636F. This manuscript has been held in high regard by editors of Rochester and, after Osborn b 105, is the second most important contemporary source for his poems. It attracts through the elegant bravura of its hand, a pleasingly virtuosic exception to the blandness of much Restoration bookwork. Its contents, both Rochesterian and non-Rochesterian, overlap considerably with Osborn b 105, the poems not found in the Yale collection being mostly of a libertine or indecent nature. However, its texts are uneven in quality, despite the fact that it was compiled perhaps as early as December 1679. Once again we have an independent compilation from separates, linked groups and small sub-collections, which were already in general circulation. No further work deriving from this archive has so far been identified, though there is a tendency for it to group in collations with texts from the Edinburgh aggregation.

(d) The Danchin manuscript. This professionally written manuscript was acquired in Paris by Pierre Danchin and published by him in facsimile.[73] Although the excision of sexually objectionable material has left it seriously defective, it would seem to belong among the 1680 manuscripts. Its latest datable item is Scroope's

[72] This relationship was first pointed out by Vieth, *Gyldenstolpe manuscript*, p. xxvi.

[73] 'A late seventeenth-century miscellany—a facsimile edition of a manuscript collection of poems, largely by John Wilmot, Earl of Rochester', *Cahiers Élizabéthains*, no. 22 (Oct. 1982), 51–86.

'While *Phaon* to the flaming *Aetna* flies' in what appears to be a transcription from the Dryden–Tonson *Ovid's epistles, translated by several hands* (1680), which had been published by February 1680.[74]

(e) The Edinburgh aggregation. Edinburgh University Library MS D C 1 3, an oblong folio, is an unusual compilation which appears to record the contents of six separate smaller collections. They were copied throughout by the same scribe, who has given the texts a strong infusion of Scotticisms. Each sub-collection has its own title page and index, and the presence of a certain degree of overlap between the collections supports the premise that this was not simply a scribal convention to break up an otherwise unmanageable corpus of verse. Errors in pagination suggest that at least the first two collections were present in a consecutively written exemplar. With the exception of the sixth collection, which is solely composed of songs, the contents are a somewhat incoherent mixture of libertine verse, earlier state poems and current satire. Compilation would seem to have taken place late in 1683 though the bulk of the material dates from prior to 1680. The texts of the poems are, where tested, very poor: all the elements of the aggregation seem to stand at the end of a long succession of copyings. The manuscript appears to preserve the archive of an Edinburgh scriptorium, some of whose exemplars may well have come north with courtiers attending on York or Monmouth during their periods of residence in Scotland.

(f) The Dublin manuscript. A second regional compilation is represented by National Library of Ireland MS 2093, a professionally written pocket manuscript, principally of verse by Rochester, which is shown to be posthumous by the presence of Flatman's 'As on his deathbed gasping Strephon lay'. The collection draws partly on separates from the London scriptoria (its text of 'An epistolary essay' is from the same source as that of Harvard MS Eng. 636F) and partly on otherwise unrecorded material which appears to

[74] The volume is advertised in the *True domestic intelligence* for 10 Feb. 1680. The derivation is suggested by the sharing of an obvious error in the last line: 'But lett thy [for 'my'] Life here wth. thy Letter end'.

derive directly from the Rochester circle.[75] The most likely point of origin would be the vice-regal court at Dublin, a mimic Whitehall presided over by the elderly Duke of Ormond, one of whose daughters-in-law is the subject of a poem.

TOPICAL SATIRE OF THE 1680S

As mentioned earlier, the publication of the 1680 Rochester *Poems*, fairly late in that year, and its many surreptitious reprintings destroyed the market for collections solely or substantially devoted to court-libertine verse. From the following year court-libertine poems generally occur intermingled with political satires from the Marvellian and current traditions. An early example of these transitional volumes is Leeds University Library MS Brotherton 54, which was originally written by two scribes (later additions may be ignored for our present purposes).[76] The base collection (items 1–8 and 24–59) is an anthology of pre-1680 court-libertine verse with a strong contribution from Rochester; however, interpolated within this is a sub-collection of state satires of 1679–80 (items 9–23), all of this material being the work of hand A. The second collection, written by hand B, consists of state satires from 1683 to 1687 in rough chronological order, intermixed with some earlier libertine verse.

Alongside the collections which mixed current with retrospective lampoons, and which became increasingly prominent as the century progressed, other compilers concentrated on presenting volumes of material illustrating recent and current production, often with the items arranged chronologically. An example from the early 1680s (a boom period for lampoons[77]) is the pair BL MS Harley 6913 and Nottingham University Library Pw V 38, collections of topical satire from 1679–83, which, as Vieth was the first to point out, are substantially identical in contents and sequence. Both follow the example of the Gyldenstolpe manuscript by commencing with Ashton's 'Gentle reproofs have long

[75] In addition to three unique Rochester items listed by Beal, there is 'Chloe to Sabina', attributed to Mrs Jean Fox, whose title alludes to 'Artemisa to Chloe'.

[76] The manuscript is described and indexed in Hammond, 'Robinson miscellany'.

[77] Contemporary references to this are cited in *The prologues and epilogues of the Restoration 1660–1700*, ed. Pierre Danchin (Nancy, 1981–8), iii, pp. xviii–xix.

been tried in vain' but do not appear on present evidence to be textually dependent on the Gyldenstolpe archive. Lincolnshire Archives Office Anc. 15/B/4 shares a sequence of items with the pair. Another important source, National Library of Scotland Adv. MS 19.1.12, preserves three pre-existing compilations of which the first, covering 1680–84, survives independently as Nottingham University Library MS Portland Pw V 45. The second is a collection of state and libertine verse ranging from the late 1660s to 1680. At the end of this the scribe has copied the explicit of his exemplar, reading 'Exiatur. Fin de premier tome'.[78] The third collection opens in a new hand as a continuation of the second but then reverts to the first hand to become a continuation of the first. Within each section an attempt has been made to place the poems in chronological order, with dates given for most post-1677 items. Two further professionally written anthologies of topical satire are BL Add. MS 34362, containing satires from the late 1670s and early 1680s, and Yale MS Osborn b 113, a collection of the early 1680s with two token Rochester items from the earlier repertoire.

Although the publishers of these volumes have yet to be identified, the names of some individuals involved in the trade are known from a number of sources including the satires themselves. Robert Julian continued to market lampoons through the first half of the eighties. In the prologue to Ravenscroft's *The London cuckolds*, believed to have been first performed in October 1681, a lively picture is given of an outburst of lampoon writing:

> Now Fop may dine with Half-wit ev'ry noon,
> And reade his Satyr, or his worse Lampoon.
> *Julian*'s so furnished by these scribling Sparks
> That he pays off old Scores, and keeps two Clarks.[79]

And, indeed, it would seem from the evidence assembled by Harris and Randolph that his role at this period was more that of publisher than scribe. He waited personally on his upper-class clients both supplying newly copied lampoons, conveyed in his pockets, and collecting the contributions of authors for future copying. He would also deliver billets doux for a fee, wrote

[78] F. 109^{r}. Ff. 109^{v}–110^{v} are blank, the text resuming on f. 111^{r}.

[79] Danchin, *Prologues and epilogues*, iii. 329.

newsletters, and is reputed to have done some pimping on the side. An anecdote concerning Joe Haines indicates that he would pay, when necessary, for promising new copy.[80] In 1684 he finally succumbed to the law. On 31 May he was charged in the court of King's Bench and in November of that year fined and sentenced to the pillory 'for publishing several scandalous libells'.[81] He also suffered the humiliation of having one of his ears cropped. Unable to pay his fine, he remained in prison until the following June when an appeal for clemency to James II proved successful, no doubt because of his former sea service under James as Admiral. If he returned to his old trade, it was in an appropriately surreptitious fashion. The appearance of a burlesque epitaph in 1688 would suggest that this was the year of his death, were it not that Jack Howe's 'An epistle to Somerton', dated by Cameron 'possibly just before, but more probably just after the Revolution' speaks of him as alive and still working.[82]

Two other names also appear in verse addresses of the period, those of 'Captain' Warcup and John Somerton. Warcup is addressed in a lampoon of June 1686 couched in the form of advice about where writers of libels might be found.

> Here take this, Warcup, spread this up and down,
> Thou second scandal carrier of the Town;
> Thy trapstick legs and foolish, puny face
> Look as if nature meant thee for the place.
> In this vocation should grow greater far
> Than e'er should do by stratagems of war.[83]

Warcup has been convincingly identified by the editor of the satire, J. H. Wilson, as Captain Lenthal Warcup of the First Foot Guards, a son of the Whig justice, Edmund Warcup. Why an army officer would have traded in manuscripts is not clear—perhaps his role was rather that of a social circulator of lampoons—yet one

[80] In Tobyas Thomas, *The life of the late famous comedian, Jo Hayns* (London, 1701), pp. 45–6, Haines is said to have sold Julian a manuscript of 'On the three dukes killing the beadle' ('Near Holborne lies a park of great renown').

[81] Narcissus Luttrell, *A brief historical relation of state affairs* (Oxford, 1857), i. 319–20.

[82] 'Epitaph on the secretary of the muses' in *Poetical recreations . . . Part II* (London, 1688), p. 66 and several manuscript sources. A 'notched' scribe, suggestive of Julian, is referred to in the introductory epistle to 'The divorce' (1691), *POAS (Yale)*, v. 534. For 'An epistle to Somerton' see ibid., v. 535–6.

[83] Wilson, *Court satires*, p. 159.

large collection can be circumstantially linked with a regimental colleague of Warcup, Charles Robinson.[84]

Somerton is more mysterious. Howe's 'An epistle to Somerton' (1688–9) addresses him in terms that imply that he was a competitor of a still active Julian:

> Dear Somerton, once my beloved correspondent,
> Since scandal's so scarce, though the world is so fond on't
> That poor Brother Julian of pay does miscarry
> As well as the List, Civil, and Military,
> And the brains of our poets as empty are grown,
> As his Majesty's coffers, or (faith) as their own . . .[85]

The use of 'correspondent' suggests that Somerton may have moved into the lampoon field from being a newsletter writer—a logical enough progression. Our only other information comes from one of Tom Brown's *Letters from the dead to the living*, published in 1702, which is a reply from Will Pierre to the by then undoubtedly deceased Julian.[86] This tells us that 'since your death, and your Successor *Summerton*'s Madness, Lampoon has felt a very sensible decay'. An early hand has entered Somerton's name together with that of 'Bhen' on the title page of Bodleian MS Firth c 16, a substantial miscellany covering the years 1682–8. The title of the volume, *Astrea's booke for songs & satyr's*, confirms the connection with Aphra Behn, but leaves Somerton's role unclarified. The manuscript as originally copied contained 132 items. It is written in three main hands, two of them skilled book hands and the third a hurried and careless script, legible but revealing little concern with appearance. Mary Ann O'Donnell has identified the most frequent of the book hands as that of Aphra Behn, a discovery that greatly increases the interest of the volume but still leaves a mystery surrounding its function.[87] One explanation would be that it was the archive of the Somerton

[84] Leeds MS Brotherton Lt 54 contains two notes of direction to a Captain Robinson whose address is given as 'att Cpt Eloass [Elwes] near ye Watch house in Marlburrough street'. Assuming the reference was to a military and not a naval officer, Charles Robinson is the most likely candidate.

[85] *POAS (Yale)*, v. 535.

[86] (London, 1702), pp. 69–70.

[87] 'A verse miscellany of Aphra Behn: Bodleian Library MS Firth *c.* 16', *English manuscript studies* 2 (1990), 189–227.

(Behn?) scriptorium, similar to the great books of Starkey and Collins, with new items entered on acquisition by whichever scribe was available. What the book is not is a finished professional product intended for sale; but then neither is it a random, personal commonplace book: the concentration throughout is on topical, vendible lampoons.

As a coverage of satire to the eve of the Revolution, Firth c 16 can be grouped with Bodleian Douce 57 (second element) and Harvard Eng. 585 under the generic title of 'accession miscellanies'. By this is meant collections that present retrospective surveys of the satire of a particular reign or reigns on the occasion of the beginning of a new one. While the precise intentions of their compilers can only be guessed at, it is likely that the gathering of large numbers of potential customers in London for a coronation or first regnal parliament would create a demand for collections of this kind.

The wide readership achieved by scriptorial satire at this period is indicated by the casual way in which knowledge of particular scribally published pieces is assumed by writers for the theatre. An address to the 'Scribbling Beaus' in the epilogue to Aphra Behn's *The lucky chance* (1687) attempts a riposte to '*the late Satyr on Poetry*'—probably the 'Satyr on the poets' ('Wretch whosoe'er thou art that longst for praise') found in manuscripts of the Cameron scriptorium.[88] Southerne in the prologue *Sir Anthony Love* (1691) works a reference to a current lampoon into a lament for the absence of male theatregoers at the war in Ireland:

> *Some weak amends this thin Town might afford,*
> *If honest Gentlemen would keep their word.*
> *But your lewd* Tunbridge-*Scandal that was moving,*
> *Foretold how sad a Time wou'd come for Loving.*
> *Sad Time indeed when you begin to write:*
> *'Tis a shrewd sign of waning Appetite,*
> *When you forget your selves, to think of Wit.* [89]

Dryden's more general reproof in the prologue to *Amphitryon*

[88] Danchin, *Prologues and epilogues*, iv. 613. Danchin's candidates, two printed satires, were each several years out of date by this time. The context suggests strongly that lampoon-writers were intended.

[89] *The works of Thomas Southerne*, ed. Robert Jordan and Harold Love (Oxford, 1988), i. 172.

(1690) is linked by Richard Elias with the circulation of 'The female nine' ('What chance has brought thee into verse').[90] Lampoons of this kind, as well as proliferating in written form, were quickly appropriated by a culture of gossip shared between the male coffee house and the female tea table. News of the accusations made in a new lampoon would promote the desire to obtain a copy.

THE 1690S

Whereas the reign of James II had seen the satirists concentrating their venom on the court, the 1690s saw the recurrence of a healthy diversity of views, with Whigs and Tories, Williamites and Jacobites, belabouring each other in collections which display a surprising catholicity of viewpoints. The 'court Whig' tradition (so called to distinguish itself from its 'country' counterpart) was in many ways a derivative of the Buckingham circle in the 1670s. It is customary to think of the court of William and Mary as a rather dour place; but that was not the case as long as Purcell was in charge of its music, Kneller in charge of its art and Dorset in charge of its writers. Re-established at court in 1688 as Lord Chamberlain, a post he held until April 1697, and with the large revenues generated by that office at his service, Dorset moved into the last and most splendid decade of his career as a patron. With Fleetwood Sheppard as his *fidus Achates*, and Matthew Prior, Charles Montagu and George Stepney as protégés, he was once more at the centre of English literary culture, occupying a position not all that different from Newcastle's in the years following 1660, as an elder statesman of letters who was also a respected practitioner: moreover, he was younger than Newcastle had been, turning forty-five in the year of the Revolution. His circle included old Whig friends such as Shadwell, for whom he secured the laureateship stripped from Dryden, and Sedley who found a new lease of life as a translator and epigrammist; but he was also generous to former foes such as D'Urfey, a ready convert to the new order, and the unrepentant Jacobite, Dryden, whom Dorset personally recompensed for the loss of his official positions.

[90] *Works*, xv. 227; *POAS (Yale)*, v. 202–10.

The impact of the court group shows clearly in the miscellanies, especially those of the 'Cameron' scriptorium. Dorset remained one of the star authors, represented in the anthologies by the immense 'Faithful catalogue' of 1688 and a sprinkling of slighter satires and of the elegantly turned songs that were his forte.[91] However, although his influence was a strong one at the beginning of the decade, it was eventually to fade. In moving from opposition to become part of the establishment, the Dorset circle had offered itself as a target to both the Tories and those factions of his own party who were offended by Dorset's determination to extract every available guinea from his office. His master William III was also, on the whole, rather roughly handled, with the satirists routinely accusing him of a homosexual relationship with his favourite, Bentinck. Otherwise the satire of the decade reflects the vigour and many-sidedness of its politics. With a relatively small number of exceptions, of which the most notable is Yale MS Osborn b 111, a collection of 'Loyal poems' prepared for the exiled James II, the surviving miscellanies are unpartisan in their representation of competing points of view. Far from being factional collections they suggest a sophisticated interest in the political debate as debate, and in the artistry and malice of the satirist irrespective of the particular message. The satire in turn remains oppositional in a general tendency to denigrate those who currently hold power, but never seems able to speak with the authority of a movement which knows its time has come.

THE 'CAMERON' SCRIPTORIUM

The work of this scriptorium was first identified by W. J. Cameron while editing texts for volume 5 of the Yale *Poems on affairs of state* series, and was described by him in an important article of 1963 which has already been extensively cited.[92] Cameron's discussion of his material is extremely condensed, representing a preliminary report on a topic that would have justified a book-length study. While the essence of his method lay in the integration of textual, physical and historical data, his most telling evidence was derived

[91] For these, see Harris, *Charles Sackville*, and *Poems*, *passim*.

[92] Cameron, 'Scriptorium'; see also *POAS (Yale)*, v. 527–38.

from collations for the Yale edition, which the editorial policy of the series only permitted to be included in reduced form. Hopes that he might have returned to this material or given a fuller account of his evidence were dashed by his unexpected death in 1988.

In summarizing his findings I intend to begin where he did with an unusual manuscript in the Folger Library, MS M b 12, which is an aggregation of three originally separate manuscripts of state and libertine verse. The first two of these manuscripts were written by different scribes, with the third a joint effort in which the first-volume scribe was responsible for pp. 1–253 and the second-volume scribe for pp. 257–315. The care and similarity of the hands and the disciplined method of presenting the texts both suggest a conscious effort to achieve what Cameron calls 'an impersonal, professional norm' (p. 31). When the three manuscripts were originally written, there had been some overlap of contents between them, but, as part of the process of aggregation, the duplicated poems, along with some others, had been removed by a complicated mixture of excisions and pasteovers. Cameron had no trouble in demonstrating that the three sub-volumes represented the archive of a scribal publisher who offered his customers a choice of three different styles of miscellany, giving rise to what Cameron called the 'William' group, the 'Venus' group and the 'Restoration' group. Each of these groups is represented by a number of surviving manuscripts copied prior to the pruning of the archive and its incorporation into a single volume. These groups will be considered, as Cameron does, in the reverse order of their representation in the Folger manuscript, which will have the advantage of placing the most clearly defined group first and the most problematic last.

The 'William' group consists of satires of the reign of William and Mary and William alone and was continually updated during that reign. The earliest surviving member is Huntington MS Ellesmere 8770 whose title page reads: *A Collection of the best Poems, Lampoons, Songs & Satyrs from the Revolu[ti]on 1688. to 1692.* The other volumes known to Cameron were University of Nottingham Library MS Portland Pw V 47 (1695), Earl of Leicester's MS Holkham 686 (1695), BL Harl. MS 7315 (second element, 1701), Portland Pw V 48 (no date but also circa 1701),

University of Chicago MS PR1225f H5 c 7 (written after William's death in 1702), and Portland Pw V 44. The title page of the Folger sub-volume gives a date-range 1688–99 to which '1703/4' was later added, which the contents indicate was the date at which compilation ceased. Portland Pw V 44 is of the same period but Cameron was able to show that it derives from Folger as it was prior to its mutilation (or an immediate ancestor) and therefore preserves texts of the items excised during reconstruction. Detailed comparisons of watermarks made by Cameron provide strong evidence of origin within the scriptorium for all except the Chicago and Harleian manuscripts, which he classifies as extra-scriptorial copies ultimately derived from Pw V 48. Most of the manuscripts have the items in chronological order of years, with dates supplied when known, but this regularity sometimes breaks down towards the end of a manuscript.

The William group represents a continually evolving collection to which new items were regularly added and from which old ones were regularly discarded, a classic case of what I call a 'rolling archetype'. Beginning as an anthology of topical writing, it eventually turned into an 'accession' miscellany, recording the whole political history of William's reign and opening the way for a new topical compilation covering that of Anne—though it is not clear whether this was ever attempted. A manuscript unknown to Cameron was Leeds University Library Brotherton MS Lt q 38, which is a twin of BL Harl. 7315/2, though not in the same hand.

Cameron's second group, which is also represented second in the Folger manuscript, is a collection of chiefly libertine verse with a strong pornographic element. Its contents are signalled and its identity established by its opening item, the (otherwise innocuous) 'Venus her enquiry after Cupid'. Other manuscripts from this group, listed by Cameron, are Nottingham University Portland MS Pw V 42, Ohio State University MS Eng. 15, Princeton MS Taylor 2 and Bodleian MS Firth c 15. Cameron reports that there is much less variation in contents than in the case of the William group, but much variation in order within a broadly chronological arrangement. Portland Pw V 42 may well preserve the content of the Folger element as it was prior to mutilation. Watermark evidence confirms that all manuscripts originated within the scriptorium.

The third group is simultaneously the smallest, and the one that gave rise to the most substantial manuscripts. Called by Cameron the 'Restoration' group, it is an accession miscellany of libertine verse and state poems from the early 1670s to 1688, embracing much of the content of the 'Venus' group. The most imposing representatives of this group are Österreichische Nationalbibliothek MS 14090 and Victoria and Albert Museum MS Dyce 43, collections which in their original numbering contain 880 and 841 pages respectively. These are versions, in two different hands, of the same miscellany, except that the Vienna manuscript omits a few items found in the Dyce.[93] Selective collation shows that initially both scribes were working from a common exemplar; however, in at least some of the later texts Vienna is a descendent of Dyce. Vienna is also the less formally written, with such extensive use of contractions that it would have been difficult to make a completely accurate copy from it. The other representatives of the group, which are Folger MS M b 12 (first element) and Nottingham University Library Portland Pw V 43, represent selections from the earlier and the later part respectively of the huge primary compilation, the first ending with item 162 of the Dyce manuscript and the second beginning with item 164. (These are Cameron's numbers: mine would be 164 and 166; the corresponding numbers in the Vienna MS are 155 and 157.[94]) The contents of a lost manuscript are preserved in BL Harl. MS 6914, pp. 1–158, which is a copy made outside the scriptorium of fifty-seven poems from the Dyce/Vienna compilation.

In addition to the groups given, Cameron also identifies two other products of the scriptorium, a manuscript, Nottingham Pw V 46, and a printed book, *Poems on affairs of state: from Oliver Cromwell to this present time. Written by the greatest wits of the age . . .*

[93] Eighteen in Cameron's count and 22 in mine. (This discrepancy may arise from our differing definitions of an item.) The most likely reason for the omission is that the scribe of MS 14090, writing a larger hand than that of Dyce 43, was dropping material from time to time in order not extend what was already an enormous collection. (There is evidence in the index and the text itself (f. 40ᵛ) that some of the omitted material was available in his exemplar.) The Vienna scribe recognized and removed one appearance of a poem ('Satyr on the court ladies') that occurred twice in Dyce 43.

[94] See Rudolf Brotanek, 'Beschreibung der Handschrift 14090 (Suppl. 1776) der Nationalbibliothek in Wien', in *Festschrift der Nationalbibliothek in Wien. Herausgebeben zur Feir des 200jährigen Bestehens des Gebäudes* (Vienna, 1926), pp. 145–62.

Part III (London, 1698). The manuscript, compiled in 1695, is most closely related to the William group, but contains a preliminary selection of poems from previous reigns. A related manuscript which was unknown to Cameron was Bodleian MS Eng. poet. c 18, which differs only slightly in content and order from Pw V 46. A third manuscript linked with these is BL Add. MS 21094, a much larger anthology written in the reign of Queen Anne, and once owned by Fielding's uncle, the Earl of Denbigh. Items 82 to 162 of this are a selection, appearing in the same sequence, from the earlier compilation. Cameron classifies Add. MS 21094 as a 'copy of a scriptorium MS with additions' (*POAS (Yale)*, v. 542) and as descended from Portland Pw V 46 in respect of poems they have in common.[95] When the Nottingham and the Bodleian manuscripts were being written, two leaves were left blank at the same point in the sequence, presumably to permit the insertion of a text not currently available. In Eng. poet 18 (ff. 158^{r}–60^{r}) the first page of the first blank leaf was eventually filled in with a document dated 1718; in Pw V 46 (pp. 306–13), however, the gap was used, circa 1703, for a group of satires on the death of William III and the accession of Anne, four of which are present at the corresponding position in Add. MS 21094 (fols 129^{r}–30^{v}). The hands of Eng. poet. 18 and Pw V 46, while not the same, have enough detailed similarities to suggest that one was a conscious imitation of the other, which itself indicates a common origin.

The importance of the scriptorium manuscripts lies in the fact that their texts derive from a single archive of exemplars whose growth and decay can be mapped from the mutations of its products. The order of items is usually chronological with a high proportion dated by year of composition, though not always accurately. While there is a great deal of variation in order between anthologies, even sometimes when of similar date, most of this is within the limits of the year, suggesting that the publisher filed his material as far as possible in annual bundles. As these were untied to permit copying there would be inevitable changes of order, but as the separates would be returned after copying to the same bundle, the general shape of any later compilation would remain the same.

[95] Other poems are described as descending from a nonextant scriptorium collateral (*POAS (Yale)*, v. 554); see also 568, 585, 592–3, 595, 599.

The greater variability of the material in the Restoration group would be explained by the publisher being less certain of specific dates (certainly fewer appear attached to poems). The concern with dating also suggests something about the interests of readers. The scribally published state poem and court lampoon had come to comprise a kind of secret history of political events from the Restoration to the Revolution and beyond, which was in many ways more revealing than the conventional histories so far available. Huge compilations such as the Vienna and Dyce manuscripts were also a celebration of the scope and variety of the scribal medium which could still in the 1690s claim to have produced more satire of real distinction than had so far appeared in print. In each case the productions of the present gained in interest by being linked to those of the past, and, while topicality remained the *raison d'être* of the newly composed lampoon, the spirit of the large compilations is close to being an antiquarian one.

Before leaving the manuscripts it is necessary to mention one major anthology that Cameron certainly knew, but chose to exclude from his scriptorium—BL Harl. MS 7319. This has quite a high level of overlap in content with authentic scriptorium manuscripts and resembles them in its style of presentation; however, as far as I have tested the matter, I would agree that its texts do not derive from the scriptorium master copies. Two other questions I must defer are whether the scriptorium may also have published copies of single poems or small linked-groups of poems as separates, and scribal editions of prose texts. My expectation would be that it did both these things, but that, again, is a matter for further research.

THE SCRIPTORIUM AND THE BOOK TRADE

Having summarized and reviewed Cameron's findings, it is now necessary to consider whether the story of the scriptorium can be taken further than where he left it. Cameron's reconstruction of the work of his scriptorium rested on close physical examination of key manuscripts (including virtuoso analysis of watermarks), content and sequence analysis, and the meticulous collations prepared for his Yale *POAS* volume. Although none of this information (except that relating to watermarks) is reproduced in full in either of his two publications on the subject, he provides a magnificent platform for further study both of this and other scriptoria of the period. He also provides immaculate biographical and political annotations to the scriptorium texts included in his edition. What he does not do is to look at the work of his scriptorium within the larger context of scribal publication or writing for the scribal medium. Since the story is one that brings us close to the time when scribal publication ceased to be a major means of public communication, it will be useful to review his findings from this perspective.

The consolidation of the dispersed scriptorial activity of previous decades into the hands of a dominant well-organized agency poses an interesting parallel with tendencies in print publication which were seeing the emergence of large-volume specialist publishers such as Jacob Tonson and Thomas Parkhurst, along with the beginnings of wholesaling and the consolidation of much pamphlet publication into the hands of trade publishers such as Samuel Briscoe and John Morphew.[96] The period was also seeing a more co-operative attitude towards the marketing of copyrights and a tendency on the part of smaller booksellers to join together in congers to obtain a share in large-scale publication. Even as the regulatory power of the stationers' company declined, the trade was being restructured by a new body of co-operative relationships forged by the requirements of capitalist book production. Given this new context of mutuality, and the extent to which the scribal anthologies of the 1690s are dominated by the products of the Cameron scriptorium, it is tempting to hypothesize that the master of the scriptorium was not a furtive opportunist working on the fringe of the book trade, but a known specialist who could be approached by any bookseller who had received enquiries about such material. The distinguishing mark of such a businessman would not be his supervision of a writing room but his control of a body of exemplars and ability to obtain scribes willing to copy on a piecework basis.

This leaves us with the paradox that the master of our scriptorium may not in fact have had a scriptorium. That the archive was carefully preserved, regularly updated, and kept in

[96] Processes discussed in Feather, *A history of British publishing*, pp. 60–77.

good order is clear enough. The master had tidy habits and made sure he kept abreast of the market. The other thing he controlled was the paper used for copying. Cameron's 'Scriptorium' article gives us the results of very patient and detailed studies of watermarks, even going so far as to indicate when paper from the same pair of moulds is to be found in separate volumes. The judgement that a particular volume derived from the agency rather than being a secondary copy can be made with a high degree of certainty on the basis of this evidence.[97] But this does not mean that the master was the permanent employer of his scribes: simply that he found it wise to relieve them of an unnecessary overhead and ensure that a suitable grade of paper was used for these expensive products. In doing this he would again be following the practice of print publishers, who were expected to provide the printer with the paper required for a book.

The crucial question, then, becomes one of hands, and here the evidence falls well short of allowing us to posit a semi-permanent scriptorium with a stable staff. I note for a start that Cameron never himself claims that any two manuscripts from his list are written in the same hand. It is possible that he did not have the facilities for making proper comparisons, but if this was the case it would have been uncharacteristic of him not to tell us so, and I prefer to believe that this was a problem he had reserved for more mature consideration. Without having examined all the surviving scriptorium manuscripts, and being in no position to declare finally on this issue, I believe that a careful comparison would reveal at least fifteen distinct hands, and probably more. The only scribe whose work unmistakably recurs in more than two manuscripts is the one who wrote Portland Pw V 42, 43 and 44, which seem, in any case, to have been designed from the start as a group. Two scribes shared the work on the three Folger anthologies, and Bodleian Firth c 15 and Ohio State University MS Eng. 15 *may* have been written by a single hand, though, once again, the possibility cannot be ruled out that one versatile scribe was imitating the work of another.

Of course, judgements of this kind are often difficult to make.

[97] I take this opportunity to thank Dr Bryan Ward-Perkins of Trinity College, Oxford, and formerly librarian at Holkham Hall, for kindly listing the watermarks of Holkham 686 for me and assisting in the preparation of beta-radiograph prints.

Scribes of the period could frequently write a variety of hands quite distinct from each other; hands could vary greatly over time; institutionalized hands can be so conventional that the palaeographer may become hypersensitive to difference and blind to the weight of similarity; lastly, the surviving manuscripts may not be representative, in their variety of hands, of the total output—which is impossible in any case to quantify. But, on the evidence currently available, it seems unlikely that there was any permanent staff of scribes in the service of our scribal publisher. What seems more probable is that scribes were brought in on piecework rates whenever a new volume was bespoke, or that the work was contracted out to whichever scrivener, moonlighting scrivener's apprentice or newsletter scriptorium offered the lowest quotation.

CONCLUSION

What we have been following in this chapter is the origin and growth to maturity of one particular tradition of scribal publication. We have seen how the transmission of Restoration scriptorial satire began in the mid-1660s with the circulation of separates by author and user publication. From the mid-1670s we have evidence of professional involvement in the copying of court-libertine verse, and can assume the same with some confidence for the even more widely circulated state poems. 1679–80 sees the copying of the earliest surviving anthologies as enterprises of evanescent scriptoria with no apparent relationship to each other apart from that of drawing on a common stock of separates. From this period too the author-publisher yields place to the organized entrepreneur, selling directly to a clientele established through personal contact or to the customers of a particular bookseller but not, apparently, through the book trade to the public at large. The 1690s saw a decisive centralizing of activity into the hands of the Cameron scriptorium, a development that also suggests an integration of the production of manuscript books into the regular commerce of bookselling. With this the process is complete which has led us from the exchanging of single poems among friends to the writing of 800-hundred page anthologies by skilled professionals.

The development described in the publication of satirical verse is one which is paradigmatic for all scribal publication of topical texts. A tradition would evolve through a series of transitions of which the most important were the professionalization of writing and transmission, and the consolidation of scattered separates into substantial anthologies, which, by preserving many items which would otherwise have been lost, would widen the field of choice for subsequent compilers. The crucial factor in bringing about this latter transition was the growing mass of material available. If whole books of lampoons did not appear until the late 1670s it was largely because enough good satire was not yet in circulation to fill books. Once this was the case, the opportunity existed to present collections that were both current and retrospective, and which may well have been valued as chronological *aide-memoires* as well as for their polemics. The historical impulse was to prove a powerful incentive to purchase, as was the desire to present a whole tradition in its development. The same pattern will be found in other progressive compilations, such as collections of parliamentary reports and viol fantasias. Here we need to acknowledge the status of the scribally published text as a collectible alongside the better documented passions for coins, paintings, tulips and antiquarian manuscripts.

However, the professionalization of copying may well have been more advanced with regard to these highly saleable commodities than in the case of most other kinds of scribally circulated material. For this we can thank the aristocracy, who seem to have been the principal buyers of the large books. The humbler separate and newsletter drew their customers from the coffee houses and the unfailing hunger of country readers for fresh information from the town. In London itself the court lampoon had a place in the culture of gossip that ensured both that new compositions would be widely talked about and that women as well as men would be keen to secure copies. Once these avenues of transmission were in place, they could be manipulated in order to give special prominence to texts expounding a particular political position, Robert Julian's alliance with the 'Whiggish peers' being one example of this. A lampoon could be brought to attention by being displayed or discarded in places where it was likely to be read. Equally, one could be suppressed by the simple means of destroying copies or refusing access to exemplars.

The final stage in the life-cycle of the lampoon tradition was its transition to print. The work of the Cameron scriptorium, at the same time as it marks the culmination of a long tradition of scribal anthologies, also bears unmistakable signs of decadence. This is particularly evident in the 'Restoration' group whose two major representatives are monstrous in bulk and entirely retrospective—aged rakes grown fat and garrulous. Increasingly, the distinctive function of the scribally published lampoon—that of providing an arena of uninhibited critical expression within a culture premised on the strict control of public utterance—would join the other functions of script already appropriated by the press. A new generation of poets, by rejecting the outspokenness of lampoon for a manner based on irony and indirection, would show that a separate medium was no longer necessary for the performance of such a critique. Satire of the Popean kind could be publicly available through print while preserving a 'reserved' status by veiling its full import from those who had not acquired certain specialized reading skills. Meanwhile the lapse of time was making the older lampoon repertoire available to any bookseller bold enough to print it, in suitably censored versions, for the sake of its historical interest.

There is as yet no comprehensive study of the process by which this repertoire was progressively made available in printed form. A volume such as the 1680 Rochester *Poems on several occasions* is of little significance since it was simply a scribal miscellany in typographical dress. In the same way the various turn-of-the-century *Poems on affairs of state* volumes (one of which, as we saw, actually originated from the Cameron scriptorium) do little more than bring a mass of material together on an *omnium gatherum* principle. Greater interest attaches to Jacob Tonson's 1691 edition of Rochester in that its aim was to accommodate the writings of a scribal classic to an innovative print-publisher's conception of what constituted a vernacular literary 'works'—a field that Tonson was to make a specialism. In order to fulfil this aim, Rochester had to be reformulated ideologically as well as in terms of medium. To start with, '*every Block of Offence*' had to be removed, so that the volume might '*not unbecome the Cabinet of the Severest Matron*'.[98] And, while comparisons with Horace and Virgil

[98] *Poems, &c. on several occasions: with Valentinian, a tragedy. Written by the Right*

might seem far-fetched, a status that was both patriotic and elevated could be claimed through the prefacer's judgement that: '*Whatever Giant* Boileau *may be in his own Country, He seems little more than a Man of Straw with my Lord* Rochester' (p. A5^{v}).

Artistically the problem was how to confer an appearance of unity on the *œuvre* of an impenitently occasional writer—a solution being essayed through making him, in both his strengths and his weaknesses, an exemplary case of the aristocratic poet (as he was to remain). Whereas Horace had enjoyed the advantage of having his poetry '*over-look'd*' by 'Pollio, Mecænas, *and* Augustus, *the greatest Men, and the best Judges*', Rochester's high status left him with '*no Body of Quality or Severity so much above himself, to Challenge a Deference, or to Check the ordinary Licences of Youth, and impose on him the Obligation to copy over again, what on any Occasion had not been so exquisitely design'd*' (pp. A3^{r-v}). Yet there was a compensation for this special status in that '*No Imagination cou'd bound or prescribe whither his Flights would carry him*' (p. A6^{r}). Tonson also rearranged the poems into broad generic groupings of lyrics, satires, translations, and addresses (including the prologues and Bendo's bill), concluding with the tragedy *Valentinian*. This seems to reflect a conscious design to lead the reader progressively from the private and intimate to the most public of forms, the drama. There had also to be a renegotiation of class interests, for the readership of such editions was now a much broader one. Thus the Restoration court is roundly censured for its '*Ribaldry and Debauch*' (p. A3^{v}).

Insofar as these print-engendered values could be imposed upon the Rochesterian corpus (or that part of it that was allowed to appear) this was done. And yet for some time Tonson's major outlet for the publication of new poetry was to remain the miscellany, in the series that began with Dryden's *Miscellany poems* of 1684 and concluded with the sixth volume of 1709. In this respect print publication had still to find its own organising principles to supplement the scribal anthologists' delight in mixture. The way in which these principles eventually evolved might be studied through patient comparison of the scribal

Honourable John late Earl of Rochester (London, 1691), 'The Preface to the Reader', p. A6^{v}.

compilations detailed in Beal's volumes of the *Index of English literary manuscripts* with their printed counterparts; and by tracking both the manuscript and print appearances of satires recorded in David Foxon's *English verse 1701-1750: a catalogue of separately printed poems with notes on contemporary collected editions.*[99] But in the present study, it seemed more fruitful to look at the interactions of the two media in the work of a single writer, Jonathan Swift, who more than any other, was to recreate the political values of the scribally published text within the triumphant rival medium.

[99] 2 vols (Cambridge, 1975).

7

THE AMBIGUOUS TRIUMPH OF PRINT

THE city of Melbourne, where this book was written, is the home of a form of football played with four goalposts at each end of the field and eighteen players on each side. Although sometimes described as a cousin of Gaelic football it is in fact of at least as great antiquity, its origins having been scrutinized in this respect by a distinguished historian.[1] In the earlier years of the game the leading clubs had their grounds in working-class suburbs close to the city centre and drew their support from their own territories, matches at this stage having something of the quality of inter-tribal warfare. Like that of most team sports, the game's history has been one of continual subtle evolution within an overall dialogue between the framers of rules, whose intentions were sometimes conservative and sometimes reformist, and creative players and coaches, whose aim was to develop match-winning innovations, bending the rules when necessary. One important period of innovation occurred during the 1960s, a decade in which the teams' support base was transferred to a more dispersed constituency scattered through a vast exurbia.[2] Subject to new competitive pressures and an increased need to attract as a television spectacle, the game modified in the direction of greater player mobility, fewer interruptions to the movement of the ball, and enhanced physical skills, a process that still continues. Trevor

[1] Geoffrey Blainey, *A game of our own: the origins of Australian football* (Melbourne, 1990).

[2] This phase of the game's development, along with the attendant change from semi-professional to fully professional status, is the subject of David Williamson's drama, *The club* (Sydney, 1978). In performance the play has been adapted to other football codes, emphasizing that the predicament was a universal one.

Grant, in an article from which this section draws most of its material, has compared AFL football to 'a hyperactive child forever burrowing into unexplored territory' for whom 'the constant search for something new has rendered the past largely irrelevant'.[3]

Largely but not completely. While many of these changes, being a response to changing conditions, would have occurred anyway, there is a consensus that the essentials of the modern game were first formulated by a single, far-sighted coach, Len Smith (d. 1967), whose dicta are still treasured by present-day coaches. A friendly, civilized man in a brash profession, Smith did not himself win a premiership during his years as coach, but laid the tactical foundation for the later success of his own club Richmond and of Melbourne, the club coached by his brother Norman. Sporting coaches have always had a tendency to compile lists of 'do's' and 'dont's' for players and to keep written notes of their ideas about the game. In Len Smith's case the ideas were set down in eighty-eight pages of a black-covered exercise book.

From time to time other coaches were allowed to make transcriptions from this book. In 1965 Allan Jeans, then coach of St Kilda, went to see Smith for advice on how to prepare his team for an imminent grand final appearance. 'I remember hopping on the train', he told Grant, 'and going out to see Len at his place in Essendon. He welcomed me with open arms and brought out this old exercise book in which he had made all his coaching notes. I went through and jotted down everything he had written on confidence. I passed it on to the players and it formed the basis of the notes I used in the years to come.' Jeans's own notes, incorporating material from Smith's, were later deposited with the Victorian Coaches Association. Another coach, Colin Kinnear, went for advice some years after Len Smith's death to his brother Norm. Norm, he recalled, 'sat down with me for five hours and wrote out in longhand all those ideas from his brother's book', also adding some of his own. A third coach, John Northey, who had himself been coached by Len Smith, preserved notes received from him in a cardboard box. After a time Smith's text became a kind of cult object to be consulted for reasons other than immediate

[3] 'The father of modern football', *Sunday herald*, 22 Apr. 1990, p. 41.

practical advice: Kevin Sheedy described it as 'the sort of notes I look to when things aren't going right and I want to refresh my memory'. By 1990, according to Grant, a league coach who had not read some of the 'Smith manifesto' was a rarity. Smith's notebook may itself have incorporated material received from earlier coaches or during his own playing career. Certainly some of the principles quoted by Grant ('True friendship—one for all and all for one') have a time-honoured ring. But it is also clear that the game, at a period of transition but with a long history of orally transmitted football wisdom to draw on, was ready for the written *summa* that Smith provided. If he had not supplied it in so acceptable and forward-looking a form, some other coach would sooner or later have filled the vacuum.

What has just been described is a kind of scribal authorship and publication which should by now be perfectly familiar. Once the existence of Smith's manual came to be known, it was recognized as a means of winning games against coaches ignorant of its precepts. The ideal situation was one in which its reserved status was retained through certain coaches having access while others were denied it or given only partial access. For this reason it was deliberately withheld from the typewriter, the stencil duplicator and the photocopier. Personally generous, Smith was prepared to show it to enquirers of whom he approved but not, it would seem, until after he had retired from active coaching. His brother, to whom the book passed on Len's death, was also careful to restrict transmission. John Northey, although he was later to coach Norm's own club, Melbourne, could not be allowed to make his own transcription: instead Norm painstakingly copied out what he thought proper the younger man should receive. This was also a way of emphasizing Len Smith's status as a guru whose wisdom should not be undervalued through being acquired too lightly. Not all enquirers were interested in the entire document: Allan Jeans's special concern was material on building confidence. Ideas from the manual circulated back to players in a form analogous to seventeenth-century separates through coaches' notes and memoranda. Larger-scale copying seems generally to have been a form of re-creation as successive coaches incorporated their own insights into the received script and adjusted it to take account of new developments in the game. Fragmentary and interpolated transmission led to a position where Smith could be invoked by partisans of contradictory views—e.g. as favouring the 'flick pass', later declared illegal by the rule-makers because it made the game *too* fast-moving, and as deprecating handball as a poor alternative to kicking. All of this can be parallelled in the scribal transmission of earlier wisdom literatures, and must certainly have counterparts in the histories of other modern team sports.

The example is given to show that even in an age when, with the aid of the photocopier, the personal computer, and the modem, reserved publication can be conducted quite effortlessly without resort to the pen, transmission of texts through handwritten copies still persists where there is a demand for its special capacity to integrate privilege and presence. As late as the nineteenth century the cultural role of scribal publication was still an important one. During the lifetime of Gerard Manley Hopkins his writings were distributed in a manner not essentially different from that employed by Orinda in the seventeenth century, through separates and small collections sent to a circle of readers, with only the occasional appearance in print.[4] Even a text as important as Wordsworth's *The prelude* could only be read by those to whom the poet was prepared to give access to the manuscript. In our terminology, recalling Donne's circulation of *Biathanatos*, it would count as a case of author publication through one copy. The scribal newsletter survived in the form of the handwritten ships' newspapers produced on the lengthy intercontinental voyages of this period: examples were also to be found in the trenches of the first world war. Trevor Grant's article on Len Smith appeared in a journal that was a successor to a handwritten newspaper circulated on 1 January 1838 by John Pascoe Fawkner in Melbourne. The political role of the scribally published text remained an important one in Ireland until the present century, and continues to be reasserted wherever the freedom to promulgate ideas through the print and electronic media is denied. Samizdat publication in the Soviet Union used the typewriter for Cyrillic texts but had no alterative to the pen for those in Western languages.

The examples just given of late occurrences of scribal

[4] Since Hopkins also insisted that the true medium of his poetry was recitation, not silent reading, he might well count as a case of what Ong calls the 'residual orality' of the handwritten word.

publication could be enlarged very considerably; and yet it would be impossible to deny that in England, since 1800 at the very least, publication of this kind has been regarded as aberrant, or was the consequence of constraint rather than choice. In Hopkins's case, the choice of scribal publication was not his own, but forced on him by his religious superiors. Wordsworth, too, while reluctant to have *The prelude* printed while he was alive, fully intended to have it appear once he was dead. Handwritten newspapers, including Fawkner's, turned themselves into printed newspapers whenever it was possible to do so. This devaluation of the scribal medium can be detected as early as the reign of George I in the decline (though not total disappearance) of the entrepreneurially published newsletter and lampoon. The major writing of his reign was all circulated through the press, something that would not have held true for that of his predecessor, Anne, and certainly not for the reigns of Charles II and James II. What was kept in manuscript was increasingly what lacked the quality required for print publication. The taxing of newspapers from 1 August 1712 should have been of benefit to scribal publishers, and Defoe, in a passage quoted at the beginning of Chapter 1, foresaw it as likely to encourage a revival of 'Written Scandal' and an 'inconceivable Flood of written News-Letters'; but there is no evidence to date that this prediction was fulfilled.[5] More generally we can say that, while the institution survived the death of Anne, its centrality to the ideological debates of its society did not. It will be the task of this chapter to enquire why and how this happened.

'PRESENCE' AND 'AURA'

The most obvious reason is the rapid physical expansion of the printing trade during the early years of the eighteenth century and the accompanying diminution of the control governments were able or willing to exercise over it. The growth in the number of printers active, combined with the keenness of competition between them, led to an increase in surreptitious printing under fraudulent imprints, while the emergence of the trade publisher (usually a bookbinder or failed bookseller) permitted the real

[5] *A review*, viii. 708.

publishers of controversial works to hide their identities behind a third party.[6] Both of these developments encouraged the print publication of oppositional texts of a kind which would earlier have been circulated in manuscript. Inability to check the tide of pamphleteering led to competition for the services, or the silence, of the most able writers—those who could not be secured by money being courted, as in Swift's case, with flattery and the promise of preferment.[7] J. A. Downie's study of Harley's relationship with the press shows how an astute political manager could make use of this multiplicity of monitory voices for his own ends, influencing the conduct of his opponents' journals as well as those of his own party.[8] Harley's recognition of the need for political control of the press was no less keen than that of Clarendon or Danby; but he differed from them in appreciating that censorship and licensing were inefficient, self-defeating methods of achieving this.

Print and print culture were also extending their geographical spread. Terry Belanger has pointed out that by 1790 the aspiring author could send material to a local or a London newspaper or periodical, self-publish with a local or a London printer, or deal through a local or a London bookseller. In addition, the operations of the regional book-trade were supported throughout the kingdom by a vast mass of printing and publishing of a non-book kind. But prior to the expiry of the Licensing Act in 1695 the situation had been very different: even in London the newspapers were rudimentary, and magazines and journals rare, while outside London, with very few exceptions, they were simply absent.[9] That this was the case so long after the introduction of printing into

[6] For trade publishers, see Michael Treadwell, 'London trade publishers 1675–1750', *Library*, 6:4 (1982), 99–134. Where the trade publisher was a binder, he had a defence against prosecution in that, unlike the printer and the bookseller, he could not be assumed to have read the book that came out under his name (pp. 130–1).

[7] The subvention of writers by political factions is documented in Alexandre Beljame's *Le public et les hommes de lettres en Angleterre au dix-huitième siècle 1660–1744*, 2nd edn (Paris, 1897); English trans. by E. O. Lorimer as *Men of letters and the English public in the eighteenth century 1660–1744: Dryden, Addison, Pope* (London, 1948), pp. 212–22, 317–41. The practice declined sharply after Walpole's rise to power in 1721.

[8] *Robert Harley and the press. Propaganda and public opinion in the age of Swift and Defoe* (Cambridge, 1979).

[9] Terry Belanger, 'Publishers and writers in eighteenth-century England' in *Books and their readers in eighteenth-century England*, ed. Isabel Rivers (Leicester, 1982), p. 6.

England is a tribute to the efficiency of scribal methods of performing their functions; but it also points to the effects of repression and restricted literacy. Certainly after 1700 the domain of the pen contracts noticeably.

Citing Belanger's findings, Alvin Kernan, in an influential study of the social roles of the handwritten and the printed word in eighteenth-century England, goes on to consider the emergence of a 'print culture' based on 'print logic'.

> In this general transformation to a print culture, letters and the entire world of writing, which were directly and continuously involved with printing, underwent radical, even revolutionary, changes. To mention only some of the most familiar print-related changes in letters at this time, the novel became the major literary form, and prose challenged poetry as the most prestigious medium; the author's copyright was legalized and censorship was nearly abolished; enormous numbers of literary works, both new and old, were printed and made available to readers; large public and private libraries became common; criticism became a standard literary genre; patronage nearly disappeared as authors began to be able to live by selling their writing; literacy increased and a new public audience of readers appeared; literary histories were written for the first time. Changes of this magnitude were cumulatively as revolutionary in the world of letters as the events of 1688 and 1789, with which they were socially co-ordinate, were in the political world, and like the related political changes, the literary changes were not random but followed a particular logic.[10]

The 'print logic' which Kernan sees as powering these changes is that defined by McLuhan as 'the mechanical spirit of movable types in precise lines', whose effects may be further sublimed into abstraction, uniformity, repeatability, visuality and quantification.[11] In this Kernan's conclusions are close to those of Ong as outlined in Chapter four, though each has found his own way of accommodating the insights of McLuhan.

In another part of his study, Kernan distinguishes between the impact of manuscript and that of print by reference to Walter Benjamin's notion of 'aura'. Benjamin's argument defines aura as that quality possessed by a work of art while it remains unique in its

[10] *Printing technology*, p. 49. Kernan's concept of print-culture values is developed in Julie Stone Peters, *Congreve, the drama, and the printed word* (Stanford, Calif., 1990).

[11] Kernan, p. 50, citing McLuhan, *Gutenberg galaxy*, p. 244.

'Hier und Jetzt' but which is lost once it is multiplied through reproduction.[12] Benjamin's actual concern is with the relationship of theatre to film and painting to photography; but there is an obvious analogy with that between the manuscript exemplar for a printed book and the resultant edition. 'Aura' is also an outcome of the cult-status of the art-object, whether that status is conferred by magical or religious ritual or by its modern substitutes, the secular cult of beauty and the 'negative theology' of art for art's sake.[13] The transition from manuscript to the anonymous multiplicity of print deprives the book of its privileged uniqueness within a religiously valorized world, while simultaneously exposing it to the operation of the 'critical, judging spirit'.[14] The wider availability of books in the early decades of the eighteenth century led not only to an intensification of this spirit but a belief that anyone from the gentleman who writ with ease to the lowly Grub Street hack had the capacity to set up as an author.[15] To Kernan the problem of the eighteenth-century was to find a way of re-sacralizing printed texts, and 'rescuing them thereby from the imminent danger of being no more than ephemeral print commodities for sale in the marketplace' (p. 158).

Kernan's acceptance of 'aura' as that characteristic of the handwritten text which is lost by the transition to print is the main point of difference between him and Ong who allots that role to 'presence' in the sense established earlier. Both agree that *something* is lost and would relate it their own ways to the sacred, but these ways lead to quite different accounts of the change, one grounding it in loss of uniqueness and the other in greater remoteness from the human agents responsible for the creation of the text and document. From the point of view of a study of scribal publication, Kernan's view is less fruitful than Ong's. The notion of aura has little application to the most characteristic products of

[12] Walter Benjamin, *Das Kunstwerk im Zeitalter seiner technischen Reproduzierbarkeit* (Frankfurt, 1966), p. 12; English text as 'The work of art in the age of mechanical reproduction', in *Illuminations*, trans. Harry Zohn (London, 1973), pp. 219–53. Zohn's translation of the German phrase ('here and now') as 'presence' would have been confusing in the present context.

[13] *Illuminations*, p. 226.

[14] Kernan, pp. 152–4. See also McLuhan, pp. 69–71, drawing on Mercea Eliade's notion of 'desacralization'.

[15] Kernan, p. 155. Cf. *Illuminations*, pp. 232–4.

seventeenth-century scribal publication, the single or half-sheet separate and the private commonplace book. Even their enshrinement within rare-book libraries cannot disguise the functional, everyday quality of these documents. A few skilfully written miscellanies might enter a claim to aura on grounds of appearance, but it is one that, as Chapter 6 has shown, is usually undercut by their content. Dorset's lines from 'A faithful catalogue of our most eminent ninnies'

> Thy rammish, spendthrift buttock, 'tis well known,
> Her nauseous bait has made thee swallow down,
> Though mumbled and spit out by half the town.
> How well (my honest Lexington) she knows
> The many mansions in thy f—ing house;[16]

represent an extreme of desacralization in which the sacred (in this case the words of Christ in John 14:2) is subjected to obscene parody. (Dryden's parodies of Biblical language in the scribally published *Mac Flecknoe* are among many other examples which could be cited of the same tendency.) If volumes containing such passages were to be assimilated to a cultic conception of the inscribed word, it could only be by invoking a carnivalesque inversion of the sacred which acknowledged its privileged status even in the act of parody. By contrast, the notion of presence is one that has an immediate relevance to our physical experience of the manuscripts, at least in the non-philosophical sense that they retain much more intense traces of the human agents involved in their production and consumption than printed books. This is not said in order to deny validity to Kernan's argument, but simply to stress that it has less applicability to the matter in hand than Ong's.

A further difficulty is posed by Kernan's espousal of the idea that it was print and more specifically 'print logic' that was responsible for the emergence of a 'critical, judging spirit' in the writing of the early eighteenth century. Here the contention that such a spirit was dominant at this period is not in question—the careers of Swift, Addison and Pope would of themselves be enough to demonstrate it; but it is equally the case, and has been demonstrated many times in this book, that in a seventeenth-century context it was script and

[16] ll. 138–42, in *POAS (Yale)*, iv. 198. Harris, *Poems*, p. 141 incorrectly emends 'buttock' (= mistress) to 'buttocks'.

not print that was the critical, subversive medium. To some extent, as we saw in Chapter 5, this was the effect of state censorship. Attempts to use print in a critical role were ruthlessly suppressed whenever the authorities had the power to do so, and when they did not possess this power an oppositional print literature was quick to manifest itself. But the scribal medium must also be granted an inherent orientation towards a critical stance. The reserved nature of scribal publication and the fact that the initial readership of the scribally published text was usually a circle sympathetic to the author meant that opinions were uttered with a freedom and directness that would have been highly imprudent in print. It was also likely to be the case that the scribal community was a political community of an oppositional kind. The development of the lampoon as the most characteristic form of scribally published verse and the fact that a Suckling and a Rochester could devote their considerable talents to that genre is itself a strong objection to Kernan's model: we should also note the huge body of scribally published state poems, reaching back to the reign of James I, which collectively represent the most comprehensive and outspoken body of oppositional verse we possess from the Stuart century. If this tradition is to be reconciled with Kernan's reworking of Benjamin's insight it can only be in the form that a deprivation of aura experienced through print led to a critical reaction conveyed through script. As it stands, however, Kernan's model does not accommodate the historical phenomenon of scribal publication.

FROM LAMPOON TO SATIRE

What can be demonstrated, though, is a procedure by which as the vitality of scribal publication declined, a determined attempt was made to rescue forms of oppositional discourse which had been nourished within the scribal arena for use within the print medium. It will be maintained that the character of print culture was irreversibly changed as a result. The beginning of this process can be seen as early as Dryden's *Absalom and Achitophel* (1682), a print-published poem that draws boldly on the language and manner of the scribal lampoon. The opening lines, in their presentation of Charles II as an amoral libertine, strike a note which, while alien to print, was familiar from a long series of scribally published attacks:[17]

In pious times, e'r Priest-craft did begin,
Before *Polygamy* was made a sin;
When man, on many, multiply'd his kind,
E'r one to one was, cursedly, confind:
When Nature prompted, and no law deny'd
Promiscuous use of Concubine and Bride;
Then, *Israel*'s Monarch, after Heaven's own heart,
His vigorous warmth did, variously, impart
To Wives and Slaves: And, wide as his Command,
Scatter'd his Maker's Image through the Land. (ll. 1–10; *Works*, ii. 5)

The anti-clerical tone of these lines, their libertine critique of marriage, and their blasphemous inversion of Biblical language and values were features previously restricted to the scribal medium and must have had a considerable shock effect when first encountered in print.[18] The logic of lines 7–10 (recapitulated in 13–16), which, once applied to the year 1682, required Dryden's first readers to accept that the more Charles II committed adultery the more like God he became, represents a quite remarkable reversal of the teaching of the Church of England with regard to honourable marriage. The passage can certainly be read as ironic, but its irony is of a distinctly two-edged kind. In a printed text, some degree of irony would need to have been posited by a contemporary reader even to explain that it was being openly sold. Did not, after all, both civil and ecclesiastical courts exist to prosecute those responsible for the public utterance of blasphemies? But encountered in manuscript such lines would be accepted as a perfectly sincere statement of a familiar libertine critique of marriage as a human invention designed to privilege interest over nature. Where exactly then *did* Dryden stand in this puzzling mixture of discourses which were usually segregated off into separate media?

[17] A selection of these is given in Ch. 5, n. 81.

[18] The only exceptions to this would be surreptitious printed editions of scribal texts, such as the 1680 Rochester *Poems on several occasions*, and the speeches of theatrical villains, such as Don John in Shadwell's *The libertine*, in printed plays. While some mildly libertine philosophizing in plays (e.g. that of Phraartes in Crowne's *The destruction of Jerusalem*) is given to sympathetic characters, most was neutralized by either punishment or repentance.

Having seized our attention with his lampoon-style opening, Dryden swiftly withdraws into less disconcerting forms of discourse. Even when the lampoon manner is revived for the gallery of Charles's enemies in lines 543–681, print decorums are generally maintained. Still more reassuringly, by the end of his poem Dryden has become engaged in a full-scale exercise of resacralization—the presentation of the royal utterance in its by this time little-credited role as the metaphorical voice of God.[19] To return to the opening lines is to reveal that the poem is profoundly heteroglossial, exposing the reader to a variety of competing discourses and media (the vocal, the scribal and the typographical) with competing claims to authority. A discrepancy which has been noted by several commentators is that between the ironic use of 'godlike' in the reference to Queen Catherine as Michal

Michal, of Royal blood, the Crown did wear,
A Soyl ungratefull to the Tiller's care:
Not so the rest; for several Mothers bore
To Godlike *David*, several Sons before. (ll. 11–14; ii. 5–6)

and its 'serious' use in the concluding lines of the poem:

Henceforth a Series of new time began,
The mighty Years in long Procession ran:
Once more the Godlike *David* was Restor'd,
And willing Nations knew their Lawfull Lord. (ll. 1028–31; ii. 36)

The notion that these two usages need to be reconciled, or that one has to be valorized at the expense of the other, is a misconception: Dryden's poem is one whose unity lies in its acceptance of disunity, in its being a counterpoint of irreconcilable voices. This was in turn to be the condition of all writing in which what we would define, in Ong's or Kernan's sense, as script values were transferred into the medium of print, creating productions whose rationale was to question the certainties of print logic even as these were being invoked.

A critical perspective towards print was already established within the scribal medium through a fashion for texts parodying either the substance or the visual appearance of print forms. An early example is Francis Beaumont's 'Grammar lecture', a section

[19] Cf. Ch. 4, pp. 160–73.

by section send-up of William Lily's Latin grammar.[20] The Rochesterian *The destruction of Sodom* and *Actus primus, scaena prima* are burlesques not simply of conventional sexual mores and the conventions of the heroic play but also of the way these plays were set out on the page with their attendant title-pages, prologues and stage directions. The group of mock-commendatory verses circulated in 1669–71 on Edward Howard's *The British prince* and *The new Utopia* are an explicit example of scribally published burlesques directed at a printed text. Rochester's mock-songs and obscene lyrics mimic originals, both specific and generic, which formed the staple of the printed verse miscellany, while two of his satiric epistles appear to parody the Dryden-directed translation of *Ovid's epistles* (1680). The particular force of these parodies lies not simply in their somewhat mechanical reversals of received values but in their exposing the compromises and falsifications which had to be accepted by the print-publishing writer in order to take a stand in the public arena. From its shifting, indeterminate world, which is also, however, because it relies on penstrokes rather than machines for its perpetuation, a more human and in the Libertine sense 'natural' world, script mocks at the soulless fecundity of print. Dryden's scribally published *Mac Flecknoe* is in ways which have never fully been appreciated an anti-print poem, picturing a world choked up with the mighty yet evanescent products of the press:

> No *Persian* Carpets spread th' Imperial way,
> But scatter'd Limbs of mangled Poets lay:
> From dusty shops neglected Authors come,
> Martyrs of Pies, and Reliques of the Bum.
> Much *Heywood*, *Shirly*, *Ogleby* there lay,
> But loads of *Sh*— almost choakt the way.
> Bilk't *Stationers* for Yeomen stood prepar'd,
> And *H*— was Captain of the Guard. (ll. 98–105; ii. 56–7)

The press is a monster which once set in motion can never be halted—a perpetual action machine whose function, in a metaphor which was later to be adapted by Pope in *The dunciad*, is to convert mind into mountains of inky sheets. Being libertines in principle as well as in politics, the scribal poets of the Restoration

[20] Text in Mark Eccles, 'Francis Beaumont's *Grammmar lecture*', *RES* 16 (1940), 402–14.

were in no doubt that the print medium was their enemy; yet they must also have realized that it was ultimately unassailable through any medium but its own, and it was this project they handed on to their successors.

SWIFT, SCRIPT AND PRINT

The three eighteenth-century writers whose work reveals the sharpest sense of the relationship of the two media are Swift, Richardson and Sterne. It is interesting to note that both Swift and Sterne belonged to circles that engaged in some degree of scribal publication, Swift firstly as a Scriblerian and later as an exchanger of social verse with his friends Delany and Sheridan, and Sterne as a member of the Crazy Castle clique, presided over by John Hall Stevenson.[21] Richardson, paradoxically a printer by trade, was a compulsive letter-writer. Richardson's and Sterne's particular perception of the relationship emerges through an insistent foregrounding, within the fictional narrative, of the act of inscribing: their readers are rarely out of hearing of the scratching of a nib. In Sterne's case we should add his creation of a mode of storytelling which contradicts everything that has been proposed about print logic.

The case of Swift is especially pertinent in that his career spans the exact period in which the scribal medium ceased to be a central vehicle for ideological debate within the governing class and was reduced to a marginal function. What we see in the course of this career is a series of experiments by which the critical and parodic stance which had been perfected by writers for the medium is recreated within the culture of print. Born in 1667 he would undoubtedly have had some contact with the vigorous scribal culture of the closing decades of the century, though the links have yet to be explored in detail.[22] Certainly his own satirical verse is

[21] Apart from the handful of 'Jeux d'esprit of the Scriblerus club' (*The poems of Jonathan Swift*, ed. Harold Williams, 2nd edn (Oxford, 1958), pp. 184–8), the scribal phase of the circulation of Swift's Scriblerian writings is undocumented. For an interesting speculation that would assign elements of third voyage of *Gulliver's travels* to this period, see Christopher Worth, 'Swift's 'Flying Island': buttons and bomb-vessels', *RES* NS 42 (1991), 343–60. Manuscript circulation is recorded for several of the Irish pieces in the third volume of the *Poems*.

[22] It has not to my knowledge been suggested that his 'A pastoral dialogue' (*Poems*, 879–82) is a parody of Horace, *Carm.*, III. ix ('Donec gratus eram tibi'), but a connection

often very close to the manner of Rochester, Dorset and their school. Poems such as 'The lady's dressing room', 'The problem' and 'A beautiful young nymph going to bed' would have been welcome additions to the archive of Robert Julian. They also have an obvious parodic target in the idealizing love poems which were the staple of the printed anthologies.

An equally important part of Swift's education was an initiation into the duplicity of the print medium provided by his encounter with John Dunton's Athenian Society. The Dunton episode shows a surprisingly print-naïve young Swift falling into exactly the kind of literary trap he was later to set himself with consummate skill. Through a lively imagination, an incessantly active pen and a masterly manipulation of the delusive authority of the typographic page, Dunton had succeeded in conjuring into existence a largely chimerical society of savants whose lucubrations, issued and reissued in a variety of publications, so far prevailed upon Swift in his isolation at Moor Park that he was moved to salute them with an ode, his first published work, which was given pride of place in *The supplement to the fifth volume of the Athenian gazette* on 1 April 1692. There is no trace of irony in this poem. Swift's tribute to Dunton's semi-imaginary college (he did have his advisers but they were scarcely the master-spirits pictured by Swift) appears to be a perfectly sincere one. How soon after the publication of the ode Swift was undeceived about the real nature of Dunton's operation is not clear, but that the undeceiving was a bitter one is suggested by the taunting reference in *A tale of a tub*, where Dunton is accused of planning to publish 'a faithful and a painful Collection' of the gallows speeches of criminals in twelve volumes in folio.[23] But Dunton had at least taught Swift that, despite its prim visage and air of impersonality, print could be made to lie and would be much more effective in its lying than script or voice because in its mechanical methodicalness and freedom from presence it seemed to carry a guarantee of objectivity that was not available to its more exposed and patently human rivals. Swift was himself in *Gulliver's travels*, the *Modest proposal* and the Bickerstaffe papers (to look no

between the two poems would be more evident if we could introduce as an intermediary term a cant version of Horace's ode ('Whilst thou hadst all my heart and I had thine'), widely circulated in manuscript, in which the speakers are a Restoration rake and a prostitute.

[23] *Prose works of Jonathan Swift*, ed. Herbert Davis *et al.* (Oxford, 1939–68), i. 35.

further) to prove himself the most adroit of liars in print but always with the subsidiary aim of undermining the reaction by which readers unthinkingly attribute impersonality, authority and stability to the printed word. (We should take particular note here of his mastery of the parody title page.)

Swift's savaging of print genres and conventions may seem a strange attitude for an Anglican clergyman whose faith was anchored in the printed text of the Bible and the *Book of common prayer*. For reasons that will emerge, this was not as serious a problem as we might expect it would be; but it did complicate the profounder problem of how the democratically distributed sacred texts were to be protected from partial, sectarian interpretations. Here Swift's response was simply to deny that they should be interpreted at all. For a writer whose own works pose such stringent hermeneutic challenges he was surprisingly conservative in his overt attitude to the texts of others. His stylistic ideals, largely acquired from Sir William Temple, rest on admiration for a dignified plainness of expression, while his theological principles reflect an undeviating, churchmanly regard for the thirty-nine articles of the Churches of England and Ireland. Any Modern rash enough to cast doubt on either of those ideals was likely to be very vigorously handled. With regard to the Bible Swift exhibits a positively Brobdingnagian hostility to interpretation, branding it as impious, unorthodox and abhorrent to good sense 'to attempt explaining the Mysteries of the Christian Religion'.[24] Clive Probyn has pointed to the significance of his *Abstract of Mr C—ns's discourse of free-thinking* to an understanding of this attitude.[25] Anthony Collins's *A discourse of free-thinking, occasion'd by the rise and growth of a sect called free-thinkers*, published in 1713, had argued that Biblical meanings were incapable of final determination either at the philological/codicological level (due to uncertainties about the meanings of ancient words and the large number of variants among the source manuscripts) or at the interpretative where he denied the right of a self-perpetuating caste of hierophants to

[24] *Prose works*, ii. 77.

[25] ''Haranguing upon texts': Swift and the idea of the book', in *Proceedings of the first Münster symposium on Jonathan Swift*, ed. Hermann J. Real and Heinz J. Vienken (München, 1986), pp. 187–97. See also his 'Swift and typographic man: foul papers, modern criticism, and Irish dissenters', in Peter Shakel ed., *Critical approaches to teaching Swift* (New York, 1991), pp. 1–17.

impose their reading on the world as the only valid one. In the light of this he argues for the liberty of individual readers to generate their own meanings in a way which, if not quite permitting the free play of meanings, was at least in accord with the principles of free trade.[26] To reduce Probyn's argument to its simplest terms, Collins's aim was to free the English Bible from an institutionalized and legally sanctioned form of closure imposed by the Anglican clergy and Swift's aim to reimpose closure both on the Bible and on Collins in a way that would protect the clerical hegemony over interpretation. This was not solely a matter of occupational self-interest on Swift's part: in his nostalgia for an originary signified, he seems genuinely to have regarded the urge to interpret what he saw as the plain and evident sense of the scriptures as a preliminary symptom of madness.

Division over such matters was not new even within the Church of England. The Bible, after having been both transmitted and interpreted by various communities of hierophants for 1500 years in the case of the New Testament and some centuries longer in the case of the Old, had unsettlingly been made available in the vernacular and distributed in enormous numbers by the printing press. Printing and, in England, the issue of an 'authorized' translation had brought a stability to the text to replace the disagreements over readings endemic to manuscript transmission, while also endowing it with a new kind of authority by virtue of Kernan's 'print logic'. After the Reformation, the Church of England, having rejected the Roman Catholic canons of Biblical interpretation resting ultimately on Papal authority, was in the awkward position of having to create a comparable consensus for its own, a task at which it was never particularly effective. (An acute analysis of its problems from a contemporary Catholic point of view will be found in the second part of Dryden's *The hind and the panther*.) Differences over the role of the bishops in controlling the interpretation of the text led first to the Puritan secession and then, following the Puritan victory in the Civil Wars, to the actual dismantling of the state church; however, the Puritan movement was itself already divided into a Presbyterian wing which favoured the supervision of interpretation by a national assembly and an

[26] *A discourse of free-thinking* (London, 1713), pp. 46–7 and *passim*.

Independent wing which defended the right of the individual congregation and individual believer to interpret the text as they were directed by inner conviction. 1660 and the years following saw the state church restored, interpretation once more under the supervision of the bishops, and a ruthless purge of all clergy who would not accept episcopal direction. But, since the motives behind this purge were as much political as theological, the dominant tone with regard to interpretation was increasingly set by the Church's rationalist, Latitudinarian party for whom knotty questions of faith were to be ignored as disruptive of social order or reduced to the lowest common denominator of reasonableness. In such a climate the way was open to assault from a more radical rationalism—a secular Independency judging by the light of sense rather than that of inspiration. It is to this movement that Collins belongs. Like earlier independents, in the expanded sense of those whose aim was to democratize interpretation, he set out to encourage a personal liberty of enquiry in all matters relating to the text. Swift's aim, on the other hand, was to deny Collins's pretence to authority (including the authority of print) while, at the same time, not yielding ground to those other arch-foes of mainstream Anglican divinity, the Papists and the Dissenters.

In performing this task, the last thing that Swift wished to do was to validate Collins's criticism by engaging him in his own rationalistic and historiographical kind of discourse. Others, including Swift's other foe, Richard Bentley, did do so and were able to identify flaws in Collins's scholarship and mastery of his sources, but were in this conceding his point that the authority of the Bible *could* be assailed on codicological, historical and philological grounds. One should add that Collins's emphasis on the transmissional instability of the Bible had been anticipated by the Catholic, Père Simon, whose *Histoire critique de la vieux testament*, translated into English in 1682, was praised by Dryden but deplored by Evelyn who rightly saw it as a serious threat to a faith premised on a belief in a stable, unvarying text preserved in the pristine purity of print.[27] Swift may also have anticipated difficulty in rebutting an attack on the rightness of a clerical

[27] Letter to Bishop Fell, 19 March 1682, *Diary and correspondence of John Evelyn Esq., F. R. S.*, ed. William Bray and H. B. Wheatley (London, 1906), iii. 410–13. Dryden's approval is signified in *Religio laici*, ll. 224–75.

monopoly of interpretation when he had himself argued in very similar terms to Collins in the history of Peter in *A tale of a tub*. The target therefore was not to be Collins's ideas but his claim to the authority of print logic—that is his claim to be speaking freely, rationally and objectively. To this end Swift, in an unashamed *tu quoque*, countered Collins's image of the clergy as self-interested manipulators of the sacred text with one of a burlesque Collins sputtering out his anti-clerical heterodoxies in a restructured version of his own phraseology through which, in Probyn's words, 'the formal dignity of the printed text' could be driven back into 'the disordered personality of an individual ego' (p. 190). The self-proclaimed man of reason is transformed, if not quite into an intellectual yahoo, at least into a recognizable variant of Swift's other satirical protagonists, the mad Modern author and the monomaniac projector.

Swift's strategy in this case is essentially one of transposing Collins from the medium of print into the medium of voice. Reordered and abstracted, his *Discourse* becomes a kind of monodrama—a performance text. Voice, because it is instinct with presence, permits discriminations to be made concerning sincerity and truthfulness that are not possible through print. To hear the voice of a printed text, whether that text was a discourse of freethinking or the Bible itself, was therefore essential to a proper appraisal of its moral tendency. It is likely that much 'silent' reading at this period was still strongly subvocal. Probyn suggests that Swift may himself have read in this way, citing *Thoughts on various subjects*: 'When I am reading a Book, whether wise or silly, it seemeth to me to be alive and talking to me.'[28] What was heard was not just the sound of the word but its wisdom or silliness.

Where the Bible was concerned we need to remember that most seventeenth-century readers had heard the principal passages read aloud many times in the course of divine service before they ever saw them on the page. Much Anglican theological literature, even if not in sermon form, must likewise have been reconstituted subaudially in the impersonal tones of the pulpit and lectern. Vocal

[28] Probyn, p. 190; *Prose works*, iv. 253. Cf. 'My Lady's lamentation and complaint against the Dean', ll. 155–6 which implies that Lady Acheson was also accustomed to read to herself aloud. This would be no more than a continuation of the medieval practice of vocal reading described in Chaytor, *From script to print*, pp. 5–21.

reading of this kind had internalized its own kind of institutional closure which protected the reader from the dangerous freedoms offered by the text that was merely scanned. The danger of Collins's text was that it came without a voice: few if any of its potential readers had ever been to a freethought sermon or had any clear idea what freethinking words should sound like. Collins and his kind used print as if it was somehow independent of voice, an assumption that must have been seriously disorienting to readers with Swift's kind of training in language. Freedom from voice implied a freedom from presence that helped activate the impersonality of print logic. Swift sets about the task of demolishing Collins by searching for the kind of voice that would have been audible if it were not hindered by the typographical filter from reaching the reader's ear, discovering that it was that of a prating buffoon. Probyn sums up the matter perfectly in describing the essential technique of Swift's satirical metafiction as being 'to expose those texts which seek to blur the reader's awareness of a medium, or narrative personality, or identifiable voice behind the authority of the printed word' (p. 90). The Bible was to be defended by essentially the same means, but with the aim of revealing an authoritative, originary voice rather than an unauthoritative and deferred one.

THE BIBLE AS MANUSCRIPT

But countering Collins in this way had not answered his central point that the Bible, despite having made the transition to the world of print logic, remains, when all is said, a printed manuscript and as such subject to all the indeterminacy of scribal transmission. This was an argument that Swift could hardly contest since it was, again, one he had used himself, most notably in *The battle of the books*. But there was no reason that he would have wanted to, since the *Battle* itself provided a sufficient answer to Collins.

Whatever Swift may have learned from the scriptorium poets about the unstable nature of scribal transmission will undoubtedly have been reinforced by the events that gave occasion for the *Battle*. As is well known, his patron, Sir William Temple, had announced (in print) his admiration for the *Epistles* of Phalaris as representing a noble simplicity characteristic of the earliest and most laudable period of Greek civilization. A Greek text of the work had been edited by Charles Boyle with the help of Atterbury and other Oxonians, only to be savaged by Cambridge's Richard Bentley on the grounds that the *Epistles* were not the work of a genuine 'ancient', but were a late-Greek forgery, an opinion which despite a spirited reply by the Oxford party has never since been doubted. The dispute raised the issue of the relative authority of print and script in an unusually acute way. The manuscripts of Phalaris were shown to be deceptive not only in the uncertainty of their readings but in their language, morality and ascription. The authority of Temple's printed essay had thus been subverted by the mendacity of its sources in much the same way as Collins was later to argue the Bible was vitiated by the ambiguities of the scribal medium. Bentley's superior acumen, on the other hand, was obviously a product of the print medium in that it rested on an understanding of the historical development of the Greek language which had been impossible to acquire before an immense corpus of ancient writings had become available in printed editions to the individual researcher.[29] Moreover, the press had not only provided the huge bodies of data that fuelled Bentley's phenomenal learning but had also fostered the spirit of enquiry which was so brilliantly exemplified in his critique. It was only to be expected that, as we will see in Chapter 8, Bentley scorned the evidence of manuscripts in favour of *ratio et res ipsa*.

In terms of the values that underlie the *Battle* things, as seen at first glance, are disastrously the wrong way round. Truth, identified by Swift with the ancients, with an unproblematic simplicity, with wax and honey which produce sweetness and light, comes to us tattered and torn while the arrogance of modern error, whose reality, according to the *Battle*, is the flybane and cobweb of speculation, comes clothed in the seamless garment of mechanically multiplied letterpress. Surely in a just world it would have been the thoughts of the ancients which would have enjoyed the authority and permanence of the printed page, while the egotistical whimsies of the magotty-headed moderns would have found their proper outlet in the labile, quizzical medium of script? In the case of the *Battle* and its companion tracts, Swift sets out to

[29] A point made by McLuhan, pp. 142–3.

reverse the cruel joke played by history, and by doing so to make a point about the nature of ancient truth and modern error which goes some way towards righting the reckoning in favour of the offended party.

Swift, as far as is known, never publicly conceded the duplicity of the chirographic medium in this instance, maintaining an unswerving allegiance to Temple's and Boyle's original judgements; but his method of assailing Bentley in the *Battle* shows that at a deeper level he had taken his lesson very much to heart. Whereas later with Collins the design would be to collapse the authority of print back into the vulnerability of voice, his technique with Bentley is to assert the proposition that *all* alphabetically reproduced texts are subject to the imperfections of manuscript. In the course of his career he was to devise several ways of doing this. In the *Battle*, the moderns (including the modern 'author' of *A tale of a tub* and editor of the *Battle*) have been for once consigned to their proper medium through Swift's insistence that his own printed text is only a transcript of a defaced and imperfect manuscript. His victims, Bentley, Wotton and their allies, become figures in a garbled, chirographically transmitted epic, their history degenerating, as the text proceeds, into a progressively more fragmentary state until in the end they are swallowed up in a *hiatus valde deflendus*. The ancients of the *Battle* are equally victims of the ravages of time and the lability of language in scribal transmission, but can be shown—now that the conditions of transmission are equalized—to be better equipped than the moderns to survive the rigours of transmission, because their ideas are simpler, stronger and less subject to manic elaboration (a line of defence also applied by Latitudinarian scholars to the imperfections of the Biblical text). Since the basic values of the ancients, like the fundamental values of Christianity, are so much more hiatus-proof than the complexities of the moderns, these very transmissional hazards may be seen as a test of truth—fatal to the speculative and intricate, which for Swift is also the false, if not the mad, but incapable of distorting the truths that emanate from an ancient or a divine simplicity. That where a modern was subjected to the rigours of chirographical transmission the result must be a very imperfect account of his thought is further demonstrated by the companion tracts, especially *A tale of a tub* and *The mechanical operation of the spirit*. A hiatus in *A tale of a tub* is supplied with the footnote: 'Here is another Defect in the Manuscript, but I think the Author did wisely, and that the Matter which thus strained his Faculties, was not worth a Solution; and it were well if all Metaphysical Cobweb Problems were no otherwise answered'.[30]

Chirography, then, can be used to explode the presumptions of print through the satirical device of a facsimile manuscript; but it can also serve as a kind of sieve which will not harm simple and clear conceptions but will do irreparable damage to over-complex ones. Finally, and crucially, it can remind us that the printed text only pretends to have entered an autonomous sphere of print logic, for there can be no printed text that can be anything more than a copy of the author's manuscript, and truth, if it resides anywhere, must do so in the original, not the copy. Moreover, in the course of print production the readings of the manuscript may suffer from a multitude of additional causes. At a vital moment of *The mechanical operation of the spirit* we encounter the 'editorial' rubric: '*Here the whole Scheme of spiritual Mechanism was deduced and explained, with an Appearance of great reading and observation; but it was thought neither safe nor Convenient to Print it*' (i. 181). Captain Gulliver's prefatory letter to his *Travels* reveals an even more deplorable situation. Cousin Sympson and his assistant, a young graduate, entrusted with preparing the text for print publication, had cut, interpolated, and so 'minced or changed' circumstances (xi. 5) that Gulliver hardly knew his own work:

> I find likewise, that your Printer hath been so careless as to confound the Times, and mistake the Dates of my several Voyages and Returns; neither assigning the true Year, or the true Month, or Day of the Month: And I hear the original Manuscript is all destroyed, since the Publication of my Book. (xi. 7)

Additional errors include the consistent mis-spelling of '*Brobdingrag*' ('for so the Word should have been spelt, and not erroneously *Brobdingnag*') (xi. 8). Sympson, in his separate prefatory letter, impenitently insists that the book would have been twice as long if he had not removed large quantities of purely nautical information. The joke is not sustained beyond these missives, but the strategy is the same as in the cases just

[30] *Prose works*, i. 107.

considered—to remind us that a printed book is nothing more than a printed manuscript and may distort that manuscript just as radically as any chirographic transcription. Indeed, the greater amount of collaborative work involved in print publication means that a whole variety of parties—censors, capitalists, publishers, booksellers, compositors, pullers, beaters and binders—may all have an opportunity to influence the fidelity of what is transmitted. But fidelity to what?—in Swift's case it was fidelity to blatant lies which none the less took it upon themselves to assume the truth-conferring dress of typography.

Pertinently, Swift was to find that the printed text of his own *Travels* required manuscript emendation.[31] Equally pertinent is an episode which has also been studied by Probyn involving the first Dublin printing of the 'Verses on the death of Dr Swift'.[32] When these were printed, large white spaces were left in the notes, apparently signalling material that might get the printer into trouble, but also pointedly reminding the reader of the fact that the completion and truth of the text must reside in the manuscript original, not the printed edition. What is interesting is that, although many of these white spaces were filled in by hand in the surviving copies, the chirographical supplementations are never complete and never quite coincide. Whoever was responsible took care that the full version of the notes, preserved in Swift's manuscript, was never made available in any single copy of the edition, thereby ensuring that the derived status of the printed text could never be ignored.

CONCLUSION

The final point that needs to be emphasized is that Swift's two strategies for countering print logic, the reduction to voice and the reduction to script, are themselves dependent for their effect on being conducted through the medium of print. It is possible, as a thought exercise, to imagine the answer to Collins's discourse performed as a monodrama and the *Modest proposal* circulating as a scribal separate; but this would be to deprive them of something

[31] See David Woolley, 'Swift's copy of *Gulliver's travels*: the Armargh *Gulliver*, Hyde's edition, and Swift's earliest corrections' in *The art of Jonathan Swift*, ed. Clive Probyn (London, 1978), pp. 131–78.

[32] 'Swift's *Verses*', pp. 47-61.

which is an essential part of their power—a sense that dignity is being withdrawn not just from the victim but from the medium, or, if we like, that the power of the medium is being turned against itself. In their burlesques of a misused authority they are themselves the work of a great misuser, a hijacker of genres which in an ideal world would always be exercised with the seriousness and objectivity promised by print logic, but which have now become untrustworthy both at the level of the ostensible authors, the philosopher and the projector, and that of the unknown ventriloquist who pulls the strings and does the voices. Whoever this ventriloquist is, he can surely not be the disembodied spirit of print logic: indeed the whole basis of his art is that he sets out to deceive us from within a form of inscription that (falsely) promises truth.

The force of Swift's satire, then, can be seen to depend crucially on his involvement in the historical project of translating script values into the medium of print. The emergence of the ironic mode in satire was itself an effect of this transference. Prior to 1700 satirists had no particular need of irony for the simple reason that most of their work was directed toward the scribal medium, where views could be expressed without disguise. The decorum of the lampoon was one of outspokenness in all things, a fact that helps explain why so productive a genre produced so few lasting masterpieces. That, among the print-publishing satirists, John Oldham, Robert Gould, Richard Ames and Tom Brown should cultivate a similar bold directness is a token of their parallel involvement in scribal publication and a wish to appeal to patrons (principally Dorset) who were themselves scribally publishing satirists. Where irony makes an appearance in scriptorial satire it is usually in the form of heavy sarcasm. One satire of 1680 is actually headed 'An ironical satire', as if this was necessary to prevent its statements being taken seriously; but its 'irony', quickly discarded, amounts to no more than a bare mechanical, reversal of the writer's true opinion of Charles II:

> Not Rome in all her splendour could compare
> With those great blessings happy Britons share.
> Vainly they boast their kings of heav'nly race:
> A god incarnate England's throne does grace.
> Chaste in his pleasures, in devotion grave,

To his friends constant, to his foes he's brave;
His justice is through all the world admir'd,
His word held sacred, and his scepter fear'd.
No tumults do about his palace move,
Freed from rebellion by his people's love.[33]

This kind of thing is chainsaw-like in comparison with Pope's scalpel in *To Augustus*. Not to speak one's mind in a genre whose whole rationale was the speaking of minds about topics forbidden to the print medium was to invite total misunderstanding.

Print, even when used surreptitiously, encouraged greater subtlety in addressing readers, who in turn soon learned to read below and against the surface of the writing. Lois Potter's account of the reading habits of Cavaliers during the interregnum explores an earlier case in which readers were prepared to master strategies for placing a private, partial interpretation on outwardly innocuous public utterances.[34] But the decoding of Swiftian satire is of a different nature, resting on the recognition that an authorial persona valid in the print medium has been usurped by a malicious imposter who is consuming it, caterpillar-like, from within. Having communicated this primary awareness, each separate text then develops its own rules for decoding attitudes, which the reader has to be smart enough to discover. At a very simple level this procedure is made necessary by the fact that the satirist, having taken his stand in the forum, has to discover acceptably disguised ways of uttering the unacceptable truths he has come to deliver; but in Swift's case it is also the consequence of his desire to subvert the pretensions of print logic.

The important aspect of this subversion, as far as the present study is concerned, is that it was conducted in the name of another medium which had never claimed to be other than personal and partial in what it uttered. Writers such as Swift who had come to maturity in the age of the scribally published lampoon remained fifth-columnists for the medium of frankness long after they had abandoned it as a mode of addressing readers. By contrast, the irony of Pope, younger and less marked by scribal consciousness, is socially rather than inscriptionally based and reveals no discomfort

[33] *POAS (Yale)*, ii. 200.

[34] Potter, *Secret rites*, pp. 38–71 and *passim*.

about the print medium as such. It is also the case that Pope's irony is usually resolvable into a coherent authorial attitude whereas Swift's draws the reader towards deeper and deeper contradictions. Yet Pope was eventually to create the *Dunciad variorum* (the four-book version of the poem) which, through the medium of an elaborate burlesque of the typographical conventions of scholarly editions, was to deliver the most crushing of all attacks on the culture of print publishing as it existed in his time.[35] It is hard to see how the poem could have been written without some knowledge of the lampooners, even if it was only through the heavily censored anthologies in which their verse was eventually brought to the press. What Pope regained for satire in *The dunciad* was the sense of an inscriptional space in which attitudes could be expressed without reservation and disguise. In the previous century that space had existed within the scribal medium; by the mid-eighteenth century it had been re-established within the print medium, and perceptions of that medium definitively altered as a result. After the work of Swift and Pope, print could no longer pretend to be innocent.

The triumph of print, then, was an ambiguous one which, while it left 'print logic' intact, saw readers fully alerted to the fact that the printed word was always an irredeemably self-interested word, and instinct with disguise—as it remains.

[35] Cf. McLuhan, pp. 255–63.

PART III

EDITING SCRIBALLY PUBLISHED TEXTS

8

EDITING SCRIBALLY PUBLISHED TEXTS

THE manuscripts considered in this book offer a huge field for editorial work. We cannot go on for ever reading important writings either in early printed texts taken from randomly encountered manuscripts, or modern editions taken from such early printed texts. If we wish to know what Sir Robert Cotton was really arguing in *The danger in which this kingdom standeth and the remedy* we will need to edit the text from the fifty or more copies rather than supinely relying on Rushworth, *Cottoni posthuma* or the incredibly corrupt 1628 printings. The capacity of scribes to turn sense into nonsense should never be underestimated. The name of a man who called himself 'Wolseley' appears in the fourteen surviving scribal texts of Dorset's 'A faithful catalogue of our most eminent ninnies' as 'Wolesley', 'Woosely', 'Worsley', 'Woosly', 'Wosly', 'Oosly' and 'Oosy', with the best represented form being 'Oosly'.[1] What Rochester put into circulation as something like

> The great man's gratitude to his best friend,
> King's promises, whores' vows—towards thee they bend,
> Flow swiftly into thee and in thee ever end.

emerges at the end of one line of descent as

An earlier version of some of the material of this chapter appeared as 'The editing of Restoration scriptorial satire' in *Editing in Australia*, ed. Paul Eggert (Canberra, 1990), pp. 65–84.

[1] Sources in Beal, *IELM*, ii/1, pp. 357–8. Fiennes, *Journeys*, in referring to the place of that name (mod. Wolseley), employs the additional variants: 'Woolsely', 'Woolsley' and 'Woolsly'.

The Great Mans gratitude to his best Friend,
Court promises, *Whores* vows tow'rds thee, I bend,
Flow Swift, Fly into Thee, and severs in the End.[2]

Errors no less grave but simply less apparent lurk in many texts which have entered modern anthologies and collections of documents.

The scribes' difficulties arose from the average human brain's maladaptation to the task of exact copying.[3] In most historical situations, copying took place by transient memorization of a section of text either read or heard. The scribe would place a group of words in short-term memory, and the transcription would be made from the memorial record, not the original. Medieval evidence suggests that scribes would sometimes mumble the texts aloud to themselves as they often did in normal reading: in this case the intermediate record would be part aural, part visual and part muscular.[4] Touch-typing and the ability to write without taking one's eyes from the exemplar reduce copying from a three-stage to a two-stage process but disable the capacity to monitor what is being inscribed. While the record is held, it is subject to the process by which short-term memories are recorded for longer-term memorization as impressions or ideas—in effect a translation from the *parole* of speech to a highly generalized *langue* which is unavailable for conscious inspection. Thus, by the time the brain has to retrieve a word from late in the memorial group, that word may already have been processed, so that what is retrieved will be a reverbalization of the original concept. There will also be a tendency for the scribe's own verbal or syntactical preferences to override those of the author, even at the level of the initial perception and memorization. Added

[2] 'Upon nothing', ll. 49–51 in my own modern-spelling text and that of *Upon nothing. A poem* (London, 1679; A version), a pirated printing of a casually encountered manuscript. For the relationship of the two, see my *The text of Rochester's 'Upon nothing'*, Monash University Centre for Bibliographical and Textual Studies, Occasional papers, no. 1 (Melbourne, 1985).

[3] The standard guides to the psychology of copying are J. Stoll, 'Zur Psychologie der Schreibfehler', *Fortschritte der Psychologie* 2 (1913), 1–133, and Eugène Vinaver, 'Principles of textual emendation' in *Studies in French language and medieval literature presented to Professor Mildred K. Pope* (Manchester, 1939), pp. 351–69; repr. in *Medieval manuscripts and textual criticism*, ed. Christopher Kleinhenz (Chapel Hill, NC, 1976), pp. 139–66. See also Vinton A. Dearing, *Principles and practice of textual analysis* (Berkeley, Calif., and Los Angeles, 1974), pp. 25–58.

[4] See Chaytor, *From script to print*, pp. 13–21.

to this is the problem of relocating one's position in the exemplar (the source of eyeskips and repetitions of whole blocks of text) and mishaps in the largely autonomous functioning of the reflexes involved in the act of writing. The operation of all these systems will be further affected by the degree of care and responsibility the scribe brings to the task: the careless copyist may not even register the words of the exemplar correctly. Where copying is performed with complete accuracy, it will usually be because of rigorous systems of training which arise from a high cultural value placed on textual stability. The involvement of legal clerks in scribal publication would sometimes ensure this, but even they would often have had different standards for a separate and a writ. Scribes who realized that an error had been made would often delete it and continue with the correct text. Study of errors thus made and redeemed by a particular scribe will suggest what kinds of uncorrected errors may still lurk in the document.[5]

Apart from their involuntary lapses from accuracy, scribes would often have been active in adapting, repairing and revising texts. As we saw in Chapter 3, the document in chirographic transmission was open at every copying to purposive changes whose aim might be to refine or modernize expression, to remove perceived difficulties of meaning or to meet the expectations of new readers. Moral and political censorship was common, as was its opposite—the desire to make the text more shocking or more oppositional.[6] Many of these purposive changes are fascinating historical data in their own right, which is another reason why even workaday scribally published texts will often justify careful scholarly editing; but they greatly complicate the search for the authorial text. Variation, both involuntary and purposive, is particularly marked in texts whose scribal transmission was interrupted by episodes of oral transmission. The astonishing mutability of Rochester's 'I' th' isle of Great Britain' can only be explained on this assumption.[7]

The editor's first challenge is to locate the surviving copies—a

[5] For an example of this kind of analysis, see Peter Holloway, 'Scribal dittography: Daborne's *The poor man's comfort*', *Library*, 6:3 (1981), 233–9.

[6] Cameron (*POAS (Yale)*, v. 532) instances miscellanies of the 1690s whose compilers doctored texts 'in order to increase the force of Jacobite hatred of William and his new regime'.

[7] Walker notes (*Poems*, p. 185) that 'The texts are so divergent and corrupt I have not set out a table of variants, except in the case of the title'. Cf. Chaytor, pp. 125–9.

matter for which available bibliographical aids are still far from adequate. The indexes to the Historical Manuscripts Commission reports and the Calendars of State Papers are likely to be the starting point for most historical enquiries, with the *Index of English literary manuscripts* the source of first resort for literary scholars. *IELM* covers only a restricted canon of writers, but is of value for its brief descriptions of the sources in which their writings are contained. Used intelligently it will indicate which sources require to be searched for manuscripts of non-canonical writers. The work of earlier editors and scholars, bibliographies of special collections, union lists of manuscripts, the published catalogues of the major libraries and record offices, and whatever more specialized finding lists are relevant to the particular enquiry must be searched diligently. At the next stage, letters of enquiry need to be sent to all likely repositories. The value of these will depend on whether the library possesses a full author and title index to its corpus of texts held in manuscript: where it does not a personal visit may well be necessary to search all likely compilations. Scribal anthologies sometimes have contemporary tables of contents or even indexes, which can be obtained on microfilm. The value of these is limited by their endemic inaccuracy and the number of times texts appear with variant titles or ascriptions, but they at least give a sense of the scope and date range of a collection. Items in private hands, items in early printed collections, and items known only from appearances in auction catalogues all pose their own special challenges which will not always be solvable. It is always valuable to be able to tap the memories of experienced scholars and scholar-librarians in the field concerned: the world of manuscript studies is on the whole a friendly and co-operative one. The most serious problems likely to be encountered by the searcher are those posed by texts which are scattered through compilations of various kinds, since it is quite likely that they will also appear under unpredictable titles. It is also common for such texts to be misattributed or to appear without attribution. Here it is important that the editor's interest in a particular title is adequately advertised to other scholars.

Having assembled one's sources, to the very best of one's ability, there remains the crucial problem of choosing between the many ways by which a text might be presented to readers. Where there is only one source, facsimile is always to be preferred, with facing-page transcriptions when appropriate; but where there are several sources crucial questions of editorial choice arise. My aim in the present chapter is to address three topics which are at once the most challenging and the most contentious. The first is the value of genealogical reasoning to the editing of scribally transmitted texts in early modern English. There has been much negativism over this matter in recent decades, but it seems to me that the difficulties are not nearly so acute as is sometimes assumed. My second topic will be the special challenges posed to the constructor of transmissional histories by composite texts, such as miscellanies and anthologies. Finally it will be necessary to consider a range of problems attending the choice and treatment of the reading text. These topics will be raised at the appropriate points in a more general introduction to editorial procedure.

The work of editing begins with the collation of all manuscript and, when necessary, printed witnesses in order to prepare a list of variant readings, which must be both complete and totally accurate. A partial collation is useless for purposes of textual analysis and an inaccurate one a positive menace. It is the usual practice for editors to record only 'substantive' variants (those which actually affect meaning), ignoring spelling and punctuational differences as dependent on individual whim; but an exception can and should be made whenever an 'accidental' variant seems likely to have evidential value, as in variant spellings of an unusual proper name.[8] Study of the distribution of variant spellings of the same word over a group of texts can also be revealing. The master text for comparison is chosen purely for convenience and there is no reason for it to be the same as any eventual copy text, assuming that this method of editing is found appropriate.[9] In order that the dangers of comparing via a transient memorial image are avoided, a photocopy of the master text should be scrolled down the page bringing correspond-

[8] Cameron notes in *POAS (Yale)*, v. 529: 'When the texts in this volume were collated, all accidentals as well as substantive variants were recorded. Each text was established by applying Greg's principles, but before the text and its textual apparatus were modernized, the ranking of the textual witnesses according to their relative general authority was reviewed in the light of the evidence provided by the accidentals. Many modifications to the stemma were made clearer or more authoritative by the exercise.'

[9] Useful guidance on choice of base text and various practical aspects of collation will be found in John Whittaker, 'The practice of manuscript collation', *Text* 5 (New York, 1991), pp. 121–30.

ing verse lines or prose sentences into physical contiguity. The master is then moved laterally so that each individual pair of words can be sighted and compared as a single image. Collating from right to left will protect against the anticipation of known readings but inhibits the continuous reflection on matters of principle and detail which is the foundation of editorial wisdom.

Variations may be recorded in standard footnote form, in which the lemma is followed by a closing square bracket and the variants are separated by semi-colons

great] large *G*, *P2*; wide *Y9*

or in the more ample form invented by Greg:

10 thy pow'r *B2 uncorr.*, *B15 uncorr.*, *B22*, *BB*, *HE*, *I*, *LA*, *L31*, *W1* : the Nothing power *B4*, *C3*, *Y10* : thy Nothinge Pow'r *B15 corr.*, *L2*, *79A*, *79B* : thy mighty power *B7*, *B18*, *H7*, *H8*, *L11*, *L9*, *LO*, *W2*, *Y*, *YY*, *80*, *91* : at first thy power *E*, *G*, *P2*, *Y9* : att first thy Pow'rs *H6* : *om. W2*

In this case, where the best attested variant in the variation contains less than half the total number of sources, its members have to be specified in full; but, where it contains more than half the sources (which means that it has ceased to be of interest to the editor), it should be placed first in the record without its members:

5 When Σ(-W2) : by *B15*, *I*, *LA*, *79A*, *79B*

Here Σ indicates 'all sources not specified singly' and (-W2) instead of, say, '*om.* W2' that a source is not a witness for the passage that contains this reading (something that is not adequately signalled by many lists of variants). Greg's method, whether in the full or more condensed form, is to be preferred for the editor's own record, and 'footnote' format for the published collation. The well-equipped editor will have the variations entered on disk and a range of macros to shift entries from one format to another as required by the various stages of editing.[10]

[10] Computer packages also exist which assist with the collation of texts, recording of variants and the preparation of printer's copy. At the time of writing, Peter Shillingsburg's *CASE* programs, marketed by him through the English Department, Mississippi State University, and Peter Robinson's *Collate*, available from the Oxford University Computing Service, are the best-known and most versatile of these.

Sources are indicated by whatever sigla the editor regards as appropriate. In this case manuscripts are cited under a condensed library code and printed texts under the last two digits of the date of publication. Although more cumbrous, there is a lot to be said for the system by which manuscripts are cited under a truncated version of the call number, so that, for instance, Harvard MS Eng. 636F becomes *He36*. Sigla should remain constant throughout all the items of an edition so as not to impede the analysis of relationships between composite sources: the only exception to this would be when, as a temporary measure, an editor wants to approach a tradition without any influence from prior assumptions. In recording variants, there will often be a choice between using a whole phrase as the lemma, or breaking it down into a sequence of single-word variations. The second method is more exact in its indication of differences but may make it more difficult for the reader to grasp the gist of the matter. The longer example given above is a compromise: it does not have separate entries for the variants 'thy : the' or 'power : Pow'rs' but it does divide the 'nothing' and 'at first' variations between two separate entries. The assumption is that the reader can perform the requisite acts of integration or differentiation mentally; but this would not be true of a computer, and an editor who wishes to experiment with stemma-building software of the kind advocated by Vinton Dearing will need to specify variations with greater minuteness.[11] Since our first example is clearly an important variation one would expect to find a note explaining its significance.

After our list of variants between sources has been completed it is of the utmost importance that every reading on the list is rechecked for error against each one of the manuscripts. Once this is done, a few variants that occur in only one source may still have been overlooked but the chances will have been greatly reduced of any agreement *between* texts failing to be recorded. A list which has not been subjected to this test cannot be regarded as reliable. Since many published collations, whether for this or other reasons, are

[11] For Dearing's rules for defining variations see his *Principles and practice*, pp. 25–58. This book presents the result of long and deep reflection on editorial problems and has much to offer the reader who is prepared to grapple with its difficulties; but its larger theoretical claims are open to challenge. See also his 'Textual analysis: a kind of textual criticism', *Text* 2 (New York, 1985), pp. 13–23.

inaccurate or incomplete in their record of agreements (some grossly so), trial collations should be undertaken as a check on editors' work before it is made the basis of a textual argument.

GENEALOGICAL REASONING

A testimony to the low current status of the genealogical method is some words by Keith Walker from the introduction to his edition of Rochester:

> The various versions of Rochester's texts . . . have been charted with increasing fullness and precision by Johannes Prinz, V. de Sola Pinto, James Thorpe, and David M. Vieth, but much is still to be investigated about their relation to each other. We do not even know the relations that Harvard MS Eng. 636F (which contains the texts of some twenty-seven of Rochester's poems), Nottingham MS Portland PwV 40, the recently available Leeds MS Brotherton Lt. 54, Victoria and Albert MS Dyce 43, and the Gyldenstolpe MS (merely to cite some of the largest of such collections) bear to each other. I hope that my tables of variants may stimulate enquiry upon these lines.[12]

The interesting point here is that Walker, although meticulous in his recording of variants between his many manuscript sources, did not himself regard the matter as worth pursuing. Rochester, as we saw in the previous chapter, was primarily a scribal-publishing poet. This would not trouble an editor if autographs of the poems had survived in any number, but this is not the case: shortly before his penitent death in 1680 he authorized the burning of his manuscripts, only a few stray leaves surviving.[13] The text of Rochester, then, like that of so many scribally publishing authors, has to be reconstructed from contemporary separates and manuscript miscellanies.

The collections that Walker mentions, along with Yale Osborn b. 105 and National Library of Ireland MS 2093, since they appear to have suffered least from corruption, are the ones on which—pending new information from Peter Beal—our texts of Rochester must chiefly depend. But they are very far from being the only manuscript sources. In an ideal world, where scribes always

[12] Walker, *Poems*, p. xvi.

[13] United in Nottingham UL, Portland MS Pw V 31, which is discussed in Vieth, *Attribution*, pp. 204–30.

introduced unique and irreversible alterations into the texts they copied, one could aspire to prepare a family tree (stemma) for each individual poem showing where each of its sources stood on lines of descent from their lost common ancestor. Armed with this information we might then look for evidence of wider relationships between the miscellanies, bearing in mind that these would be unlikely to be simple ones. But the world in which copies are made is not an ideal one in this respect: the scribe may not only fail to provide the kind of evidence that the method requires but make changes that lead the editor to wrong conclusions. One endemic problem is that of conflation (or contamination) which occurs when readings characteristic of one branch of a tradition are imported into a text descending in another branch. This may happen memorially as well as through the comparison of two written copies. In its simpler forms it is identifiable through a text wishing to appear at two (or three) different points in a stemma; however, when a tradition is largely or wholly composed of conflated texts, the whole rationale of the genealogical method is destroyed and the editor has to find other ways of divining the readings of the archetype.[14] Walker's reticence reflects a view widely held among Rochester scholars that no adequate methodology is available for dealing with these difficulties. Indeed, one might say both of his edition and that of David M. Vieth—the great reformer of the text and canon of Rochester—that they were prepared in an atmosphere of intense institutional suspicion of the genealogical method.

The origins of this suspicion are to be sought as early as the time of Karl Lachmann (1793–1851) who, in his capacity as an editor of Latin and Greek texts, is often credited with being the inventor of the method. Prior to his time editors of ancient texts had either placed their main reliance on a single favoured manuscript, or, in the tradition represented in England by Richard Bentley (1662–1742), had emended boldly on the basis of context and linguistic usage. If they explored the genetic relationships of

[14] The traditions of a number of Latin and Greek texts are radically conflated in this way. On the other hand, among 17th-cent. English texts circulated in manuscript, relatively uncontaminated traditions will often be found, with what conflation has taken place easy to diagnose. Genealogical analysis works best with new, rapidly expanding traditions and with those ancient traditions whose surviving copies derive from a single ancestor of the medieval or early Renaissance period.

manuscripts it was only to divide them loosely into 'families' defined by shared readings. The generation of Lachmann was the first to realize that under favourable circumstances the readings of the most recent common ancestor of a family of surviving texts could be restored through a systematic analysis of those of its descendants.[15] But Lachmann worked also on medieval German texts and was well aware that these were much less amenable to genealogical analysis than those of ancient authors. The reason arises from the circumstances of transcription. Classicists begin the work of analysis by deciding that certain readings are authentically ancient and others are scribal errors. They can do this because they are dealing with sources which were copied by scribes who were not speakers from birth of the tongues in which their texts were written, and whose alterations are therefore often easy to identify. Contemporary copyists of vernacular texts, on the other hand, can be assumed to have had just as good an understanding of the language as the author, which makes their interventions much harder to spot. They are also much more prone to alter the text in a purposive, creative way. The agreements in variation of vernacular texts, then, will often be too complex to permit the construction of clearly articulated trees ascending to an apex. On the other hand, such traditions are less likely to have been vitiated by conflation than texts which have been in scribal circulation for many centuries. Much of course depends on whether the surviving texts really descend from a single, finalized archetype, an assumption that is always risky to make in connection with a living vernacular tradition of author publication.

The greater lability of the vernacular text was one of the reasons which led first Joseph Bédier and later Eugène Vinaver to attack the very basis of the genealogical method as it had been applied to the editing of medieval French poetry. Bédier's initial misgiving, first stated in 1913 and developed in 1928, arose from the perceived reluctance of editors to include multi-branched junctions in their

[15] Traditional methods of textual criticism used by editors of Greek and Latin texts are described in Paul Maas, *Textual criticism*, trans. Barbara Flower (Oxford, 1958). For a fuller account of the history and varieties of the genealogical method, the reader is referred to G. Thomas Tanselle's magisterial 'Classical, biblical, and medieval textual criticism and modern editing', *SB* 36 (1983), 21–68. Michael Weitzman's 'The analysis of open traditions', *SB* 38 (1985), 82–120 searchingly surveys the major non-genealogical methods of textual analysis.

stemmas. Somehow when lines diverged (representing separate copyings from a single lost exemplar) it was nearly always into two rather than any larger number of branches.[16] Bédier accounted for this by editors wishing to enlarge their field of choice, rather than letting head-counting carry the day. But the more unsettling criticism, developed in his 1928 paper, was that in any situation where three manuscripts agreed in the patterns AB:C, AC:B and BC:A, four quite different stemmas could be offered to explain the phenomenon.[17] This reason for this had already been established by W. W. Greg in his analysis of 'the ambiguity of three texts'—a matter to be considered below.[18] Bédier's solution to the problem was that editors should eschew genealogical reasoning in favour of what is known as 'best manuscript' theory. Guided by this, they would simply reproduce the source that was judged to preserve the text in its most authentic form, emending its readings only when they were unmistakably in error.

> Aussi la méthode d'édition la plus recommandable est-elle peut-être, en dernière analyse, celle que régit un esprit de défiance de soi, de prudence, d'extrême 'conservatisme', un énergique vouloir, porté jusqu'au parti pris, d'ouvrir aux scribes le plus large crédit et de ne toucher au texte d'un manuscrit que l'on imprime qu'en cas d'extrême et presque évidente nécessité: toutes les corrections conjecturales devraient être reléguées en quelque appendice.[19]

There remain many cases in which such conservatism is thoroughly justified.

Vinaver, in 1939, while accepting Bédier's critique of the genealogical method, recommended a more interventionist approach. Rather than relying on the readings of a single preferred text, the editor should use an understanding of the mechanics and psychology of copying to distinguish original readings from derived ones.[20] However, editors should still not aim at 'restoring

[16] Bédier's views are to be found in the introduction to his edition of the *Le lai de l'ombre par Jean Renart* (Paris, 1913) and his 'La tradition manuscrite du Lai de l'ombre, *Romania* 54 (1928), 161–96 and 321–56. Paul Maas, *Textual criticism*, pp. 47-8 questions the validity of Bédier's first criticism, but does not engage with his second.

[17] 'La tradition manuscrite', p. 338.

[18] W. W. Greg, *The calculus of variants. An essay on textual criticism* (Oxford, 1927), p. 21.

[19] 'La tradition manuscrite', p. 356.

[20] 'Principles of textual emendation', pp. 139–66.

the original work in every particular' but restrict themselves to 'lessening the damage done by the copyists'. In consequence Vinaver's attitude towards emendation was still relatively conservative: readings which were probably the result of scribal error were to be restored but 'improbable' readings which might or might not be those of the author were to be retained.[21]

A radical development of this view was adopted by George Kane and E. Talbot Donaldson for their editions of the A and B texts of *Piers plowman*, one of the most dazzling, but controversial, intellectual achievements of twentieth-century editing.[22] Their method involves the preparation of a conjectural text on the basis of one-by-one analyses of variations, and then accepting the existing text which most resembles this as their authority for spelling and minor grammatical variants. Variants are identified as original on the basis of an understanding of the psychology of copying and familiarity with the writer's *usus scribendi*. The result of this process, if it were wholly successful (which the editors do not pretend it could be), would be to reconstruct the author's own text of the work without any aid from genealogical controls: indeed, Kane and Donaldson argue, reversing the usual order of things, that a stemma can only be drawn *after* the work has been edited.[23] A claimed ability to distinguish Langland's own manner of writing from that of his scribes is the foundation of this approach. The high-risk status of such an assumption is acknowledged but the method is defended as the only one that makes the editing of this notoriously problematic text possible.[24] In the case of the A-text some groupings of texts are accepted as being genetic

[21] Ibid. 157–9. On this point, he takes issue with the still more interventionist Housman (pp. 158–9). The most influential study of the issue has been Greg's 'The rationale of copy-text', *SB* 3 (1950–1), 19–36 and in his *Collected papers*, ed. J. C. Maxwell (Oxford, 1966), pp. 374–91.

[22] *Piers plowman: the A version. Will's visions of Piers plowman and Do-well*, rev. repr. (London, 1988) and *Piers plowman: the B version. Will's visions of Piers plowman, Do-well, Do-better and Do-best* rev. repr. (London, 1988); originally pub. in 1960 and 1975 respectively.

[23] 'In this situation lodges the ultimate absurdity of recension as an editorial method: to employ it the editor must have a stemma; to draw the stemma he must first edit his text by other methods. If he has not done this efficiently his stemma will be inaccurate or obscure, and his results correspondingly deficient; if he has been a successful editor he does not need a stemma, or recension, for his editing' (*B-text*, pp. 17–18, n. 10). However, this only makes sense in terms of Kane and Donaldson's atomistic view of what constitutes 'successful' editing.

[24] *A-text*, pp. 54–64; *B-text*, pp. 130–1.

but are regarded as useless, because of convergent variation and other anomalies, for Lachmannian head-counting.[25] With the B-text, Kane and Donaldson insist that the incidence of genetically non-indicative variation is too great to permit anything more than a division of their eighteen sources into two families, one of which contains only two members.[26]

In its practical effects, this approach resembles that of the great but often mistaken Richard Bentley. Bentley maintained the view '*nobis et ratio et res ipsa centum codicibus potiores sunt*' ('meaning and content are more important to me than a hundred manuscripts'); a principle that he applied with great success to Greek texts, more controversially to Latin ones, and disastrously to Milton.[27] The difference between Bentley and the twentieth-century editors is the greater insight of the latter into the psychology of copying and the care with which the strengths and limitations of their method are explained to the reader. Their discussion is also valuable for its merciless demonstration that the Lachmannian method cannot be expected to work when applied to texts whose agreements lack the degree of genetic indicativeness necessary to support it. The weakness of their approach lies in its atomistic quality—decisions have to be made with regard to the individual reading without the editor possessing any theory of its relationship to other readings found in the same source. D. C. Greetham goes as far as to argue that the *Piers plowman* editions are not just prize examples of Bentleyism revived, but should be viewed as irrepressible outpourings of post-structuralist *jeu*, or, to put it less kindly, the eclectic method gone completely over the top.[28] In the end the only real recommendation for the Kane and Donaldson approach is the one they advance so passionately themselves: that dire straits call for desperate remedies.

[25] *A-text*, pp. 65–98.

[26] *B-text*, pp. 16–69.

[27] This maxim is quoted in Latin by Humphrey Palmer, *The logic of gospel criticism* (London, 1968), p. 61 and in English by R. F. Jones, *Lewis Theobald* (New York, 1919), p. 41, but in neither case with an indication of source. The sentiment, though not the precise wording, will be found in Q. *Horatius Flaccus ex recensione et cum notis atque emendationibus Richardi Bentleii* (Cambridge, 1711), p. c1^{v}. For an account of Bentley's editorial method, see R. Gordon Moyles, 'Iconoclast and catalyst: Richard Bentley as editor of *Paradise lost*', in *Editing poetry from Spenser to Dryden*, ed. A. H. de Quehen (New York, 1981), pp. 77–98.

[28] Greetham, 'Textual and literary theory', pp. 11, 13-14, 23.

What makes this tradition pertinent to the present discussion is that the editing of Rochester—not quite so desperate a case—was conducted under these influences. Vieth, who published with Yale University Press, was advised early in his career by Donaldson, and took some years to struggle free from that influence.[29] He uses what is in effect the *Piers plowman* method of (1) creating a 'tentative text' by judging between variants on a one by one basis, and (2) accepting the existing text in closest sympathy with this as authority for indifferent readings. Genealogical reasoning was used during the first part of this process, but Vieth's general comments reveal the strong scepticism characteristic of the Yale school.[30] Walker, working at University College, London, under the long shadows of Kane and Vinaver, chose a form of 'best manuscript' theory closer to Bédier's ideal than Vinaver's in that it also involved fidelity to copy-text spelling and punctuation—Vieth's text being modernized. Walker, as well as being kind enough to reprint one of my own stemmas, sought advice during the preparation of his text from the distinguished textual theorist, Michael Weitzman, but emerged from this convinced that Weitzman's computer analyses of variation were merely confirming decisions he had already made on conjectural grounds. The editorial methods used in these two editions remain valid and workable models for editors of scribally published texts, and will continue to be used when circumstances are appropriate, but should not be regarded as the only ones available.

The scepticism towards the genealogical method which we see in Vieth's (1968) and Walker's (1984) editions of Rochester, but also much earlier in V. de Sola Pinto's (1953), was a pity for at least two reasons. The first is because one of the earliest things any Rochester scholar encounters is one of the great triumphs of

[29] An influence acknowledged by Professor Vieth in correspondence. Vieth's later 'Dryden's *Mac Flecknoe*: the case against editorial confusion', *Harvard Library bulletin*, 24 (1976), 204-44, shows how well he could employ genealogical reasoning when he set his mind to it.

[30] *Complete poems*, pp. xlvi–xlvii. They include the remark: 'Some aspects of textual criticism raise surprisingly philosophical questions, in this instance whether the universe (not to mention the human mind) is fundamentally rational' (p. xlvii). In the six-stage method of editing described on pp. xlix–li the earlier stages leading to the 'tentative text' are only of significance as a means of selecting the copy text, which is then awarded the authority of a 'best manuscript' whose readings are to be retained unless 'there is substantial reason to substitute a reading from other texts' (p. li).

genealogical reasoning in modern scholarship. I refer here to James Thorpe's demonstration of the genetic relationship of the editions of the 1680 Rochester *Poems on several occasions*.[31] Thorpe not only succeeded in establishing that what had once been regarded as a single edition was in fact no less than thirteen editions with near identical title pages; but successfully predicted that a mixed copy would be found combining sheets from the British Museum A and Sterling editions—which has since been done.[32] A further reason why this scepticism is to be regretted is that in 1963 W. J. Cameron, in an article already discussed at length, had presented a convincing account of how a sizeable group of manuscripts could plausibly be linked to a particular scriptorial archive.[33] Cameron provides a model of how the kind of enquiry Walker describes might be conducted using a combination of genealogical analysis, of which he is an enthusiastic advocate, with historical evidence, content analysis, bibliographical description and comparisons of watermarks.

Yet, despite these shining examples and the hardly less shining precedent of the Oxford English Texts editions of Donne (1952–78) and Suckling (1971), both of which laid strong reliance on the use of genealogical reasoning,[34] there was a widely-held assumption among editors of the 1950s, 1960s and 1970s that manuscript traditions of scribally published texts were too prone to non-genetic agreements and too sketchy and capricious in their documentation of the processes of change to be handled other than by free conjecture or some version of the 'best manuscript' approach. (More culpably some editors were still not prepared to edit from a manuscript at all, preferring the convenience of a

[31] *Rochester's Poems on several occasions*, ed. James Thorpe (Princeton, NJ, 1950), pp. xiii–xxii.

[32] See Nicholas Fisher and Ken Robinson, 'The postulated mixed "1680" edition of Rochester's poetry', *PBSA* 75 (1981), 313-15. There is rarely any difficulty in applying the genealogical method to printed sources.

[33] Cameron, 'Scriptorium', pp. 25-52.

[34] For the Donne editions, see Ch. 1, n. 5. *The works of Sir John Suckling* is in two volumes, *The non-dramatic works* edited by Thomas Clayton and *The plays* edited by L. A. Beaurline (Oxford, 1971). Beaurline's 'An editorial experiment: Suckling's *A sessions of the poets*', *SB* 16 (1963), 43–60 is one of very few studies available of the transmissional history of a representative scribally published text and the implications of this for editorial method. (J. B. Leishman's "You meaner beauties of the night': a study in transmission and transmogrification', *Library*, 4:26 (1945), 99–121 remains at the level of impressionism.)

printed copy text even when this was wholly unauthoritative.[35]) Editors of these persuasions did not try to apply genealogical reasoning, and in doing so waived the possibility of developing new methods specifically geared to the problems of traditions of this kind and period. In the pre-Cameron volumes of the Yale *Poems on affairs of state* series little effort is made to establish transmissional histories, and what there is often leads to wrong results. Collations of variants throughout the series are so skeletonic that some editors do not even give a full record of the emendations made to their copy texts. The editors of the 1628 *Proceedings and debates*, working from the same university, display an even more marked disdain for the genealogy of sources, announcing baldly that they have 'not tried to discover "families" among the manuscripts'—'families' obviously being a dirty word.[36] Here they are explicitly rejecting the precedent of Notestein and Relf, who, while hampered by a primitive method, had at least made a serious attempt to establish the main distributional groupings of their sources.

There was also the problem in the 1960s and 1970s that editorial theorists such as Vinton Dearing, Dom Froger and G. P. Zarri who all accepted the validity of genealogical reasoning were also intoxicated by the possibility that otherwise intractable volumes of textual data might be analysed by computer.[37] This committed them to a search for ways in which genealogies could be constructed by purely quantitative means using very simple algorithms. This was not a very plausible project at the time, and has since come to appear even less so. Its effects can be followed in

[35] Examples are cited in Beaurline, 'An editorial experiment', p. 43.

[36] *CD 1628*, p. 7. They also reveal that one manuscript has been rejected from consideration because it was a 'late copy' (p. 4) and another because of 'major defects' (p. 5); however, neither factor in itself prohibits a source from being the sole bearer of an archetypal reading.

[37] See Vinton A. Dearing, 'Computer aids to editing the text of Dryden' in *Art and error: modern textual editing*, ed. Ronald Gottesman and Scott Bennett (Bloomington, Ill., 1970), pp. 254–78; Dom. J. Froger, *La critique des textes et son automatisation* (Paris, 1968); and G. P. Zarri, 'Algorithms, *stemmata codicum* and the theories of Dom. H. Quentin' in *The computer and literary studies*, ed. A. J. Aitken, R. W. Bailey and N. Hamilton-Smith (Edinburgh, 1973), pp. 225–37. W. Ott, 'Computer application in textual criticism' in the Edinburgh volume, pp. 199–23, is of greater value since it restricts the role of the computer to ordering data for decision-making rather than actually making the decisions. Weitzman, 'The analysis of open traditions', includes a critique of several of the methods proposed.

the writings of Vinton Dearing who devoted a very great amount of intellectual energy to discovering that gold could not, after all, be made out of sea water.[38]

The result of all this is that the theory of how the genealogical method is to be applied to scribally published texts is still pretty much where Greg left it in 1927. Greg's main innovation was his insistence that, before any decisions were made about the priority or posteriority of readings, the relationship of the sources should be expressed as a non-directional stemma, i.e. one that, excluding all assumptions about the direction of change, groups and filiates sources as a synchronic not a diachronic system. For Greg it is necessary that we determine the distributive relationships of texts before we attempt to show one as derived from the other. Of course, there will often be situations where directional judgements have to be made in order to resolve ambiguity or conflict in the evidence for distribution or where the relationship of the two kinds of judgement is a reciprocal rather than a linear one. But where evidence is plentiful and there is no serious problem with conflation, Greg's method of procedure is more satisfactory than the older alternatives.

Because of this many editors of medieval and Renaissance English texts with manuscript traditions still try to use *The calculus of variants* as a manual of editing. Unfortunately, this is something it was never meant to be. Greg does throw in some advice about the practical problems, but his aim in writing the book was a much more specialized one. What the *Calculus* is concerned with is the methods to be used in the formal analysis of variants within an ideal tradition in which all agreements are genetically significant—a tradition in which there is no irregular agreement and no conflation. His acknowledged intellectual influences were not editorial theorists but philosophers, particularly the team of Russell and Whitehead, though he also mentions Wittgenstein.[39] What we are given is a study in the logic of variant groupings, not

[38] See Tanselle, 'Classical, biblical, and medieval textual criticism', pp. 31–5 and Michael Weitzman's review of Dearing's *Principles and practice* in *Vetus testamentum* 27 (1977), 15–35. Dearing's reply to Weitzman, *VT* 29 (1979), 355–9, only partly deals with his criticisms. Dearing's method of eliminating conflict by breaking 'rings' at their weakest point leads not to a solution but to an endless deferral of the problems that the editor should be prepared either to resolve or to declare unresolvable.

[39] Greg, *Calculus*, pp. v–vi.

a manual of editorial practice. He does not deal systematically with how we are to determine the direction of change or with how genetically indicative variants are to be distinguished from those that are not. A further problem is that Greg's method is basically one of deductive investigation of the consequences which flow from a range of hypothetical stemmas. He is not a good guide to how one is to reason inductively from the evidence of real-life agreements (which can never be as clearcut as his examples), or how hypotheses derived from the textual evidence are to be tested against that same evidence, which is a crucial issue in editing of this kind.

Certainly the method described in the *Calculus* needs a great deal of development before it can help us with large, vernacular manuscript traditions. One crucial question is how we are to strike a balance between positive evidence and negative evidence. A very simple example is the process by which sources are classified as either terminal or intermediary. A terminal source is one that stands at the end of a line on the stemma, like the terminus of a railway line, while the intermediary is one of the stops or junctions along the line. (A textual railway line will often have a lot of little branch lines going for a stop or two.) The two are distinguished on the basis that a terminal source will possess unique variants which are not found in any other text, while an intermediary will possess no such variants. Now, while this is all perfectly logical, the two judgements are being made on the basis of two different, and incommensurate, criteria. Terminal status is determined by a presence and intermediary status by an absence. The positive argument is satisfied whenever evidence is to hand, irrespective of the length of the text, but the negative argument is much more cogent for a long text than for a short one. And, in any case, how is one to treat the manuscript that, as so often, shows two or three easily reversible unique variants—the one that could go either way? The problem here (as Bédier realized) is that when the two modes of argument come into collision it is usually the positive argument that wins. Yet any diagnosis of radial copying (where a number of manuscripts have been copied from a single exemplar) will inevitably rest on an argument from absences. These are real problems in the kind of traditions I am describing where there was probably a great deal of radial copying from scriptorial archetypes.

Under such circumstances one needs to give a special weight to negative evidence; but the problem is how this is to be done.

Here we encounter another cognitive problem not considered by Greg, which is the insufficiency of any linear model of textual reasoning. The issue is not simply that cases of irresolvable conflict over either distributive or directional evidence can only be dealt with by declaring certain agreements indicative and others non-indicative, but that the precise significance of some agreements must remain unclear until it is conferred by the stemma. (A simple example would be when what appeared initially to be a strong agreement has to be revalued in the light of fuller evidence that places the texts concerned at mutually remote arms.) In other words, decisions made at one stage of reasoning may have to be reviewed in the light of conclusions reached at a later stage which is itself dependent on those earlier decisions.[40] Until we have a sense of a possible structure, the data is only patterns without significance; and yet it is also the case that the structure is discovered through an analysis of that very same data. In this as in so many other aspects of historical scholarship it is difficult to escape from the hermeneutic circle. So while it is often possible to demonstrate a textual conclusion by means of linear argument, it is rarely that the conclusion has actually been arrived at in this way. Instead, 'hee that will

> Reach her, about must, and about must goe;
> And what th'hills suddennes resists, winne so . . .

RANKING OF VARIANTS

One mode of textual circumambulation is to divide the record of variation into two groups—a smaller one containing those classes of variation which one's experience of the particular tradition suggests can usually be relied on as genetically indicative, and a larger group of indifferent or trivial variations which are not, considered singly, an adequate basis for textual reasoning. The point here is that while members of this larger group are individually unable to provide a foundation for argument, they will still, collectively, tend to align themselves with the broad

[40] Vieth's Step 5 (*Complete poems*, p. li) is a rare acknowledgement of this.

genetic divisions of the tradition. So one can use the smaller group to generate hypotheses (the more of them the better) that can then be tested against the larger group. In cases where there is no smaller group of putatively more reliable variations, or where the agreements between those that there are radically contradict each other, one has to work statistically from the whole body of variants—a much more difficult matter.

The criteria that should govern the acceptance of some variants as likely to be indicative and the rejection of others as less likely or positively unlikely have been analysed by me with some care elsewhere and will only be given here in outline.[41] The most prized variant reading is that which is (1) likely to mark not only the members of a particular 'family' within the overall tradition, but *all* of the members of that family, and which (2) is not likely to appear either spontaneously or through conflation in another family. We may call the first of these criteria 'stability' and the second 'unrepeatability'. The criterion of stability requires that the reading should fit plausibly into its context. The persistence of a glaring and obvious error (providing it is not of the kind to repeat itself independently) is excellent evidence that the texts that contain it stand in a close genetic relationship; but such a reading, because of its vulnerability to correction, is unlikely to identify all the texts of its group. The criterion of unrepeatability would give a reduced value to variants produced by the commonly encountered mechanisms of error—e.g. anticipation, perseveration, metathesis and eyeskip—since there must always be a likelihood of the same change being made by another scribe.[42] In many cases such changes are context-promoted and will inevitably be repeated if copying continues for long enough. Greg argues that 'the easier it is to explain how an error arose, the less valid the assumption that it only arose once'.[43]

The proneness of a reading to be transported to another family by conflation must always be difficult to assess on probabilistic grounds, but help may be had from the insight expressed by Greg

[41] 'The ranking of variants in the analysis of moderately contaminated manuscript traditions', *SB* 37 (1984), 39–57. See also my 'The text of "Timon. A satyr"', *BSANZ Bulletin* 6 (1982), 113–40, and *The text of Rochester's 'Upon nothing'*.

[42] These mechanisms are discussed in Stoll, 'Zur Psychologie der Schreibfehler'.

[43] *Calculus*, p. 20 n.

in the two forms: 'What usually happens is that collation and "correction" are confined to some of the more striking variants' and 'where conflation is suspected, the value of variants as an indication of ancestry is in inverse proportion to their intrinsic importance'.[44] Our ideal reading, then, should not be too obtrusive—with obtrusiveness a criterion that has to be derived afresh for each new work or tradition studied. In a religious text it might be the theologically charged word that required to be so defined whereas in verse the position of the word in the stanza might be significant. Where memorial contamination is suspected, the obtrusive word is simply the memorable word. A risk of conflation should also be assumed whenever the reading of the group of sources under consideration is notably superior to that of other groups—this assumption being necessary to allow for the case where a scribe, dissatisfied with an inferior reading, might come searching for a better alternative.[45] Our ideally indicative reading therefore would belong to a variation in which all the variants were plausible in their own way (as often happens as the result of authorial revision).

If some variants are to be preferred, others are firmly to be avoided. One should note, as stated earlier, that variations in spelling, since they depend so much on individual whim, are only of value in special instances. In practice the same volatility affects many kinds of variations which are formally classified as substantive. These include purely dialectical variations, many variations involving grammatical function words, most variations in which alterations to meaning are brought about by small changes to spelling or punctuation, and most variations in the wording of material ancillary to the text proper, such as titles, marginalia, author identifications or stage directions. To this we should add all variations involving words such as 'the', 'that', 'and', 'which' and 'when', which were frequently written in contracted form, and most variations between singular and plural forms,

[44] *Calculus*, p. 57. He continues: 'To the herd of dull commonplace readings we must look for the genetic source of the text, to the more interesting and striking for the source of the contamination. Nothing can be more misleading than to seek to "place" a manuscript on the evidence of a few "test" readings'.

[45] Maas (p. 8) notes the complementary principle that 'obvious corruptions, particularly *lacunae*, may easily be transmitted in the direct line but are hardly ever transferred by contamination'.

many of which appear to arise from the misreading of final 's' as a decorative flourish or of a decorative flourish as final 's'. The problem with such readings is that they are highly prone to reversal to the prior form (usually without any conscious awareness on the part of the scribes) and to spontaneous replication. Taken singly, variants of the kinds just described offer no basis at all for textual reasoning, though taken collectively, as has already been explained, they will show a general tendency to conform to the genetic distribution. Variations composed of synonyms or near-homonyms have some value but can still easily reverse more than once during a series of copyings, the vulnerability applying to both variants in the variation. In assessing the genetic indicativeness of variant groupings, it may be helpful to use an informal arithmetical scale with values assigned according to the criteria of stability, unrepeatability, obtrusiveness and relative plausibility.

CONSTRUCTING THE STEMMA

Our application of these principles begins with the investigation of distributional relationships expressed through a non-directional stemma. The variants are sorted out by hand or computer program into singletons, pairs, threes and so on, but with the full list always available for consultation, for the evidential value of an individual variant is always a function of its context in the work and the variation, and no two variants are exactly equivalent in this respect.[46] The editor must then classify each source as terminal, intermediary or ambiguous. A terminal text is defined, as we have seen, by the possession of unique readings and an intermediary by their absence. However, an easily reversible unique reading, or even a whole series of these, is not firm evidence of terminal status. Where this possibility cannot be excluded, one should withhold

[46] For pencil-and-paper analysis, this can be done by a simple computer program that rewrites the variations in the form 'list of sigla—line number—variant' and then resorts the list of sigla alphabetically, reverse alphabetically or from any given letter of the alphabet as required. If logical investigation of groups of sigla is undertaken by computer it should be solely with the aim of producing a range of hypothetical solutions to be tested against the actual readings. Before processing, each variant should be assigned an arithmetical estimate of indicativeness to be used in resolving conflict. The program should then produce a list of instances in which these estimates have been overridden.

judgement until more stable evidence is obtained. A helpful method is to grade variants for stability on a scale of 0, 1 and 2, with the 0 variant being that lacking real evidential value, and the 2 variant that least amenable to reversal. A 2-score variant would carry the evidential weight of a whole string of zeroes. The presence of copious evidence of terminal status in the earlier part of a text should not be made an excuse to suspend the testing of variants, in case the scribe may have switched to another exemplar.

The editor now turns to the variations which have been selected as most likely to be genetically indicative. Within these, some groupings of texts should immediately stand out as consistent and well attested. (Anomalous groupings among these texts, which can be assumed to be the result of non-genetic agreement, should be examined as evidence for the kinds of transmissional 'noise' likely to be encountered in the particular tradition.) Other groupings will be less certain, while at the lower extreme there will be agreements represented by only one or two trivial occurrences. A weakly attested pair may be non-evidential, or it may represent a true genetic link between two relatively invariant sources. Examination of other agreements involving each source should indicate which of these is the case. True genetic groups with a large number of members may never be attested by any single agreement, but always appear minus family members or in the company of interlopers. Irreconcilably conflicting groups will undoubtedly present themselves. Some conflicts will be the result of the same alteration being made independently or the spontaneous reversal of changes, but other cases will result from conflation, progressive copying, or successive copying from two exemplars. Conflation can usually be diagnosed when it has happened only once and sometimes if it has happened twice, but a source containing more than two levels of conflation is likely to remain inscrutable. It should not be included in the stemma but discussed separately. Note that a source which contains a large number of unique variants is also likely to enter into a large number of inconsistent agreements with other texts. This need not indicate conflation (which tends on the whole to reduce variation) but is simply what we would expect on a chance basis.

Beginning with the well-attested groups, we now construct our non-directional stemma. This relies primarily on the principle of intermediation, which holds that when three sources stand in the relationship A—B—C, they will generate the agreements AB and BC but not AC. Texts are arranged in order according to their membership of fields and sub-fields defined by the possession of common variant readings. The principle is the same as governs the use of Venn diagrams—which are another way of expressing the relationships concerned, as are the quasi-algebraic expressions used by Greg in *The calculus of variants.* It is often helpful to begin by placing texts along a linear 'spectrum' with vertical lines of division tagged with the indicative variants. One tries to begin with a well-attested and uncontradicted pair of texts which will be written as in Diagram 1. The existence of larger groups ABC and ABCD would permit us to extend the diagram to the form given in Diagram 2. In these diagrams it is assumed that all texts are terminal. If C, for instance, was an intermediary, it would be placed on the line instead of on a branch from it. The existence of additional groups DEF and EF would allow us to complete or stemma according to Diagram 3.

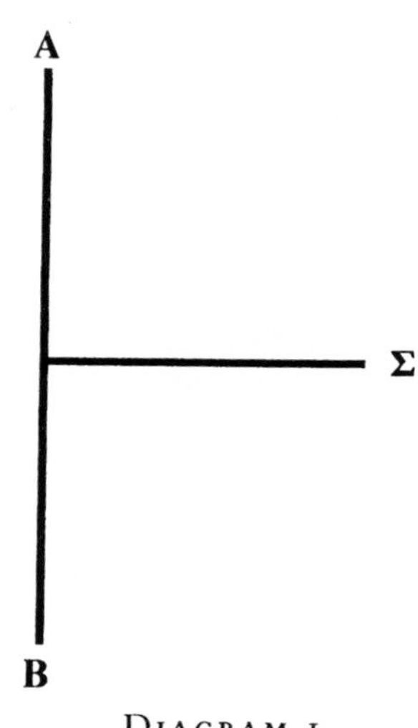

DIAGRAM 1

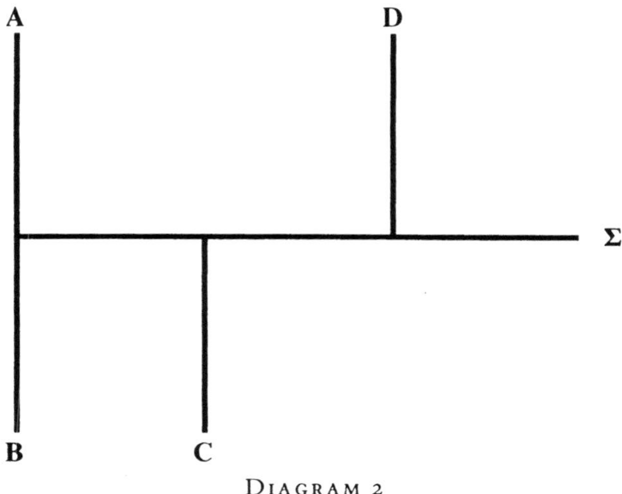

Diagram 2

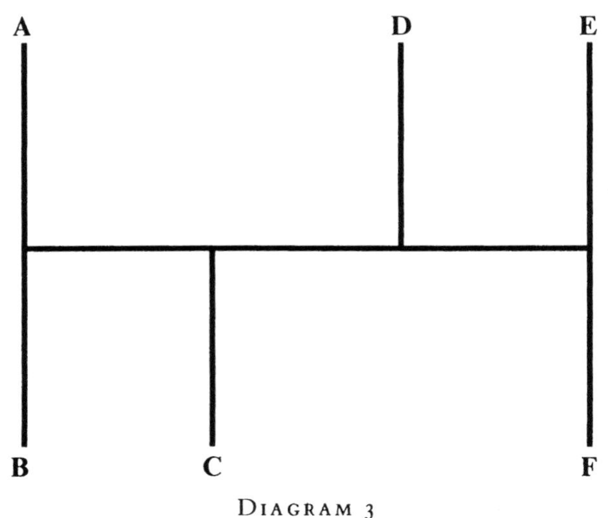

Diagram 3

There is a certain fairy-tale quality about these examples, since in practice it may be hard to find pairs (let alone larger groups) that are both well-attested and uncontradicted. A little thought will show that the structure illustrated in Diagram 3 might well produce the pairs AC and BC as well as AB, and DE and DF as well as EF: all that would be required would be for the larger groups ABC and DEF to lose a member due to the mutation or reversal of a reading in one of the extreme pairs. In some instances, a large tradition will divide spectacularly at some key point into a series of consistent subfamilies characterized by a particular reading, greatly easing the work of the editor.[47] At other times we must work patiently from the smaller units up to the larger until we finally arrive at a testable hypothesis concerning the totality. Remember that at this stage relationships embody no assumptions about priority. The ancestor of the group could be at any point on the stemma or external to it.

To have a full appreciation of the significance of our diagram and how it is and is not to be used it will be necessary to give some consideration to what Greg called 'the ambiguity of three texts'. In its simplest form this is simply to say that the relationship of three terminal texts consistently agreeing AB:C, AC:B and BC:A may be any one of the four quite different directional stemmas shown in Diagram 4. This arises from the variety of points at which it is possible to insert the exclusive common ancestor of the pair. Inscribed on the non-directional stemma these are as indicated in Diagram 5.

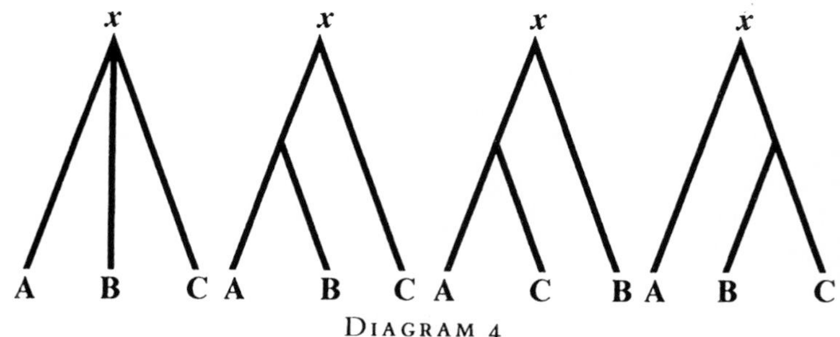

DIAGRAM 4

[47] In Rochester's 'Upon nothing' this occurs with the variant at line 10 quoted earlier in this chapter. The sources divide into four major groups arising from the loss of a word or words before 'power'. The variation does not indicate which, if any, of the variants is original. See my *The text of Rochester's 'Upon nothing'*, pp. 22–31.

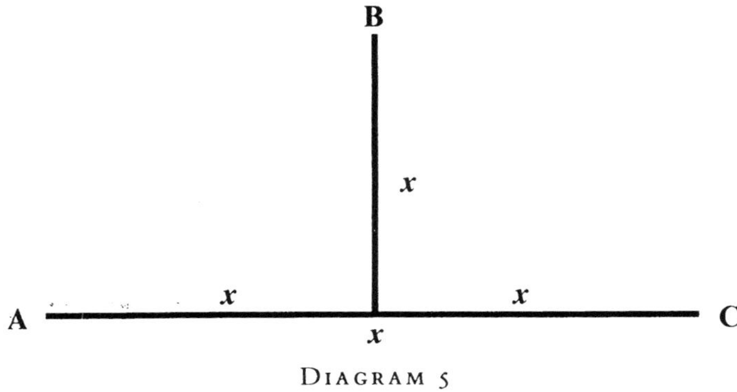

DIAGRAM 5

It will be seen that the term 'ambiguity of three texts' is inaccurate: the problem only arises when we try to insert the further text or texts that we require to supply the ancestor and any missing internal junctions or sub-ancestors. Greg realized, and Hruby has demonstrated more rigorously, that the presence of a larger number of texts in the non-directional stemma does not remove the problem, but simply alters its scale.[48] Thus, to borrow an example from Greg, a group of six terminal texts agreeing A:B:C:D:E:F (i.e. without any agreements in higher groups) permits one directional stemma in which all texts descend independently from the ancestor and a range of others which supply an intermediate common ancestor for all the sources except one.[49] Kane refers to the same problem when he warns against assigning a notional sub-ancestor to 'agreements in right readings, which are not evidence of descent from an exclusive common ancestor and would grievously mislead'.[50] In other words the relationship, ABCD:EF is equally satisfied by Diagram 6 and Diagram 7—to look no further. The moral of this is that all junctions entered on the non-directional stemma must be regarded as provisional, and that some may never be determined. What the stemma plots is intermediation, not filiation.

[48] Greg, *Calculus*, pp. 46–7; Antonín Hrubý, 'A quantitative solution of the ambiguity of three texts', *SB* 18 (1965), 147–82.
[49] *Calculus*, pp. 21–2.
[50] *A-text*, p. 63.

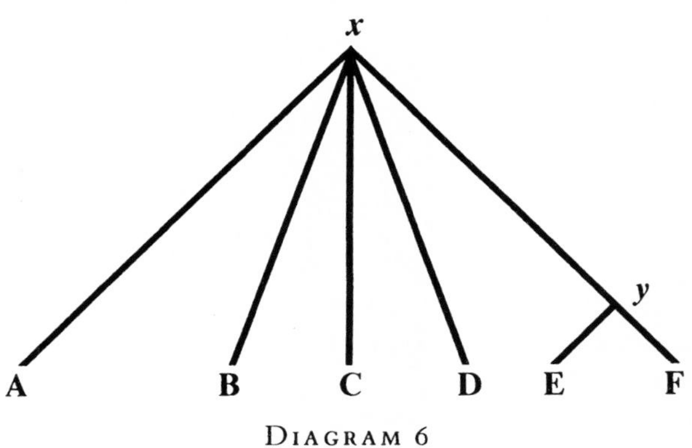

DIAGRAM 6

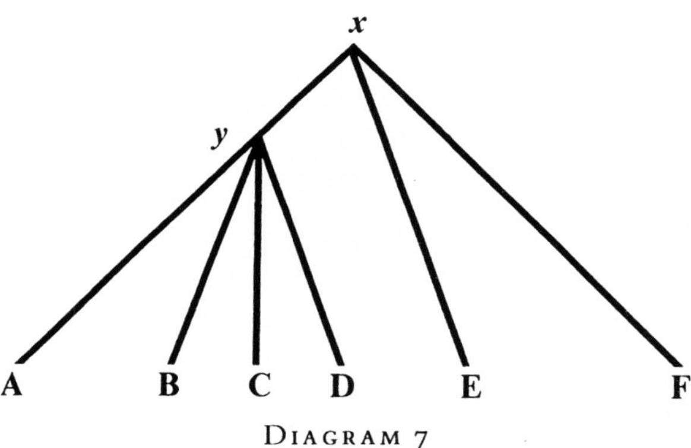

DIAGRAM 7

The next stage in stemma construction is the systematic examination of directional evidence in order to determine the position of the archetype and the nature of its relationship to the other surviving texts. As at the earlier stages we will almost certainly have to adjudicate cases of irresolvable conflict, and it is vital that our decisions in these instances and the considerations that led to our making them should be fully laid open to the reader. Reliable directional evidence is much less common than the school of Vinaver would have us believe.[51] For one thing, as has long been recognized, we have to be cautious about giving priority to a variant because it is 'better' than the alternative. Kane and Donaldson lay great stress on their ability to recognize Langland's *usus scribendi*; but this can never be more than an editorial construct from the fallible transcripts. In any case, the aim of recension is not to restore the author's lost autograph but simply the most recent common ancestor of the surviving copies—which may well itself have contained errors. Moreover, there is no reason why scribes should not be quite as good as editors in spotting a slip by one of their predecessors and either repairing it or replacing it with a plausible sophistication. Disappointingly, evidence often tends to diminish as we approach the position of the archetype. This is because a relatively good text gives the scribe a much better chance of producing an accurate copy than one riddled with oddities, errors and non-sequiturs, which will tend by their very nature to excite further alterations. The presence of conflation should have revealed itself at the stage of distributional analysis, but the matter of whether authorial revision has taken place is one that should be considered along with evidence of direction. We must also remain alert for evidence of progressive copying (discussed in Chapter 3) and mixed exemplars. Moreover, scriptorial exemplars could be altered between copyings—not an easy matter to diagnose but probably common enough. Some texts are found with readings from a second source entered marginally: subsequent copyists might well make their own selection of these. In others errors might be corrected between copyings, or attributions added or removed.

This will also be the point to review the evidence for the placing of intermediaries and the number of texts to be linked up to the various junctions within the stemma. Directional evidence will frequently permit resolution of these ambiguities.[52] However,

[51] A point searchingly considered in John M. Bowers, 'Hoccleve's two copies of *Lerne to dye*: implications for textual critics', *PBSA* 83 (1989), 437–72.

[52] Hrubý, 'A quantitative solution', offers an ingenious mathematical method to assist in the identification of intermediaries. This rests on the hypothesis that independent derivation (i.e. with no intervening sub-ancestor) will produce a different frequency of occurrence of the groupings ABC, AB:C, AC:B and BC:A than what he calls 'successive' derivation. ABC in this context represents the unaltered readings common to the three texts. The rates of occurrence of each of these groupings are expressed as decimals of the total number of

even when this evidence is clear and ample, there will sometimes be cases where the principle of intermediation permits texts to be isolated as a group but the evidence for branches within the group is irresolvably conflicting. Here the editor should simply box the texts on the stemma, sternly resisting any attempt to force the evidence of filiation within the box. Alternatively, the evidence could be presented in the form of an intermediation spectrum—still a useful tool—rather than a stemma of the Lachmannian type. Cases of less severe doubt should be footnoted so that readers are duly warned and can dissent as they see fit. Information about the historical circumstances of production is also of value in determining direction and derivation. Examples of this will be considered in the next section of this chapter.

Throughout our investigation, we will be looking for the directional stemma, or partial stemma, which yields the maximum plenitude of explanation, secured with the minimum need to declare agreements anomalous. If the truth of the matter fails to conform to this prescription it is unlikely that it will ever be known. The method of procedure will, as before, be one of reciprocal adjustments of models and data. Having established a hypothetical stemma or stemmas on the basis of the purportedly indicative subset, verification is sought by returning to the excluded variations and working through them one by one. If our hypothesis is correct, we will find that most of these conform to the predictions of the provisional stemma and that the remainder generally fail to do so as the result of some explicable scribal mechanism. Any completely anomalous variations should be checked at this point against the sources to make sure they have been correctly recorded: the discovery of an error that brings a reading into conformity with the stemma, while a sign of earlier carelessness, may none the less be reassuring to the editor. If this kind of fit is not encountered, the hypothesis should be regarded as

possible changes which is quantified as one. If the rate of ABC is given as $f1$, that of AB:C as $f2$, that of AC:B as $f3$ and that of BC:A as $f4$, the formula

$$\frac{f1^2}{(f1+f4)\,(f1+f3)\,(f1+f2)}$$

should return a value of one in the case of independent variation and not one in the case of successive variation. However, it has never been shown how this might be applied in practice.

having failed and further possibilities be considered. When, as often happens, a choice between hypotheses rests on the interpretation given to two or three crucial variations, this should be explained to users of the edition in a way that makes it easy for them to review the editor's decision.

Our conclusions about these matters will always remain hypotheses even if they should be vastly more probable ones than any others we have been able to devise. Kane and Donaldson speak eloquently on this subject:

> In any case our edition, as a hypothesis, continues subject to the classic test: whether it is the simplest that can be devised to account convincingly for the phenomena to which it applies. Like all hypotheses it is also essentially presumptive, that is subject to modification by the emergence of new data, or to replacement by a superior hypothesis.[53]

Having come so far, we will be as close to and as far from certainty as the facts of copying in the real world usually allow. It must be stressed that the theoretical aim of creating a full enough stemma to assist in the reconstruction of the readings of the archetype will by no means always be achievable. But this does not mean the exercise has not been worthwhile. To the extent that we are able to construct a convincing argument about the origin and growth of the tradition we will have gained a valuable aid to the other kinds of editorial decision making. We may also have acquired information that will cast light on other manuscripts and traditions.

THE TEXTUAL RELATIONSHIPS OF MISCELLANIES

Our discussion of the role of genealogical reasoning in the editing of scribally published texts has so far been concerned with single texts considered in isolation. But while these texts may well be encountered as separates, they will also as a rule be found as part of larger units. The simplest form of this is what W. J. Cameron called an 'aggregation', meaning a volume formed by binding together materials of diverse bibliographical origin.[54] Most surviving examples are the creations of later generations of

[53] *B-text*, p. 212.
[54] 'Scriptorium', pp. 27–9.

librarians, but collections will sometimes be found which were bound up in their own time, and there would have been many which were kept together by their original owners without actually being bound. For collections entered by their owners in a book reserved for that purpose, Beal's term 'personal miscellany' should be used rather than the traditional 'commonplace book', which should be reserved for actual collections of commonplaces in alphabetical order. 'Miscellany' is also to be used for all scribally published collections which would not more suitably be described as 'anthologies'. Little attention has so far been given to the significance of these larger units for the editor. Our starting point must be the realization that they possess a structure which is at once particulate, aggregative and, in many cases, evolving. Let me begin by explaining what I mean by these terms.

If one should wish to establish the textual relationship of two seventeenth-century manuscript miscellanies, whether of prose or verse, there would be no other way than by collating all the surviving copies of all their constituent items. This would yield a series of stemmas which might or might not be complete or, indeed, reliable, and which might or might not be consistent with each other. The chances are that they would not be complete, because there would probably be situations in which the available evidence would not support the procedural requirements of the method. But, assuming these stemmas were complete *and* reliable, they might still be inconsistent with each other. The reason, as we have seen, is that the compilers of these miscellanies, as well as acting as publishers for writers who brought them new material, were drawing on a body of separates already in circulation. Even when new pieces were sent to a scribal publisher by their authors, this would have nothing to do with their subsequent history, or with the condition or sequence in which they would be picked up by other scriptoria. So there is theoretically nothing to prevent each individual item from our pair of miscellanies having followed a different set of paths from agency to agency, or indeed for traditions of some complexity to have arisen within particular agencies through progressive copying. It is in this sense that the miscellanies are particulate.

But one would almost certainly find that a certain proportion of the contents of the miscellany had already been circulating as smaller sub-collections prior to their inclusion, that is as linked groups, sometimes consisting of several items on a particular topic, and sometimes of an item followed by others written in response to it.[55] It is in this sense that the miscellanies are aggregative. So as well as building stemmas for individual items, we would need to investigate the relationships of these linked groups. Moreover, when a number of versions of the same collection were the work of the same scribal agency, we would need to consider the overall collection as a transmissional unit. We are speaking, remember, of manuscript anthologies which are always one-off affairs. Of course they might be replicated in near-identical volumes with regard to their contents—though even here there will always be some alteration of readings—but it is much more common to find that collections issued by the same agency vary through items being added or removed. It is in this sense that they can be thought of as evolving. Because each manuscript is a separate production, the publisher can work in new material the moment it is acquired and discard the old the moment it grows out of date. There is also the opportunity to supply each customer with a product which is in some respects unique, or, less nobly, to force the purchase of material already possessed in order to secure the new and desired.

The moral of this is that, when dealing with the transmission of texts that were widely copied into composite sources, it can never be enough simply to analyse the transmissional history of the individual item. If that item has circulated as part of a linked group, then one must also study the history of that group through its growth and decay. If the miscellany exists in a series of evolving recensions one must also try to discover the sequence of those recensions. And then one has to see whether the three different histories agree or disagree. If they disagree one has to decide whether this is the result of a mistake in one's own analysis or whether the disagreement points to some undetected complication in the process of transmission. Not all these questions will be answerable.

To discuss these phenomena, we will need some terminology. The overall body of materials from which any particular volume is

[55] For linked groups of satires, see Vieth, *Attribution*, pp. 26–7, 76–80 and 322–52. The principle applies to all forms of scribally published composite texts.

compiled we have already called the *scriptorial archive*. Sometimes this archive would have been entered in a large book, as was done by Starkey and Collins and the creators of Folger MS M. b. 12. In this case there would have been a tendency for items to remain in the same order in any copy. But in other cases, as we saw in our discussion of the Cameron scriptorium, it is likely that the scriptorial archive existed in the form of separates—that is, of single leaves, half-sheets, folded sheets and small, stab-sewn booklets. In these cases, material removed from the archive might be lost permanently, and it would be a very easy matter for the order of items to become disturbed, either accidentally or by design. A scriptorial archive of this kind is in genealogical terms an archetype, but it is not a static archetype: I have called it a *rolling archetype*, and if it rolled long enough and vigorously enough it could even produce offspring that had no actual items in common.[56] The value of the terms scriptorial archive and rolling archetype is that they help us replace a very difficult question ('What is the transmissional history of this miscellany in respect both of its whole and its parts?') with a considerably simpler one ('Is there a known agency to which the production of this miscellany can be assigned?'). When the knowledge that given manuscript texts of a work derive from such an archive can be used in connection with the genealogical method, with each set of data serving as a control on the other, we can reason pretty conclusively.

The search for scriptorial archives and rolling archetypes makes use of many different kind of evidence. For a start there may be documentary information, of the kind considered in earlier chapters, about the publishers of texts. There will also be bibliographical evidence concerning such matters as hands, layout styles, quiring and bindings. Watermarks and countermarks can offer evidence for common scriptorial origin. The composition dates of the items will also need to be considered: seeing the bulk of scribally circulated material is highly topical it is usually not hard to determine these. In addition much material in the sources is itself supplied with dates, which if they are not those of composition will

[56] The analogy would be with a bus or train which began its journey with one set of passengers and ended it with a completely different one, or with the turnover of staff within an organization.

at least be those of transcription or of the event that inspired the item. Most important of all, naturally, are the content of the collection and the order in which items appear, though it is necessary to realize that evidence of this kind is not always conclusive. Miscellanies will show strong similarities in content and also frequently order when they derive from the same scriptorial archive; but they will also show similarities whenever independent compilers of archives have been acquiring more or less the same items (including linked groups and formed sub-collections) over more or less the same period. Moreover, some compilers of retrospective miscellanies liked to impose a chronological arrangement on their material. In these cases order may not in itself offer a means of distinguishing the work of individual scriptoria. An obvious point is that collections formed in one scriptorium may become embedded, either in whole or in part, within a larger anthology produced by another scriptorium. Compilations of political and parliamentary material include many examples of this, as do the verse anthologies discussed in Chapter 6.

Otherwise, the challenge is to extend the methods of genealogical analysis from individual items and linked groups to embrace whole collections of items. Once again, we will try, by using the more reliable evidence, to generate hypothetical models and then test those models against the whole body of data. One strongly indicative pattern is when particular groups of sources maintain their integrity from stemma to stemma while appearing in constantly varying intermediary and terminal relationships with other identifiable groups. A fluidity of relationships *within* such a group may also be significant when it suggests the possibility of progressive copying. (When the fluidity arises from unexpected reversals of readings, these could well be due to a scriptorium scribe's memory of earlier copyings.) All this can yield no more than probabilities, but they can become powerful ones when we look at them, interactively, with other classes of evidence—the historical, the bibliographical and considerations of order and content. Once we are able to link miscellanies with particular scribal agencies, we possess a powerful tool for evaluating variants in items within those miscellanies in a way which will no longer be circular because it will now be conferred from a higher level of structural understanding. An example is the Rochesterian 'Signior Dildo', where problems of editorial judgement are vastly eased by the knowledge that all but three of the collections which contain the poem are derived directly or at second hand from the archive of the 'Cameron' scriptorium. Naturally, we should always be watchful for the possibility of a scriptorium's possessing two genetically unrelated copies of the same item.[57]

TEXT AND APPARATUS

The kind of edition that has been presented as an ideal in this chapter is one that represents the most probable hypothesis a present-day scholar is able to devise about what a seventeenth-century scribally-publishing author wrote. But the information necessary for a proper assessment of the edited text can only with some difficulty be displayed on the same page as that text. By the use of diacritic signs of the kind invented by Hans Walter Gabler for his edition of Joyce's *Ulysses*, successive stages in the linear evolution of a work can be presented graphically—allowing the reader, in effect, to become the true editor of the text.[58] But the problem in our case is the very different one of recovering a lost text from the evidence of its descendants—something that is not merely a matter of the arrangement of states but rests on the construction and presentation of an argument. The challenge to the editor is to present that argument in such a way that the reader can appropriate it and if necessary revise it with the minimum of effort.

Such an aim requires that the data on which the argument rests—the list of variations—should not simply be presented but interpreted, whether it is by an introduction, physically separate explanatory notes, or notes and symbols embedded in the list itself. An uninterpreted list of variants is of very little value: only another editor is likely to be able to make much sense of it and even then it

[57] An example is the two highly variant texts of the Restoration 'Satyr on the court ladies' ('Curse on those critics ignorant and vain') in V&A MS Dyce 43, pp. 215–19 and 360–4, a product of the 'Cameron' scriptorium. Both are in the same hand. In the collateral manuscript, Österreichische Nationalbibliothek 14090, the first occurrence has been omitted.

[58] James Joyce, *Ulysses. A critical and synoptic edition*, ed. Hans Walter Gabler with Wolfhard Steppe and Claus Melchior (New York, 1984).

may take many hours of work before it can be put into usable form.[59] In practice, few editors do much to make their processes of reasoning intelligible. Many openly refuse accountability, presenting their text as the outcome of arcane processes of intellection which must always remain a mystery.[60] Such an approach is not only a manifestation of bad faith towards the reader, but leads to an unjustifiably final status being claimed for the resultant reading text. In fact the heart of the edition is not its text but the judgements that underlie the text. The edition that makes these judgements available for inspection will also acknowledge the necessarily provisional status of any reading text both with regard to the hypothetical nature of editorial decisions and the determining role of editorial policy. Here Kane and Donaldson provide a salutary model. As D. C. Greetham has pointed out 'the degree of license assumed by the editors requires that *all* of the evidence for reconstruction of the text be made available so that the editorial rationale can be continually tested against the documentary witnesses'.[61]

Having once accepted this primacy of the argument, the editor is rewarded with a considerable latitude in adapting the reading text to the requirements of its users. This can affect both substantive and incidental readings. Literary readers by and large are happy with the notion of the eclectic text constructed from a variety of witnesses; but there will always be strong resistance among historians towards this ideal since such a text has ceased to be what they would recognize as a document—i.e. something firmly assignable to a particular place and time.[62] In such cases it is

[59] The listing of variations in the form in which the lemma is the reading of the edited text is itself a source of confusion as it renders the variation less amenable to analysis. The form used by Greg for the demonstrations of *The calculus of variants* would be the ideal one with some typographical means used to single out the preferred variant.

[60] As in Vieth, *Complete poems*, p. xlvi: 'Although Rochester scholarship has shown encouraging progress in recent years, its level of accomplishment does not yet warrant incorporating into this edition a complete textual apparatus, including lists of all variants in the independently descended versions of each poem and a detailed account of the procedure, sometimes quite elaborate, by which these variants were used to establish text'.

[61] D. C. Greetham, 'Normalisation of accidentals in Middle English texts: the paradox of Thomas Hoccleve', *SB* 38 (1985), 123 n.

[62] This attitude is both defended and assailed in the papers presented in *Literary and historical editing*, ed. George L. Vogt and John Bush Jones (Lawrence, Kan., 1981). The wider ramifications of the debate are considered in Mary-Jo Kline, *A guide to documentary editing*

probably kindest to reserve speculation concerning the readings of the archetype for the report on transmissional history and provide a reading text which is a particular scribal version from as close as possible to the origin of the tradition, presented with only minimal intervention. But this will not be 'the text' so much as a means of interrogating the transmissional history, first of all for evidence as to the nature of the archetype, and secondly (and perhaps more importantly in a historical text) for the story of how the text has been conceived, promulgated, used, misused, understood, misunderstood, and revised to suit new circumstances. In other words, the critical old-spelling edition compiled (where practicable) on genealogical principles is not only a concatenation of hypotheses about what might once have been written but a record of the various forms in which the text was *read*—and rewritten—by its contemporaries.

As an example of the way in which records of variation illuminate the use of the text by its first readers, I would like to take two cases from poems by the sixth Earl of Dorset. A state poem of the Stuart century normally emerged from within a political clique which had highly privileged information about circumstances at court or in parliament, but whose aim was not to share this information so much as to use it as the basis of a sophisticated kind of disinformation which would influence the future course of events. From the point of view of the clique, the poem would soon be rendered obsolete by their acquiring hotter information and adopting new political strategies. But long before this happened, the satire would have moved out into circles which did not possess the privileged information of the writer and where readers would indulge in various kinds of creative *mis*reading in order to adjust the text to their own understanding of politics and desires to influence the future. They would do this by altering names, by filling in deliberate blanks with their own guesses, and, of course, by rewriting what seemed to them to be meaningless so that it made better sense—to themselves.

Dorset's 'Colon' is a satire on Charles II and his mistresses, written when the leading royal mistress, the Duchess of Ports-

(Baltimore, 1987), pp. 8–21 and G. Thomas Tanselle, 'Historicism and critical editing', *SB* 39 (1986), 1–46.

mouth, was under attack from parliament. The writer imagines that Portsmouth has resigned from her post, and that Charles is holding interviews to select her successor—the poem being a narrative of these interviews. At lines 56-9 we find the following passage:

> Next in stepp'd pretty Lady Grey,
> Offer'd her lord should nothing say
> 'Gainst the next treasurer's accus'd
> So her pretense were not refus'd:[63]

Elias Mengel in Volume two of the Yale *Poems on affairs of state* cites a variant reading for the third line ' 'Gainst next the treasurer's accus'd'.[64] He further suggests that if, as is quite likely, the poem was written between December 1678 and March 1679, the variant would allude very precisely to the plight of the then treasurer, the Earl of Danby, who had been saved from impeachment only by the proroguing of parliament on 30 December and was attacked at once by the new parliament which met on 6 March, dismissed from his post and on 16 April sent to the Tower. Mengel presents this simply as a piece of dating evidence, but the variation in the line can also be seen as marking a shift in the relationship between the text and the events it was both recording and trying to influence. We might refine this insight further by proposing that the change corresponds to a movement outwards of the satire from an internal court faction, to which Dorset belonged and for whom the poem was an attempt to influence internal court politics, to a wider public who would read it, in Whig terms, as an attack on the court as an institution. So the variant reflects both misunderstanding of the precise allusion intended by the writer, and a wresting of the poem by its new readers to an altered political function.

The second example is from Dorset's 'A faithful catalogue of our most eminent ninnies', dated 1686 and 1687 in some manuscripts but assigned by Brice Harris and Galbraith Crump to early in 1688.[65]

[63] *POAS (Yale)*, ii. 170–1.

[64] Ibid. 171.

[65] *Poems*, ed. Harris, p. 136; *POAS (Yale)*, iv. 190. Line 17 addresses Charles II (d. 1685) as if he was still living. The text given here is Crump's. Harris's contains several misprints as well as being marred by retention of inferior readings on a 'best manuscript' basis. His record of variants is much fuller than Crump's but still incomplete, as well as containing

Proud Oxford justly thinks her Dutch-built shape
A little too unwieldy for a rape;
Yet, being conscious it will tumble down,
At first assault surrenders up the town;
But no kind conqueror has yet thought fit
To make it his belov'd imperial seat;
That batter'd fort, which they with ease deceive,
Pillag'd and sack'd, to the next foe they leave;
And haughty Di in just revenge will lig,
Although she starve, with any senseless Whig . . . (ll. 368–77)

Early in the process of transmission, the fourth couplet of the passage was omitted and then added at the foot of the page with a mark to indicate its proper position. As a result of failure to observe the mark, the majority of the manuscripts have it in the wrong position, creating the following:

But why to Ireland, Braithwait? Can the clime,
Dost thou imagine, make an easy time?
That batter'd fort, which they with ease deceive,
Pillag'd and sack'd, to the next foe they leave.
Ungratefully, indeed thou didst requite
The skillful goddess of the silent night
By whose kind help thou wast so oft before
Deliver'd safely on thy native shore. (ll. 394–9)

The error is obvious enough to modern readers with the full textual history of the poem available and should also have been obvious to a reader in 1688 since the errant couplet would have had no relationship to its context. But most of the surviving manuscripts are from anthologies written in the 1690s, and for their scribes the couplet would have seemed a perfectly apt, if somewhat oddly phrased, comment on the state of Ireland in the aftermath of William's invasion. In this case a sexual insult in a poem attacking members of the court of James II has been metamorphosed into a sneer at Anglo-Dutch conduct in Ireland.

Textual change of this kind has to be recorded because it is itself a part of the historical process. The Yale *Poems on affairs of state* series has good explanatory notes which illuminate many issues of

inaccuracies. Neither editor gives a proper record of the sidenotes which the manuscripts show were an integral part of the work.

this kind; but it is only in the Cameron and Ellis volumes that a real attempt is made to illustrate and explain transmissional histories. If a parallel series of the political poetry of the earlier part of the century should ever be attempted (now a major desideratum) it is to be hoped that the nexus between an understanding of textual genealogies and an understanding of how the text was used and understood by its early readers will be foregrounded for attention. The same should also apply to editions of historical documents. A precedent for this is the Notestein and Relf edition of the 1629 *Commons debates* which anticipates a number of techniques of present-day *textes génétiques*. In this, as in other respects, it is vital that the reader should not be confined to walking the decks of the edited text but should be given easy access to both the bridge and the engine room.

The secondary status of the reading text *vis-à-vis* the textual argument will also be reflected in the choices to be made concerning spelling and punctuation. It will be helpful in sorting out the issues if we return to the case of Rochester and the way in which the problem has been handled by his two most distinguished editors, Vieth and Walker. Vieth's edition of 1968 starts from the premise that what readers are primarily interested in is the personality of Rochester. The poems are grouped under sections headed Prentice Work, Early Maturity (1672–1673), Tragic Maturity (1674–1675), and Disillusionment and Death (1676–1680). The more substantial poems are introduced by headnotes relating them in a more particular way to the biography of the poet. For instance, at the beginning of 'Leave this gaudy gilded stage' Vieth has the note: 'It is tempting to imagine that this lyric, which survives in Rochester's own handwriting, was addressed to some actress who was his mistress, perhaps Elizabeth Barry'—which makes it rather difficult *not* to read the poem in a biographical way, or at least to test the offered proposition as one reads it.[66] An apparent inconsistency of the edition, in view of its strong assertion of the authorial rationale, is that it uses modern spelling and heavy, often actively interpretative, modern punctuation. Vieth's argument for modern spelling is that 'there is virtually no basis for an old-spelling text of Rochester's poems'—an

[66] *Collected poems*, p. 85.

argument which looks rather odd now that Walker has produced such a text.[67] But clearly what Vieth meant by an old-spelling edition was an edition that preserved the author's own accidentals, rather than simply accidentals from the historical period. This choice of modern spelling and punctuation is one of a number of features of Vieth's edition—the headnotes are another—that tend to submerge the personality of the author under that of the editor. In other words, it represents an arbitrary choice which is in conflict with the wider rationale of the edition. But my concern here is not to criticize that choice, but to use it to illustrate the kind of latitude which is validly available to the editor who acknowledges the secondary and provisional status of the reading text. Any disappointment felt with this edition will not be over its radical rehandling of incidentals but in its failure to provide its readers with a usable record of transmissional history.

Walker's edition of 1984, which deserves always to be remembered with gratitude as the first to present an *apparatus criticus*, was based on the alternative assumption, accepted much earlier by de Sola Pinto, that what is interesting about Rochester is his contribution to the development of the major genres of Augustan poetry. So in this case the text is arranged in sections headed Juvenilia, Love Poems, Translations, Prologues and Epilogues, Satires and Lampoons, Poems to Mulgrave and Scroope, and Epigrams, Impromptus, Jeux d'Esprit etc. Walker presents versions which are very faithful to their manuscript copy-texts, except when the accidentals of these would pose severe difficulties for a modern reader. This gives his edition a valuable sense of the flavour and variability imparted by scribal publication. Walker has also, very commendably in my view, included whole variant manuscript texts of a number of poems, and also poems by other writers which formed part of linked groups to which Rochester contributed, again emphasizing the conditions of the poems' first circulation as scriptorial satire. Yet here one is again conscious of a conflict of rationales. In de Sola Pinto's case the texts had been based on the edition of 1691, which was the form in which they were probably read by most later Augustan writers. This is clearly an advantage if one is looking at Rochester as a

[67] Ibid., p. xlv.

source of influences on the subsequent history of the genres he pioneered, and was one of a number of other policies which might legitimately have been chosen.

Both editors had their reasons for these choices which they would wish to defend. None the less, the choices actually made suggest the possibility of others which might have been considered. In Walker's case, a text presenting the accidentals of a series of 'best manuscripts' might well have ordered its contents not under genres but under the sources in which the poems made their first or most significant appearance. Vieth likewise might have reinforced the biographical thrust of his edition by using a synthetic spelling system based on Rochester's known preferences as revealed by the handful of verse holographs and, more revealingly, the manuscripts of the correspondence. As it happens, Rochester was remarkably consistent in both his spellings and his punctuation and such an approach would be perfectly feasible for a new edition. This could have been done either in a conservative way as in the Latham and Matthews *Pepys*, which uses spellings characteristic of the author when known but otherwise modern spelling, or more radically by employing the method accepted for the text of Hoccleve's *Regement of princes* in which probabilistic methods are used to replicate the author's use of variant spellings for the same word.[68] Such a choice would not be made on the assumption that one was actually restoring what the author originally wrote, but in the belief that, since some arbitrary system had to be used, it could more usefully be one the author approved of than modern spelling. Once again, these comments are not meant as criticisms of the choices actually made by Walker and Vieth, to both of whom future editors of Rochester will owe an immeasurable debt, but simply to illustrate the range of possibilities open to all editors of scribally published texts who set out to do more than reproduce a particular historical document.

Behind the freedom available in suiting or not suiting the accidentals to the wider aims of the edition lies Greg's liberating argument in 'The rationale of copy-text' that the authority for accidentals need not inhere in the same text as the authority for substantives.[69] His aim in proposing this was to ensure that the text

[68] *Diary*, i, p. cl; D. C. Greetham, 'Normalisation of accidentals', pp. 121–50.

[69] *SB* 3 (1950–1), 19–36. This modest paper has spawned a huge secondary literature, for

which best preserved the author's accidentals was available to be used as copy-text for the edition. In the cases just considered, and indeed most of the writings discussed in this book, there is no authorial text available in the first place, nor in many cases any text which is known to stand sufficiently close to the authorial fair copy as to preserve anything of its accidentals. Indeed, the authors of the majority of scribally published texts remain unknown or only to be guessed at. This makes the degree of options available unusually wide—even to the extent of abandoning any notion of copy-text in Greg's sense and supplying a conjecturally reconstructed text with editorial accidentals. One would not, of course, wish to see freedom degenerate into caprice. All things considered, it is preferable that the choice of a system of accidentals for the edition should grow from a sense of its function and purpose, and that this should also govern the ordering of items and the relationship established between the textual apparatus, the explanatory notes and the words on the page. But where there are good reasons for departing from this principle of consistency, they should be followed. What makes this freedom possible is a view of editing which sees its central and defining function not as the presentation of a text but the creation of an argument or a series of arguments embodied in a record of transmissional history. My own rider to this view is simply that the argument should be presented in a form which allows the reader to monitor and where necessary to revise its conclusions. A bare list of variants is of little use when the tradition is of any complexity. Editors must explain not only their general policy concerning the texts, but how and why they have chosen to resolve particular cases of conflict. This can best be done by direct annotation of the record of variation.

which see G. Thomas Tanselle, 'The editorial problem of final authorial intention', *SB* 29 (1976), 167–211.

BIBLIOGRAPHY OF MAJOR REFERENCES

What are here listed are secondary, and a few primary, sources of major relevance to the topic, and those which are referred to by short title at scattered locations throughout the text. Other sources may be located through the index.

ASHBEE, ANDREW. 'A further look at some of the Le Strange manuscripts'. *Chelys* 5 (1973–4), 24–41.

AUBREY, JOHN. *'Brief lives', chiefly of contemporaries, set down by John Aubrey, between the years 1669 and 1696*, ed. Andrew Clark. 2 vols. Oxford, 1898.

BAUMAN, RICHARD. *Let your words be few: symbolism of speaking and silence among seventeenth-century Quakers*. Cambridge, 1983.

BEAL, PETER, comp. *Index of English literary manuscripts. Volume 1 1450–1625* and *Volume 2 1625–1700*. London, 1980– .

BEAUMONT, FRANCIS and JOHN FLETCHER. *Comedies and tragedies written by Francis Beaumont and John Fletcher gentlemen*. London, 1647.

—— *The dramatic works in the Beaumont and Fletcher canon*, gen. ed. Fredson Bowers. Cambridge, 1966– .

BÉDIER, JOSEPH. 'La tradition manuscrite du Lai de l'ombre'. *Romania* 54 (1928), 161–96 and 321–56.

BELANGER, TERRY. 'Publishers and writers in eighteenth-century England' in Isabel Rivers, ed., *Books and their readers in eighteenth-century England*, pp. 5–25. Leicester, 1982.

BELJAME, ALEXANDRE. *Men of letters and the English public in the eighteenth century*. London, 1948.

BENJAMIN, WALTER. *Illuminations*, introd. Hannah Arendt, trans. Harry Zohn. London, 1973.

BRAUNMULLER, A. R., ed. *A seventeenth-century letter-book*. Newark, Del., 1983.

BRETT, PHILIP. 'Edward Paston (1550–1630): a Norfolk gentleman and his musical collection'. *Transactions of the Cambridge Bibliographical Society* 4 (1964), 51–69.

CAMERON, W. J. 'A late seventeenth-century scriptorium'. *Renaissance and modern studies* 7 (1963), 25–52.

CHAYTOR, H. J. *From script to print: an introduction to medieval vernacular literature*. Cambridge, 1950.

COMENIUS, JOANNES AMOS. *Orbis sensualium pictus*, facsim. edn, introd. James Bowen. Sydney, 1967.

Commons debates for 1629, ed. Wallace Notestein and Frances Helen Relf. Minneapolis, 1921.

CORAL, LENORE F. 'Music in English auction sales, 1676–1750'. University of London Ph.D. thesis, 1974.

CRESSY, DAVID. *Literacy and the social order: reading and writing in Tudor and Stuart England*. Cambridge, 1980.

CROFT, P. J. *Autograph poetry in the English language*. 2 vols. London, 1973.

CROFT, PAULINE. 'Annual parliaments and the long parliament'. *Bulletin of the Institute of Historical Research* 59 (1986), 155–71.

CROSFIELD, THOMAS. *The diary of Thomas Crosfield*, ed. Frederick S. Boas. London, 1935.

CUST, RICHARD. 'News and politics in early seventeenth-century England'. *Past and present* 112 (Aug. 1986), 60–90.

CUST, RICHARD, and ANN HUGHES, eds. *Conflict in early Stuart England: studies in religion and politics 1603–1642* (London, 1989).

CUTHBERT, DENISE. 'A re-examination of Andrew Marvell'. Sydney University Ph.D. thesis, 1987.

DANCHIN, PIERRE, ed. *The prologues and epilogues of the Restoration 1660–1700*. 7 vols. Nancy, 1981–8.

DAVIES, JOHN, OF HEREFORD. *The complete works of John Davies of Hereford*, ed. Alexander B. Grosart. Edinburgh, 1878.

DAVIES, ROY. 'The creation of new knowledge by information retrieval and classification'. *Journal of documentation* 45 (1989), 273–301.

DAWSON, GILES E., and LAETITIA KENNEDY-SKIPTON. *Elizabethan handwriting 1500–1650*. London, 1966.

DEARING, VINTON A. *Principles and practice of textual analysis*. Berkeley, Calif., and Los Angeles, 1974.

DE BEAU CHESNE, JOHN, and JOHN BAILDON. *A booke containing divers sortes of hands*. London, 1602 (facsim. repr. Amsterdam, 1977).

DEFOE, DANIEL. *A review of the state of the British nation*. London, 1712 (facsim. ed. A. W. Secord, New York, 1938, book 21).

DERRIDA, JACQUES. *Of grammatology*, trans. G. C. Spivak. Baltimore, 1976.

D'EWES, SIR SIMONDS. *The autobiography and correspondence of Sir*

Simonds D'Ewes, Bart., during the reigns of James I and Charles I, ed. James Orchard Halliwell. London, 1845.

DODD, GORDON, comp. *Thematic index of music for viols.* First instalment (London, 1980), with further instalments 1982, 1984 and 1987.

DONNE, JOHN. *Letters to severall persons of honour.* London, 1651.

DORSET, CHARLES SACKVILLE, EARL OF. *The poems of Charles Sackville, sixth earl of Dorset*, ed. Brice Harris. New York, 1979.

DOUGLAS, DAVID. *English scholars 1660–1730.* 2nd rev. edn. London, 1951.

DOWNIE, J. A. *Robert Harley and the press. Propaganda and public opinion in the age of Swift and Defoe.* Cambridge, 1970.

DRAYTON, MICHAEL. *The works of Michael Drayton*, ed. J. William Hebel. 5 vols. Oxford, 1961.

DRYDEN, JOHN. *The works of John Dryden*, gen. eds. H. T. Swedenberg, jun., and Alan Roper. Los Angeles, 1956– .

DUGDALE, SIR WILLIAM. *The life, diary, and correspondence of Sir William Dugdale*, ed. William Hamper. London, 1827.

EVELYN, JOHN. *The diary of John Evelyn*, ed. E. S. de Beer. 6 vols. Oxford, 1955.

FEATHER, JOHN. *A history of British publishing.* London, 1988.

FIENNES, CELIA. *The journeys of Celia Fiennes*, ed. Christopher Morris. London, 1947.

FINLAY, MICHAEL. *Western writing implements in the age of the quill pen.* Wetheral, 1990.

FLETCHER, HARRIS FRANCIS. *The intellectual development of John Milton.* 2 vols. Urbana, Ill., 1961.

FRASER, PETER. *The intelligence of the secretaries of state and their monopoly of licensed news 1660–1688.* Cambridge, 1956.

FULLER, THOMAS. *Ephemeris parliamentaria.* London, 1654.

—— *The history of the worthies of England.* London, 1662.

GAIR, W. R. 'The politics of scholarship: a dramatic comment on the autocracy of Charles I' in David Galloway, ed., *The Elizabethan theatre III. Papers given at the third international conference on Elizabethan theatre held at the University of Waterloo, Ontario, in July 1970*, pp. 100–18. Waterloo, Ont., 1973.

GASKELL, PHILIP. *A new introduction to bibliography*, rev. impression. Oxford, 1974.

GOLDBERG, JONATHAN. *Writing matter: from the hands of the English Renaissance.* Stanford, Calif., 1990.

GREETHAM, D. C. 'Normalisation of accidentals in Middle English texts: the paradox of Thomas Hoccleve'. *SB* 38 (1984), 121–50.

GREETHAM, D. C. 'Textual and literary theory: redrawing the matrix'. *SB* 42 (1989), 1–24.

GREG, W. W. *The calculus of variants. An essay on textual criticism*. Oxford, 1927.

—— *A companion to Arber, being a calendar of documents in Edward Arber's 'Transcript of the registers of the Company of Stationers of London 1554–1640'*. Oxford, 1967.

—— 'The rationale of copy text'. *SB* 3 (1950-1), 19-36. Also in his *Collected papers*, ed. J. C. Maxwell, pp. 374–91. Oxford, 1966.

GUBAR, SUSAN. '"The blank page" and the issues of female creativity' in Elizabeth Abel, ed., *Writing and sexual difference*, pp. 73–93. Brighton, 1982.

The Gyldenstolpe manuscript miscellany of poems by John Wilmot, Earl of Rochester, and other Restoration authors, ed. Bror Danielsson and David M. Vieth. Stockholm, 1967.

HABERMAS, JÜRGEN. *The structural transformation of the public sphere: an enquiry into a category of bourgeois society*, trans. Thomas Burger with the assistance of Frederick Lawrence. Cambridge, Mass., 1989.

HAMMOND, PAUL. 'The Robinson manuscript miscellany of Restoration verse in the Brotherton Collection, Leeds'. *Proceedings of the Leeds Philosophical and Literary Society, Literary and historical section*, 18/3 (1982), 277–324.

HARBAGE, ALFRED, rev. S. SCHOENBAUM and SYLVIA STOLER WAGENHEIM. *Annals of English drama 975–1700*. 3rd edn. London, 1989.

HARINGTON, SIR JOHN. *Nugae antiquae: being a miscellaneous collection of original papers*. 2 vols. London, 1769–75.

—— *A supplie or addicion to the catalogue of bishops, to the yeare 1608*, ed. R. H. Miller. Potomac, 1981.

HARRIS, BRICE. *Charles Sackville, sixth earl of Dorset, patron and poet of the Restoration*. Urbana, Ill., 1940.

—— 'Captain Robert Julian, secretary to the muses'. *ELH* 10 (1943), 294–309.

HEAL, SIR AMBROSE. *The English writing-masters and their copy-books 1570–1800: a biographical dictionary and a biography*, introd. Stanley Morison. London, 1931.

HEAWOOD, EDWARD A. 'Papers used in England after 1600. I. The seventeenth century to *c.* 1680'. *Library*, 4:11 (1930), 263–99.

HECTOR, L. C. *The handwriting of English documents*. 2nd edn. London, 1966.

HOBBS, MARY. 'An edition of the Stoughton manuscript (an early seventeenth-century poetry collection in private hands, connected with Henry King and Oxford) seen in relation to other contemporary poetry and song collections'. London University Ph.D. thesis, 1973.

HOBBS, MARY. 'Early seventeenth-century verse miscellanies and their value for textual editors'. *English manuscript studies 1100–1700* 1 (1989), 182–210.

HRUBÝ, ANTONÍN. 'A quantitative solution of the ambiguity of three texts'. *SB* 18 (1965), 147–82.

HUGHES, EDWARD. 'A Durham manuscript of the *Commons debates* of 1629'. *English historical review* 74 (1959), 672–9.

HYDE, HENRY, SECOND EARL OF CLARENDON. *The correspondence of Henry Hyde, Earl of Clarendon, and of his brother Laurence Hyde, Earl of Rochester*, ed. Samuel Weller Singer. 2 vols. London, 1828.

JENKINSON, SIR HILARY. *The later court hands in England from the fifteenth to the seventeenth century*. 2 vols. Cambridge, 1927.

JONSON, BEN. *Ben Jonson*, ed. C. H. Herford and Percy and Evelyn Simpson. 11 vols. Oxford, 1925–52.

JOWETT, JOHN. 'Jonson's authorization of type in *Sejanus* and other early quartos'. *SB* 44 (1991), 254–65.

KAY, DENNIS. 'Poems by Sir Walter Aston, and a date for the Donne/Goodyer verse epistle "alternis vicibus".' *RES* NS 37 (1986), 198–210.

KELLIHER, HILTON, comp. *Andrew Marvell, poet and politician 1621–78. An exhibition to commemorate the tercentenary of his death*. London, 1978.

KENYON, J. P. *Stuart England*. 2nd edn. Harmondsworth, 1985.

KERNAN, ALVIN. *Printing technology, letters and Samuel Johnson*. Princeton, NJ, 1987.

KINNAMON, NOEL. 'The Sidney psalms: the Penshurst and Tixall manuscripts'. *English manuscript studies 1100–1700* 2 (1990), 139–161.

KIRKMAN, FRANCIS. *The unlucky citizen: experimentally described in the various fortunes of an unlucky Londoner*. London, 1673.

LANGLAND, WILLIAM. *Piers plowman*, ed. George Kane and E. Talbot Donaldson. *The A version. Will's visions of Piers plowman and Do-well*. London, 1960 (rev. repr. 1988). *The B version. Will's visions of Piers plowman, Do-well, Do-better and Do-best*. London, 1975 (rev. repr. 1988).

LASLETT, PETER. 'The gentry of Kent in 1640'. *Cambridge historical journal* 9 (1947–9), 148–64.

—— 'Sir Robert Filmer: the man versus the Whig myth'. *William and Mary quarterly*, 3:5 (1948), 523–46.

—— *The world we have lost: further explored*. Cambridge, 1983.

LEMMINGS, DAVID. 'The student body of the Inns of Court under the later Stuarts'. *BIHR* 58 (1985), 149–66.

LE STRANGE, SIR NICHOLAS. *'Merry passages and jeasts': a manuscript* jestbook of Sir Nicholas Le Strange (1603–1655), ed. H. F. Lippincott. Salzburg, 1974.

Letters addressed from London to Sir Joseph Williamson while plenipotentiary at the congress of Cologne in the years 1673 and 1674, ed. W. D. Christie. Camden Society publications, NS, 8–9. 2 vols. London, 1874.

LEVY, F. J. 'How information spread among the gentry, 1550–1640'. *Journal of British studies* 21 (1982), 11–34.

LILLYWHITE, BRYANT. *London coffee houses: a reference book of coffee houses of the seventeenth, eighteenth and nineteenth centuries*. London, 1963.

LOVE, HAROLD. *Restoration literature: critical approaches*. London, 1972.

—— 'Preacher and publisher: Oliver Heywood and Thomas Parkhurst'. *SB* 31 (1978), 227–35.

—— 'The text of "Timon. A satyr".' *BSANZ bulletin* 6 (1982), 113–40.

—— 'The ranking of variants in moderately contaminated manuscript traditions'. *SB* 37 (1984), 39–57.

—— 'Manuscript versus print in the transmission of English literature, 1600–1700'. *BSANZ bulletin* 9 (1985), 95–107.

—— 'Shadwell, Flecknoe and the Duke of Newcastle: an impetus for *Mac Flecknoe*'. *Papers on language and literature* 21 (1985), 19-27.

—— *The text of Rochester's 'Upon nothing'*. Monash University Centre for Bibliographical and Textual Studies. Occasional Papers, no. 1. Melbourne, 1985.

—— 'Scribal publication in seventeenth-century England'. *Transactions of the Cambridge Bibliographical Society* 9 (1987), 130–54.

—— 'Scribal texts and literary communities: the Rochester circle and Osborn b. 105'. *SB* 42 (1989), 219–235.

—— 'The editing of Restoration scriptorial satire', in Paul Eggert, ed. *Editing in Australia*, pp. 65–84. Canberra, 1990.

—— 'Richard Flecknoe as author-publisher'. *BSANZ bulletin* 14 (1990), 41–50.

LOVELACE, RICHARD. *The poems of Richard Lovelace*, ed. C. H. Wilkinson. Oxford, 1953.

LUTTRELL, NARCISSUS. *A brief historical relation*. 6 vols. Oxford, 1857.

MAAS, PAUL. *Textual criticism*, trans. Barbara Flower. Oxford, 1958.

MACCOLL, ALAN. 'The circulation of Donne's poems in manuscript', in A. J. Smith, ed., *John Donne: essays in celebration*, pp. 28–46. London, 1972.

MCKENZIE, D. F. *The Cambridge University Press 1696–1712: a bibliographical study*. 2 vols. Cambridge, 1966.

—— *Bibliography and the sociology of texts*. London, 1986.

McKenzie, D. F. 'Speech–manuscript–print', in Dave Oliphant and Robin Bradford, eds., *New directions in textual studies*, pp. 87–109. Austin, Tex., 1990.

McKenzie, D. F. and J. C. Ross, eds. *A ledger of Charles Ackers: printer of 'The London magazine'*. Oxford, 1968.

McLuhan, Marshall. *The Gutenberg galaxy: the making of typographic man*. Toronto, 1962.

Marotti, Arthur F. *John Donne, coterie poet*. Madison, Wis., 1986.

Marvell, Andrew. *The poems and letters of Andrew Marvell*, ed. H. M. Margoliouth, 3rd edn, rev. Pierre Legouis with the collaboration of E. E. Duncan-Jones. Oxford, 1971.

Maslen, K. I. D., and John Lancaster. *The Bowyer ledgers*. London, 1991.

Monson, Craig. *Voices and viols in England, 1600–1650. The sources and their music*. Ann Arbor, Mich., 1982.

Morison, Stanley. *Politics and script*, ed. Nicholas Barker. Oxford, 1972.

Morrill, J. S. 'William Davenport and the "silent majority" of early Stuart England'. *Journal of the Chester Archaeological Society* 18 (1975), 115–29.

Moxon, Joseph. *Mechanick exercises on the whole art of printing (1683–4)*, ed. Herbert Davis and Harry Carter. 2nd edn. London, 1962.

Muddiman, J. G. *The king's journalist 1659–1689: studies in the reign of Charles II*. London, 1923.

Nashe, Thomas. *The works of Thomas Nashe*, ed. R. B. McKerrow, rev. F. P. Wilson. 5 vols. Oxford, 1958.

Nicholl, Charles. *A cup of news: the life of Thomas Nashe*. London, 1984.

North, Roger. *The life of the right honourable Francis North, Baron of Guilford*. London, 1742.

—— *Roger North on music*, ed. John Wilson. London, 1959.

—— *General preface and life of Dr John North*, ed. Peter Millard. Toronto, 1984.

O'Day, Rosemary. *Education and society 1500–1800: the social foundations of education in early modern Britain*. London, 1982.

Ong, Walter J. *Fighting for life: contest, sexuality, and consciousness*. Ithaca, NY, 1981.

—— *Orality and literacy: the technologizing of the word*. London, 1982.

Patterson, Annabel. *Censorship and interpretation: the conditions of writing and reading in early modern England*. Madison, Wis., 1984.

Pearl, V. L. and M. L. 'Richard Corbett's "Against the opposing of the Duke in parliament, 1628" and the anonymous rejoinder, "An answer to the same, lyne for lyne": the earliest dated manuscript copies'. *RES* NS 42 (1991), 32–9.

PEBWORTH, TED-LARRY. 'John Donne, coterie poetry, and the text as performance'. *SEL* 29 (1989), 61-75.

PECK, LINDA LEVY. *Northampton: patronage and policy at the court of James I.* London, 1982.

PEMBROKE, MARY, COUNTESS OF. *The triumph of death and other unpublished and uncollected poems by Mary Sidney, Countess of Pembroke (1561–1621)*, ed. G. F. Waller. Salzburg, 1977.

PEPYS, SAMUEL. *The diary of Samuel Pepys*, ed. Robert Latham and William Matthews. 11 vols. London, 1970–83.

PETER, JOHN. *Complaint and satire in early English literature.* Oxford, 1956.

PETTI, ANTHONY G. *English literary hands from Chaucer to Dryden.* London, 1977.

PHILIPS, KATHERINE. *The collected works of Katherine Philips*, ed. Patrick Thomas. Stump Cross, 1990– .

PINTO, DAVID. 'The music of the Hattons'. *RMA Research chronicle* 23 (1990), 79–108.

PLANT, MARJORIE. *The English book trade. An economic history of the making and sale of books.* 2nd edn. London, 1965.

Poems on affairs of state. Augustan satirical verse, 1660–1714, gen. ed. George deF. Lord. 7 vols. New Haven, Conn., 1963–75.

POTTER, LOIS. *Secret rites and secret writings: royalist literature, 1641–1660.* Cambridge, 1989.

POWELL, WILLIAM S. *John Pory 1572–36. The life and letters of a man of many parts.* Chapel Hill, NC, 1977.

PRITCHARD, ALLAN. 'Marvell's "The garden": a Restoration poem?'. *SEL* 23 (1983), 371–88.

PROBYN, CLIVE. '"Haranguing upon texts": Swift and the idea of the book', in Hermann J. Real and Heinz J. Vienken, eds., *Proceedings of the first Münster symposium on Jonathan Swift*, pp. 187–97. München, 1985.

—— 'Swift's *Verses on the death of Dr Swift*: the notes'. *SB* 39 (1986), 47–61.

Proceedings of the short parliament of 1640, ed. Esther S. Cope in collaboration with Willson H. Coates. Camden Society, 4:19. London, 1977.

RANDALL, DALE B. J. *Gentle flame: the life and verse of Dudley, fourth Lord North (1602–1677).* Durham, NC, 1983.

RANDOLPH, MARY CLAIRE. '"Mr Julian, secretary of the muses": Pasquil in London'. *N&Q* 184 (Jan–June 1943), 2–6.

Reports of cases in the courts of Star Chamber and High Commission, ed. S. R. Gardiner. Camden Society, NS 39. London, 1886.

ROCHESTER, JOHN WILMOT, 2ND EARL OF. *The complete poems of John Wilmot, Earl of Rochester*, ed. David M. Vieth. New Haven, Conn., 1968.

—— *The letters of John Wilmot, Earl of Rochester*, ed. Jeremy Treglown. Oxford, 1980.

—— *The poems of John Wilmot, Earl of Rochester*, ed. Keith Walker. Oxford, 1984.

ROSTENBERG, LEONA. *English publishers in the graphic arts 1599–1700. A study of the printsellers and publishers of engravings, art and architectural manuals, maps and copy books.* New York, 1963.

SAUNDERS, J. W. 'The stigma of print: a note on the social bases of Tudor poetry'. *Essays in criticism* 1 (1951), 139–64.

SAVILE, GEORGE, MARQUESS OF HALIFAX. *The works of George Savile, Marquess of Halifax*, ed. Mark N. Brown. 2 vols. Oxford, 1989.

Scriveners' company common paper 1357–1628 with a continuation to 1678, ed. Francis W. Steer. London, 1968.

SHAKESPEARE, WILLIAM. *The complete works: original spelling edition*, ed. Stanley Wells and Gary Taylor. Oxford, 1986.

SHARPE, KEVIN. *Sir Robert Cotton 1586–1631: history and politics in early modern England.* Oxford, 1979.

SIMPSON, CLAUDE M. *The British broadside ballad and its music.* New Brunswick, NJ, 1966.

SNYDER, HENRY L. 'Newsletters in England, 1689–1715. With special reference to John Dyer—a byway in the history of England', in Donovan H. Bond and W. Reynolds McLeod, eds. *Newsletters and newspapers: eighteenth-century journalism.* Morgantown, 1977.

SOUTHERNE, THOMAS. *The works of Thomas Southerne*, ed. Robert Jordan and Harold Love. 2 vols. Oxford, 1988.

The spectator, ed. Donald F. Bond. 5 vols. Oxford, 1965.

STOLL, J. 'Zur Psychologie der Schreibfehler'. *Fortschritte der Psychologie* 2 (1913), 1–133.

STONE, LAWRENCE. *The crisis of the aristocracy 1558–1641.* Oxford, 1965.

STYLES, PHILIP. *Sir Simon Archer 1581–1662.* Oxford, 1946.

The first and second Dalhousie manuscripts: poems and prose by John Donne and others, a facsimile edition, ed. Ernest W. Sullivan II. 2 vols. Columbia, Mo., 1988.

SWANSON, DON. 'Undiscovered public knowledge'. *Library quarterly* 56 (1986), 103–118.

SWIFT, JONATHAN. *Prose works of Jonathan Swift*, ed. Herbert Davis *et al.* 14 vols. Oxford, 1939–68.

TANSELLE, THOMAS. 'Classical, biblical, and medieval textual criticism and modern editing'. *SB* 36 (1983), 21–68.

THOMPSON, ANN and JOHN. *Shakespeare: meaning and metaphor.* Brighton, 1987.

THOMPSON, ROBERT P. 'English music manuscripts and the fine paper trade, 1648–1688'. London University Ph.D. thesis, 1988.

TREADWELL, MICHAEL. 'London trade publishers 1675–1750'. *Library*, 6:4 (1982), pp. 99–134.

TURNBULL, G. H. *Hartlib, Dury and Comenius: gleanings from Hartlib's papers.* Liverpool, 1947.

VIETH, DAVID M. *Attribution in Restoration poetry: a study of Rochester's 'Poems' of 1680.* Yale studies in English, no. 153. New Haven, Conn., 1963.

—— 'Dryden's Mac Flecknoe: the case against editorial confusion'. *Harvard Library bulletin* 24 (1976), 204–44.

VINAVER, EUGÈNE. 'Principles of textual emendation', in *Studies in French language and medieval literature presented to Professor Mildred K. Pope*, pp. 351–69. Manchester, 1939; repr. in Christopher Kleinhenz, ed., *Medieval manuscripts and textual criticism*, pp. 139–66. Chapel Hill, NC, 1976.

WANLEY, HUMFREY. *The diary of Humfrey Wanley 1715–1726*, ed. C. E. Wright and Ruth C. Wright. 2 vols. London, 1966.

WATSON, ANDREW G. *The library of Sir Simonds D'Ewes.* London, 1966.

WEITZMAN, MICHAEL. 'The analysis of open traditions'. *SB* 38 (1985), 82–120.

WHALLEY, JOYCE IRENE. *The pen's excellencie: a pictorial history of Western calligraphy.* New York, 1980.

WILKINSON, D. R. M. *The comedy of habit.* Leiden, 1964.

WILLETTS, PAMELA. 'Sir Nicholas Le Strange and John Jenkins'. *Music and letters* 42 (1961), 30–43.

WILLIAMS, FRANKLIN B., jun. 'Commendatory verses: the rise of the art of puffing'. *SB* 19 (1966), 1–14.

WILLIAMS, WILLIAM P. 'The Castle Ashby manuscripts: a description of the volumes in Bishop Percy's list'. *Library*, 6:2 (1980), 391–412.

WILSON, JOHN HAROLD, ed. *The court wits of the Restoration.* Princeton, NJ, 1948.

—— *Court satires of the Restoration.* Columbus, Oh., 1976.

INDEX

Index